HOW THE

Arabian Nights

INSPIRED THE

AMERICAN DREAM,

1790–1935

SUSAN NANCE

How the
Arabian Nights
Inspired the
American Dream,
1790–1935

The University of North Carolina Press

Chapel Hill

© 2009 The University of North Carolina Press

All rights reserved

Manufactured in the United States of America

Set in Quadraat and Caliph
by Keystone Typesetting, Inc.

The paper in this book meets the guidelines for permanence
and durability of the Committee on Production Guidelines for
Book Longevity of the Council on Library Resources.

The University of North Carolina Press has been a member of the
Green Press Initiative since 2003.

Library of Congress Cataloging-in-Publication Data
Nance, Susan.

How the Arabian nights inspired the American dream, 1790–1935 /
Susan Nance.

  p. cm.

Includes bibliographical references and index.

ISBN 978-0-8078-3274-5 (cloth: alk. paper)

ISBN 978-1-4696-1495-3 (pbk: alk. paper)

ISBN 978-0-8078-9405-7 (eBook)

1. United States—Civilization—Arab influences. 2. Arabian nights.
3. Arab countries—Foreign public opinion, American.
4. Orientalism—United States—History. 5. United States—
Civilization—1783–1865. 6. United States—Civilization—20th
century. 7. Performing arts—Social aspects—United States—History.
8. Popular culture—United States—History. 9. Capitalism—Social
aspects—United States—History. 10. United States—Economic
conditions. I. Title.

E169.1.N314 2009

909'.0974927—dc22   2008047299

contents

illustrations

After a half century of near invisibility, since 2001 West and South Asian Americans have become increasingly prominent in comedic and dramatic entertainment, advertising, and journalism in the United States. This notoriety is only one aspect of the public attention people have recently begun giving to those who came to the United States as a result of the 1965 Immigration Reform Act. The descendants of these new immigrants have in turn thought long and hard about how to come across as native-born Americans by their appearance, speech, politics, and more. For entertainers in this group, building a career in show business has been especially tricky. Audiences have been deeply affected by the "War on Terror," the nation's often-troubled relations with various governments in the Muslim world, and the debate over the Palestinian-Israeli conflict. These issues can make it nearly impossible for desi, Iranian, or Arab American performers to get work playing anything but bewildered migrants, religious radicals, or foreign terrorists.

To make their way as entertainers and citizens, West and South Asian Americans often use humor to step outside the portrayals of Muslims in news broadcasts and cautionary television dramas. Prominent among these ventures is the "Axis of Evil" Comedy Tour. Featuring comedians of Iranian, Egyptian, and Palestinian descent—but "still looking for a North Korean," their publicity material teases—comics like Maz Jobrani depict themselves as normal people living in complicated times. One of Jobrani's most famous jokes revolves around the common scenario of the Iranian American who reveals his ethnic background to a group of acquaintances for the first time. "You're Iranian?!" they ask with alarm. "No . . . ," he says with a smile. "I am Persian, like a carpet. I am soft and colorful, you can lay down on me. Go ahead, take a nap." Here Jobrani reminds us of an older American tradition of interpretation wherein the Muslim world was not a national security concern or subject to invasion by American companies or armies but a familiar provider of contented consumer experiences. In insisting he is Persian, Jobrani brings to the fore again an interpretation of Eastern lands that actually predominated for the first 150 years of American history. In those years, most people interpreted an Eastern persona not through the lenses of American imperialism or national security policy but through capitalism.

The consumer's interpretation of the Muslim world never completely went away, of course; it has lingered with us for the last sixty years. The fortune earned by the Disney film *Aladdin*, for instance, shows that people continue to seek out depictions of West and South Asia as a site of incredible riches, romance, and happy endings. Yet when the American moment in the Middle East began in 1933 with the Arabian American Oil Company's Saudi oil concession and expanded during the 1956 Suez Crisis, older consumerist networks of understanding focused on ease and plenty began receding into the background, while Cold War strategic concerns and political news came to define the Muslim world in American public culture. This book is about what came before that moment, a century and a half that could certainly be difficult for entertainers but for vastly different reasons. It reconstructs the knowledge of artists, both native and foreign born, amateur and professional, who sought to depict a spectrum of nations stretching from Morocco to India by way of Eastern personae and to understand how and why audiences used these performances to devise ways of displaying their own identities through consumption.

My stubborn mission to document this group of creative people has been humored and helped along by many people, and I am really glad to be able finally to thank them publicly. I learned an enormous amount about what to do with this topic, and about how to become a good reviewer myself, from the smart people who read and commented upon various drafts and parts of the manuscript and/or supplied intellectual guidance during the research stages of this project: Karen Ferguson, John Munro, William Cleveland, Mark Carnes, Tim Marr, Ussama Makdisi, Hilton Obenzinger, Donald Malcolm Reid, Leslie Peirce, Beshara Doumani, Paula Fass, Ann Swidler, the members of the University of California, Berkeley, intellectual history reading group, and my mentors at Berkeley, David Hollinger, Mary Ryan, and Darcy Grimaldo Grigsby. A special thanks also goes to the faculty and staff in the Department of History, University of Guelph, for taking me in in 2004 and making completion of this book so much easier. Mostly, though, I need to tip my hat to Elaine Maisner and the other staff at the University of North Carolina Press as well as the two very wise and helpful anonymous reviewers who pitched in. All of these folks somehow saw potential in the first draft I offered and supplied advice that made all the difference.

Nor would this project have been completed without the help of the generous agencies and institutions that provided grants or helped fund conference papers contained here: the University of California, Berkeley, Graduate Division; Riordan and Schubert History Fellowships; Prince Alwaleed Bin Talal Bin Abdulaziz Al Saud Center for American Studies and Research at the American University of Beirut; and Department of History and College of Arts of the University of Guelph. My humble thanks go to the patient staff of the inter-library loan departments of the University of Guelph and University of California, Berkeley, for tracking down all the strange things I requested. My students have also been important to the process of getting this book to the end point, though they may not have realized what they were doing. Since I first was a teaching assistant for Bill Cleveland's introductory course in Middle East history many moons ago, I have taught almost two thousand students whose questions and interests always remind me why history is important.

There were many times I was sure I had bitten off more than I could chew by taking on this project, but somehow my family and friends never gave up hope. The following individuals thus deserve a big round of applause: Jack Nance and Penny Gallagher, who always told me "Keep going!"; Brett Korteling, Bonnie and Laura Dobb, Gerda Bako, Jane, Jeff, and Greg Styles, who supplied logistical and intellectual support and/or computer equipment along the way; Margit Nance, whose labors as a filmmaker helped me understand the lived experiences of creative people, and who supplied endless encouragement; Pokey Jones, Priscilla, Trixie, and Myokie Bobtail, none of whom ever asked me about this project even once; and lastly, my best friend and husband Wes, who is delighted this book is finished.

HOW THE

Arabian Nights

INSPIRED THE

AMERICAN DREAM,

1790–1935

Playing Eastern

As a historian, I have studied intercultural communication for many years. I have been most compelled by the workings of the entertainment business and the men and women whose bread and butter was live performance. This interest has driven me to consider a phenomenon I seem to find hidden in plain view everywhere I look in the American past but especially between 1790 and 1935: Why did so many choose to perform in the guise of persons from the East? And what practical and cultural rules governed who could speak for North Africa, West Asia, or South Asia in such a way? When we look for them, we can find tens of thousands of such performers in the United States in those years. They all claimed special knowledge of an ethnically and religiously diverse spectrum of predominantly Muslim lands stretching from Morocco to India: poets and travelers who wrote homegrown imitations of the stories in the *Arabian Nights*, traveling admirers of Sufism and Eastern fraternal orders, impresarios and merchants from the Ottoman Empire, dancers, acrobats, turban-wearing magicians, spiritual missionaries from India, and even members of the fraternal order known as the Ancient Arabic Order, Nobles of the Mystic Shrine, or Shriners. To borrow a phrase from Philip Deloria, all these people were engaged in the art of playing Eastern.

For the first 150 years of American history, the most broadly influential people to speak about the Eastern world were people who played Eastern by presenting themselves in Eastern personae—or "Oriental" or "Moslem" or "Hindoo" persona as the patter might have required. Some of these individuals were native-born Americans, some were migrants or immigrants from North Africa, West Asia, and South Asia. They included equal numbers of professional and amateur entertainers, some of whom performed in a serious attempt to depict foreign peoples, some of whom performed a kind of Eastern minstrelsy only in jest. In character, these performers told stories about affluent abundance, guilt-free leisure, spiritual truth, natural manhood, the mysteriously exotic, feminine self-discovery, romantic love, racial equality, and the creative possibilities for individuation in a market economy.

The men and women who performed in Eastern guise worked in a creative context largely defined by the standards of the commercial entertainment industry, whose comedic and dramatic logic was premised upon the performance of cultural difference. Within this expressive economy, the act of playing Oriental, along with blackface, ethnic, and gender caricature, was only one way of speaking about life and identity in a globalizing nation among the endless opportunities for sincere consumer self-fashioning the nation offered. Nevertheless, Eastern personae were uniquely important among the options for professional and consumer individuation in the United States because the leisure, abundance, and contentment many perceived in Eastern life was the same vision promised by the consumer capitalist ideology that would come to define the American dream.[1]

The arts of playing Eastern percolated out into American life by way of two parallel modes: professional personae, normally in performances observers understood as staged entertainment, and nonprofessional personae, which viewers found in contexts that implied that the performer was expressing a sincere sense of him or herself whether this was true or not. In both cases, performers needed to come across in a way that balanced personal motivations and audience expectations. Both professional and amateur performers also shared the problem of financial viability, for the professional as a matter of making a living or financing the next show and for the amateur in using an Eastern persona to demonstrate one's success in the market, either as a breadwinner or articulate consumer. The lines dividing professional and amateur performer, persona producer, and performance consumer were always blurry, always moving. Consumers often recycled and performed their own Eastern personae to create a broader context for those professional entertainers who would follow, and vice versa. The audience was thus not just a ticket buyer at the moment of the show but a purveyor of that content to others and an active player in the meanings and uses of the Eastern world within the United States.

So how should a historian explain the phenomenon of Eastern personation in the United States up until the Great Depression? Once upon a time, one would have begun by reaching for a copy of Edward Said's influential 1978 work *Orientalism*. Said famously asserted that Western-authored representations of the Muslim world were interreferential cultural texts that flattered Western self-conceptions. These representations multiplied, each referring to the last, until by the sheer weight of their presence they came to hold great cultural and political authority in the West, to the point of defining the objective truth of the East to the world. Because of the superior economic and military power of nations like Britain, France, and eventually the United States, this tradition of knowledge, Said argued, worked to facilitate imperial expansion in Eastern territories.[2]

Certainly Edward Said had a point. With respect mostly to academic literature and the European novel, he wrote that Westerners argued for a powerful, civilized, righteous, and dynamic West by depicting the East as an oppositional "Other" that was weak, decadent, depraved, fanatical, and unchanging. Europeans and Americans used the ideological concept of the "Orient" to essentialize the ethnically, geographically, and intellectually varied Muslim world as a monolith that scholars could more easily define. Often Westerners did so by way of representations heavily loaded with sexual preoccupations that gendered the East feminine and the West masculine. Drawing from Michel Foucault and Antonio Gramsci, Said went on to create a very persuasive version of the idea that a "discourse," a body of self-referential knowledge, can wield considerable cultural authority even when not factually true, reproducing and exacerbating imbalances of power between those who create the representation and those who are represented. To describe this discursive system, Said redefined a nineteenth-century literary term, "Orientalism," that Europeans and Americans had previously used to describe the expressive style associated with Western-authored Oriental tales. Orientalists, in Said's sense then, were the academics, painters, writers, and other Westerners who assembled and authorized Orientalism as a powerful body of knowledge that often operated largely independently from, but to the disadvantage of, the actual lands and people it described.

Many see Edward Said as the most influential thinker of the late twentieth century, though to be accurate, he was part of a much larger group of academics who were similarly challenging traditional Western scholarship on the Muslim world.[3] Many scholars followed this lead and began to look anew at primary sources and scholarly literature created by Europeans, which many had taken as historically contingent to be sure but ideologically legitimate just the same. Said's work spawned a broad movement within literary scholarship and cultural analysis known as postcolonial studies. At the same time, the flaws in Said's original work, *Orientalism*, inspired many others operating from various political perspectives—and Said himself—to begin grappling with important questions about how European Orientalism exercised power over human actions, how the process might continue to the present day, the role of the non-Western "Other" in that relationship, and whether postcolonial theorists can exist outside discursive systems of knowledge themselves.[4]

With respect to our subject, the United States and the Muslim world, many scholars in various disciplines have been equally inspired by Edward Said but have pursued their analyses with far less rigor than their Europeanist colleagues. Scholars of the United States in various disciplines routinely seek out Orientalist affects in American life and culture—in the Saidian sense—to produce accounts that seem driven by ideology rather than historical evidence. Admirers of Said have looked for evidence supporting his theories in film, visual arts, travel writing, fashion and costuming, home décor design, countless novels, magazine publishing, journalism, and just about every other cultural product one can name whether nonprofit or commercial, religious or secular, official or private, influential and profitable or contemporarily ignored and forgotten. These authors undermine their otherwise insightful observations about specific cultural texts because they do not ask how audiences actually understood, misunderstood, or consciously manipulated depictions of the Muslim world. They collect all these depictions under the discursive term "Orientalism," thereby lumping them together in authorial intent and presumed political effect, suggested by Said's original theory, as part of an imperial "American" project to define and thus control Eastern lands and peoples.

More often than not, the implicit argument thereafter is that a particular cliché of the Muslim world was replicated over and over because Americans were a uniform, unthinkingly racist mass public somehow timelessly "obsessed with the Orient" or culturally invested in the proposed "imperial" project the scholarly author seeks to demonstrate at work in American history. They often make these determinist presumptions manifest by personifying Said's term (e.g., "Orientalism perceived itself as a civilizing mission") or by lazy reduction of the diversity of American experience and opinion over two centuries to "the mind of America."[5] Here a stereotyped monolithic, unchanging "Orientalism" directs all American engagement with the Eastern world for all people at all times. Its existence and power to direct human affairs has become seemingly unquestioned academic common sense—indeed, the scholarly idea of Orientalism has become its own "discourse."[6]

Yet a contradiction emerges when we look at American history from the perspective of historical actors and really press the point of *why* people chose to refer to the Eastern world *when* and *how* they did. My research has shown me that the most numerous attempts by people in the United States, native-born or foreign-born, to take on Eastern personae occurred before the American moment in the Middle East began in the 1930s. In this earlier period, U.S. political and territorial expansion was focused on the American West, Canada, the Pacific, Central America by way of Panama, and the territories of the Spanish Empire: Cuba, Puerto Rico, and the Philippines. That is, playing Oriental was most ubiquitous *before* Eastern nations or natural resources became practically or politically relevant to the bulk of the population or the U.S. government.

Certainly some have noted American missionizing in the nineteenth-century and early twentieth-century Ottoman Empire and India as well as an enthusiastic scholarly interest in the biblical archaeology of the "Holy Land." It is true that at times such activities were relatively well funded and well publicized among the Anglo-American middle classes. They were clearly of great spiritual significance, especially in New England, among those who hoped to see the "Holy Land" they imagined from reading the Bible take shape in the Ottoman Empire. The problem with seeing these Americans or their supporters as evidence of a broader imperial public interest in Muslim lands is that they represented a minority opinion, had limited practical power abroad, and were often criticized by their fellow citizens.[7]

In fact, a majority of Americans knew throughout the nineteenth and early twentieth centuries that the idea of the United States as an imperial power in the Ottoman Empire, Persia, or India was preposterous. To take one example, in 1849 the New Yorker Howard Crosby went on vacation to Egypt. He wrote from his hotel in Alexandria: "We actually found a Yankee steward [here]. . . . He had come from Marblehead, and, in direct opposition to the tide of emigration, had struck Eastward for a new home. Who knows but this may be the germ of Annexation!—the first dawning of the established series of three stages for the extension of empire, . . . viz: Colonization—Declaration of Independence—Annexation!"[8] Readers in the United States would have found this funny because Crosby was making light of the dangerous national debate around lands of actual Anglo-American immigration/invasion, namely, Texas, a former Mexican territory, then brief independent republic, now the newest state in the Union.[9] The absurdity that made the joke work came from the fact that even if some Americans hoped to trade, travel, and proselytize in the Middle East, even if they complained that someone should really "relieve" the region of "Turkish misrule" or felt that the sentiment of Manifest Destiny out west in those years was misguided, there was no actual chance of the U.S. government or its citizens colonizing any part of the Ottoman Empire, a region most acknowledged as sites of overt British, French, and Russian pressure.

Plenty of people argue nonetheless that the Americans who mattered were jealous of British or French imperial activities and sought to ape them in the Middle East and that American colonialism in, say, the Philippines or the American West made U.S. citizens subject to a generalized ethos of superiority in their contacts with all foreign peoples at all times.[10] Such blanket theories are not a sufficient explanation for the expense and effort a broad spectrum of people in the U.S., including immigrants and migrants from the lands in question, invested in depicting the Eastern world, especially through Oriental personae, over the course of 150 years.

Far more serious yet, almost without exception these writers pay lip service to "Orientalism" but do not actually engage with the full theoretical implications of Said's arguments with respect to *how* subconscious discursive power has supposedly worked through cultural texts and *how*, precisely, this is connected to the formulation of foreign policy and military or diplomatic action. Instead common scholarly interpretation sees a predatory inevitability in American engagement with the Muslim world because authors tend to focus analysis on cultural "texts" in isolation from the moment of production or live display. They do this, David Hall astutely explains, "by privileging an ideal reader (the critic's own stance) or else a particular interpretation (invariably modernist/ ideological) of a given text."[11] Do not get me wrong here. I do not mean to claim that American depictions of North Africa, West Asia, and South Asia did not operate in a global context at times or take on newly politicized meanings after 1935. The imperious attitude held by some Americans toward Easterners over the years is part of American engagement with the Muslim world. However, if we really seek to understand the specific utility of particular cultural products and performances of identity to actual people, some Americans' imperiousness is not the most prominent part of the story.

Thus, we have arrived at an intellectual moment in which academics use the term Orientalism to define American contact with the exact portion of the globe in which most Americans had no imperial aims and the U.S. government and American business little influence. I. C. Campbell has explained this phenomenon to note that scholars attempting to reconstruct situations of intercultural interaction can often operate under "a teleological fallacy: knowledge of the later outcome of contact influences perception of the nature of early contact, . . .

a history of displacement gives rise to explanations of first contact couched in terms of aggression and intrusion."[12] I agree and will stubbornly argue that it is a presentist distraction to view the cultural products of the nineteenth-century and early twentieth-century United States only through the lens of recent history, looking everywhere for evidence of present political concerns over the activities of U.S. citizens in the Arab world, Iran, or Afghanistan. Nor should our analysis simply play on the contemporary reader's sense of discomfort with obviously dated primary sources if it is to provide any real understanding of why such representations proliferated.[13] American cultural interest in the Eastern world was not the same thing as business investment, loan making, military occupation, or diplomatic arm-twisting, nor did cultural interest necessarily lead to these things.[14]

As a historian, I assume that people have agency and act for conscious reasons and that we cannot explain historical causation without explaining that reasoning. This is not a minor issue. The single most important problem historians ever tackle concerns historical causation. In this case, why did people consciously decide to depict North Africa, West Asia, or South Asia? Why did they wear those depictions on their bodies as personae when they did? Why did they believe those depictions were truthful, funny, beautiful, distasteful, or financially beneficial for producers and consumers? Why and how did they inspire imitations, elaborations, or rebuttals by other performers?

What I provide in the following pages is an attempt to recapture that knowledge, to listen to those who played Eastern. I cannot take these performances for granted and want to determine what body language, clothes, modes of speech, accents, or attitudes fell inside and outside the practices of playing Eastern as worked out at different times and at great cost of time, energy, and money by trial and error over the decades. Each person depicting the East in the United States knew that he or she could not possibly speak with omnipotent control over what audiences would take away or without consequences, at the very least the possibility of being ignored. These performers ask us to consider their work in context, racist or sexist as it all may appear today or may have appeared back then, and take seriously Mohammed Sharafuddin's advice to "take into account *what was possible in the age*."(italics in original)[15] Native-born and foreign-born performers who crossed over in Eastern personae developed many modes of performance that became adaptable staples of American entertainment for later generations of people who reworked them for their own needs. Those modes of personation would only become internationalized with respect to American activities in North Africa, West Asia, and South Asia after World War II. Especially during periods of public attention to the Palestinian-Israeli conflict, the Iranian Revolution, and oil-producing states like Saudi Arabia and Iraq, audiences might more forcefully impose new meanings on older artistic forms. To onlookers fatigued from long lineups at the gas station, Shriners fooling around in a street parade as pompous "Imperial Potentates" and "Oriental Nobles" during the 1973 oil crisis would, whether they meant to or not, appear as a comment on the power of the Saudi elite.

To make sense of the historical practices of playing Eastern, we must investigate the creative realities of those times by asking how people theorized communication and consumption in the periods in which Eastern personae were so common. Sixty years before Saidian scholarship emerged, Walter Lippmann published *Public Opinion*.[16] Influenced by his work as a government intelligence officer during World War I and his experiences as a journalist, Lippmann wrote about how culture and capitalism shaped communication.[17] He argued that perception of an event, an experience, or the front page of the local newspaper was governed by the viewer's past experience and social context. Lippmann saw that viewers' perceptions created rules for evaluating future experiences in order to make the world quick to understand and mentally organize. He borrowed the printer's technical term "stereotype" to describe those guiding preconceptions, which could include political or religious values, racist generalizations, or any other concept a person might use to make sense of the world.[18] "The audience must participate in the news, much as it participates in [theatrical] drama, by personal identification," Lippmann discovered of when and why people would pay attention.[19] More broadly, consumers found interest in cultural products, he said, because they seemed right, seemed to flatter the purchaser's common sense about how the world worked and how one could know it.

Lippmann's word—stereotype—has become incredibly ubiquitous ever since and is often misunderstood.[20] Lippmann's stereotype does not function like Said's Orientalist discourse because properly understood as Said wrote about it as a discursive system of knowledge, Orientalism imposes a predetermined meaning on cultural products defined by a body of knowledge largely independent of individual agency. In contrast, Lippmann explained that stereotypes make communication comprehensible and efficient specifically because the viewer has the power to think about a representation for himself or herself and to do the intellectual work of putting new information and past knowledge together to create meaning. Lippmann learned these lessons the hard way. He watched government information officers, newspaper editors, writers, and photographers struggle to make their messages seem credible to often-doubtful audiences who ultimately held the balance of power in communicative relationships and whose interpretive stereotypes seemed knowable one moment, unpredictable the next.

Nonetheless, Walter Lippmann observed the power of the stereotype at work in the process by which journalists of his day attempted to get their messages across to readers by using representational short cuts that helped them provide new information to readers while affirming the specific identities and values of the market segment they served. "The economic necessity of interesting the reader quickly and the economic risk of not interesting him at all, or of offending him by unexpected news insufficiently or clumsily described," he explained, tempted many to rely on dependable tropes and narratives. Moreover, market relations therefore tended to breed a kind of conservatism since innovation in communication created commercial risk. It was common knowledge among his colleagues, he said, that there was seldom found in a newspapers "sufficient space in which even the best journalist could make plausible an unconventional view." The use of common stereotypes that flattered the audience was not simply a function of capitalism, he cautioned, but was certainly exacerbated by it.[21] Lippmann's ideas were and still are revolutionary because he was one of the few people to account for the role of human agency and capitalism in the practical logistics of communication.

In fact, Lippmann was expressing wisdom long current among a group of professional communicators, an old truism circus men, dancers, magicians, lyceum lecturers, writers, and even half-drunk parading Shriners lived with. They all knew their job was to create artistically satisfying performances that were also culturally and financially viable because they spoke to the identities of those who would view them and perhaps adopt them. I call this process "crossing over," in loose adaptation of the music industry term "crossover."[22] It required performers of Oriental personae to design their performances to provide comprehensible novelty to viewers, that is, new content that still flattered preexisting attitudes of the specific audience in question. Those who performed in Eastern personae professionally tended to be working-class or middle-class individuals who had no choice but to produce financially viable performances. Their main concern was not the cultural authority of the "discourse" they constructed but daily economic survival. Sometimes their representations of the Muslim world crossed over to the right audience and paid; sometimes they did not. Sometimes the same depiction would sell out one week and go down in flames days later when new, entirely unrelated competition hit the market. This book seeks to explore the possibilities of this industry-made theory of communication to explain why playing Oriental was specifically useful to actual people when it was.

Even more, performers of Oriental personae knew that audiences were seldom influenced solely by a show's content or cultural authority but usually also by far more mundane conditions specific to the commercial nature of entertainment: the location of the venue, the ticket price, the state of one's personal finances (and by extension the ups and downs of a notoriously volatile American economy more generally), the class, sex, or race of fellow audience members, or the production value of the costumes and props. Audiences used a combination of such cultural, social, and fiscal conditions to determine the perceived entertainment value of a given performance. Those who played Oriental for these audiences consequently acted according to both personal motivations and daily exigencies, making decisions that were counterproductive and badly conceived as often as they were successful or brilliantly executed.

Scholars of performance have in fact written about the task Lippmann pondered, which I call crossing over, to see that a performance must include the conventional and the new at the same time, expectation and improvisation, stereotype and revelation. For instance, Elin Diamond explains, "Every performance, if it is intelligible as such, embeds features of previous performances: gender conventions, racial histories, aesthetic traditions—political and cultural pressures that are consciously and unconsciously acknowledged."[23] To capture the ways professional and amateur performers made this work, I have focused when possible on live performances of Oriental personae. In those cases, cultural production and consumption occurred simultaneously, so that no party was powerless and no party was omnipotent either. With respect to the circus, for example, Janet Davis explains, "In live performance, the relationship between self and Other is constantly in flux—even when the performance reinforces racist norms—because as an entertainer, one returns the audience's gaze with one's own, thus undermining the controlling function of the gaze."[24] As a mode of communication, live performance has always required a give and take between performer and audience that gives all participants a moment of relative equality. Both native-born and foreign-born performers in this situation had no choice but to use the audience's applause or boos, laughs, or uncomfortable silences to discover which clichés, narratives, costumes, accents, or patter made sense to the audience then and hopefully would again in future.

Thus, I insist on including foreign performers in this story because I do not wish to go looking for a necessarily adversarial relationship between Americans and Easterners by excluding foreigners as agents in American history. Instead I ask what experiences native-born and foreign-born performers shared in negotiating their way through the markets for performance in the United States. Although players from overseas have left us with far fewer records than native-born Americans, they can still help us examine the "Easternization" of American artistic practices by contact with foreign cultures.[25] The people and cultures of the Muslim world were not just a figment of the American imagination or a blank screen onto which people projected "imperial desires" but real, active places, peoples, and traditions that intervened into global history whether Americans liked it or not.[26] For this reason, whenever sources permit, each of the following chapters documents direct contact between Americans and those from the Eastern world, either overseas or in the United States.

Whether people witnessed performances of Eastern personae live or recorded in newspaper accounts, images, letters, or by other means, in all cases they needed to be comprehensible.[27] We can measure that comprehensibility by asking how and when audiences adapted such performances to their own lives. Anyone who tried to play Oriental was not merely attempting to portray the Eastern world as a disinterested third party or to demonize foreign people. Rather they used personalized means that required them to present *themselves* as representations of the Eastern world, whether seriously or in jest, not knowing with complete certainly what viewers would assume about the performer's actual sense of self. Audiences often adapted what they saw to their own work of individuation in the market economy as amateur performers of a sort who played Eastern as consumers.

What made Oriental personae unique in the extensive performative context of American public life was the fact that Americans were very familiar with and interested in the Eastern world, not primarily as diplomats, soldiers, or missionaries but as consumers. North Africa, West Asia, and South Asia provided and inspired among Americans a tradition of extravagant and sumptuous creativity that people found in domestic translations of the *Arabian Nights*, a classic of world literature for centuries, and its Western imitations known as Oriental tales. This artistic tradition specially privileged Eastern content among Americans over the cultural production of every other part of the globe because these tales provided unparalleled depictions of luxury, ease, and magical self-transformation in robust language that closely matched the promise of consumer capitalism as it developed between 1790 and 1935. The French political scientist Emile Boutmy would note in 1891 that capitalism seemed to define the United States as a nation even more than race, responsible government, or Protestantism: "The striking and peculiar characteristic of American society is, that it is not so much a democracy as a huge commercial company for the discovery, cultivation and capitalization of its enormous territory."[28] Commerce and production defined the United States for many, and arts informed by the Orient provided an artistic tradition that many Americans and Easterners believed could allow for incredibly ostentatious and expensive productions that celebrated consumer subjectivities and that national character. Such performances and cultural products were the primary way Americans disconnected from or disinterested in government, missionary, academic, or even newspaper coverage of political events overseas had a personal stake in their access to content inspired by or derived from the East.

By playing Eastern, amateur and professional artists often sought to create works that communicated some combination of ingredients drawn from two creative ideals: the " 'ultra-natural' (wild, untamed, passionate, chaotic, animal) and [the] 'ultra-artificial' (fantastic, androgynous, bejeweled, decorative, decadent)," as Peter Wollen has explained.[29] Both the ultranatural and the ultra-artificial were relevant to consumers' work of individuation in a market economy. The ultra-artificial came in the form of ornate Orientana,[30] spoken, written, decorative, and performed, that people used to aspire to the affluent, carefree self-transformation promised by the market. The ultranatural came in modes of consumer individuation ostensibly outside commerce because of their provenance or ancient roots in the East yet practiced only by those wealthy enough to purchase cultural products, objects, and experiences that communicated an ultranatural identity.

Such consumer interest in the Eastern world was possible because before the 1965 Immigration Reform Act brought large numbers of Africans and Asians to the United States, many people welcomed Easterners to the country as exotic visitors.[31] Nor were there obvious plans for the U.S. government to engage in war or diplomacy so as to incorporate any part of North Africa, West Asia, or South Asia into American imperial domains. Thus, were there few of the usually resulting concerns over potential "foreign" elements in the labor pool or body politic that might have complicated the meaning of an Eastern persona.[32] Because of their relative political innocence, Oriental personae had great capacity as vehicles for satire, tales of the surreal, masculine posturing, feminine power, or stories of magic and plenty presented by an authoritative person seemingly foreign to the United States who might say things an undisguised person could not. Americans continued to find playing Eastern useful over time because of this power, flexibility, and sumptuousness.

An amateur filtering and borrowing process ran parallel to the professional exercise of artistic license that allowed native-born and foreign-born people to adapt Eastern content and modes of expression to the entertainment standards of the American economy. Especially after 1880, this process would begin to include broader and broader segments of the population until people of all walks of life and regions had access to Eastern personae, even if only by way of a circus show or cigarette advertisement. As more and more Americans obtained the means to individuate themselves as consumers, they created new expectations—not without debate to be sure—about how each person might define and achieve personal fulfillment through material goods. Beginning in the early nineteenth century if not earlier, Americans also increasingly expressed a belief that consumer products and practices reflected one's identity and success in the economy. Neil Harris explains, "Materialism, in the mid-nineteenth century, was tied to both production *and* consumption. If a man desired what he could not yet afford to buy, he could either enlarge his fortune or apply his own talents to imitation."[33] Indeed, it is that imitation I seek out here, that moment in which people reinterpreted objects or ways of being to their own ends. This meant one could individuate oneself in relation to the various examples one found among peers and neighbors, certainly, but also in the marketplace of information and entertainment. The same national markets, go-ahead spirit, and transportation revolution that made the mobile, chameleon-like confidence man possible in the nineteenth century and beyond also give more honest citizens of all stripes the opportunity for personal "self-invention" by moving from place to place, learning, buying, and behaving in new ways that included periods of playing Oriental more than one might suspect.[34]

Back then, many people knew that in life as on stage, one's public persona was not necessarily the same thing as one's personal sense of self and that self-fashioning was a symptom of the myth of the self-made man in a consumer society. A number of present-day thinkers similarly argue that human identity more generally is itself a performance. Judith Butler suggests that gender, and by extension any identity component, is made manifest by individuals as "a stylized repetition of acts" and "a kind of persistent impersonation that passes as the real."[35] In performing an identity and passing, so to speak, all of us are crossing over an image of our personalities in a comprehensible form to observers. Sometimes called "self-fashioning," such individuation through consumption in the past meant more to Americans than purchasing products to display social status or dress "beyond their rank."[36] People individuated themselves through products they combined in novel ways with styles of speech, body language, dress, naming practices, and choice of venue. Their individuation communicated a sense of personal uniqueness, even if that uniqueness was in reference to a larger group of similarly unique individuals who conceived of themselves as such.[37]

Scholars of performance, identity, and consumption also explain that these personae are a compromise between one's internal landscape and the expectations of others, a give and take in which the individual must draw from common stereotypes and available resources in order to make himself or herself comprehensible to observers. Moreover, a "commodity self" emerged during the nineteenth and early twentieth centuries in which consumers who might feel powerless to challenge capitalism more broadly made the best of it by embracing a "therapeutic world view" that suggested one could find satisfaction and identity through goods and by internalizing some of the expectations voiced around them about what a native-born or foreign-born man or woman of a given class, region, or "race" could or should do, say, or own.[38]

I am most concerned here with the ways people have consciously conceived of capitalism, consumption, and identity and acted upon them by playing Eastern, a shared experience for native-born and foreign-born, professional and amateur performers. Thus, each chapter in this book follows a group of interrelated artists to see how they created performances of Oriental personae that provided observers with suggested uses of North Africa, West Asia, and South Asia. No book could document every example, so I have found the most publicly prominent, broadly accessible performers of Oriental personae to see what they had in common. I found in the process a network of exceptionally creative people who either knew one another directly or passed in the night, as it were.

To understand how performers crossed over Eastern personae we must, initially at least, accept the national, ethnic, religious, global, and other designations participants used to describe themselves and others. Americans and foreign performers linked Moroccan, Algerian, Turkish, Arab, Persian, and "Hindoo" lands and people together as "Oriental," "Moslem," or simply "Eastern," often regardless of actual religious identification or land of origin, because they perceived them to have a common cultural heritage defined by predominantly Islamic and particularly rich artistic and spiritual traditions.[39] We can be more accepting of this early perspective if we remember that native-born and foreign-born performers also lumped the inhabitants of the United States together as "Americans" in a similar project of defining cultural difference with respect to the Ottoman Empire, India, or Europe. These were years in which many talked about identity by seeking out ideal national and racial types defined by essential characteristics, not by seeking hybridity or transnational identity. The frequent assumption that Persians, Turks, Arabs, and (South Asian) Indians were whites, combined with their status as perceived inheritors of one of the world's great civilizations even if Americans said it was in decline, often translated into a kind of romantic interest on the part of many Americans.[40] Christians, Jews, and Muslims from West Asia and North Africa drew advantage from this economy of interpretation in the United States as did South Asian Muslims, often called "Hindoos" regardless of their religious affiliation.

Our story begins just after the Revolution with the more exclusive markets for book and magazine publishing, mid-nineteenth-century fraternal orders, and middle-class and upper-class domestic consumption to show where playing Oriental began as a consumer practice. The main task of these more exclusive commercial forms was to facilitate middle-class and upper-class Anglo-American self-definition with authorship in these genres largely restricted to those groups. Chapter 1 sets the stage with the story of how the *Arabian Nights* inspired the dream of contented and abundant consumption in the United States during the nineteenth century. It was in admiration of the *Nights* that Americans began to play Eastern, first in print, then as tourists in the Middle East, then at home as consumers who decorated their parlors in a cluttered Oriental-tale style that evoked ease and plenty while celebrating consumer choice. In plenty of these cases, the character of Aladdin, made suddenly rich by rubbing an old lamp, stood as an apt metaphor for the vast capitalist transformation taking place in the nation.

Chapters 2 and 3 ask how difficult it was for native-born American men to make a living by playing Eastern. First, I compare Christopher Oscanyan and Bayard Taylor, two performers of Oriental personae in the mid-nineteenth century, to explain why in those years Anglo-Americans seemed to prefer to hear about the East from other native-born Americans and how and why both native-born and foreign-born speakers so often presented information specifically about the Muslim world as new or exclusive, even when it was old and conventional. Next, I follow a group of men who cultivated the affluent if hand-to-mouth body of earners and consumers known as the Masonic public. This group of men made up the largest market for masculine Eastern personae in the nation, using those portrayals to demonstrate their affluence and success in business just as they claimed to have a brotherhood that existed outside the market grounded in a region of the world highly sacred to American Protestants. The image of the wise man of the Masonic East was so prevalent by the 1870s and 1880s that elite Masons could found a new order, the Ancient Arabic Order, Nobles of the Mystic Shrine or Shriners, to lampoon the Masonic 'East' and its boosters as well as other modes of conventionalized provocativeness characterizing middling Protestant interest in the Muslim world.

By the 1880s, with the exception of the class-conscious and race-conscious "legitimate stage," people from all walks of life began replicating and celebrating cultural difference in the commercial world of entertainment.[41] In traveling Wild West shows, the circus, carnivals and amusement parks, vaudeville, medicine shows, street parades, department stores, newspapers, advertising, and radio, people of all races and backgrounds participated as consumers and performers. Thus, Chapters 4 and 5 ask why the Eastern world was "exotic" to Americans and how Eastern personae could be both familiar and strange. I begin by examining the first opportunities a broad American public had to see or meet people from North Africa and West Asia in person and thus the earliest major interventions by foreign-born performers into the arts of playing Eastern. When North Africans and Middle Easterners came to the U.S. in significant numbers after 1870, many made their migration financially viable by speaking for the Eastern world. In the guise of Arab horsemen and self-starting acrobats in traveling circuses, wild west shows, and vaudeville, they offered portrayals of Arab athleticism that flattered American patriotism in comprehensibly exotic modes. Then at the 1893 Columbian Exposition in Chicago, Ottoman entrepreneurs and official representatives of the Sultan provided carefully managed but easily appropriated Eastern identities. Various groups played Oriental at the fair for competing American audiences, including white and black communities of Shriners who would fight over the right to make use of the personae they found on the exposition grounds.

The following two chapters similarly radiate out from the Columbian Exposition, first to examine modern female uses of the persona of the mischievous Eastern dancer as a vehicle for colloquially feminist, sexually self-aware consumer individuation. Then in Chapter 7, I uncover how South Asians and Americans argued about Eastern spirituality in such a way that the turban became a sign of masculine failure at the height of public support for the business ethic and the idea of personal responsibility for success. Chapter 8 serves as a conclusion of sorts, asking how the democratization of access to the arts of playing Eastern showed why many African Americans—traditionally the least-respected consumers in American society—saw the Eastern world and the turban as a sign of promise for the future that spoke of their autonomy as spiritual people, as consumers, and as citizens. A short note on the cinema or theater proper (beyond vaudeville): because I want to focus on modes of playing Eastern and venues less often examined, and because the cinema and Broadway deserve books in their own right with far greater detail than I can provide here, I mention cinema only with respect to the early nickelodeon films of the 1890s and the desert romance/Rudolph Valentino phenomenon of the 1920s.

From the perspective of as many Americans as possible, I will look for answers to questions about who could take on an Eastern guise and when. How did people come to know about the Eastern world, how did they evaluate people who claimed to speak for North Africa, West Asia, and South Asia, and how did they think about their place in the commercial trade in such representations? What were the politics over who could play Eastern, and what do those politics tell us about how people were arguing about just how much a person could manipulate his or her identity or persona? Why did men become interested in certain guises and women in others, or how did a particular persona become useful to both at once? When did race become critical to those guises, and whose race? Why did people find these personae funny or controversial or banal when they did? These are the questions people asked on the ground, and their answers are important if we are to know why the Eastern world mattered to Americans from all walks of life learning to live with consumer capitalism.

These particular stories have much to tell us about how and why Eastern self-presentation persisted for so long and, for the vast majority of Americans, usually overshadowed more cautionary representations of Islam or the Eastern world by those who sought to demonize cultural difference. The historical sources I examine are thus not the destination of a theory-driven textual analysis that seeks out those cautionary messages and conflict but clues about the shared experiences of creation and the constantly changing context of depictions in which governments, business people, travelers, and missionary organizations operated and were compelled to compete if they sought the sympathy of the vast bulk of the population in the United States.

While the industry-made theory of crossing over tells us about the process of communication, it does not determine the content. Eastern personae were unique because between the American Revolution and crisis of capitalism known as the Great Depression, they rested at the intersection of performance, identity, and consumption. In order to survive, all the varied performers of Oriental personae had to cross Eastern content over to audiences also coping with capitalism. The most profitable and ubiquitous performances, therefore, were those that did not openly challenge cultural difference or consumerism but functioned as idealized suggestions of how the Muslim world could be useful in the process of consumer individuation. These stories, then, are about the creative lives of all people who defined themselves by watching others perform their personae and about trying on versions of those personae to see if they fit. Whether professional entertainers looking for a dependable bit, reformers seeking to change audience attitudes, or consumers inspired to wear the exotic while looking to communicate a sense of self, playing Eastern was at its core about how to engage in self-mystification in a market economy that, in theory, promised "Oriental" self-transformation and abundance to all.[42]

chapter 1

Capitalism and the *Arabian Nights*, 1790–1892

*T*he population of the United States has always embraced a consumer ethic of one sort or another. Even before the market revolution of the early nineteenth century, historians tell of colonial subjects mobilized politically in a "revolutionary marketplace" in which their shared experiences as consumers helped a diverse population decide to support rebellion against Britain so as to protect consumer choice and domestic production.[1] Once the dust had settled, with the Revolutionary Wars resolved and the Constitution in place, shoppers in one Virginia town made a translation of the *Arabian Nights* the single most popular work of fiction sold by the local bookseller.[2] Years later, when those and other Anglo-American readers remembered the hours of enjoyment they had with the *Nights* when they and the Republic were still young, they always said basically the same thing: the *Nights* had "highly excited" their imaginations with vivid scenes of magical events and incredible wealth, "houses of gold and streets paved with diamonds."[3]

The collection of short stories known as the *One Thousand and One Nights* or *Arabian Nights' Entertainments* would continue to be in steady demand in urban, rural, and frontier parts of the United States throughout the nineteenth century.[4] The translations Americans read shared a famous frame tale in which a Persian woman named Scheherezade each night recounted to her husband, King Shahriyar, a gripping story. Fearing he would kill her the next morning, every evening she refused to reveal the resolution of her story in order to persuade her husband to leave her alive for one more day. The next night, she would finally end the previous story only to begin another right away. As the frame tale went, Scheherezade saved herself for one thousand and one nights through her stories, most famously the tales of Aladdin and the magic lamp, Ali Baba and the Forty Thieves, the Seven Voyages of Sinbad the Sailor, and tales of the venerable Haroun al-Raschid, powerful but generous "governor of old Baghdad."

The mind-boggling luxuries described in the *Nights* contrasted sharply with the modest, hard-working lives of those readers. For citizens who had just fought a war for economic and political independence, the *Nights* provided colorful metaphors of the potential contentment and plenty they might enjoy as consumers in a nation that, by 1840, was becoming a global powerhouse rivaled only by Britain. Here was a nation undergoing dramatic cultural and economic changes, especially in cities crowded with foreign and domestic rural immigrants, and open to expanding global trade. Increasing access to the world's cultures, products, and people also meant that Americans increasingly had more ways by which to consider and display personal identity.[5] Many took to heart the antebellum consumer ethic of individuation by which people strove for self-improvement and economic autonomy displayed through the appropriate clothing or household reading materials, for instance, while endorsing the perceived democracy inherent in a market society that promised prosperity for all citizens.[6]

In the beginning, Americans looked specifically to the Muslim world and the *Arabian Nights* for prototypes of luxurious consumption and transformation that served as metaphors for democratic capitalism. Americans gained access to Eastern literature as translated adaptations of the *Nights* and stories created in imitation of the *Nights* known as Oriental tales or "tales of the East." Between the Revolution and 1892, middle-class and upper-class Anglo-Americans would use these sources and forms to construct an Orientana of the "ultra-artificial" that endorsed capitalism through compelling modes of consumption that allowed anyone to play Eastern. These Eastern characters endorsed hedonistic consumption and a consumer's Oriental tale to help people think about the romantic promise of magical self-transformation, repose, and contentment to be found in the market.

The consumer possibilities Americans would see in the *Nights* and other Oriental tales are an important part of the answer to the question of "how 'the consumer' arose," as Frank Trentmann asks of why people chose to think of themselves *as* consumers in the nineteenth century.[7] Americans saw their acquisitive desires brought to life in the *Arabian Nights* and developed a consumer's Oriental tale to enact fantasies of contented, leisured consumption that was useful in both modes of market participation: as producers of goods and services that made the United States a capitalist power and as consumers seeking self-fulfillment and personal expression in a society of abundance. The consumer's Oriental tale was not in effect a protest against materialism or industrialization or capitalism but a way of participating in these developments in ways that seemed creative and authentic to the emerging identities of many individuals. As Colin Campbell and others explain, the romantic consumer ethic that emerged beginning in the nineteenth century was no anomaly but a tool Americans needed in order to internalize both a productive "Protestant work ethic" and a romantically expressive, hedonistic consumerism.[8]

Consequently, this chapter is about a couple of firsts in American history, the first opportunities Americans made to play Eastern by writing Oriental tales that imitated the *Arabian Nights* and the first opportunities Americans took to play Eastern as consumers by enacting the scenes of ease and plenty they found in the *Nights* in their own lives and houses. Between 1790 and the 1890s, Anglo-Americans cherished the *Arabian Nights* deeply, seeing it as a literary classic that coexisted with the Bible in helping people interpret West Asia. Though the politics over who can use what to express himself or herself have changed in many respects today, Americans coping with capitalism in 1830 or 1880 did not often worry about whether they should draw inspiration from the *Nights* or some other cultural product from the East but rather how to do so in authentic and meaningful ways. They sorted these values out first by writing Oriental tales, stories in imitation of the *Arabian Nights* through which they talked about material abundance, leisure, and self-renovation. People used the Oriental-tale style as a "creative notion" and artistic practice that they could carry over into mutually promoting forms directed at middling consumers including poetry, travel narratives, parade decoration, advertising, retail space design, and common colloquialism.[9]

For most Anglo-Americans who were not professional writers, painters, or travelers, amateur attempts at replicating what they read about usually took place through consumption of goods that carried similar retellings of the consumer's Oriental tale. People would try the tale on for size by playing Eastern at home in order to make the most of the vast material transformation of the United States, casting themselves in the role of an incredulous Aladdin made wealthy in an instant. The metaphor of American capitalism as Oriental tale would not be without its critics, but it carried on throughout the nineteenth century nonetheless because so many people found it specifically useful for coping with the market revolution, western expansion, and the industrial revolution, all of which seemed to promise great riches and happiness but so often supplied financial panics, disappointment, and personal obscurity.

THE *ARABIAN NIGHTS* IN TRANSLATION AND ADAPTATION

To understand how the *Nights* became useful to Americans, we need first to explode the myth that Western adaptations of the *Nights* were crude appropriations of some pristine Arab cultural tradition. Instead we can see Americans who played Eastern as part of the global story of the *Nights* as a shared tradition.[10] The land depicted in the *Arabian Nights*—from Egypt through Persia to India and China—had always been a global trade and travel crossroads. As artists and storytellers transmitted the root stories behind the *Nights* through this network of societies, the tales were never a static text. In every place and time, borrowing, plagiarism, and recycling of material have been at the heart of the creative process, a reality the *Nights* could not escape. Often orally transmitted, thousands of people reworked and adapted the tales to suit their particular language, audience, and time. Only in the hands of Arab storytellers and European compilers would the tales take the form of the *Thousand and One Nights* as Americans knew them.[11]

The Western part of this story began during the "Age of Discovery" in the seventeenth and eighteenth centuries. It was a period marked by new global travel and trade between Europeans, Americans, and the Muslim world, resulting in what Schwab calls an "Oriental Renaissance" that reinvigorated Western art and literature.[12] By the late eighteenth century, a new generation of writers on both sides of the Atlantic were rejecting the conventional "pietistic Calvinism" of sixteenth-century and seventeenth-century sermons and miracle stories, which made up the bulk of reading material then. Instead they wrote "gay stories and splendid impieties of the traveller and the novelist," Royall Tyler, author of famed American antislavery novel *The Algerian Captive* (1797), explained of his cohort.[13] The *Arabian Nights* was a great inspiration to these authors, a global masterpiece of imagination so complex and varied that one could find characters, plot lines, or narrative styles to suit any conceivable situation of adaptation. Thus, some early American reviewers pronounced the *Nights* superior even to Shakespeare in literary importance.[14]

Anglo-American interest in adapting the *Nights* to domestic audiences was also a product of plain logistics. The United States had the highest literacy rates in the world and a changing economy that allowed more and more people free time for reading.[15] A burgeoning publishing industry served and expanded this readership, giving more people access to aspects of Asia's creative arts by way of books, lectures, magazines, newspapers, and inexpensively replicated portraits and landscape images. The prices of such printed materials came down between 1750 and 1850, creating an "explosion of printed matter" and markets for authors that were never before possible.[16]

In the midst of the publishing boom in the United States, Edward W. Lane's highly praised English translation, The Thousand and One Nights, commonly called in England, The Arabian Nights' Entertainments (1839–41), emerged as the state of the art.[17] Lane's edition exposed the open secret that the Arabian Nights could be made locally relevant because the stories existed at the intersection of history and artistic license. Indeed, for Western translators even to make the Nights available to non-Arabic consumers in the first place required the stories to be reworked and adapted to a substantial degree, defying even the possibility of a culturally neutral translation in any language, and some contemporary readers talked openly about this. American fans appreciated Edward Lane's translation because it surpassed the first translated adaptation most Anglo-Americans might have seen (if they could read French), Antoine Galland's Les Mille et Une Nuits (1704). Galland had attempted the difficult task of translating the stories into French prose that was not mechanical and literal but rather, like all good translations, attempted to convey the narratives in French prose that appealed to his early eighteenth-century audience. Translated into English, reprinted and bootlegged for decades thereafter, Galland's rendition came across as burdened with French idioms and sounded to Americans more French than anything else.[18]

By contrast, Lane created an English-language adaptation for a broad middle-class and upper-class readership that was more literally translated to capture and celebrate, he hoped, the creative agency of Middle Eastern artists. It came with ample footnotes that described the stories as the performance art of actual Egyptian storytellers and sought to engender the reader's sympathy toward a part of the world routinely criticized by Europeans.[19] "Public taste has changed since [Galland's day]; we prefer to preserve the Oriental coloring of manner and style," Atlantic Monthly said of the contemporary standards of evaluation and Lane's timeliness.[20] Lane's edition seemed more Middle Eastern because it restored "the spirit and style of the original," one early review explained.[21] That is, Lane used prose that endorsed the important artistic assumption that, in contrast to plain-speaking Americans, real Easterners past and present used flowery and pompous language that expressed their heightened love of beauty, leisure, and ceremony.

Of course, non-Arabic speakers with no access to the Arabic manuscripts or contemporary Egyptian popular culture could not have verified whether this was true, but the belief prevailed that Lane's version was most accurate, nonetheless, in communicating the "truth" of the *Nights* as art. Other copiously footnoted, scholarly looking editions, "With an Explanatory and Historical Introduction by G. M. Bussey. Carefully Revised and Corrected, with some Additions," for instance, extended historical and documentary claims for the stories, which gave them an appealing authenticity despite the artistic license involved in their production.[22] Moreover, all American authors routinely applied scholarly historical pretenses to their fiction for one very simple reason: history sold better than any other genre of published material because it could come across to readers as entertaining and educational, and it had earned men like Washington Irving great fortunes.[23]

Thereafter, translated adaptations of the stories continued to emerge throughout the nineteenth century, some serialized in newspapers and magazines, some sold as inexpensive chapbooks, and some printed in Europe and exported to the United States or bootlegged by American printers, and each person could choose a favorite.[24] Among these were expensive editions owners would only display on a shelf, their high prices a crucial part of the design for highly respected titles.[25] Others served primarily as a vehicle for the work of well-known artists, for which "the essential requirement was to provide copy that would be familiar and that could be satisfactorily illustrated," as editorial wisdom went at the time.[26] As a rule, European and American translators did not work from the scarce Arabic manuscripts readers falsely believed Galland had found in Cairo but from Galland's or Lane's editions, themselves conglomerations of various manuscripts located in Paris.[27] Still, every editor/translator sought to reproduce the truth of the *Nights* in his or her version of the stories, though what that truth needed to be was culturally contingent. That is, compilers and sellers of the *Nights* did not have complete creative freedom but had to answer to their particular audiences' comprehension of the *Nights* in order to recoup the money invested in their production.[28] One compiler explained thusly: "he frankly acknowledges he has taken many liberties with the stories" in choosing to "abridge the duller parts, or occasionally modify customs and sentiments, which rendered his heroes less estimable and more tedious."[29]

Especially important was making editions of the *Nights* acceptable to parental audiences because for most Americans that century the *Arabian Nights* was first and foremost children's literature. Young Anglo-Americans read highly censored, moralistic, but sumptuously written editions, such as Harper Brothers' 1848 volume "translated and arranged for family reading," received as gifts from parents.[30] One 1848 puff piece for a Harper Brothers edition suggested to book buyers that even adults should not be embarrassed if they found it difficult to shake from their minds the *Nights* depictions of "the fictitious wealth and supernatural agency which . . . enchained the youthful mind and enchanted the senses," pronouncing the stories the most influential in world history and a necessity for kids and their nostalgic parents.[31]

The American love affair with the *Nights* additionally involved some conflation of the *Nights* with and plagiarism of other translated works emanating from the Muslim world: Arabic or Persian poetry, Sufi philosophy or Turkish fable in the form of the *Tales of Nassrudin*, and the Qur'an. George Sale's translation, *Koran, Commonly Called the Alcoran of Mohammed* (1734), in particular seemed to mirror the over-the-top prose style found in Lane's *Arabian Nights*.[32] Likewise, the 1859 Fitzgerald translation of *The Rubaiyat of Omar Khayyam*, poetry attributed to the twelfth-century Persian mathematician and philosopher Omar Khayyam, was, like the *Nights*, a translation with no definitive original. Some American readers believed the *Rubaiyat* expressed a distaste for religious dogma and a love of the simple pleasures in life, from which the Western world gained the phrase, "A Jug of Wine, a Loaf of Bread—and Thou."[33] With his down-to-earth sympathy for the creative process, Lawrence Levine advises us that American uses of Shakespeare—likewise known for their inclusion of new characters, new dialogue, and new humor—were similarly flexible. In his case or ours, the hybrid arts thus produced were "not diluted or denigrated" versions of the originals, he advises us, but "*integrated* into American culture" to create forms "rendered familiar and intimate by virtue of [their] context"(italics in original).[34] That is, the translated adaptations of the *Thousand and One Nights* that would sprout up throughout the century were necessarily crossed over to domestic audiences by their inclusion or exclusion of both foreign and home-grown elements that made them comprehensible.

PLAYING EASTERN IN PRINT

Translated adaptations of the *Arabian Nights* were seldom simply read and forgotten. They were sources repeatedly reread and raided for plot ideas, stock characters, and styles of writing either out of artistic admiration or pressing editorial deadlines. The temptation had begun right away. The dramatic appearance of Antoine Galland's French edition had quickly been "succeeded by a swarm of preposterous imitations pretending also to be translated from oriental manuscripts," an early history of the form explains.[35] These Oriental tales were different only in degree, not in kind, from those translated adaptations of the *Nights* transformed by heavy artistic license. Famed European authors like Thomas Moore and Lord Byron—read in rural Michigan as well as New York and Philadelphia—gave the form great credibility as an invitation to amateur writers hoping to demonstrate their mastery of creative writing.[36]

American Oriental tales appeared as poems or short stories, allegory, fantasy, or pun. They could be satirical, romantic, or moralizing, shockingly subversive or blandly conventional, a celebration of the Muslim world or a nasty debunking of those Westerners who admired it, or any combination of these elements depending on the interpretation of the reader.[37] The charm of Oriental tales among Anglo-American writers and literary magazine readers had especially to do with its recognizable purpose of offering unsolicited moral advice. Oriental tales were defined by highly allegorical, formal, and prolix language derived from Lane's and other editions of the *Nights*, which provided an appealing disguise for the communication of criticism or controversial content that, if stated plainly, might be too heavy handed to be well received or heeded.[38]

Americans just then also had increasing access to many kinds of "moral tales," most of them set in Western locations and distributed by the religious tract societies that would prosper especially during the Second Great Awakening.[39] Ali Isani nicely explains how the two trends of moral writing and the Oriental tale came together at the turn of the nineteenth century: "Orientalism was spreading, and particularly through the medium of the magazine. Articles and poems on the East with full-page illustrations were appearing, enthusiasts were flourishing such Oriental pseudonyms as 'Selim' and 'Orasymn,' one writer of moral essays (possibly a minister) took to signing himself 'Almanzor,' and a Vermont mother given to reciting the poetry of [Thomas Moore's] Lalla Rookh named her child 'Selim.'"[40] These writers in effect used the Oriental tale style to play Eastern in print. Thus, for instance, did Washington Irving write letters to the *New York World* in 1805 as a supposed Tripolitan wag, "Mustapha Rub-a-Dub Kheli Khan," satirizing independent Anglo-American ladies by lampooning fictional North African women.[41]

The utility of the Oriental tale was particularly contingent upon this kind of deceptive literary role-playing, wherein the speaker came across in Eastern voice in order to comment tactfully on contemporary life in ways comprehensible because they flattered the readers' knowledge of Eastern literature and its imitations. A first vogue for literary Oriental tales came and went before 1810, but the style surged again as a vehicle for stories about tyranny and political "slavery" at home during public outrage over the impressment controversy around the War of 1812, in which Britain had defied U.S. sovereignty by arresting as traitors to Britain sailors on ships flying the American flag. The American wars with the North African states in the first two decades of the nineteenth century renewed the currency of the form for authors who wrote stories of Americans taken hostage in North Africa to critique the enslavement of blacks at home.[42] Thereafter, romantically satirical "Oriental Maxims" written in Eastern voice remained popular and later were colloquially known as the "Abou Ben Adhem" genre of poetry and prose after James Henry Leigh Hunt's 1838 poem by the same name.[43]

By the 1840s, domestic authors and readers had developed the Oriental Tale into a creative practice that produced works more seemingly "Oriental"—as Western artistic notion—than *Arabian Nights* translations themselves. Works by Lord Byron, Thomas Moore, Washington Irving, John Greenleaf Whittier, and others served as models to be imaginatively polished not challenged as authors embellished those aspects of the form that seemed most appealing. For the amateur or professional artist needing practical rules about what made a given work recognizably "Eastern" or "Oriental," this meant Persian, Turkish, or Arabic character and place names (or at least ones that sounded as such), plot lines concerning a quest for riches, wisdom, romantic love, or magical transformation as well as elaborate descriptions of colorful processions, pomp and ceremony, utter contentment, or extraordinary beauty. It required "a picture of Eastern luxury from beginning to end—a feast of roses and a flow of fountains, in which we look for nothing but sighs and perfumes," as one reviewer advised in 1852.[44] One also needed a few stock characters: benevolent but powerful potentates like Haroun al-Raschid, fakirs, dervishes, geniis, beautiful but wily women, merchants, wise sages, and of course dancing girls or "houris." One could also employ famous phrases, philosophies, or stories drawn from the Qur'an, Middle Eastern poetry, or translations of the *Nights* to add perceived authentic details to a homegrown creation.

For our analysis of performance and individuation in Eastern guise, the most critical component of this American artistic practice was a style of expression I call Eastern or Oriental voice. This mode of speech was a language of fantastic self-indulgence by which Americans first tried on perceived Eastern styles of personhood defined by excess and consumption. To creative people and their

THE VISION OF AGIB.

AN EASTERN TALE.

The caravan slowly passed on its way through the desert, while the sands glowed like a furnace, and the sun looked hotly down, the travellers voices becoming every moment less animated, and the camels step more heavy. Rich stores were crossing the scorched waste, but as the thirsty and weary merchants toiled through that vast and burning plain, and sickened in the unbroken and fiery glare which surrounded them, they felt that the wealth they bore with them, would be a cheap exchange for the repose and the gentler climate they had left behind. But the distance which stretched before them was now less than that they had already traversed, and they pursued their way with an endurance suited to its evils.

Agib, the nephew of the rich merchant Hussein, accompanied the caravan. The merchandize of Agib was more valuable than that of any of his companions. The richest goods filled his packages—silks for the maidens of Yemen, and jewels of the highest price, and most exquisite workmanship; for his uncle, the wealthy Hussein, had associated him with himself in trade, and they were celebrated in all the bazaars of the east, as dealers in the costliest articles of commerce. This, however, was the young merchant's first journey to Yemen, and of course its dangers and its toils were new to him. Early left an orphan in the house of his uncle, he had been carefully bred up in all the accomplishments of the East; and, habituated to the society of the merchant's only daughter, the beautiful Zarah, he had so won upon her youthful affections, and become himself so much attracted by her early loveliness, that Hussein had resolved to unite these objects of his deep solicitude, and to live in the enjoyment of their continual society. But first, anxious to test the ability of his future son for his own profession, he had, as we have seen, adopted him into partnership with himself, and insisted on his making the journey to Yemen. Greatly did Zarah repine at the separation, nor had the luxury of his early life prepared the young Agib for this trying delay, or the fatigues of the desert Arabia. Yet these he had hitherto borne at least without complaint, and the hoof of his spirited steed had been still among the foremost in the caravan. So with such tales or converse as might beguile the way, the travellers toiled on to the noon of the weary day.

About this hour, however, a cry from the rear of the caravan aroused the young merchant from a day dream of love and Zarah, and, looking back, he beheld, approaching with a rapidity which divested him at once of the power to think, one of those huge and flying pillars of sand, of which he had from time to time heard frightful accounts from the camel drivers. Onward it whirled with furious velocity. A consciousness of

ceived that the spot on which he lay was covered with fresh verdure, and that beside him a copious spring sent forth a stream of pure and pellucid water, which wandered through a beautiful oasis, its banks fringed with palms and pomegranates, and its light ripples disturbing the repose of fragrant amaranths and white lilies, which bent their heads to partake its coolness. Large masses of rock raised themselves around the spring, except on one side, where they were lowered to permit the overflow of the bright and foamy cascade which supplied the rivulet. Immediately on leaving this little cataract the brook became tranquil, and led its waters silently onward through the grass and bloom of the quiet scene.

Agib gazed around him with amazement. He remembered the sand storm of the desert, and was unable to account for his present situation.

"Alla be praised, however," he said at length, as he crept to the clear source of the stream, "for in whatever manner I may have been transported hither, the gracious decree of the eternal only could have provided such an awakening from that sultry slumber." He tasted the waters, and leaned against the rocks with a delicious sense of refreshment and repose.

"But where am I?" he said. "Have I crossed the narrow bridge? Am I already in the gardens of the blessed?"

A strain of music, soft indeed, but clear, liquid and distinct as the voice of the nightingale, now stole upon the ear of the astonished merchant. For some moments it continued like the harmonious warbling of a thousand birds. It ceased.

"Prophet of the faithful!" murmured Agib, "these birds could only sing in Paradise!"

From an aperture in the rock, hitherto unobserved by the enchanted merchant, now issued a form of matchless grace and delicacy. No veil obscured the splendor of features, beautiful beyond the brightest dream of imagination, and the light folds of a thin white robe fell gracefully around a figure, the just proportions of which it did not conceal.

"Alla! Alla!" whispered Agib, fearful by a sound to dispel the illusion. "It is an Houri, beaming with the glory of her immortal existence." The being approached, and Agib yielded his senses to the musical voice which clothed words of welcome with a charm till now unknown.

"Stranger," said this beautiful apparition, "thou art weary—thou hast suffered. Repose awaits thee in my dwelling. Unconsciousness to-day released thee from the pang of a burning death. Enter with me, and refresh thy returning senses with delight."

She turned and signed to the merchant to follow her.

"I obey thee, Glory of Paradise," he said, "for doubtless I behold in thee the loveliest of the Houris?"

"Not one of those blessed immortals am I," said the stranger with a smile as soft as the voice in which she

An Oriental tale written in Eastern voice, a language of sumptuous excess, by an American author playing Oriental in print. *Southern Literary Messenger,* 1837.

audiences this meant verbose or metaphorical diction that summed up Anglo-American perceptions of how Arabic, Persian, or Ottoman Turkish sounded to native speakers, past and present.[45] The author's practice of speaking in Oriental voice, a way to play Eastern in print, was a crucial step in broadening the appeal to Anglo-Americans of Eastern personae that in the future would be enacted in naming practices, speech styles, costuming, lyceum and parade performance, and consumption patterns.

In translations that seemed credible to Anglo-Americans, Eastern voice reproduced the commonly appreciated "flavor of Oriental sentiment and adventure, . . . magic, drollery, wit, and passion," one reader of the *Arabian Nights* said.[46] This was "the pompous language of the East,"[47] as Americans would have described it back then, something James Gill has more recently identified as a kind of "faux-archaic prose."[48] When they spoke in Oriental voice, readers, editors and writers gave immense cultural authority to a number of soon prevalent clichés about Easterners' supposed proclivity for verbose language, pomp and formality, a language of the ultra-artificial.[49] Of course, the frequency with which Anglo-American authors adopted these purportedly Eastern forms for their own creative arts meant that in effect these colorful practices were utterly American. They demonstrated Anglo-Americans' own innate creativity and desire for gaudiness and formality, even if many were in denial about it in order to believe that the cultural difference represented by Eastern voice was real.

In the nineteenth-century sense, then, the artistic practice of writing or speaking in Eastern voice to play Eastern in print constituted literary "Orientalism." In spite of its ubiquity, Americans were not uncritical producers or consumers of the form. "Strictly speaking, Orientalism is a mode of speech," the *Knickerbocker* had famously revealed in 1853, "Orientalism . . . is a complex idea, made up of history and scenery, suffused with imagination and irradiate with revelation. . . . We frame to ourselves a deep azure sky, and a languid, alluring atmosphere; associate luxurious ease with the coffee-rooms and flower gardens of the Seraglio at Constantinople. . . . We see grave and revered turbans sitting cross-legged on Persian carpets in baths and harems, . . . This is Orientalism . . . as it swims before the sensuous imagination." It was an ultra-artificial form that described, the author admitted, a romantic East that was only a prized remnant of historical Asian nations whose modern descendants he actually saw in grave decline. He warned that to compare the real Muslim world to the fantasy was pointless, for "to analyze it is to dissolve the charm."[50] As a literary practice, the goal of the Oriental tale was to perfect the "idea of the

East," Mohammed Sharafuddin tells us, that made sense for a given author and for his audience.[51]

As the *Knickerbocker* described them, the standard tools of the practice were hard at work in American Oriental tales, not toward the subversion or questioning of the form's conventions but in perfection of them. Chris Steiner tells us that such replication can make a new form iconic and thus more authentic than unique or older cultural products because oft-replicated or mass-produced cultural products "effectively produce [their] own canons of authenticity." Audiences and artists then come to believe that effective new productions reassert accepted information about the genre as a whole.[52] In making the conventions of the Oriental tale seem authentic and natural, many creative people attempted to reproduce the "gorgeous East" that readers sought by providing over-the-top renditions of the "Oriental warmth of feeling and richness of imagery" that defined the genre.[53] Thereafter, the task with most Oriental tale–style creations was to assemble a combination of those components that reproduced the audience's current expectations, that seemed perfectly Oriental but in a slightly novel way. The descriptions of Eastern riches Americans admired became more ornate and over the top, the supposed verboseness of Eastern voice more extravagant and wordy, the stories of romantic love more sentimental and breathless, and the jokes redirected at contemporary topics to keep them funny.

The industry in Oriental tales was so large among Anglo-Americans that many readers were not always entirely sure when they were reading translated adaptations of an Eastern source or a domestic imitation.[54] Interpretation and debate over the form would split along the lines of "high" versus "low" art, scholarly genre, or commercial form in ways evident in other modes of American cultural expression. As professional academic Orientalists staked their claim on specialized knowledge of the East, some complained that well-meaning but thinly researched commercial Oriental tales gave short shrift to the literatures of Asia. One irritated reviewer warned of an 1865 compilation in which, "specimens of Oriental thought and fancy run one after another in the accidental order of a commonplace book, without attempt at arrangement of any kind by subject, by country or by period, . . . and this is a much more serious defect—of heterogeneous character, translations from Oriental originals, translations from Oriental imitators, and original imitations of Oriental thought and style [juxtaposed]." More to the point, of the work's American editor the reviewer asked, "How know we that he is so penetrated with the Oriental spirit that all he gives us is genuinely Oriental? May we not be taking in a larger share of [the editor] Mr. Alger himself than we at first suspect, or than we care to receive?"[55] Well-to-do translations could only come across as intelligent and respectful to their originators if their components were properly attributed and the reworking of the prose through translation explained in the footnotes. For the "commonplace book" and other more middling commercial products, the limits of artistic license tended to be less obvious because a given work referred back to a domestic tradition of imitation for authority.

Originally, the sardonic value of early Oriental tales was a product of the half-disguised literary passing an author used, knowing his audience would know Easternized satire when they saw it. As people polished and replicated the conventions of playing Eastern in print, for a new generation of readers the distinctions between the supposed originals and their Western imitations became hazier with time. After half a century, satire replicated often enough became romantic cliché, which could in turn promote the idea, person, or practice earlier authors had set out to critique. Indeed, Oriental tales continued to be useful and intelligible to readers by pleasing the cynical and romantic at the same time, depending on the reader's inclination. Take, for example, "The Oriental Merchant," a short story published in *Harper's New Monthly Magazine* in 1854. The hero of the tale, Hamed, is initially tricked by a group of women including "a very young maiden, who after having laughed [at Hamed] with the rest, had flung herself carelessly on a pile of cushions under a tree . . . [and] seemed annoyed that her beauty, which was great, did not amaze him." Here we see key components of the form—leisure, romance, wittiness. When, by the end of the narrative, the author resolves the sexual tension between Haj Hamed and the young woman by reassuring the reader that "she settled down into a most prudent and exemplary wife—which relieves our mind," it must have dawned on many readers that the tale was a satire on contemporary courtship rituals.[56]

Nonetheless, some readers, perhaps all those young women noted for their enthusiastic consumption of romance novels that decade, might have read "The Oriental Merchant" as a serious romance story. Indeed, the heroine was clever, assertive, affluent, and beautiful and did win the heart of the eligible hero in the end. Either reading would have drawn on many readers' understandings of the famed ingenuity of the *Nights'* female characters, who displayed appealing modes of personal autonomy to plenty of nineteenth-century women.[57] New audiences came to know Oriental tales as romance stories, a process that would help increasing numbers of people internalize the visions of ease and plenty inherent in playing Eastern and adapt them to the ideology of consumer capitalism as a way to a kind of personal autonomy.

Because of this kind of flexibility of interpretation, wherein the same piece could be moral tale or burlesque depending on the reader, Oriental tales would continue to be regular features in a diverse body of publications beyond *Harper's*, where the style became a dependable bit that writers of any stripe could use to get a laugh or sentimental identification. What many of these cultural products had in common was the fact that by the mid-nineteenth century, the phrase "as fantastic as anything in the Arabian Nights" and analogous similes served as shorthand for everything deemed astonishingly beautiful, richly luxurious, or simply unbelievable. Such over-the-top metaphors were not available in any other tradition of world literature and certainly not in any with such cultural authority among "the reading public." One contemporary author defined this group of Anglo-American consumers: "those whose leisure or tastes, and professional habits, lead them to peruse all new books, or all belonging to certain departments of literature or science." These readers he contrasted with a more popular market of rural middling or working-class readers who cherished the Bible but might be uncritical of what he perceived as the "doubtful or pernicious character of lighter literature" in the penny press or dime novels.[58]

By 1850, newly accessible opportunities for consumption had appeared in the form of theaters, dime museums, department and variety stores, peddlers' wagons, circus tents, and the pages of mail-order catalogs. With a burst in increasingly efficient or even mass production, people could take advantage of volume sales and lower prices on all sorts of consumer products, from newspapers to clothing to curios.[59] In this atmosphere, Anglo-Americans were drawn to Oriental tale–style stories of rapid transformation, satisfaction, and wealth, which had entirely new currency because they helped people articulate their hopes, worries, and astonishment over the benefits and hazards of capitalist transformation. After the successful end of the war with Mexico and the advent of the California gold rush, to many Anglo-Americans the United States appeared to have limitless potential, rich in land and in natural resources out west with booming wheat, timber, and cotton economies, overheated stock exchanges (until the panic of 1857), and a growing white population. Once-nascent American sectors like railways, manufacturing, insurance, credit, retailing, journalism, and publishing were swiftly developing components of a newly industrial nation. Various people noted the "go-ahead spirit" of entrepreneurship and speculation that seemed to drive these changes.[60]

Thus, for journalists and other public speakers in those days, Easternized tales of sudden transformation and incredible riches were useful metaphors making up a kind of Orientana of capitalism. In 1851, a *New York Times* piece typically suggested that the Gold Rush boom overflowing from California "almost surpass[es] in reality the gorgeous fictions of the Arabian Nights."[61] The tale of "Aladdin and the Magic Lamp" became a particularly tempting model and comprehensibly exotic form of self-flattery for those Anglo-Americans who stood to benefit most from these developments. Readers knew that in the *Nights*, the impoverished character Aladdin finds a genie living in a disused brass lamp. The genie emerges from his container to materialize incredible wealth in gold, gems, and other priceless items as well as a palace for Aladdin, though these riches cause Aladdin significant personal trouble he must struggle to overcome.

In a typical use of this metaphor in 1853, the publisher and journalist George Putnam sought to play Eastern storyteller in homage to the tremendous commercial growth of New York City, with its stores full to the rafters with merchandise, sidewalks crowded with people, streets undergoing an architectural rebirth and a building boom:[62] "Yet this story [of Aladdin] which dazzled our childhood's eyes with unimaginable splendors, grows daily tamer and tamer, before the passing wonders of the days in which we live. We also are Aladdins, and for us the Genii of the lamp are working. For us too the farthest Indian shores and the Eastern isles yield their treasures gladly, gold, frankincense and myrrh, diamonds and pearls, rubies, . . . carpets in which the foot sinks as in moss, perfumes that load the winter air with summer, . . . and dainties which make our democratic tables groan with the profusion of Lucullus and the splendor of [caliph Haroun] Al Raschid."[63] By way of a homegrown Aladdin tale told in Eastern voice, he offered to romanticize the raw productive and commercial power of the city in the classic mode of a romantic Eastern tale.

Putnam also used his Oriental tale in the moral tale mode to urge reform in persuasive language that contrasted his Eastern voice above with a more down-to-earth prose that compared a wealthy but worried Aladdin to a New York City burdened with "the mean and unsuitable docks and markets, the filthy streets, the farce of a half-fledged and inefficient police, and the miserably bad government, generally, of an unprincipled common-council, in the composition of which ignorance, selfishness, impudence, and greediness seem to have equal share." Here was the Gilded Age in a nutshell, apparent to Putnam already in 1853 and voiced as a moralizing Eastern tale. His contrasting of fantasies of riches and beauty with the leaden inner reality of a capitalist city was a meta-phor that could encapsulate both the potential and the often-disappointing actuality of the nation.

THE TRAVELER'S ORIENTAL TALE: SHOPPING IN THE OTTOMAN EMPIRE

Although the majority merely engaged with North Africa and West Asia as armchair travelers through printed matter, cheap illustrations, or lyceum lectures, Americans of means went to see the lands of the *Arabian Nights* for themselves. Beginning in the 1840s, culture, technology, and commerce came together to give many increasing access as consumers to the world beyond North America. Anglo-Americans would thus transform playing Eastern in print into a performed consumer practice enacted through imported goods and their domestic imitations. In the beginning, this transformation required that Americans tour the Ottoman Empire, usually as a diversion from a European tour. Anglo-American access to the Middle East was a product of the discovery of the "increasing tourist potential" of the region by entrepreneurs various countries, not least in the Ottoman Empire itself.[64] Growing personal wealth for some as well as blooming communication and transportation industries that integrated the telegraph, postal service, publishing, and rail with the new international steamer service made a Middle Eastern visit much more doable for Americans in terms of time, money, and health risks than, say, India, Rhodesia, or the Philippines. For instance, in 1860 over 19,000 Americans would cross the Atlantic, and five hundred of them toured Egypt.[65] A typical route saw Americans voyage in winter to Alexandria by ship, south through Egypt by boat on the Nile and back, then by camel and horse caravan across the Sinai to Palestine, Syria, and perhaps Anatolia.

Though exact proportions are difficult to know, a large minority of these tourists had the skills with which to compose publishable travel narratives and the business or social connections with which to secure publication deals. Many traveled abroad only due to the sponsorship of a newspaper or of magazines like *Harper's Monthly*. They often published work on other subjects, laboring for newspapers and literary magazines to pay the bills. Narratives of travel soon became enormously popular and constituted some of the most ubiquitous and profitable of all nonfiction available to a growing readership stateside. Cumulatively, it had the effect of promoting Middle Eastern tourism to Anglo-

American readers as a realistic vacation possibility. Writers celebrated the interpretive agency of the American traveler, and by extension the reader, while often minimizing the ingenuity and personhood of foreign peoples for patriotic American readers who wished to imagine U.S. citizens as independent actors abroad.[66]

Authors also needed to flatter the knowledge of Anglo-Americans immersed in other cultural products describing the history, people, and landscape of the Middle East, often as a Protestant "Holy Land," most especially one other piece of highly manipulated yet supremely authoritative piece of Eastern literature—the Bible. Most Anglo-Americans knew the book inside and out and had spent many hours imagining what Palestine or Egypt had looked like in biblical days. A fortunate few were able to venture overseas to look for evidence of biblical truth in the people and landscapes of the Ottoman Empire.[67] In contrast to the *Arabian Nights*, which inspired literary masquerade and performed Eastern impersonation, people would never write satirical "biblical tales" or in time decorate their homes in a style restaging the Last Supper because the Bible, as they read it, did not celebrate the increasingly influential capitalist ideals of acquisition, contentment, and leisure, only the work ethic and self-denial parts. Many Protestants further argued that although the Holy Land might be located in the Middle East, the Hebrew cultures and history it represented were not culturally "Oriental" like the *Nights* nor was the Bible because it was not characterized by romantic stories of extravagant consumption, fantasy, or guilt-free hedonism but cautionary ones.[68] That is, in the hands of middling and affluent Anglo-Americans, the Bible advocated work, production, and restraint, while the *Nights* advocated play, consumption, and self-expression. Thus did the two works share a bedside table in many households.

To put their foreign experiences in a comprehensible form for these readers, travel writers often employed Eastern voice, either for romantic or satirical purposes. Take Ross Browne, a young Kentucky satirist who had seen California and the East African coast before setting out for the Ottoman Empire with a publishing deal for foreign letters with the *Daily National Intelligencer*.[69] His 1855 travel narrative *Yusuf: A Crusade in the East* was widely popular and was excerpted for promotional purposes in *Harper's New Monthly Magazine*. While in the Ottoman Levant, Browne had speculated on the attitude his donkey held toward him and joked that the animal had a number of times intentionally fallen into ditches simply to humiliate his rider. To the American tourist on his back Browne suggested that the animal had said, "Bismillah! you are in the mud now! See how I throw dirt on you! You needn't think to impose upon me because I'm little. By the beard of the Prophet! A pretty fellow you are, truly! Two hundred pounds' weight, nearly, riding on a little chap like me! But don't think because you're a bigger ass than I that you can lord it over me in this way much longer. I won't stand it."[70] Here were a number of the necessary ingredients common to the genre: a sense of hauteur, ample references to God or Anglicized Arabic phrases, and emphatic interjections derived from the classical Arabic of the Qur'an such as "verily" or in this case "truly." Browne may have hoped his beast of burden, speaking in Oriental voice, would get across the sometimes cynical sentiment he found among tourism workers in the Middle East. He also provided an opportunity for the reader, if he or she chose, to laugh at the arrogance of Western travelers—the cliché of the tacky tourist was fast becoming current in those days—or chuckle in agreement with Browne's satire of Anglo-American reverence for Oriental tales, reduced to the words of an "ass."[71]

Browne's satirical Eastern voice was a minority one though, and most American visitors to the Ottoman Empire who played Eastern in print did so in order to write about their experiences out of romantic affectation. Some authors went so far as to imagine themselves literally adding "a new leaf from the 'Arabian Nights,'" as one author suggested, to celebrate picturesque or satisfying moments on the road that helped them forget how tired or homesick they were in an age when travel went by boat or pack animal and was hard work. In time, whole travel narratives would appear in American periodicals framed as Oriental tales. Authors and editors could explain a voyage down the Nile as "Ethiopian Nights Entertainments" or a trip to the Tigris River as a visit to "The Land of the 'Arabian Nights.'"[72] The cumulative effect of such recorded performances of playing Eastern abroad was probably the ethnological verification of Eastern voice and the historicity of Eastern tales, which were mostly a domestic invention. Indeed, there had long been doubt about the folkloric accuracy of the *Arabian Nights*, although plenty of people who actually visited the region still believed that the *Nights* contained "pretty accurate ideas of Eastern social life," as an 1848 promotional review promised.[73] An *Atlantic Monthly* writer agreed in 1889, echoing a century of scholarly and middle-class belief grounded in a sense that old world nations had a timelessness to their cultures and artistic production, "For Eastern customs remain long unchanged, and what one now observed in a Cairo khan may have occurred a thousand years ago in a Bagdad bazaar."[74] American tourists did not really expect to see geniis or Ali Baba moving about in Cairo or Damascus, but many did hope to see things that reminded them of the material abundance, formality of social relations, and romantic beauty they read about in the stories. Plenty of these travelers would thereafter argue for the historicity of the *Nights* in order to lend authenticity to the personae they drew from the stories and the actual Middle East.

Traveling writers used the Oriental tale mode to make their narratives relevant to American readers by emphasizing those aspects of the Empire that a particular person found beautiful, which one might describe as the true spirit of the East. Thus, in the interest of flow, an author could reserve criticism of those aspects of the place he or she did not appreciate, which writers might describe as a recent Muslim imposition, evidence of a "corrupt" Ottoman administration, or an imposing Western influence, for other pages. In the Middle East, when American tourists found the *Arabian Nights* alive and well it was in very specific, mostly urban locations. Some curious travelers came right out and asked locals about the stories while in Egypt or Syria and were delighted to find that local people knew them. One advised readers in 1856, "The old Arabian tales are learned chiefly by oral repetition, and by frequent hearing; [and] it is not easy to find in Damascus Arabic copies of the 'Thousand and One Nights,'" although rumor had it Egyptian governor Muhammad Ali's government had put the stories in print again.[75]

Others saw the essence of the *Nights* in regional architecture or interior design in affluent Middle Eastern homes. During a visit to Egyptian governor Abbas Pasha's palace and residence, the Rhode Island native Jane Eames, like others who visited the homes of the Ottoman and Egyptian elite, marveled at its décor and luxuries that "brought to our minds passages in that wonderful book, 'the Arabian Nights.'"[76] Since many of the *Arabian Nights* tales take place in urban settings, Americans often ascribed a romantic charm to the cosmopolitan environments of West Asian cities. "Altogether, [Damascus] is considered the most Oriental city of the world," a Fetridge's *American Travelers' Guide* characteristically explained: "Nearly every house has a beautiful garden, fragrant with orange-flowers and rose-buds, a sparkling fountain fed by the waters of Abana or Pharpar. The ceilings are arabesque, walls mosaic, and floors marble. . . . The spirit of the Arabian Nights is prevalent in all its streets [where] the bazaars still retain that poetry and romance which looks you in the face from out every page of the Arabian Nights."[77] The elegant houses and public buildings in that city "seemed to realize all the legends of the days of Haroun Al Rashid," while "Aladdin's palace might seem but an imperfect copy of the mosque of El Amwy," a *North American Review* piece concurred.[78] Travel to the Ottoman Empire provided the first opportunity for middle-class or upper-class Americans to verify the *Thousand and One Nights* in person. This was a make or break moment in which Americans might have been disabused of their ideas about an abundant and luxurious consumer Orient. For some this was exactly what happened when they saw the very real poverty there. Yet most Americans complained about some aspects of the Empire but enjoyed traveling there nonetheless, in part by consuming local goods and services that made them feel privileged.

To many travelers, a trip East offered what Bayard Taylor, an exceedingly popular travel writer in the 1850s, called "delicious rest," a leisured prototype of the consumer's Oriental tale.[79] Eastern repose was a mode of playing Eastern in which one could justify sitting around or taking a nap as an enactment of an age-old remnant of good taste that showed worldliness and confidence. The (in)famously pious and abrasive American author William Prime wrote from Egypt in those days of common knowledge of "the reception of guests in the East [which] has been so frequently described that I may run the risk of a repetition," he said, excusing his own passage praising the rituals of coffee drinking, pipe smoking, and leisured conversation.[80] New Yorker Jesse Spencer had already written about "Romance of Life on the Nile" in 1848, in which he improvised a leisured Eastern persona. From his boat he reveled in "[the] dreamy stillness of the atmosphere, the air of repose, . . . splendor of the starry vault of heaven," and the other chances he had had on the trip for laying about with pipes and coffee, imagining himself a philosophical character in "the glowing stories of the "Thousand and One Nights.""[81] Many embraced such scenarios because they too accepted their premise, which juxtaposed the essentialized work ethic of the American against a similarly romanticized Eastern appreciation for leisure.

Although Americans perceived some people they met in the Middle East—unhelpful officials or indifferent merchants and dragomen mostly—to be lazy fatalists indulging in "ignoble ease," they found the ideal of Oriental repose appealing as a way to mystify and make respectable American habits of leisure.[82] International tourism gave tourists, and writers on working vacations, ways to voice dissatisfaction with life at home that William Leach argues were "symptomatic of changes taking place within Western society—and especially in cities—that had little to do with imperialism or with the desire to appropriate somebody else's property, but that symbolized a feeling of something missing from Western culture itself, a longing for a 'sensual' life more 'satisfying' than traditional Christianity could endorse."[83] Smoking, coffee drinking, and idle time spent lying on some carpet or pile of cushions suggested ways of being productive of cultural meaning while indulging oneself at the same time and of exposing aspects of one's personality that might have seemed trivial or inappropriate in other contexts. Back in the United States, beginning in the 1850s, this mode of playing Eastern was especially an affectation of young men who wished to appear more manly, evident in the fashions for smoking jackets and gentlemen's lounges where one donned a fez.[84]

Venturing out to local markets with their guides and dragomen, American tourists sought out specific souvenirs that seemed quintessentially Oriental in their evocation of particular scenes in Eastern tales. On their trip up the Nile, William Prime's party purchased "match-boxes, cups, and plates, vases, and like articles, which are curious and even beautiful in appearance, and with which we loaded ourselves as we returned to the boat."[85] In Damascus, too, Eastern Christians produced "those splendid, gold-embroidered shawls and scarfs, which some travellers have set down as among 'the lost arts' of Damascus," another said.[86] Jane Eames delighted in animated Cairo markets that could "dazzle the eye, and tempt the fingers to open the purse."[87] There she and other American travelers sought out local clothing, fabric, carpets, brassware, swords, ink stands, and hookah (narghile) water pipes.[88] In the same bazaars, the Philadelphia minister Benjamin Dorr and his party sat crosslegged "à la Turque" just like the locals did, he said, to inspect fine silk and embroideries. Access to these products, which were indeed expensive luxuries if imported into the United States, reinforced Dorr's perception that the Middle Eastern past might be as luxurious and fantastic as many believed, the markets serving as a portal to the "true" East of the *Nights*.[89] There was a large grain of truth to such an attitude since the Middle East had long been a highly developed, often affluent trading center for consumer products. The nineteenth-century North African or Middle Eastern *suq* or bazaar offered a shopping experience unlike any in the United States, with its vast square footage, many shops crowded together in bustling, narrow streets, and products stacked in piles monitored by dozens of shopkeepers.[90]

The fictionalized Oriental merchant, now available in person, seemed like a dream of the *Nights* come true to many tourists. He was also a testament to the salesmanship and business sense of many Ottoman subjects who facilitated touristic consumer choice and convenience. American sailor and entrepreneur

William Francis Lynch was always on the lookout for trade opportunities and wrote of visiting one like-minded business owner: "Mehemet Effendi, a Turkish dealer in perfumes and embroidery. . . . In his neat back shop we were always sure to be regaled with pipes, coffee, and a cool, delicious preparation of cream. He seemed to possess Aladdin's lamp, for we could call for nothing that was not immediately forthcoming, from a jasmine pipe-stem to the golden embroidery of Persia; from the attar of roses to the Indian cashmere."[91] Bayard Taylor similarly told of his own shopping excursions and "the picturesque merchants and their customers" he found. In Damascus he purchased a sword marked "Hegira, 181, which corresponds to A.D. 798. This was during the Caliphate of Haroun Al-Rachid, and who knows but the sword may have once flashed in the presence of that great and glorious sovereign—nay, been drawn by his own hand!"[92] The contemporary artisan or shopkeeper who probably mystified the sword with such an inscription referring to Arabian Nights–era Baghdad might have predicted that when Taylor paid for the sword, he would also buy a vicarious participation in the stories.[93]

Many Ottoman subjects looked upon such situations and chose to facilitate travelers' desire for anteekeh, the colloquial Arabic term derived from the robust trade in household objects, ancient pottery, stonework, scarabs, papyri, mummy parts, and carpets. As the 1840s and 1850s passed, tombs and gift shops were emptied of their contents and actual antiquities became more rare, so that travelers were just as likely to purchase "antique novelties" of recent local or even European manufacture.[94] Ottoman and European entrepreneurs were also quick to size up the foreign market, exporting many high-quality products that bypassed "misguided tourists" who actually went to the land of their production. "The brilliant things are packed off for Paris, and turbans, and pipes, and slippers are bought better (the papers tell us) on the Boulevard," Harper's Monthly told American shoppers in 1853.[95]

PLAYING EASTERN AT HOME:
THE CONSUMER'S ORIENTAL TALE

Readers would increasingly be able to try out these forms of Eastern consumption at home, taking the act of playing Oriental from reading and writing through foreign experimentation to domestic practice of individuation and self-fulfillment through spending. At the same mid-century moment as American tourists to the Ottoman Empire were experimenting with a performed

Oriental tale as consumers and writing home about it, the retail landscape in the United States had begun to change dramatically. Large middle-class stores could already be found in most big cities in the North, East, and Midwest and in San Francisco, and department stores with broader selections of merchandise emerged by the 1880s. Contemporary department store designers were beginning to produce richly cluttered retail environments that praised consumer agency in picking and choosing a unique assortment from the fantasy-of-plenty windows and store interiors provided.[96] Each customer could in his or her own way encourage an "ethos of accumulation, speculation, and display" that would grow decade by decade into the incredible proportions of the 1890s.[97] All the while, shoppers in small towns and the South and West perused the pages of mail-order catalogs to make similar purchasing choices.[98] Imports of consumer items would multiply by four or five times between the Civil War and turn of the century depending upon the item, with prices dropping substantially relative to personal income.[99] Brick and mortar establishments, mail order businesses, and a growing contingent of urban import shops and auctions offered goods from around the world that encouraged customers to demand yet more novelty.

In fact, American entrepreneurs, like George Peale of Peale's Museum in Philadelphia, had been at work since the early nineteenth century to communicate the basic humanity of the foreign artist so as to promote consumption of imported products.[100] Peale's venture would be joined after the Civil War by New York import stores, some of them run by immigrants from the Ottoman Empire itself, that supplemented travelers' overseas souvenir purchases with stocks of rugs, swords, inlaid tables, brasswork, clothing, and ceramics. Several thousand Syrian Christians also immigrated to the United States in the decades following the Civil War. Many eschewed factory jobs to work as self-employed peddlers of all sorts of objects, including jewelry, "notions," Oriental carpets, and linens.[101] Often recruited directly from the Ottoman Empire, these merchants worked all over the United States living within developing Eastern immigrant communities, especially in New York City or, like Naseef Freige, camping on his own at the south end of 14th St. where residents of Fargo, North Dakota could find him in the late 1890s.[102] Some women came too, raising money to send home, and many families became middle class in the old country through these remittances.[103]

Probably the most famous of these Eastern entrepreneurs was "Far-Away Moses," the Constantinople guide famously described in Mark Twain's 1869

Innocents Abroad and Murray's Ottoman travel handbook. He and at least one family member came to the United States in 1869 and stayed over fifteen years. With his son-in-law as a partner, the two sold imported objects from the Empire, wearing their Ottoman citizenship in the form of Turkish accents and foreign clothing that helped market their merchandise. Moses came off to Americans as "tall and venerable looking, [wearing] extravagantly wide, baggy trowsers, a long, loose outer garment with wide sleeves and trimmed with yellow fur, a waist sash of variegated Persian stuff, white stockings, . . . and for head-gear a fiery-red fez." The *New York Times* said his companion was similarly "rather good looking" but wore Western dress with his fez.[104]

By then the imaginatively romantic Ottoman Empire souveniring of the 1850s had crossed the Atlantic, and domestic shoppers were transforming it into a post–Civil War consumer ethic of self-expression that appealed to various segments of the Anglo-American market: old money families, Gilded Age *nouveau riches*, and the growing middle class.[105] The most obvious space for playing Eastern for many was at home, where amateur and professional decorators would attempt to recreate Middle Eastern modes of hospitality and luxury as an oasis from the world of commerce. They fueled a broad interest in Oriental tale–style decor premised on the idea that consumption was a creative act in which the owner could arrange objects, interiors, and clothes to create a unique effect articulating personal taste. Already in the 1870s middling and upper-class Anglo-Americans often talked about such connections "between personality and setting."[106] It was not yet the fully elaborated, utterly democratic "new commercial aesthetic" James Leach has uncovered at work in turn of the century marketing theory, but an earlier, more exclusive prototype readers, writers, and home decorators were working out by acting out styles of consumption and contentment they had first read about as children in the *Arabian Nights* and later in travel narratives written in Eastern voice.[107]

Meanwhile, publishers continued to release new adapted translations of the *Arabian Nights* throughout the nineteenth century, each new edition changing to reflect the times. Domestic illustrators showed readers how to make use of products from the Empire with illustrations that crossed a new edition over by depicting the growing fashions in Easternized American living. Eastern décor could also be the style of most extreme cost and clutter, much as Eastern voice had been a language of sumptuous excess, formality, and prolixity.[108] Anglo-Americans who could afford it created "Arabian divan"–style parlors or gentleman's lounges and studios where the man of the house could smoke, fez-clad,

"Prince, we must make you amends for so many fasts."

Scene of comfort and plenty from a McLoughlin Brothers of New York edition of *Arabian Nights' Entertainments*, ca. 1885.

on cushions surrounded by provocative sculptures of odalisques. Middle-class women created more frugal but equally imaginative "Oriental cozy corners" as a home-decorating equivalent to the literary practice of the Oriental tale. There the *ottoman* footrest and generously upholstered *divan* challenged stiff and spindly Victorian chairs and settees to speak of comfort and plenty.[109] An interest in draped fabric was also crucial after the antebellum "textile revolution" that provided a vast selection of new fabrics to shoppers.[110] Once made laboriously by hand, fabric was now mass produced or imported and was displayed by some in excessive amounts, hanging over doorways, draped across the corners of rooms to frame a couch or shelf, or nailed overhead to completely conceal the ceiling. All of these uses created an aesthetic of the ultra-artificial, which people saw as rich and mysterious interiors that communicated the sense that the homeowner was living in a tent or desert caravan litter.[111] Jackson Lears explains that advertisers between 1870 and 1900 similarly used this aesthetic of Oriental repose in advertisements that placed common products in "settings of luxuriant sensuality," reinforcing the currency of Eastern-styled decorative interiors as spaces of satisfaction and contentment.[112]

Yet to really make a room come across like an Eastern divan, one needed Oriental carpets. Many Anglo-Americans believed these intricate and expensive handmade items were the most precious of all Eastern luxuries, and American tourists spoke of finding them in great profusion in hotels, shops, and mosques overseas. According to many schools of design thought, Middle Eastern carpets served as examples of pure art, embodying "the most perfect . . . color and design that can be procured," one designer advised.[113] The Oriental carpet as elite collector's item also became fashionable just as cheaper machine-made imitations were becoming available to the average middle-class consumer, a market many Americans and some Middle Eastern and Asian producers perceived as vulgar. Hand-made antique carpets in particular were supremely favorable over the tacky modern pieces: "a room whose carpet is grass-green, with large red spots or big flowers on it," the *New York Times* chided readers in 1872, was a gaudy formality some decorators perhaps incorrectly believed communicated sophistication but actually reeked of homegrown mass production.[114]

During the 1870s and 1880s, European and American artists concerned by the growing ubiquitousness of manufactured objects and art reproductions began to display Persian carpets, old ones in particular, on walls in their homes and in museums and galleries as simultaneously sophisticated and uncomplicated art, embodying "simplicity or splendour."[115] Explaining these carpets as a kind of "primitivist nostalgia" produced by noble people practicing ancient arts inspired by innate genius, many idealized the foreign contexts in which the carpets were often produced as free of labor strife or commercialism and divorced from the ostensibly effeminate and materialist world of European art schools, artists salons, and their wealthy but credulous patrons.[116] Thus did Oriental rugs epitomize the consumer's Oriental tale. As objects they spoke of independence from the market, the ultra-artificial and ultranatural at the same time, while the middling domestic imitations spoke of the democratization of such consumer individuation.

At the 1876 Philadelphia Centennial Exposition, the staff of Mssrs. Hiam, Vidal & Co. brought carpets and other products from the Ottoman Empire to sell to elite and middle-class customers, applying detailed provenances to their merchandise. Their retail environment included on-site production space, which encouraged one American to imagine "[t]he leisurely Oriental, seated before the loom in her own house, earning easily enough to satisfy her simple wants . . . with the eye of a born artist." Thus did she create art "which no steam-driven loom will allow" because of her "inevitable individuality" that rubbed off on the owner as well. Plenty of Americans responded to the marketing of carpets as items of "Oriental Home Industry" with picturesque but fictional details about the women and children who might spend months or years making a single carpet at home. Such Easterners seemed like respectably exotic Eastern workers who spoke of Oriental markets and flying carpet stories to consumers rattled by urban disorder like the 1877 railway strikes or the tramp armies riding the rails of the Gilded Age.[117] American romanticization of the cultures of Italy, Spain, or Native America functioned in similar ways to idealize objects and people, to be sure.[118] Yet the ethos of excessive, luxurious abundance people looked for in the ideology of consumption came straight from the *Arabian Nights*.

Consequently, carpet dealers stateside were as quick as their foreign colleagues to capitalize on their customers' desires to express "tasteful," richly abundant interpretations of the Eastern world in their own homes.[119] Print advertisements for carpets soon became another venue for the Oriental tale as artistic practice as illustrators employed clichéd images of onion domes, palm trees, camels plodding across star-lit deserts, or turbaned men reposing on the merchandise before a rug-bearing merchant fresh from the caravan. This was no random exoticism but carefully chosen scenes derived from the *Arabian Nights*, Oriental tales, and Ottoman Empire travel narratives that emphasized shopping as a leisured activity that flattered consumer choice, leisure, and creativity. With the boost provided by the Columbian Exposition in Chicago in 1893, Oriental carpets would continue to be dependable sellers, "a good investment," and an easy choice for the consumer seeking a compromise between financial prudence and satisfying spending.[120]

Most important, though, were the middling decorators who began buying inexpensive imports and domestic copies made in an Oriental style. One market watcher speculated on the volumes of imitation Oriental carpets American manufacturers began putting on the market: "There must be a wide number of persons to whom [the Oriental carpet's] more prominent features are to some extent *familiar and attractive*, for no one ever forged worthless paper, or borrowed a trade-mark from unpopular goods."(emphasis added)[121] Manufacturers designed a plentiful selection of Eastern-styled carpets at low prices accessible to new groups of home keepers. These buyers might desire to appear European in taste by buying such reproductions. Yet they also had the option of seeing the carpet as a souvenir of Oriental leisure, a familiar prop in Eastern tales of rich merchants' households. This interpretation drew on many Anglo-Americans' long interest—especially among women—in Eastern domestic life. Seldom reduced to the cliché of the harem before the 1890s, women more often idealized Eastern households as a privileged space of relaxed familial relations protected from masculine interests.[122]

Thus, the lady's Oriental cozy corner that emerged in American parlors in the 1870s and beyond was not a metaphorical comparison between affluent American women and the ostensible prisoners of Middle Eastern harems but a celebration of consumer creativity and freedom put over in the richest style available. Prototypes for this kind of creativity appeared in middle-class print venues like *Art Amateur* magazine, the *New York Times*, *Scribner's Monthly*, and countless women's magazines as well as design books and trade magazines like *Decorator and Furnisher*.[123] To get into these venues, information on Eastern fashions and products came by way of a network of tourism, publishing, and retailing. After the Civil War, American travel to the Ottoman Empire had only accelerated, especially with the advent of Cook Company packaged tours in 1869, increasing the volume of this information and the size of the potential audience for Eastern-styled consumer practices.[124]

Typically, in an 1877 piece promoting his travel book *Land of the Arabian Nights*, William Perry Fogg reminded *Scribner's Monthly* readers of the marketing power of West Asian bazaars, in Eastern voice, of course: "Here can be seen the beautiful fabrics of Persia and Cashmere, the jewels of India, the spices and perfumes of Arabia." He wrote of sitting on "divans" at coffee shops in Cairo and Baghdad where the staff immediately brought him "strong black coffee of most delicious flavor, and then a narghileh, a supply of which is always kept ready for use." The Arabs, he asserted, were always ready to take a break, not as lazy fatalists but as contented consumers.[125] Like travelers a generation earlier, Fogg could have emphasized the noise of these markets, the foul smells, or the donkeys that pushed pedestrians off their feet in narrow streets, but this kind of pessimistic writing was inappropriate for a middling consumer's magazine like *Scribner's*. Cautionary accounts of the Muslim world might inspire donations when delivered by missionaries or diplomats, but such appeals were death to any attempt to promote consumption of products from West Asia, products consumers preferred to interpret through an admiring aesthetic of affluent satisfaction. Instead, Fogg importantly told Americans to imagine a Middle East that still supplied a cosmopolitan leisure that anyone could purchase by way of a hookah pipe, fez, divan, or carpet—just as these products might appear advertised in the newspaper or on display in a window downtown. By this time, such attitudes were very conventional among Anglo-Americans, and Fogg included such descriptions in the promotional magazine excerpts of his work because he knew they would keep his work relevant to readers.

These readers sought individuation and celebrated the democratic pretenses of capitalism. One contributor to *Home-Maker* magazine assured readers that imported objects could facilitate amateur creativity and individual self-expression that was highly accessible, even to shoppers who aspired to luxuries they could not quite afford. She had been playing Eastern at home herself, she confided: "A most sumptuous and expensive-looking divan has for its foundation a couple of packing-boxes and a cheap mattress, over which is spread a Bagdad curtain; on this divan is a riot of cushions, my one luxurious dissipation, cushions large and cushions small, cushions grave or gay, redolent of perfumes, and inviting to the weary head."[126] This type of improvised mystification of the home turned an urban household into an imagined sanctuary in which to forget Gilded Age troubles and stood in testament to the creative agency of the compiler.

In time, consumers would combine objects emanating from North Africa and West Asia with Chinese and Japanese products, Native American handcrafts, and homegrown imitations to create distinctly globalized trends in home decoration. There middle-class and upper-class white women placed items together on shelves into "fanciful creations passed off as Moorish, Turkish, Chinese, Japanese, or a combination thereof," as Kristin Hoganson so nicely puts it, by women who tried to "stuff the entire world into their parlors."[127] This was a kind of "ethnocentric cosmopolitanism" Arif Dirlik explains.[128] To its boosters in the shops, decorating guides, women's magazines and many households, Aladdin's lamp-style décor in which one did not know what one might find in a friend's parlor seemed to express extravagant unconventionality and an appreciation for the arts of foreign lands.[129] Yet soon the style became so common that it became utterly predictable, a hackneyed fashion of Oriental abundance run amok. In 1872 a *New York Times* piece had warned that such gaudy and fantastic styles were "bad, because ridiculous; they hurt our sense of propriety, and worry the eye."[130] It was "The Age of Bric-A-Brac," the *Times* declared again seven years later. "An invasion of bric-à-brac" had turned many American

Evelyn Hughes's New York City drawing room with Oriental cozy corner, 1899. Museum of the City of New York, Byron Collection, 93.1.1.17587.

living rooms into "curiosity shops" filled with "Oriental pots and pans from the bazaars of Faraway Moses and his tribe," and the "cast-off clothing of Egyptians, Turkomans, and Bengalese," the paper sniped.[131]

Satire critiquing the perceived hollowness of self-fashioning through objects was sure to follow as commentators and novelists worked out how such consumption was shaping American life, especially the acquisitiveness of women, a common target of male satirists. Mr. March, the middle-class protagonist of William Dean Howell's character study of 1880s New York, *A Hazard of New Fortunes*, snickered at the new middle-class fashion for globalized Eastern tale–style décor. The proud hostess of one home, Mr. March observed, used imported knick-knacks and fabrics to produce an interior of complete impracticality that carried all the classic components of the fashion:

> Wherever you might have turned round she had put a gimcrack [curio] so that you would knock it over if you did turn. . . . every shelf and dressing-case and mantel was littered with gimcracks, and the corners of the tiny rooms were curtained off, and behind these portieres

swarmed more gimcracks. The front of the upright piano had what
March called a short-skirted portiere on it, and the top was covered with
vases, with dragon candlesticks and with Jap fans, which also expanded
themselves bat wise on the walls between the etchings and the water colors. The floors were covered with filling, and then rugs and then skins;
the easy-chairs all had tidies, Armenian and Turkish and Persian; the
lounges and sofas had embroidered cushions hidden under tidies. The
radiator was concealed by a Jap screen, and over the top of this some
Arab scarfs were flung. There was a superabundance of clocks. China
pugs guarded the hearth; a brass sunflower smiled from the top of either
andiron, and a brass peacock spread its tail before them inside a high
filigree fender.[132]

To many contemporary observers like Howells these displays seemed to be
random displays—pastiche cultural critics would call it today—that lumped
things together regardless of their provenance or original purpose and spoke of
nervous, dissatisfying acquisition, not the careless reverie of a Nile cruise or
rich abundance of a Damascus bazaar. Such complaints were grounded in a
soon-clichéd view of women consumers as credulous participants in a feminized, inauthentic kind of mass consumerism that aped affluent independence
from the market, as Kristin Hoganson says, "to compensate for the rawness of
post–Civil War fortunes [and] the vulgar commercialism that had enabled it to
be built in the first place."[133]

Yet to their creators, these interiors were carefully assembled. No two could
ever be alike. "The pleasure of fitting up a room for one's self, and doing the
work actually with one's own hands, will recompense the occupant for any time
and trouble expended on a room," *Ladies Home Journal* encouraged.[134] By playing
Oriental in creating these spaces, women spoke volumes about their particular
choices in adding new meaning to imported objects and crossing them over
into their own lives. The "tidies, Armenian and Turkish and Persian" might be a
gift from a friend who had traveled abroad, or an object that reminded the
decorator of childhood readings of the *Arabian Nights*. The Syrian "Arab scarfs"
from Eastern bazaars helped to distract one from a radiator and the mechanical
interior of an urban apartment, to point out to the visitor that the decorator
understood the radiator to be unsightly and had the means to hide it. Indeed,
consumerism was useful to Americans because it was premised on what Michel
de Certeau calls "poaching in countless ways on the property of others." That

is, Americans could produce comprehensible meanings for and uses of foreign goods that their producers—in whatever part of the world—could not have predicted or controlled but depended upon if they were to sell to global markets.[135]

As had many Americans, William Dean Howell's Mr. March wondered at the consumer affluence of his era, "The magic of its being always there, ready for any one, every one, just as if it were for some one alone: it was like the experience of an Arabian Nights hero come true for all the race."[136] To newly middle-class consumers of the era who had sudden access to new products and services, the revolution in consumer choice did seem like a consumer's Oriental tale that highlighted the advantages of America's capitalist transformation and global trading activity. Playing Eastern had had a century-long evolution for Anglo-Americans from speaking in Eastern voice in print to imitation abroad to self-fashioning for the middle and upper classes. The story of the *Arabian Nights* as American art form was ultimately the story of the creative lives of all Americans who engaged in performed Oriental tales through the expressive use of objects in the nineteenth century. To many, the Eastern world would seem to encourage their enthusiastic participation in the market thereafter, while people adapted the act of playing Eastern to multiple new tasks.

chapter 2

Ex Oriente Lux: Playing Eastern
for a Living, 1838–1875

*I*n an October 1865 review of William Alger's compilation *Poetry of the Orient*, an anonymous reviewer for *The Nation* asked readers, "How shall the West be brought duly to appreciate and respect the East?" It only made sense for *The Nation* to raise such an issue. Triumphant abolitionists had recently founded the magazine just as slavery had finally come to an end in the United States, and the future seemed bright for all sorts of progressive causes. However, it was not time to rest on one's laurels yet, the reviewer continued: "*Ex oriente lux* is a true enough motto for the historian and archaeologist; but with the sun riding high in heaven above our heads, . . . who feels with the Mohammedans, because they bore a chief part in bridging over the dark ages, that knowledge might pass from the classical to the modern world?" *The Nation* charged, "Our want of sympathy makes us intolerant: we depreciate their personal character, contemn their literature, and stigmatize their religion as childish superstition or as devil-worship." Muslim West Asians had a "right," he asserted, to protect their religions, languages, and political and cultural traditions from Western pressure—and Americans should help. Of the Alger volume at hand the reviewer advised, "The highest significance of such a work lies in its interest and effect in bringing the Orient to the knowledge and sympathizing regard of the cultivated in our community, the leaders of public opinion."[1]

To make his case, this writer had used the phrase "*ex oriente lux*"—"from the East comes light"—a term that had originated in the 1840s as the motto of New England transcendentalists like Thoreau and Emerson.[2] Soon it became a colloquial term that represented a tried-and-true method of crossing over supposedly controversial ideas about Eastern lands to the Anglo-American middle and upper classes, those "leaders of public opinion," as *The Nation* described them. This was not the abstracted "public" composed of political men of ideas, nor was it the plebian, democratic public of firemen's parades or beer wagon congregations on election day.[3] This public was a book and lyceum public, a particularly self-aware group of self-conceived consumers and opinion makers made up of educated, upwardly mobile Anglo-Americans living mostly in the Northeast and Midwest.

The Ex Oriente Lux mode of appealing to such consumers went like this: expose some common misconception as a straw man, then explain "the truth" of the topic, thereby giving one's message a reformist purpose while flattering the audience as enlightened consumers of knowledge. Because cultural relativism has always existed, the Lux approach seldom revealed any truly new information but instead served as a way to make old insight seem new: "the East is misunderstood; only progressive people know this." The Lux method of framing information about the Muslim world was an old standby, probably first pioneered by medieval travelers to Asia who debunked European myths about the Islamic world. Translators of Eastern literature and tellers of Oriental tales like Royall Tyler and Washington Irving had employed it when the nation was barely a generation old. By midcentury, the Ex Oriente Lux mode was appearing nightly in commercial venues across the country: magazines, books, lyceum lecture halls, museums, mass-produced illustrations, and local newspapers. In each of these places, audiences were asked to believe they were gaining instruction that set them apart from some imagined, uncritical public characterized by "common misunderstanding."

The Ex Oriente Lux mode worked so dependably because many Anglo-Americans wanted to believe they had a special understanding of the Muslim world that marked them as more diligent and more sophisticated than most. Many believed common opinion especially disparaged Muslim North Africa and West Asia because most people uncritically accepted alarmist and cautionary accounts of those lands. Sometimes these cautionary depictions came from missionaries in the Ottoman Empire looking for sympathy, donations, or volunteers stateside; sometimes they came from writers made crabby and hateful by the fatigue and the culture shock of overseas travel. Much of it also seemed to pop up in the penny press, school books, and other cultural products needing villains, whose writers fell back on residual stereotypes about tyranny and slavery materialized in the person of the "Barbary Pirate" or the "despotic Turk" and found in political talk and sailor's accounts from Revolutionary and early national days.[4]

The phenomenon of the Ex Oriente Lux mode of communication matters to our understanding of how Americans used their engagement with the Muslim world to cope with capitalism because middle-class and upper-class Anglo-American consumers used the markets for information, as well as the markets for entertainment, travel, and home décor discussed in the last chapter, to individuate themselves. Thus did these people attempt to define themselves as consumers who purchased out of an urge for diligent self-improvement, not simply pious emotion or unthinking bigotry. The heritage of distrust and misunderstanding between the West and East made the Muslim world the most controversial place on earth for some, so that one's reasoned interrogation of those regions through the right consumer products was a sign of exceptional judgment worthy of an "opinion maker." In a period when only a tiny minority of Americans would ever meet an actual Easterner, that heritage of distrust and misunderstanding Americans perceived had two mutually reinforcing components. First, there were real interactions that bred actual conflict, for instance, between the American navy and North African states during the Barbary Wars in the first two decades of the century, then between American missionaries and Ottoman subjects in the Levant thereafter. Second, and most important for our purposes here, was the talk of distrust and misunderstanding journalists, writers, and artists used as a marketing technique for cultural products that told opinion makers that the crisis of perception was far worse than it was.

This story of the Lux appeal helps us to answer some important questions. How hard was it to make a living speaking publicly about the Muslim world in the nineteenth century? Why did Americans prefer to hear about the East from other Americans when they did rather than from Easterners themselves? How did the Ex Oriente Lux mode of communicating about the Muslim world make the consumer's Oriental tale more flexible by allowing those playing Oriental to tell consumers they could engage their intellects as well as their more hedonistic selves in order to stand out from the masses? To understand when and how the Ex Oriente Lux approach prospered, we can compare two important men who thusly tried to sell their wares to American consumers, Hatchik (Christopher) Oscanyan and Bayard Taylor. The first was a native of Istanbul, the other of Pennsylvania, but their shared experiences show why mid-nineteenth-century Anglo-Americans would prefer so often to hear about the East, in this case the Ottoman Empire, from fellow Anglo-Americans. Both Oscanyan and Taylor used an Ex Oriente Lux approach to present their personae as men of the East. Audiences had sympathetic though ultimately limited interest in Christopher Oscanyan's presentations of "Anatolia explained by a Turk." His national origin restricted his understanding of American audiences' cultural logic, and while he carried certain authority as a native of the Empire, this factor circumscribed his ability to speak for any other nation. By contrast, audiences enthusiastically embraced Bayard Taylor because, more than Oscanyan, he had the main ingredients necessary for great success in the market: long-term personal relationships with important publishers, an almost self-destructive ambition typical of the era, and a native-born understanding of Anglo-American cultures that helped him cross his content over by tapping into the lyceum and book public's expectations with great accuracy.

CHRISTOPHER OSCANYAN:
EASTERN GENTLEMAN AND ENTREPRENEUR

When Christopher Oscanyan came to the United States, he found a nation undergoing considerable social and economic change. By the late 1830s, the pervasive presence of market philosophies in American social relations had persuaded many to make personal investments in the emerging order by working to prosper within that order rather than seeking to avoid it.[5] Plenty of Americans were ambivalent about these developments but nonetheless valued ambition enough to build a culture in which men would be defined by their success in business. Most blamed failure on the individual, not the system, sincerely embracing the new values: "the rational pursuit of profit, the perpetual increase of capital as an end in itself, the development of an acquisitive personality, and the belief that ceaseless work is a necessity in life," Scott Sandage explains.[6] The cultures of self-help and constant improvement were the popular manifestations of these ideas, and the consuming public found them embedded in antebellum lyceum lectures, newspapers, magazines, and books.

To determined creative men who sought to make a living as communicators, like Oscanyan and Taylor, this market culture was both an opportunity and a serious problem. The antebellum boom in publishing and its promotional integration with lyceums and other forms of entertainment was a product of new national markets, banking systems, and large businesses that characterized the changes historians call the "market revolution."[7] Oscanyan and Taylor were two of what Donald Scott describes as "a swarm of young men forced to try to carve a career out of the possession of some kind of knowledge rather than from soil or craft, . . . a large number of people for whom ideas literally had become commodities which they tried to merchandize."[8] Both labored to sell various *Ex Oriente Lux* messages about the East in a growing information and publicity infrastructure that was taking shape in the 1840s, just as they both came to public notice. Publishers were taking on the increasing costs of production, distribution, and promotion while keeping a greater proportion of the profits, then leaning on authors to cater to audience demand. Authors now had access to a national audience but also had "reasons for producing as much writing as possible as fast as possible," Daniel Bell tells us, then branding it with a unique professional persona.[9] Although one might become the person one wanted to be in this universe of self-expression and self-promotion, to stay afloat financially writers, artists, and lecturers had to gamble that their wares would please an often impossibly complex and fickle public that might want lectures by Ralph Waldo Emerson one night, a penny newspaper hoax and a timely songbook the next morning.[10]

Yet for writers and other information entrepreneurs with access to the Muslim world, there was considerable opportunity since the overwhelming majority of Americans would never actually visit the Middle East. They would, however, gladly pay to hear professional travelers explain how the Ottoman Empire looked and sounded and how it might be important or useful in making sense of Americans' own identities by showing how it had shaped the speaker's sense of self. Since authors and their readers might never meet in person in the national marketplace for entertainment and information, authors needed to define themselves for audiences by enacting what Michael Conroy describes as "an artful arrangement of self, a dramaturgy of the personality," that is, a distinct and consistently interesting professional persona carried through live and recorded performances.[11] One's persona would be all the more successful if it appeared to be characterized by independence from the market. *Atlantic Monthly* explained the ironic belief that for such public men, who usually were obliged to promote their work and earn extra money through a lyceum tour, "the work of the lecturer shall be incidental to some worthy pursuit from which [the lyceum] temporarily calls him. There seems to be a kind of coquetry in this. The public do[es] not accept those who are too openly in the market or who are too easily won."[12] For male lecturers whose specialty was the Eastern world, that often meant a persona defined by down-to-earth manliness, direct contact with foreign lands, and regular complaining about the necessity of having to participate in the entertainment and information system at all.[13]

Hatchik Oscanyan, author and entrepreneur, was probably the most well-known Eastern man in the American northeast between 1838 and 1868 and would attempt to break into American public life much in this way. He was an

ethnic Armenian born in the Ottoman Empire in 1818. As a teen he had converted to Protestant Christianity in Istanbul with his father after some association with Protestant missionaries there.[14] By age twenty, he had changed his
name to Christopher and was studying at New York University after family and
missionary friends sponsored his voyage.[15] Thereafter he would live for various
periods in the United States, London, and back in Istanbul. He was a transnational person with feet in several nations in an age when few people had roots
in both Eastern and Western countries. Oscanyan arrived in the America when
there was virtually no emigration from the Ottoman Empire or North Africa,
merely the occasional batch of sailors, a trader, or members of the Sultan's
diplomatic staff. Indeed, since colonial days the appearance of a Muslim in the
country had been cause for newspaper stories describing the person, his dress,
and his apparent attitude. Many Anglo-Americans remembered these few travelers fondly, producing half-fictionalized nostalgia pieces about them in periodicals and books.[16] Some of these visitors did stay, and the 1850 census
showed almost two hundred inhabitants of Ottoman Empire origin.[17]

Oscanyan came to public life initially through a series of lectures in 1838 for
church societies of middling folk, who probably harbored any number of assumptions and ambivalences about the Ottoman Empire and its rulers. In the
1830s, Americans had watched with great sympathy the Greek War of Independence. Public interest in Oscanyan's lectures was probably further propelled
by news coverage of the Egyptian invasion of the Levant, the arrival of the
Catherwood Holy Land panoramas in New York and Philadelphia in 1836,
missionary periodicals, and plenty of Bible reading. In each of these cases,
Anglo-Americans talked in terms of concepts like liberty and despotism when
they hashed out the pros and cons of life in the Empire, whether political or
private.[18] At his lectures, Oscanyan sized up his audience and presented highly
detailed, factual accounts explaining the Ottoman system of government, social
conventions, and more, all of it framed in an *Ex Oriente Lux* approach—although
he would not have named it such—that flattered his listeners as an enlightened
public. The religious press was an able facilitator and helped amplify his message. The *Christian Watchmen*, for one, advised that Oscanyan had come to the
United States in order to "disabuse the minds of our citizens of the erroneous
notions they have received of the inhabitants of the East, from the reports of
incompetent travelers."[19]

That year most of Oscanyan's reviews and press notices would appear in
religious periodicals, a growing genre of publication that was the bedrock of

broader information networks in the nation.[20] They duly endorsed the idea of democratic access to worldly information and intellectual self-improvement, so Oscanyan was a good fit for their pages. As a convert to Protestantism, Oscanyan could flatter their perspectives by promoting American missionary work while persuading sympathetic listeners in the voice of a native speaker that the Empire was "not so purely despotic as was generally supposed." Either Oscanyan or his reviewer at one Boston talk (it is impossible to tell which by the press notice) elaborated that the Ottoman Sultan Mahmoud "could not take the property of the meanest of his subjects, even if it was required for the public good" to demonstrate Ottoman egalitarianism, although this claim would be increasingly untrue as the century progressed.[21] Nonetheless, property rights were central to the emerging political and economic order in the United States, especially with debate growing in Boston and elsewhere about how those property rights and the proposed personal rights of American slaves might soon be reconciled. Regardless, Oscanyan got across in part because he was willing to acknowledge American reservations about the Sultan's monarchical rule while presenting new information about life in Anatolia that Americans would understand and appreciate because it asserted that at heart the people in both lands had similar values emphasizing the importance of family and prosperity.

Christopher Oscanyan's manner in these early lectures was apparently quite engaging, a factor that helped give credibility to his message. The papers said he spoke well in English and concluded his talk "by warmly thanking his audience for their attention and politeness."[22] Oscanyan performed a version of Christian Ottoman manhood that was implicitly friendly to Americans while still identifiably Eastern. Crucially, Oscanyan was no "haughty" nor "impassive Turk." The character of the stern Turkish man was a familiar fixture in Anglo-American thought about the Ottoman Empire in the nineteenth century. As for the Ottoman Sultan, his ethnically Turkish officials, and his governors throughout the Empire, American travelers often spoke of finding them overly serious or unreadable. Although he might be friendly in private with close friends and family, this character was in public marked by "dignity," "calm expression," "stiffness and formality," "the most rigid indifference," or "oriental gravity," especially before inferiors.[23] A colloquial idea that "Turks are a notably reticent people," as P. T. Barnum phrased it, was already part of show business wisdom about how, precisely, one might perform Eastern nobility on stage.[24] American educators had similarly told early American children to note how "grave" was the Turk pictured in their schoolbooks and how inscrutable was the Muslim world in general.[25] For some, such unreadability was a sign of rude arrogance on the part of the Eastern man; for others it was a sign of fatalistic stoicism. Either way, the grave Turk carried a further meaning for many audiences worried about financial or social fraud since many took an impassive visage as a defensive tactic used by the confidence man or social pretender stateside.[26]

Oscanyan's warm personal manner, his endorsement of the idea of "common misunderstanding," and certainly his conversion to Protestant Christianity probably helped him make himself comprehensible and appealing to upwardly mobile Anglo-Americans. So did the imported consumer products and mannequins he used in his lectures to demonstrate specific aspects of "the manners and customs of Turkey." One night at the Boston Lyceum he displayed "Turkish dresses, books, pipes, weapons, &c.," namely, just the kinds of things travelers to the Empire would purchase as souvenirs in later decades. He also became famous for his displays of affluent women's clothing, which appealed to Americans long curious about the privileged world of female segregation in Muslim countries, especially women consumers fascinated by foreign women's clothing styles and just then gaining access to "fashion plate" and wood cut illustrations in magazine's like *Godey's Ladies Book*.[27] That night in Boston, Oscanyan had presented "a large doll dressed like the Sultan's wife, with a long shawl over the head, reaching to the ground." The *Journal of Education* editorialized, "The rich ladies wear splendid dresses: But not one girl in a hundred knows how to read." Acknowledging this critique, Oscanyan turned it into a compliment, telling his audience, New Englanders dedicated to the idea of universal education as they were, that if expanded schooling for girls became available in the Empire thanks to the work of missionaries, "How thankful our females should be for these advantages."[28]

Americans who knew him would not soon forget Christopher Oscanyan, although it is difficult to say what effect his first lecture tour had on American life other than to give Oscanyan a chance to survey the opportunities available to him in the northeast. After some years back in Istanbul, Oscanyan returned to New York City and in 1849 married a local woman, Mari Louisa, daughter of the Rev. Dr. Skinner. Oscanyan's entrepreneurial impulses were strong, and soon he had a series of business ventures on the go, including a celebrated café and gift shop at 625 Broadway in New York City.[29] There he visited with customers who drank coffee and smoked water pipes or purchased the rose water and other imported curios he sold. A correspondent for a local paper reported that

Oscanyan normally appeared in his establishment as Eastern in a flattering sort of way, "thoroughly American in his appearance and costume, with the exception of the Turkish Fez which I hope he will always wear." Knowing his readers would want to imagine Oscanyan's shop by what they had read about shopping in the East, he warned them, "Don't imagine a Bazar à l'Orient, with its wares arranged on shelves in niches fronting the narrow street, all carefully protected by thick awnings from the rays of the sun, and its turbaned merchants in loose robes sitting cross-legged upon their counters, silent and apparently sublimely indifferent to all sublunary things, like true followers of the Prophet. O No! Out of the glare and bustle and the intense civilization of Broadway enter this unpretending door, much like every other about it, and the treasures of the East shall surround you."[30] Oscanyan appears to have been an endearing person, and he managed to tap into American interest in Eastern products in ways that were suited to New York's available retail space but still capitalized on the clichés of the consumer's Oriental tale. Visitors would apply what they already believed about Ottoman bazaars to Oscanyan's space without even being prompted to do so.

During the 1850s and 1860s, Oscanyan went back to work on the lecture circuit. His many favorable reviews explained that he had much to say about Ottoman home life and still came armed with "dolls" wearing native dress to represent women of various ethnicities and classes in the Ottoman Empire.[31] Times had changed, and now secular newspapers were picking up stories of his lectures and boiling them down into briefer, more entertaining reductions. They showed Oscanyan's growing show business sense possibly but more likely showed how the papers worked to develop interest by crossing their content over in the most comprehensible ways although still endorsing Oscanyan's Ex Oriente Lux appeal. Instead of the detailed, thoughtful summaries from the religious and educational press Oscanyan had gotten in 1838, outlets like the New York Daily Times now abruptly summarized his talks, seemingly at random: "Mr. C. Oscanyan, A Constantinopolitan, lectured at the Mercantile Library on Thursday evening on 'Turkey.' . . . Mr. Oscanyan held that foreigners, in judging of the institutions of Turkey, are too much impregnated with the prejudices of European education to decide fairly and impartially. . . . The failing of Turkey is centralization. Illustrations of the customs of the country, a description of the Sultan, and a promise to take the hearer next time into the sacred precincts of the Harem, formed the features of the lecture."[32] Here was an Ex Oriente Lux appeal adapted to the patriotic pretensions of an

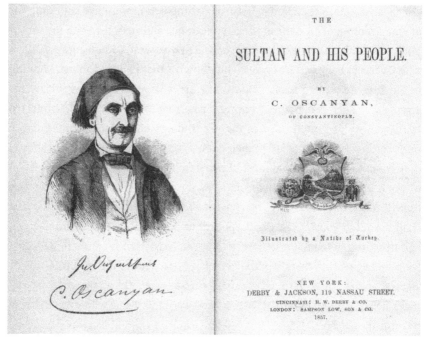

THE

SULTAN AND HIS PEOPLE.

BY

C. OSCANYAN,
OF CONSTANTINOPLE.

Illustrated by a Native of Turkey.

NEW YORK:
DERBY & JACKSON, 119 NASSAU STREET.
CINCINNATI: H. W. DERBY & CO.
LONDON: SAMPSON LOW, SON & CO.
1857.

Christopher Oscanyan's book portrait.

American newspaper and premised on telling readers they would find in their pages democratic access to a smorgasbord of information that endorsed anti-European sentiment, states rights, and intriguing but actually tame harem clichés, delivered practically in point form to save space.

Undeterred, Oscanyan pressed on with other communication ventures, and perhaps his moment of greatest public attention came with the publication in 1857 of his book *The Sultan and His People*. Oscanyan was in those days a regular in the bohemian salon of Ada Claire in midtown Manhattan, where he rubbed shoulders with a group of unconventional young Americans likewise making their way as writers by lecturing, publishing, and theater work.[33] The contacts he met there may have helped him get *The Sultan and His People* through the publication process. The book set out to answer the many questions well-to-do Westerners had about the Ottoman Empire, a nation that until 1854 had been allied with France against Russia in the Crimean War, an event that had inspired great domestic interest in the Empire. In his book, he self-identified as an immigrant, "Oscanyan of Constantinople," whose "alma mater" was New York University, creating a persona that was authentically foreign yet clearly heels with the greatest rapidity, leaving my companion in utter amazement. I endeavored to explain to him the reason of the sailor's conduct, by showing him the genuine European style of beckoning, by reversing the hand and moving the up-turned forefinger back and forth. This astonished him the more, since that motion is equivalent, in Turkey, to

that comical American gesture of placing the thumb on the tip end of the nose, and extending the fingers.

Thus things which are in themselves trifles, may lead or mislead to mighty results, and can only be appreciated when circumstances call them into action. Therefore nothing but actual nativity and

Christopher Oscanyan instructs Americans on the international language of hand gestures. *The Sultan and His People*, 1857.

connected to educated Anglo-America. Still, one reviewer worried, readers would be discouraged from reading the volume because the portrait of Oscanyan across from the title page was "a hideous caricature of the author" that did not convey his warm personal manner and "really respectable appearance." Referring to the notorious Ottoman elite military guard executed by the Sultan in 1823 and the Empire's ongoing rivalry with Russia, the reviewer complained

that Oscanyan "in this portrait looks like a Turkish janissary intent upon anni-
hilating the Russian bear."[34] Here was the specter of the stern Turk again offering audiences interpretations of Oscanyan he could not completely contain.

Regardless of this misstep, Oscanyan's book was a careful attempt to stay on
message with respect to his persona as Eastern lecturer by going systematically
through the many assumptions and clichés Americans and others held about
the Empire in order to explain them from an Armenian-Ottoman point of view.
He endorsed some common preconceptions, discussing first off the romanticism of Western Oriental tales: "Orientalism! Talisman to conjure up the shades
of the very parents of our race, . . . to array in picturesque and savage beauty the
vision of Arabian horsemen, flying steeds, vast encampments on arid plains."[35]
By "Arab" Oscanyan meant desert-dwelling Arabs, a group often misunderstood or feared by urban Ottoman subjects.[36] The Bedouins, many Americans
were convinced, were the descendants of Ishmael of the Bible and outsiders to
Christian history. Yet in secular entertainment Anglo-Americans often wished
to imagine them as inheritors of revered imperial traditions embodied in Islamic history or the *Arabian Nights*, depending on the preferences of the individual in question. Plenty of Oriental tales and rich traditions of imaginative
painting depicted chivalry in the person of the Bedouin warrior. Many poems
and paintings had as their heroes "Arab knights bearing their long muskets like
lances, sometimes in repose, sometimes hurling themselves across the desert
towards some unseen foe," as John MacKenzie tells us.[37]

As an author, Oscanyan was in a position to flatter his audience by acknowledging the Western creative practice of Orientalism, and endorsing a *Lux* appeal, while inserting his own messages in along the way. Consequently, he also
included somewhat unconventional content that he could authenticate by his
Ottoman identity and public popularity. For instance, he refused to admit that
the Ottoman Empire was hopelessly in decline, even if he did call for reform.
Nor did he argue that gender segregation was unfair to women, instead advising readers that for a woman in Constantinople to appear in public uncovered
was as inappropriate as for an American lady to appear in public in a night
gown. The book was not defensive or heavy handed, though, and Oscanyan
even inserted humorous bits to keep readers sympathetic. At one point he
explained in prose and illustration how the same insulting message might be
communicated by different hand gestures in the West versus the East.

Reviews of *The Sultan and His People* were mixed, some negative enough to
give us reason to believe they were actual critiques by magazine reviewers, not

planted "puff" pieces, the prefabricated press notices book agents often provided as free content to newspapers and magazines. They also revealed that
perhaps Oscanyan could not quite get his genial personality over on the printed
page as he did in person. The most positive evaluation came from *Putnam's
Monthly Magazine*, whose reviewer seemed to get Oscanyan's point: "On the
whole, there are few better accounts of the detail of Turkish life than this of
Oscanyan's, and he describes with a constant and natural tendency to sympathy
with his own people. He, therefore, suggests many sensible explanations of
points which are peculiar and amusing to other nations." That is, Oscanyan had
communicated the facts of Ottoman life, as he saw them, in plausible and
enlightening ways, even if some readers would be left unconvinced. Thus did
he, according to *Putnam's*, put in a bad light accounts of the Empire thrown
together by traveling hack writers, "the outer barbarians, as are all the other
tourists and authors upon that country," *Putnam's* called them, who highlighted
the incomprehensibility of foreign customs just to sell books and promote
intercultural misunderstanding.[38]

Harper's New Monthly Magazine agreed that Oscanyan addressed topics familiar to readers of travel narratives in an authentic tone, even if everything he
proposed to reveal was not necessarily news to Americans. Oscanyan's delivery
was not perfect, though, and his prose was grammatically correct but a distraction because "his style often betrays an Oriental luxuriance which needs to be
toned down in order to meet the proprieties of Western taste." Here Oriental
tale–style Eastern voice was seemingly inappropriate for nonfiction written by
an actual Ottoman subject wishing to provide believable factual information to
American readers, walking a fine line to appear just Eastern enough but not too
much.[39] Most disappointed by the book was a writer for the *North American
Review*, who complained that Oscanyan wrote in "the language of a college
sophomore" and reflected badly on New York University, he was too sympathetic to his own people to write about them objectively, and he railed against
ethnic Greeks in the Empire while too liberally praising the Ottoman Sultan:
"he makes a hero of that sick and effeminate ruler who is the heir to the honors
of Osmanli [Turkish] tyrants." Most notable to this reviewer in many ways was
that Oscanyan sought to satisfy American curiosity about the home life of the
Ottoman elite but came across as patronizing; the reviewer noted, "[Oscanyan]
vehemently combats the notions of the harem which prevail in, or rather (to use
his frequent word) *pervade*, the West" (italics in original). Here was a further
danger, that in presenting the trope of "common misunderstanding" as a prop

in his performance of Easterner with a Lux appeal, Oscanyan might over criticize or come across as such because he was a foreigner and thus offend his
audiences. Certainly there must have been a similar diversity of opinion among
readers of The Sultan and His People, a diversity Oscanyan would never completely control.

During the Civil War, Oscanyan would leave the United States again for
London, where he became involved in a $30,000 plan to found a Turkish-style
hammam, or public steam bath, as a publicly held company.[40] He would later
serve as the Ottoman consul in New York from 1868 to 1874, a period in which
he spent at least a year working the lecture circuit in England, earning larger
appearance fees than veterans of the American lyceum like E. P. Whipple, Sara
Barton, Rev. John Abbott, and Frederick Douglass.[41] In spite of these efforts to
promote cultural relativism in the United States and Oscanyan's regular appearances in newspapers up and down the East coast over thirty years, he was
less influential than many others who labored in the elite publishing universe
represented by Harper's or Atlantic Monthly and even the middling public opinion
represented by the lyceum lecture circuit. He never produced the sheer volumes
of information in easily digestible forms that most literary stars did. Nor did
he lecture on favored domestic topics like phrenology, horse training, or the
American slavery question but solely on the Ottoman Empire. He prospered by
coming across as friendly and well meaning, adopting many American ways but
remaining just Eastern enough, with his fez and Turkish accent, to flatter
American interest in cosmopolitan consumption. He suffered, or chose, a kind
of public typecasting as an Armenian Turk in order to make a living. And what
we cannot know from the published sources that remain of Christopher Oscanyan's life in the United States is whether he had any personal moments of doubt
or came to resent those Americans who for thirty years would demand that he
play Eastern as a representative for the entire Ottoman Empire.

BAYARD TAYLOR: EASTERNIZED SLAVE TO THE MARKET

Bayard Taylor was one of Oscanyan's contemporaries yet far more prolific and
broadly known, a master of the Ex Oriente Lux approach to playing Eastern. It is
not clear whether the two men ever met, but their coexistence gives us an
opportunity for comparison to see why during the mid-nineteenth century
Anglo-Americans unable to travel overseas preferred to hear about the Ottoman
Empire from native-born Americans rather than from Ottoman subjects them-

selves. In his day, Bayard Taylor was one of the nation's most popular authors and public personalities, with an ability to play Eastern for multiple domestic audiences. To his literary peers he got over in the persona of Eastern artist whose work protected him from the crass realities of the publishing business. To women and youthful male readers among the Anglo-American book and lyceum public, he appeared as a manly Eastern traveler and adventurer who seemed to endorse the myth of the self-made man. Taylor was not a transnational person to the degree that Christopher Oscanyan was since he only briefly visited foreign lands as a tourist. Yet as a native-born American he had internalized cultural logics Oscanyan could only learn about as an adult, such that Taylor could communicate his imperfect knowledge of the Eastern world in ways that seemed more authentic and meaningful in the United States because they came across with no foreign accent, so to speak, and even when Taylor had not intended it, spoke to the stereotypes and expectations of his fellow citizens in countless ways.

Born in 1825, Taylor emerged from modest means in Pennsylvania with a few undistinguished if ambitious early attempts at professional writing. At age eighteen, like many aspiring authors who tried their hand at Oriental tales, Taylor published his first poem under the Eastern pseudonym "Selim."[42] Thereafter, he would find work just about anywhere he could, publishing novels, travel books, countless reviews, and the definitive translation of Goethe's *Faust*, although he believed poetry to be his true calling. Book buyers first discovered Taylor from his *Views Afoot* (1849), a record of a year spent tramping around Europe with little money. The volume had a Horatio Alger quality about it because most European travel in those days was the privilege of the American upper classes.[43] Taylor had roughed it on the cheap, camping and walking when he could, and his optimistic tone "started thousands of pedestrians on pilgrimages," one admirer remembered, because Taylor "exploded the idea that a fortune was necessary for foreign travel."[44] A year later, during intense public interest in the gold rush, Taylor's letters from California and Mexico appeared in the *New York Tribune*, and later a book-length account, *Eldorado; or, Adventures in the Path of Empire* (1850), created similar sensation and multiple editions. *Eldorado*, as the title suggested, encapsulated common Anglo-American hopes that the conquest of California and the West was an Aladdin's lamp of easy fortune.[45]

Having earned a living for a few years and made a name for himself, Taylor then turned to African and Asian travel to find his voice as an artist. This is how

Taylor would further individuate himself professionally from the "swarm" of young writers looking for publishing deals and book sales, seeking to survive as creative people and family breadwinners by developing a branded persona. Taylor's trademark was to play Oriental in two ways, first as a spiritually content Eastern artist imbued with what Taylor called "the inspiration and the indolence of the Orient" and second as a more rugged, daring traveler, which most audiences seem to have preferred and to a large degree imposed upon him.[46] Taylor was somewhat unique in these ways. He was unlike the many missionaries and preachers who ventured to the Middle East to locate and document biblical archaeological sites for pious Protestant readers. Nor was he a cynical humorist like Ross Browne, or later Mark Twain, who sought to poke fun at Western attitudes by way of satire staged in the Ottoman Empire. In this crowded field, Bayard Taylor's specialty was to play Eastern for a living by offering audiences an Ex Oriente Lux appeal that showed American consumers how ostensibly authentic experiences of Muslim lands could inform their own identities as cultural relativists and worldly consumers defying bigotry and crudity.

In the fall of 1851, Taylor boarded a steamer and headed east. Taylor had landed financing thanks to a new publication deal with Horace Greeley that put his travel letters in the New York Tribune and some money in his pocket. He would also get immense exposure from the arrangement. Greeley delivered half his papers to addresses outside New York City and sold Taylor's letters to dozens of small-town newspapers. Taylor began playing Eastern as a translator of "Arabian sentiment and tradition," as the press would phrase it, knowing his performance would be recorded in print and broadcast to audiences across the country.[47] He argued that he had gone much further in understanding the cultures of the Ottoman Empire than most Anglo-American tourists who traveled there, segregated from local people except for their dragoman. Living close to the ground as a "happy nomad . . . masquerading in Moslem garb," Taylor said, he was out to absorb local ways and eschew what he saw as the artificiality of American social conventions that required formal clothing and social rituals that spoke of one's station and accomplishments.[48] From Anatolia in 1852, Taylor informed his publicist, James T. Fields, "If you could see me now you would swear I was a disciple of the Prophet. . . . I wear the tarboosh, smoke the Persian pipe, and drop cross-legged on the floor. . . . When I went into my bankers' they addressed me in Turkish. The other day, at Brousa, my fellow-Musselmen indignantly denounced me as damned, because I broke the fast of the Ramazan by taking a drink of water in the bazaar. I have gone into the holiest mosques in Asia Minor with perfect impunity. I determined to taste the Orient as it was, in reality, not as a mere outsider looker-on."[49] "Not as a mere outsider looker-on," Taylor said of his passing among "my fellow-Musslemen," using a then-antiquated term for Muslims. This was the rugged, daring Taylor who would jump off the page and into people's imaginations as his travel letters and books emerged.

Here Taylor was building the foundations of an *Ex Oriente Lux* argument that many Americans would find persuasive. Although potentially less authoritative than native speakers like Christopher Oscanyan, Taylor could be more credible to Americans by endorsing the comprehensible trope of the insider's account, with its sense of adventure and the forbidden, in ways that Oscanyan as a real insider could never carry off. Eastern travelers seeking to come off as experts often represented their savvy by traveling in local garb, which in some cases functioned as a sincere disguise, in others merely as an affectation. For instance, in the early 1850s, Philadelphia Minister Benjamin Dorr described running into an American in Palestine who was traveling incognito in order to avoid being approached as a tourist and asked for money by Bedouins. "His appearance was so changed by his tarboosh and long beard, that I did not at first recognize him," Dorr said.[50] It was the act of disguised passing that created the interest in these accounts because it pointed out how flexible one's persona could be and offered that flexibility to observers. Bayard Taylor would refer to the donning of local dress in the Empire as a "romantic expedient" that helped authors create dramatic tension around a transformed persona. Taylor's newspaper letters and his books celebrated events of mistaken identity; for instance, Taylor told of his arrival in one town where he was "followed by the curious glances of the people, who were in doubt whether to consider us Turks or Franks [Westerners]."[51] There was a sense here that Taylor relished being unreadable to people overseas (although in all probability he was snickered at by Easterners who saw him "gone native"). Because Taylor played Oriental abroad, his example proposed the possibility to audiences of vicariously trying on Eastern guises in their own work of individuation.

To this end, while supposedly out on assignment to collect factual content for lyceum lectures and books of travel, at one point Taylor ingested (probably too much) hashish in a Damascus hotel. The building had "once been the house of some rich merchant," Taylor said, embellishing the place with a cliché of the Oriental tale. There he produced "Visions of Hasheesh," a piece that would become an Oriental tale interlude to *Lands of the Saracen*, his Levantine travel narrative. Taylor described how he had imagined himself to be floating, then transported to the top of the pyramid of Cheops in Egypt, "moving over the Desert, not upon the rocking dromedary, but seated in a barque made of mother-of-pearl, and studded with jewels of surpassing luster. The sand was of grains of gold, and my keel slid through them without jar or sound." And so it went until Taylor finally announced that his experience allowed him to finally discover the true secret behind the mystery of Eastern voice Anglo-Americans were so determined to imitate: "Mahomet's Paradise, with its palaces of ruby and emerald, its airs of musk and cassia, and its rivers colder than snow and sweeter than honey, would have been a poor and mean terminus for my arcade of rainbows. Yet in the character of this paradise, in the gorgeous fancies of the Arabian Nights, in the glow and luxury of all Oriental poetry, I now recognize more or less of the agency of hasheesh."[52] Islamic art reduced to an intoxicated hallucination—this was patronizing to be sure. Nor is it entirely clear what middling audiences made of this, and many may have ignored this portion of his work in favor of the more seemingly pious or rugged parts. The piece was emblematic of Taylor's actually genuine admiration for the Arab framers of the *Thousand and One Nights'* incredible tales of affluence and magic. In a letter to celebrated American writer Washington Irving not long after, he would call the Arabs a "brilliant and heroic people."[53]

For Taylor, the Middle East had functioned as an artistic muse, a radical change of scene that provided fresh inspiration. Many creative Westerners found there new sights and sounds, invigorating artistic practices, respite from lecturing or newspaper and magazine work, and, for painters, clear vibrant blue skies and intense sunlight that contrasted with the grey light of industrial cities.[54] In the romantic tradition, Taylor too endorsed a common critique arguing that Anglo-American culture imposed self-restraint and anxiety upon "prosaic Christians, [who] meekly hold out [their] wrists for the handcuffs of Civilization," a culture that stifled the true artist.[55] However, after months abroad, "the Orient had left its seal on my face," he explained of the sea change in his outlook.[56]

Taylor's self-immersion in the Ottoman Empire also worked like a charm to help him create the Taylor persona of Eastern artist. Thereafter, poetry flowed forth in which he spoke of the personal transformation that would soon come to define his brand to a small audience of literary peers and consumers: "The Poet came to the Land of the East / When spring was in the air: / The Earth was dressed for a wedding Feast, / So young she seemed, and fair; / And the Poet knew the Land of the East,— / His soul was native there."[57] Intervening in the ongoing practice of Oriental tales in an attempt to put his experiences to work for his art, Taylor thereafter created a body of ostensibly Eastern poetry he called his "Orientalities," collected in *Poems of the Orient* (1855). Readers soon knew the volume for its utterly comprehensible renditions of the exotic banquets, beautiful landscapes, sage wisdom, romantic love, and chivalrous men that stocked the Oriental tale genre.[58]

Back in the United States in 1854, Taylor embarked on a more mundane lyceum lecture tour to earn more money and promote the forthcoming round-the-world trilogy, *A Journey to Central Africa* (1854), *Lands of the Saracen* (1855), and *India, China and Japan* (1855). In these works, Taylor obliged middle-class audiences with "useful" information about foreign lands in open-ended works that might satisfy the diverse tastes of many people. The American lyceum trade was no longer simply a space for democratic public access to useful information and self-improvement, as it had been in Oscanyan's early days in 1830s New York, but one venue in a network of for-profit entertainment and information ventures linked to publishing and cheap decorative illustrations.[59] Nonetheless, still touted as a "foe of bigotry in politics and religion" for the informed minority, especially city and town dwelling people under forty, lecturers knew that that venue required them to endorse the stereotypes the audience held about the lyceum public's ingenuity, productivity, and plain horse sense.[60] Lecturers also knew that these audiences and the press often "systematically misconstrued" speakers' ideas, as Mary Cayton has rediscovered, to significantly reshape the public record of a given speaker's lectures in the newspapers so as to endorse the ambitious attitudes of the upwardly mobile "commercial classes."[61] Certainly this had taken place with Oscanyan, his detailed, serious lecture reviews of the 1830s contrasting sharply with the abbreviated, matter-of-fact yet slightly sensational reviews of the 1850s.

The lyceum audiences would interpret Taylor not as a leisured Eastern gentleman who indulged in drugs and poetry but as a rugged Eastern traveler. Indeed, one Midwestern reviewer commented that the young ladies of his town should come out in force to see this worldly Pennsylvanian so that they might know "the difference between men and butterflies."[62] For these live performances, Taylor looked through his repertoire and chose material that emphasized a romantic cultural relativism, such as it was in the 1850s, that was useful for lyceum audiences because it criticized some aspect of American life by unflattering comparison with West Asian cultures.⁶³ Since his audience inhab-ited cultures saturated with biblical content and allusion, Taylor reproduced the standard Anglo-American prejudices regarding the decline of Palestinian Jews. He also duly critiqued inefficient imperial Ottoman rule, the hired guide who turn out to be an "arrant knave," worries of being robbed by Bedouins, and the lamentation that Eastern Christians had monopolized Christian holy sites at the expense of visiting Protestant American pilgrims.⁶⁴ Still, for every predictable episode Taylor did explore, he also sought out unconventionality—in a conven-tional sort of way. Thus could Taylor make hackneyed controversial statements like "the Mohammedans, it may not generally be known, accept the history of Christ."⁶⁵ Even if the reader or listener had known this, the effect was to reas-sert that he or she had specialized knowledge that less-sophisticated Americans did not. Using the Ex Oriente Lux mode in this way, Taylor additionally might get his ideas across as a sign of generational shifts in opinion by implicitly replicat-ing the stereotype that young people strove for diligent self-improvement by rejecting passé parental prejudices based in cultural misunderstanding.

Consequently, at one New York talk in January 1854 entitled "The Arabs," Taylor set about presenting a well-worn scenario: "common" opinion in the United States was mistaken about the desert inhabitants of the Middle East. Taylor warned his readers to be wary of "pious writers [who] have described what was expected of them, not what they found."⁶⁶ Instead, flattering those of the contemporary intellectual opinion that the environment shaped the charac-ter of various "races" around the globe, he explained that because of their struggles to survive the harsh desert climate of West Asia and North Africa, the Bedouin were chivalrous, generous, yet fierce to those who offended personal and family honor.⁶⁷ There was not much new in this; Christopher Oscanyan and countless Oriental tales had been saying the same thing for years.

Still, the next morning the New York Times obliged in carrying over Taylor's Ex Oriente Lux message. The paper was a good match for the lyceum crowds, representing a particularly literate and self-perceived worldly, progressive pub-lic in the Northeast in the 1850s. The Times reviewer wrote, "[p]robably no people have suffered more than the Arabs from one-sided judgment." Referring to biblical passages many took as damning evidence against Arabs as children of Ishmael, the Times presented a well-worn trope of ignorant thinking: "We have been taught to consider them an outcast race, 'whose hand was against every man, and every man's hand against them.' The Arab of our school-boy days was a lean, haggard ogre, with fierce black eyes and a sharp scimitar in his hand, ready to cut off the heads of the unfortunate Capt. Rileys, who might happen to fall into his power."[68] Taylor was right to point out that some stripes of sensationally patriotic plays and literature, like early Barbary captivity narratives (in this case William Riley's 1817 account of abduction by Algerians, *An Authentic Narrative of the Loss of the Brig Commerce*), schoolbooks, and missionary publications regularly portrayed some inhabitants of North Africa and the Ottoman Empire as "for the most part, cruel, vicious, and unprincipled."[69] Proliferating just then also were middling travel narratives that sensationally simplified the Bedouin Arabs who controlled travel networks between Cairo and Jerusalem as lawless scoundrels engaged in "Bedouin banditry" that exposed the ineffectuality of Ottoman rule.

Who among those lyceum audiences particularly wanted to hear such things? Kids and teenagers would turn out to be some of the main consumers of Taylor's works, but not for his condemnation of the Sultan or Eastern religions. These youthful readers saw in Taylor's manly Eastern persona a compelling, rugged incarnation that people sought in world travelers: desert explorer and self-made man.[70] Bayard Taylor actually identified with these young fans, a group who reminded him of himself. Like many young Americans, as a boy Taylor had gotten the travel bug by reading adult travel narratives. "I have also met numbers of bright-eyed children (God bless them!)" he wrote a friend, "who were as eager for my letters as for Robinson Crusoe, and who seem so delighted to see me and talk with me that I take my notoriety gratefully with all its annoyances."[71] Many of these young consumers indeed perceived Taylor as a model of bravery and enterprise, perhaps because they had not read his more romantic Oriental tale–style poems but merely the adventure-style excerpts that appeared in the papers.

While pious pilgrims to Palestine saw the desert landscape as proof of the mismanagement of the believed once lush and green biblical Holy Land by Muslims and the Ottoman government, young male readers and many adventure travelers in the Middle East relished the challenge of desert travel as an authentic experience divorced from the growing tourism industry there. Bayard Taylor had egged on this interpretation when in print he savored the heat and loneliness of the desert, so "excessively hot. The atmosphere is sweltering."[72] One of his young readers, Russell H. Conwell, would grow up to be a contract author of middling books like *Life of President Hayes*, *History of the Great Fire in Boston*, and *Why and How the Chinese Emigrate*. As an adult, Conwell would write an 1879 biography that captured the popular sense of Taylor as rugged desert traveler. Of Taylor's voyage to the Sudanese Nile, Conwell wrote with some embellishment: "It was a hazardous undertaking for a stranger, alone, unknown, to traverse the desert. If he was murdered, none of the authorities would care, nor would his death become known. He might contract a terrible fever. He was liable to be eaten by wild beasts, and he ran great risk of dying of thirst or hunger on the hot sands of a trackless desert. . . . But he unhesitatingly entered upon the journey . . . camping in the desert sands, riding a dromedary in the scorching sun, living upon rudely prepared food, drinking lukewarm water, with the sight of bones and carcasses by the way to warn him."[73] Taylor had never seriously been in danger in the Middle East or the Sudan nor had he really implied that he had.

Regardless, Conwell wrote from the experience of a generation of boys and young men who read travel stories and boy's adventure tales that emphasized personal triumph, rags to riches transformations, and acts of bravery.[74] For instance, Thomas W. Knox's *Adventures of Two Youths in a Journey to Egypt and the Holy Land* (1882) was authored by someone who had lived through Taylor's notoriety in the 1850s. It was part of a multivolume series called "Boy Travelers in the Far East" that suggested to younger readers how they might too become men by vicariously traveling East. The trope of the enterprising Eastern traveler had already been verified by Herman Melville's *Redburn*, in which the young male hero at church one Sunday in the 1830s spots the famous American traveler John Lloyd Stephens in the pews. By Conwell's day, Mark Twain was satirizing the persona's currency in common boyhood fantasies of being an Arab and "free son of the desert" in *Innocents Abroad*.[75] The centrality of playing Eastern in the universe of boyish adventure was something Christopher Oscanyan, as a native of a foreign country, probably did not understand as Taylor did when he thought about how to write of his travels.

In spite of these young male readers, the bulk of Taylor's fan base were made up of older members of the self-aware Anglo-American book and lyceum public. During that winter book tour in 1854, much to his own perplexed amazement, Taylor had found meeting halls overflowing with eager people, especially farm families and young women in the old Northwest and California. He wrote friends of visiting "crammed houses" that included many "breathless" women who stared incredulously at him.[76] Taylor quickly developed a troubled relationship with these audiences. During one moment of fatigue he called them "a collection of cabbage-heads."[77] Still, he complained with some pride to his writer friend R. H. Stoddard of one young lady who flattered his masculine pride during a train ride with "many advances to me, in the way of smiles, speaking looks, etc. etc."[78]

These young, heavily female audiences made material the "feminine fifties" to Taylor, a period in which male literary artists, publishers, and editors habitually claimed the market seemed to reward those who reduced their art to a cynically produced commodity. Harriet Beecher Stowe, with her blockbuster *Uncle Tom's Cabin* (1852), was only the tip of an iceberg of successful women writers who served a broad audience of yet more women, most of them ignored by elite literary magazines because so many men perceived their literature to be cheap, sentimental fodder for indiscriminate consumers. Then there was Sara Parton Willis, a.k.a. Fanny Fern, then the highest-paid male or female columnist in the United States at $100 a week for the *New York Ledger*. Her paychecks showed where money was being made in the publishing business.[79] Taylor's fame playing rugged American traveler and subject of female admiration meant that his greatest fans, rather than the refined gentlemen he hoped would contemplate his poetry or even the admiring boys Taylor humored, were plain farmers, small town book buyers, and young ladies dazzled by his masculine reputation as the "handsome lecturer."[80] "Now this is truly humiliating," he said of the buzz over his public appearances that spring in 1854. "Fame (if this is it) is not worth the trouble we take to get it."[81]

Only two years before, he had been camping through the desert playing Eastern. Now Taylor found himself schlepping across the nation on a mundane promotional trip equally crucial to the financial viability of his travel books as commercial art. To cope with this reality, Taylor played Oriental with a "coterie audience," as Mark Conroy terms it, of literary peers and intellectual consumer-admirers distinct, Taylor felt, from the mass publicity of lyceums and newspapers.[82] After his friend and fellow writer George W. Curtis released his own narrative of Ottoman Empire travel, *The Howadji in Syria*, Taylor wrote enviously from the lyceum trail in Eastern voice:

What a flood of "Syrian sunshine" burst upon me at Buffalo, with your book! My, you have been dipped in the living fountains of the East, and as I read your words, with the north wind whistling at the window and the frost on the glass, the old unutterable despair and divine longing came over me again. When Mr. Bliss knocked at the door, and I started up from the café over Parphar in Damascus, to go and lecture to miserable Christians in a Baptist Church. . . . Peace and blessing be upon you,

O Howadji! . . . Sometime—if it be the will of God—I shall get through
with these tiresome journeys, and the necessity of being nightly stared
at and pointed at and then we shall mingle the smoke of our peaceful
pipes, and give ourselves up wholly, for an hour at least, to the memories
of the Orient.[83]

Although he had traveled the world, lectured and written on dozens of topics,
and could have played Japanese or Hindu or Native American to represent his
most artistic, authentic, and unconventional self, Taylor chose to play Oriental
artist in a mode that was a greatly amplified version of any Eastern guise his
book and lyceum fans saw.

Taylor was not alone in this, and the realities of being a celebrity motivated
many male writers of the period to resort to "splitting [themselves] into an
alienable commodified self and a supposedly more authentic inner self," as
Paul Gilmore explains.[84] Especially among close friends, Taylor used his Eastern artist-self to argue for inclusion and authenticity, squaring off his "coterie
audience" against the middling book and lyceum public, themselves similarly
squared off against the rest of the nation or the truism of "common misunderstanding" that was laced through Taylor's lyceum lectures. Biographer and
contemporary Albert Smyth remembered that Taylor's Oriental persona was
"instantly recognized by every one who had read (and who had not read?)
[Taylor's] 'The Lands of the Saracen.'" The publicity materials surrounding Taylor's work and some of his private behavior combined to create "an atmosphere
of strangeness and remoteness and mystery" around him, the "mystery" being
proof that Taylor had found a way to play Eastern as someone not entirely
comprehensible yet familiar enough to be fascinating.[85] Noted literary por-
traitist Sara Parton Willis (Fanny Fern) said people called Taylor "The Oriental
Bayard."[86]

John Greenleaf Whittier, one of Taylor's audience of peers, commemorated
Taylor's Eastern persona with "The Tent on the Beach," a poem that imagined a
camping party to whom he invited Taylor, ". . . one, whose Arab face was
tanned/ . . . And in the tent-shade, as beneath a palm,/Smoked, cross-legged
like a Turk, in Oriental calm."[87] Whittier had carefully defined that "Oriental
calm," a mode of playing Eastern in which people perceived a "state of absolute
quietude—a region of ineffable calm, blown over by no winds of hope or fear.
All personal anxieties and solicitudes were unknown."[88] Taylor put on his
Eastern persona, like Christopher Oscanyan, in a way that made him appear to

be above market relations and that avoided conflation with the hackneyed and unreadable impassive Turk. Taylor derived his "Oriental calm" from the consumer's Oriental tale that imagined wealthy Easterners as utterly content and easing in luxury, an interpretation that was helping to sell the idea of consumption to the American middle and upper classes just then.

Bayard Taylor's Oriental airs were a way for him to live with a paradox inherent in consumer capitalism by expressing distaste for a machine of commercial publishing and promotion he actually relied upon to make a living. Taylor and fellow writers like R. H. Stoddard, Thomas Bailey Aldrich, E. C. Stedman, and George Curtis made up the "Genteel Circle," less famous today than the men celebrated as the first great American writers (Washington Irving, Nathaniel Hawthorne, William Cullen Bryant, or James Fenimore Cooper) or those associated with the American Renaissance of the 1850s (Ralph Waldo Emerson, Walt Whitman, David Thoreau, Herman Melville, and Nathaniel Hawthorne) but still well known and respected in their own day. Paradoxically, genteel artists often rejected the go-ahead spirit of the age in their poetry and other writing—writing nonetheless loaded with fantasies of repose and affluence derived from the consumers' Oriental tale. That is, they eagerly participated in the market, Paul Wermuth explains, aspiring to "the upward mobility of the middle class. The values of money, hard work, and success—and its rewards, comfort, and respectability—were all involved." Mimicking the lifestyles of English or southern gentry, for instance, they strove to acquire country estates where they could entertain and make a refuge from the commercial work that paid for that lifestyle. Taylor would do just so, pretentiously naming his property in Pennsylvania "Cedarcroft."[89]

Then, in the waning days of his 1854 lyceum tour, a portrait of Taylor entitled "The Author of 'Visions of Hasheesh'" appeared in *Putnam's Monthly Magazine*.[90] Designed to promote Taylor's forthcoming travel narratives while keeping *Putnam's* relevant to book and lyceum audiences and to the magazine's upper-class readers, it conformed to a familiar portrait style for worldly men. It asked them to recall the famed poet Lord Byron, who had himself been similarly depicted in Grecian dress before dying nobly, many believed, at battle in the Greek War of Independence.[91] It also foreshadowed what one author has called a "rash of publications" in the United States after 1850 discussing cannabis and hashish use. Excerpts of Taylor's own encounters with the drug had duly appeared in magazines reprinted in local newspapers like the *Brooklyn Daily Eagle*.[92]

Certainly the image was another way for the publicity infrastructure to

Bayard Taylor as Eastern traveler. *Putnam's Monthly Magazine,* 1854.

deliver the famous Bayard Taylor to those "ladies" who imagined him as a manly traveler or the young readers who may have noted his hand resting on a dagger—which he might brandish at any moment!—they may have speculated. Still, the "Visions of Hasheesh" image also throws into high relief the difficulty in knowing where Bayard Taylor's professional persona as Easternized artist ended and his industry persona as rugged adventure traveler began. Legend has had it since at least the 1950s that Taylor in fact performed many of his lectures "dressed in his colorful Arab costume with a scimitar at his side."[93] Intriguing as this possibility is, the letters and newspaper accounts documenting Taylor's lecture appearances make no mention of any Eastern dress. Nineteenth-century Americans were deeply fascinated by foreign costume, and contemporary travel accounts in book, magazine, and newspaper work, including Taylor's, accordingly described the dress of the North Africans and West Asians in great detail. If Taylor had played Eastern on the lyceum stage in costume, his appearance would have elicited considerable comment. Consequently, the confusion over Taylor's garb may emanate from Taylor's success in translating his Oriental artist of mystery persona into rich popular graphic and print forms like the *Putnam's* image, a talent that suggests that he attempted to impose his authentic artistic self on the public, though with limited control of what they would do with it.

Less than two years later, Thomas Hicks's famous work depicting a reclining, fez-clad Taylor smoking a water pipe on a Damascus rooftop emerged in the National Academy of Design, later to be sold in large numbers as mass-produced reproductions. The portrait complied with the "turk reposing" genre that spoke of the perceived leisured consumption patterns of the Ottoman elite and Taylor's persona as Eastern traveler.[94] More pious viewers may also have noted that the act of relaxing on rooftops is a common element in Bible stories, and as such, Taylor was helping them picture life in the modern Holy Land.[95] In an era when many of Taylor's readers would have been customers of panorama shows at which observers stood or sat stationary while viewing a city or landscape scene that scrolled past them on an enormous canvas, the Hicks portrait also presented Taylor in a comprehensible mode to Americans who had vicariously visited the Ottoman Empire at a panorama or dime museum.[96] Most importantly, Taylor's promotional portrait could have portrayed him as a plainly dressed lecturer at the podium, bent over a writing desk or sitting on his luggage at some Ohio train station—namely, working for a living. Instead, sold in large numbers as a commodity like the *Putnam's* image, the Hicks portrait offered an idealized Taylor who spoke of the consumer's Oriental tale, an Eastern artist who worried and worked not but promoted consumption of his books and lectures far better than any laboring Taylor could.

After the Hicks portrait hung in the National Academy of Design, one biographer reminisced, "During the Quixotic Quarter-Century (1850–1875), the Hicks portrait was [a] familiar a household object . . . [in which] one may study the romantically bronzed profile, the lean cheek, the flashing eye, and the Asiatic accouterments of burnoose and narghile which thrilled a generation of prosaic Americans."[97]

The genius in all this was that Taylor branded his writing and lyceum performances for his peers with a persona of Eastern gentleman enjoying Oriental calm and for middling audiences of adults and kids with a persona of rugged traveler while competing vigorously in saturated markets for commercial cultural products. "Rest has no meaning to our ears; what we consider rest is merely something not so fast as usual," Taylor had written.[98] He worked twelve-hour days much of his adult life in order to pay for his sumptuous home and the required entertaining out at Cedarcroft where "providing for the expenses of an estate vexed him," his wife remembered.[99] In 1860 he even wrote to Horace Greeley for a loan, asking, "Could you lend me $400, or even $300, or even $200, until the first week in July? You see I count upon *something* from The Tribune."(italics in original)[100] While many Americans complained about the increasing speed of life and the degradations of the market to an artist's spirit, Bayard Taylor actually lived that reality as a soul-crushing series of lyceum tours and constant journalistic work. "He was the most faithful and honest of workmen, but his friends knew him to be overworked," *Harper's Monthly* said on Taylor's passing in March 1879 at the age of fifty-three.[101]

Bayard Taylor and Christopher Oscanyan were only two examples of many people who marketed themselves by performing as debunkers of "common misunderstanding" with respect to Muslim North Africa and West Asia. That the Anglo-American book and lyceum public responded to their *Ex Oriente Lux* appeals, even in diverse ways that saw audiences rework, misconstrue, or even criticize these men, was evidence of a parallel universe of commercial communication coexisting with the *Arabian Nights* and Oriental tales. The consumer could have both, playing Eastern as a prototype for the promises of magical self-transformation, ease, and plenty that came with consumption in a market economy while also enjoying performances and information presented within an *Ex Oriente Lux* message that supposedly criticized the alarmist stereotypes about the East that persisted in the markets for entertainment and information. Enough middling consumers believed that crass and narrow-minded people reviled the Muslim world above all other places that they embraced the Ottoman Empire, or at least investigated it vicariously by consuming performances of professional travelers, in order to enact a more authentic identity defined by cultural relativism while spending money mightily to demonstrate that exclusivity nonetheless.

chapter 3

Wise Men of the East and the Market for American Fraternalism, 1850–1892

After the Civil War, it was male audiences who were particularly compelled by accounts of the Eastern world marketed by a native-born man in Eastern persona because to them West Asia and North Africa were utterly masculine spaces. The pattern had already begun with men like Christopher Oscanyan, who performed as Eastern Christian man for mixed Anglo-American audiences. Bayard Taylor similarly played Eastern artist to sell books and cope with the lyceum trade inadvertently attracting young male and female fans impressed by his reputation as a manly traveler. Among their audiences, a few men would in time play Oriental themselves, writing poems or travel narratives in the Oriental tale style. Even more played Eastern at home in their wives' Oriental cozy corners, their own Arabian-styled lounges, or a department store decorated to remind customers of the abundance portrayed in the *Arabian Nights*. Thousands more would go a big step further, combining the old *Ex Oriente Lux* message with a spiritual persona to create the appearance of wise man of the East. This character was often specifically Muslim, and Americans articulated him in two ultranatural incarnations: the brotherly Arab mystic and the libertarian Arab warrior.

In the late nineteenth century, American fraternal orders like the Freemasons constituted the most numerous purveyors of the wise man of the East persona. Had we lived one hundred years ago, most of us would have had a dad, uncle, brother, or boss who played Eastern through their rituals and celebrations. We would have known the location of their lodges, seen their charities at work, and witnessed their costumes and performances in street parades downtown. Fraternalists made up a consumer base of great affluence and great demand, spending liberally on regalia, lodge space, books and periodicals, food, drink, and more in support of their activities. Much as Christopher Oscanyan and Bayard Taylor had catered to their publics, many an entrepreneur would play wise man of the East to make a career by appealing to the fraternal market segment.

Fraternal wise men of the East carried an *Ex Oriente Lux* message too, arguing for the existence of "common misunderstanding" regarding the Muslim world among nonfraternalists and arguing that Masons especially knew that the men of the Arab Middle East held ancient wisdom that could save American men from spiritual decline. The fraternalists' *Ex Oriente Lux* message crossed over familiar Masonic philosophies as a kind of secret masculinist Oriental tale. These mystical traditions were thus tied to a region deeply sacred to Anglo-American Christians yet still outside the feminized economy of the church. Indeed, the masculine nature of the Middle East was obvious to most observers, who noted that Freemasons and other fraternalists chose from among the world's cultures with great specificity in order to flesh out their subcultures. Certainly the Odd Fellows reenacted a masculinist Medievalism in their lodges, while members of the Improved Order of Red Men played Indian to take on rejuvenating, autonomous manhoods grounded in perceived warrior cultures.[1] Equally, the white American fraternal universe contained no orders themed on, say, Chinese, Filipino, Dahomian, or Mexican cultures, all lands many people believed were characterized by ignoble or weak masculinities inappropriate for manly ritual performance.[2]

Freemasonry, with its one million members and foundational legends set in the biblical Holy Land, was the most prolific of all the fraternities. Masonry coexisted with at least a dozen "Arabian" and Oriental tale–style brotherhoods that provided men even more opportunities to play Eastern or Muslim. By the 1870s, the fraternal wise man of the East and his *Ex Oriente Lux* appeal was so common that his currency would inspire broadly accessible satire. Soon the most famous men using the guise were the campy, teasing amateur performers of recreational fraternal orders, most importantly the Ancient Arabic Order, Nobles of the Mystic Shrine, or Shriners. The wisecracking members of these orders would lampoon the fraternal East and broader middle-class veneration of things Oriental to show how contentious the Easternization of American life could be to plenty of people.

This chapter, then, is about the men who, between 1850 and 1892, made use of one the most common Eastern personae in United States history. It tells the stories of professional Masons Rob Morris and Albert Rawson, prominent examples of men who cultivated the fraternal public in order to cobble together a living. I also explain further how rank and file Masons in reply created burlesquing Oriental-style performance art bent on critiquing the romantic Masonic Middle East and middling Orientana of the Gilded Age. Generations of men put enormous time, money, and effort into these performances. They did not play Eastern or Muslim in a narrow attempt simply to demonize or feminize a Muslim "Other."[3] Rather, American fraternalists sought to enjoy two identities at once: authentically masculine wise man of the East and successfully affluent man of the West. They worked in a long artistic tradition marked by "love and theft," as Eric Lott has described other kinds of ambivalent double-identity performance. Like the arts of blackface or playing Indian, in which whites performed in hybrid guises, wise men of the East wore a guise that similarly adapted Arab and Middle Eastern masculinities to Anglo-American identities in ways that "mediat[ed] white men's relations with other white men."[4] As wise man of the East, whether professional traveler, hometown Masonic initiate, or prank-pulling Shriner, Anglo-American men were not falsifying their identities or putting on random personae solely in jest. Many actually used a masculine Eastern guise to expose aspects of themselves that were inappropriate in other venues dominated by family or work responsibilities.

MAKING THE MASONIC PUBLIC: ROB MORRIS

Who were the main audiences for the fraternal Ex Oriente Lux message and the main adopters of the wise man of the East persona? Coming of age in the two decades before the Civil War, many white men had accumulated (for periods of time at least) the social standing and disposable income to become Freemasons, Red Men, Odd Fellows, Knights of Pythias, or members of the approximately 300 other fraternities in the country. Masons and Odd Fellows alone would account for 2 million in membership by 1900.[5] These men shared a common culture, available through lodge attendance, increasingly voluminous fraternal literature, and public appearances of members in parades and newspaper announcements. Because of their frequent function as relief and insurance societies, all these fraternal associations also spoke of the precarious nature of many men's affluence. A number of prominent orders were known to open their meetings with the request "Does any brother know of a brother or a brother's family in need?"[6] Indeed, for many, once inside the doors of the lodge, fraternal ritual and sociability offered an escape from the competitive individualism and nonstop work of Anglo-American life.[7]

Fraternal activity was simultaneously a preeminent venue for male consumerism and signified one's success as a producer of wealth because, collectively, fraternalists were an enormous market of generous spenders. They were representative of the fact that Anglo-American men, not women, were the preeminent consumers of the nineteenth century. They did most of the paid labor in the country, had access to those earnings before other family members, and were willing to spend up to 15 percent of the household income for clothing, food, and entertainment, while their wives frugally cooked and sewed at home to meet the rest of the family's needs.[8] Fraternal participation alone required payment of ritual fees, yearly dues, charity donations, the purchase of costuming and paraphernalia, and tickets for fraternal travel, banquets, and picnics.[9] Fraternalism was in these days "systematically marketed," Mary Ann Clawson writes, to a relatively predictable imagined community of like-minded consumers of spirituality and brotherhood.[10]

In the mid-nineteenth century, Rob Morris was one of the most famous of these people to appeal specifically to a group he called the "Mason Public."[11] Famous Masonic publisher/authors like Morris, Albert G. Mackey, Albert Pike, and Robert Macoy had been instrumental in facilitating communication among this self-aware consumer community, as had dozens of mobile professional recruiting agents for newer fraternities, as well as countless regalia, book, and periodical salesmen. This was a geographically broader national group than the reading public of literary magazines and lyceum lecture halls and yet was a more exclusive community made up of middle-class and upper-class Anglo-American men, Democrat and Republican, in big cities and small towns across the nation. The emergence of the Masonic public was not an inevitable development of American culture and marketing theory but a result of the labors of thousands who made the idea of wise man of the East specifically useful as a consumer antidote to the pressures of a volatile economy and family responsibility. It was in effect an Easternization of masculine spirituality that came from the increasing access Americans had to the actual Middle East.

The career of Rob Morris is illustrative of how and why this market emerged and why the East was useful to him in developing his professional brand as a lecturer, traveler, and promoter of Masonry in the United States. Like Oscanyan and Taylor, Morris and hundreds of other men hoping for "professional and intellectual careers," Donald Scott explains, "frequently made their way by moving into and through a series of institutions, places, and activities that had not even existed when they started out and that they themselves often had to invent. . . . [They shared] a common need to secure or even create the audience necessary to sustain them." Morris was indeed an intellectual jack-of-all-trades and worked long hours to "improvise a career" in and beyond the Masonic public.[12] He dabbled in more than just Masonic material, contracting for all the different kinds of work writers and entertaining lecturers routinely took to pay the bills. Morris had published his own antislavery novel, *The Faithful Slave*, just as *Uncle Tom's Cabin* emerged to public acclaim in 1852, for instance, and would also tap into the boy-adventurer segment of the book market with his own children's travel narrative, *Youthful Explorers in Bible Lands* (1870).[13]

Rob Morris's greatest claim to fame, however, was as self-promoting "Poet Laureate of Masonry" and traveling advocate of American fraternalism. A Past Grand Master (governor) of Kentucky lodges, he visited, lectured to, and recited Masonic poetry for Masons all over the Northeast, South, and Midwest, wrote and marketed his own Masonic publications, and raised the money for all of it. "His face is recognized in more than 3,000 lodges," one obituary later said of his notoriety.[14] Indeed, Morris's greatest labor was in developing the Masonic public as an audience that could make his precarious entrepreneurialism toward the Ottoman Levant financially viable. To this end, Morris had served briefly as chair of Ancient and Modern History at the Masonic University of Kentucky, a short-lived institution funded by the fraternity, and had assembled one of the largest contemporary collections of books on Freemasonry. He was also the founder of the Masonic auxiliary for women, the Order of the Eastern Star. Then in 1859, Morris had started an even more controversial group called the Conservators' Movement, wherein he sent mysterious communications to Masons asking them if they sought to protect Freemasonic ritual from innovation, asking for money and complete confidentiality. Many Masons rejected the Conservator's Movement, especially those in the competing, proslavery Knights of the Golden Circle order, and little came of Morris's reform attempts once the Civil War broke out. Morris thereafter served as a traveling agent for several fraternities during the Civil War, including the unionist Strong Band Association.[15]

In each case, Morris used the then-current bookseller's technique of promoting his products by alerting potential customers to the existence of the larger community of preexisting readers.[16] One typical Morris appeal was directed at northern Masons and explained his career as one of reciprocity with the Masonic public, his work repaid by Freemasons who served collectively as his patron: "The events of the civil war, that have borne so hardly upon us all, have totally wrecked Bro. Morris. His dwelling has been burned by midnight incendiaries, the patrimony of his wife (lying in Tennessee) has been confiscated and lost, and in these trying times, when the best of us find it so difficult to get along, he stands with a large family, his own health impaired, and his business prostrate, homeless and impoverished. Shall the Masonic fraternity permit this?"[17] Morris crafted this appeal to Masons by explaining how the purchase of his books strengthened the Freemasonic brotherhood as a whole. Thus could he create a sense of urgency over a tradition ostensibly under siege in order to reassure Masons who thought about the early nineteenth-century attacks on Freemasonry as a dangerous and antidemocratic secret society and of the divisiveness of the Civil War.

Rob Morris of course proposed to Masons that he go to the Middle East himself to collect information and objects that would embellish and illuminate Masonic knowledge. Morris's famous lodge lectures in support of the endeavor used the Ex Oriente Lux appeal to cultivate a specific, dependable market for his services, telling this audience that they were exclusively wise and specially related to the East. The lectures began with Morris spending up to two hours reciting Masonic poetry, much of it available in his publications. Thereafter, he pitched his idea for a Masonic pilgrimage to the Holy Land to find evidence of the origins of Masonry and its masculinist teachings, by which he would produce books, lectures, poetry, and mystic souvenirs through which his patrons might display their own Easternized Masonic identities. Morris offered for a payment of ten dollars to provide to the payee a selection of specimens of "woods, waters, earths, coins, fossils, etc., from Palestine," all carefully arranged and labeled in a cabinet, which would inspire and educate Masons in the United States, he said. Just as pilgrims to the Holy Land believed that the study of the manners and customs of contemporary locals would serve as a portal into the biblical past, Morris sought out illumination on Masonic lore and ritual based in the ancient Middle East through contemplation of the modern East, in turn offered to fellow Masons—at a reasonable price.[18]

The men who responded to Morris did so because the foundational legends of Freemasonry take place in the Middle East barely at arm's length from the sacred events of the Bible. Members explained the idea of a brotherhood of "Freemasons" by the ritual story of the killing of renowned workman Hiram Abiff at the site of Solomon's temple in biblical Palestine. Masons discussed thereafter whether the principles demonstrated in the lessons of Solomon's temple emanated from the ancient Israelites and were specific to Judeo-Christian tradition or whether they originated even earlier in ancient Egypt and broader Asian traditions, a stream of interpretation known as Ancient Craft Masonry.[19] Thus, to Masons, the East could be simultaneously a Protestant Holy Land and a site of inherently Christian Masonic philosophies or part of a more challenging global tradition of manly Gnostic understandings of God. Many Americans were actively questioning all sorts of received wisdom and dogma then. Most were loyal Christians who dutifully went to church on Sundays with their families or were even ministers themselves but spent evenings at the lodge entertaining spiritual ideas that opposed white middle-class Protestantism by emphasizing man's ability for self-salvation through intercultural investigation.[20]

Whatever combination of interpretations of Masonic philosophy a man chose, he participated in a brotherhood that privileged men as "the principle moral actors" in a nation that publicly reserved such a position for women and the church.[21] That is, Masonic orders, while existing publicly as mutual service organizations, espoused to many initiates the idea of an exclusively male tradition of mystical interpretation of the Middle East. "You see, my brother, what is the meaning of Masonic 'Light,'" Masonic scholar Robert Pike's canonical work instructed: "You see why the East of the Lodge, where the initial letter of the Name of the Deity [G] overhangs the Master, is the place of Light. Light, as contradistinguished from darkness, is Good, as contradistinguished from Evil: and it is that Light, the true knowledge of Deity, the Eternal Good for which Masons in all ages have sought."[22] Freemasonic ritual and philosophies reminded members constantly of the East as geographical reality and as Gnostic metaphor. Masonic initiates to the first degree of Freemasonry, Entered Apprentice, walked from the western towards the "most noble" eastern wall of the lodge during their initiation as a spiritual voyage towards true identity.[23] "Each of us," one Mason explained, "has come from the mystical 'East,' the eternal source of all light and life, and our life here is described as being spent in the 'West.'"[24] Fraternal commercial culture reasserted the existence of the manly Masonic East with books like Lester's Look to the East and the countless other Masonic products that imagined things Eastern as imbued with brotherly mystical wisdom.[25]

Even more, Morris's plan for a Masonic pilgrimage to the Holy Land came across in the broadly comprehensible language of Anglo-American interest in the Ottoman Empire's landscape. The nascent field of biblical archaeology and the more frank entrepreneurialism of men like Morris were two sides of the same coin of American activity in the Levant in the nineteenth century. Celebrated publications emanating from studies such as Edward Robinson's Biblical Researches in Palestine and the Adjacent Regions: A Journal of Travels in the Years 1838 and 1852 (1856) and William Thomson's blockbuster The Land and the Book; or,

Biblical Illustrations Drawn from the Manners and Customs, the Scenes and Scenery of the Holy Land (1859) inspired many Americans to visit, or aspire to visit, the Holy Land seeking verification of the historicity of the Bible.[26] Morris sought similarly to venture to the Ottoman province of Palestine under the auspices of the American Holy Land Exploration Society, a group of archaeology enthusiasts who financed research trips to the west side of the Jordan River with a parallel outfit called the Palestine Exploration Society financing surveys to the east of the river. These agencies collected objects and information from local inhabitants about the possible locations of biblical events and disseminated that research in the United States.[27]

This Masonic and archaeological biblical interest overlapped with the bustling travel narrative trade, much of it concerned with the practicalities of travel, subjective accounts of shopping, sightseeing, and conversations with dragomen or fellow travelers but not mystical Masonic topics. Accordingly, at his promotional talk Morris promised listeners he would tread new ground and avoid "wasting time in merely playing the tourist" like the publishers of the "scores and hundreds of books of travel in Palestine," instead seeking out previously overlooked information that only a Freemason would fully comprehend.[28] Through his promotional lectures he acquired subscriptions totaling over $9,600 for souvenirs and the eventual published account of his travels, *Freemasonry in the Holy Land,* a sum almost sufficient to pay for his trip and provide a stipend to support his family while he was away. We know this because Morris prefaced his resulting travel narrative with a detailed financial accounting of his promotion and capitalization of the book, exposing his immersion in a common culture with readers saturated by market relations and bamboozling investment schemes. In 1868, Rob Morris had managed to make it to the Ottoman Levant where he followed his dragoman, making observations and notes over an itinerary typical of Westerners in the Holy Land in those days.

Back in the United States, Morris lectured his way around dozens of lodges to tell Masons what he had learned about "symbolic Freemasonry," namely, the mystical and secret parts of the order's traditions that members experienced by way of ritual and discussed at length in fraternal literature but never in public. One of Morris's main insights was that Masonry was not just a Christian tradition for whites but was an international brotherhood of wise men that included Muslims. Morris explained Islam with an *Ex Oriente Lux* approach crafted for the Masonic public by asserting that in his opinion, informed by overseas travel, "Avoiding the doctrinal points, and read in the spirit of fraternal love, all illustrated in the lectures of Freemasonry, that remarkable book, the Koran, might justly be taken as a comment upon the much older, far wiser, and most remarkable book ever written, The Old Testament of the Hebrew dispensation. To those who are accustomed, without the slightest examination, to denounce the Koran (as well as its author), I will simply say, . . . an unprejudiced mind will admit, not only that the Koran contains far more quotations from and references to the Bible, but is absolutely imbued more with the spirit of the inspired word than a dozen of the best 'Saints' Books' found on the counter of any Catholic bookstore in New York.[29] Indeed, in those days Masonic lodges accepted Protestants and Jews, but not Catholics, men who tended to congregate in Knights of Pythias fraternity.

Morris's appeal to the old trope of "common misunderstanding" played to Masons who noted anti-Islamic feeling among Protestants, which, especially when inflamed by missionaries or the clergy, came across as a pretense to hiding the true brotherhood of man in order to fool the masses into paying tithes that made churches wealthy.[30] It was common for Anglo-Americans to talk about the Prophet Muhammad, who received the revelation of the Islamic scripture, as an "imposter" or false prophet. Still, plenty of mystical seekers nonetheless saw clues to Masonic wisdom in the Qur'an and broader Arab life that indicated mystical ancient practices.[31] About the *salat*, or five times daily Muslim prayer, Rob Morris told his audiences, "To a Freemason, to whom all ancient national usages have (or had in their origin) important symbolical references, these Mohammedan services of prayer are worthy of the closest attention. Divested of their references to the arch-Imposter of the Orient, Mohammed, how beautifully appropriate would be these entire forms of worship in the Freemasons Lodge." Whether any of Morris's listeners took seriously the possibility of adding the Muslim prayer ritual to Masonic practice is hard to say, but the Shriners would do just that—in jest, to be sure—within a generation. In the meantime, Morris was using the same techniques Oscanyan and Taylor had used to get across, flattering listeners' existing knowledge to introduce them to new information in a comprehensible way.

What the Muslims Morris met in the Levant would have made of all this is less clear. At the time, there were Muslim men in the Ottoman Empire who also entertained esoteric and freethinking ideals, by way of domestic mystical brotherhoods to be sure, but also through their own experimentation with Freemasonry. First by way of French lodges these men visited in Paris, then in

Persia and the Ottoman Empire, a few Easterners sought out fraternal activity as a mode of worldly political and spiritual reform.[32] Far from being a reason for suspicion, as monotheists and native-born inhabitants of the land in which many Masons believed their philosophies to have originated, to many American Masons the Muslim identity of Eastern Freemasons privileged them as fellow travelers into Masonic light and truth and cast them as brotherly Muslim mystics.

Morris would play Eastern by seeking out such men and claiming brotherhood with them. To flatter domestic Masons as part of a cosmopolitan brotherhood, he told his audience he was endlessly impressed with the Ottoman Masons he met. For instance, Morris met the Governor General of Syria and Palestine, Mohammed Raschid, casting him as a "brave, wise, and learned" man and dedicating *Freemasonry in the Holy Land* to the Ottoman official. Meeting Raschid was not Morris's biggest coup nor were his contacts with expatriate American Masons he found in Smyrna or Jerusalem. His prize was the famed Abd el-Kader. An Algerian, Abd el-Kader had first become known in the 1830s when he led men in resistance to the French. Through English-language accounts of his life, many had come to interpret Abd el-Kader as a libertarian Arab hero who defended his desert people from European colonialism. Public opinion in the United States and Britain had generally opposed the French invasion, especially when the French imprisoned Abd el-Kader for five years after he finally surrendered after twelve years of terrible fighting. To those Anglo-Americans paying attention to North African and European politics, Abd el-Kader was appealing as a free son of the desert, a liberty-loving chief driven, one American newspaper said, by the "volcanic fire of patriotism" and "20,000 daring Arab horsemen." These enthusiastic portrayals predated the cowboy and strenuous manhood tropes of the 1880s and 1890s, drawing on ideals of Eastern manhood that countered self-interested French government depictions of North Africans as barbaric fanatics.[33] Muslims in this scenario were "bound . . . by oath upon the Koran," chivalrous in their loyalty to ancient traditions. Americans often portrayed them at prayer not in the mosque but alone in the desert, a space of solitary male realization and triumph. Even in acts of violence such men were justified if they sought to protect their honor from colonialism, capitalism, or even against the more vague abstractions of "Mohammedan fanaticism" or "Turkish despotism."[34]

There was more to the story, though, since Morris and other Americans additionally celebrated Abd el-Kader for his efforts in Damascus some years

American illustrators often portrayed Muslim men at prayer, not in the mosque but alone in the desert, a space of solitary male realization. Albert Rawson et al., *What the World Believes*, 1886.

later. After his release from prison in France, Abd el-Kader had been exiled to the Ottoman province of Syria. When devastating violence broke out in 1860 between the Druze and Maronite Christians in the region, Abd el-Kader and a small militia made up of other expatriate Algerians took in or had escorted from the city hundreds of Christians who were suffering disproportionately in the violence.[35] Among those saved was the local American Consul, who stayed at Abd el-Kader's home. The press made much of these events, and thereafter, many renowned travelers made a point of visiting and befriending Abd el-Kader, including celebrated travelers Isabel and Richard Burton, and Lady Anne Blunt.[36]

Eventually Rob Morris would visit too, although there is no record of how Abd el-Kader actually received him. Of course, Morris gave an overwhelmingly positive account of the meeting to sensationalize his own perspective and the ostensible reputation of American Freemasons among Easterners. To Morris, el-Kader was both brotherly Muslim mystic and chivalrous Arab warrior, a "splendid specimen of the Arab race" and "great admirer of George Washington . . . one of the finest horsemen and swordsmen of the East," he told his Masonic public. Morris said that even though his Arabic was minimal, as Masonic brothers their communication had been easy and the two had "exchange[d] the secrets of Freemasonry," saying of Abd el-Kader's apparent majestic countenance and foreign costume, "I could not help recalling my images of Abraham."[37]

Abd el-Kader's father also happened to be a chief of the Qadiriyya Sufi brotherhood, its influence described sympathetically in some English publications on Islamic mysticism, giving Abd el-Kader further interest to American Masons curious about exclusive Muslim sources of manly philosophy. Back in 1788, a Pennsylvania Masonic body, the Select Committee and Grand Lodge of Enquiry, had translated Ignatius Mouradgea d'Ohsson's *Oriental Antiquities and General View of the Othoman Customs, Laws, and Ceremonies* into English, giving American Masons plenty of information on Middle Eastern brotherhoods. The volume promised in the subtitle to explain "Various Rites and Mysteries of the Oriental Freemasons," the phrase "Oriental Freemason" being an early term for Sufi orders.[38]

By Rob Morris's day, John P. Brown's 1868 *The Dervishes; or, Oriental Spiritualism* had taken d'Ohsson's place in Masonic libraries in providing an extremely detailed accounts of the various Sufi orders, their founders, philosophies, and mystical rituals. To Anglo-Americans, the brotherly Sufi or "dervish" could be one and the same with the imagined Arab warrior, as was the case with Abd el-Kader, or could come across in less militaristic ways as a mendicant or cosmopolitan mystic. The brotherly Muslim mystic was a carrier of pre-Christian masculine wisdom who, like the Masonic public, supposedly struggled on in the face of clerical dogma and popular superstition. These kinds of messages about West Asian and North African men were not terribly obscure. For instance, the copy of The Dervishes currently in the University of California, Berkeley library had been at some point previously owned by the Odd Fellows Library Association of San Francisco, and their librarian stamped the volume with their seal in several places. Such markings and usages speak of general fraternal interest in Eastern mystical brotherhoods, even for orders themed in a Medieval European mode like the Odd Fellows. Masonic literature throughout the nineteenth and early twentieth century was sprinkled with ample references to and information about Muslim beliefs in a tone that assumed the reader's expertise regarding Islam and a proposed single mystical truth that exists in all male cultures linked to West Asia.[39]

While contemplating more esoteric representations of the Middle East as a land of fraternity and chivalry, American fraternalists still found cautionary accounts of the Muslim world in the daily newspaper, church sermons and missionary tracts that paternalistically asserted Anglo-American civilization was the height of human progress. Consequently, Morris also presented his research on the Eastern origins of Masonic truth and his meetings with Eastern Masons, not as a flirtation with conversion to Islam but as a form of masculinist missionizing by which Masons might somehow renew themselves spiritually by protecting their mystical Eastern brothers as a way to bring them over to Christianity in time. Morris said that his experiences had inspired him to think "of the good time when the Mason-craft will yet build up Jerusalem and the GOD we worship be worshipped there and everywhere."[40]

To this end, a friend and fellow Masonic scholar, Henry R. Coleman, would similarly publish a narrative of his own "Masonic pilgrimage" to the Holy Land in 1881 that carried similar veneration of Eastern men and a grain of paternalism. Coleman dedicated his volume to Rob Morris and similarly used the durable Ex Oriente Lux approach to point out to the reader that "avoiding the beaten and hackneyed course of tourists, I have endeavored to say what is new, true, and useful"(italics in original).[41] Coleman set about to prove the "Oriental theory of Masonic origin" by both looking for archaeological evidence of the building of the Temple of Solomon and seeking out locals, as Morris had, who likewise practiced the "Mystic Craft" in the Holy Land. He called his published account of the trip *Light from the East*.[42] Coleman and a number of other Masons further founded the Oriental Order of Pilgrim Knights, a superlative fraternity for men within the Masonic public interested in wise man of the East–type missionizing. Through participation in the rituals and meetings of such elite orders, select American Masons played wise man of the East in the mode of mystical quasi-Muslim brother in order to claim to have internalized those aspects of Eastern manhood and spirituality that transcended mainstream Masonic philosophy. Indeed, people would pay to support such fraternities since the *Ex Oriente Lux* marketing technique always reserved space for communications with smaller and smaller audiences in concentric circles of exclusivity, each group believing that they were defying some common misunderstanding.

SAINT AND SCOUNDREL: ALBERT LEIGHTON RAWSON

Invitational orders like Coleman's Oriental Order of Pilgrim Knights blurred the line in an open-ended way between fraternal outreach, mystical Masonic research, and self-employment. From this overlap, playing Oriental developed in two parallel directions; first, entrepreneurial mystical Masons like our next subject, Albert Rawson, used their new access to foreign lands to market ancient wisdom; second, the Shriners and other recreational orders performed a broad satire of the *Ex Oriente Lux* approach to the Muslim world and the people who peddled it. Their satire would be funny because it was a critique of American awe for the Orient and the Easternization of American manhood within Masonry, showing that there was always debate about how people could find authentic identities and personae in a globalizing market economy. Playing Oriental to represent an ultranatural manhood was specifically useful to all these people because it appealed to the deeply sincere and the deeply cynical. Both groups would use a wise man of the East guise to cross over with like-minded people who perceived themselves to be above the credulous mainstream.

Professional wise man of the East Albert Leighton Rawson is important to our story in seeing that consumers who observed men playing Eastern evaluated and critiqued those performances. Rawson showed that the same man performing as brotherly mystic could come across alternately as wise man or trickster depending upon the experiences of his audience. There had always been a hazy overlap between the saint and the scoundrel within the worlds of Masonry and other alternative spiritual traditions. For instance, the Italian

Allesandro Cagliostro (1743–1795), "prince of Masonic imposters," became notorious in fraternal history for having founded the Egyptian Rite of Free-masonry and having claimed initiation in Mecca and various Egyptian loca-tions. His order was later "exposed" as a fraudulent money trap, one that had persuaded a number of wealthy and well-known European noblemen to pay Cagliostro great sums for initiation. Cagliostro is still remembered today by some as misunderstood mystic, by others as the quintessential fraternal con artist.[43] Moreover, all Americans knew of the saint/scoundrel character bearing an *Ex Oriente Lux* appeal in the person of the mobile Oriental-style-notion street huckster, who offered the "theme of self-transformation that would be taken up by patent-medicine salesmen and peddlers of self-improvement guides," as Jackson Lears explains.[44] Thus could a man like Rawson potentially be both believer and opportunist at the same time, telling members of each group what they wanted to hear about his Eastern persona but not convincing every individ-ual of the authenticity of his information.

Like Morris and so many others, Rawson had taken what work he could, laboring as writer, researcher, and illustrator for both esoteric and broader public audiences. Rawson exhibited some of his illustrations at the National Academy of Design in 1858 and managed to get them published in *Harper's Weekly*. Thereafter, for middling consumers of subscription encyclopedias and travel narratives, Rawson wrote or cowrote popular and quasi-scholarly books on religion, various European and Middle Eastern languages, and archaeology, though they appear to mostly be lost now.[45] He also made a living as a re-searcher and lecturer. In 1873, Rawson accepted a speaking engagement at the American Geographical Society of New York. That year, the scholarly study of West Asia, mostly by way of ancient languages, had only just become substan-tial enough to allow for the first international gathering of scholars then known as "Orientalists."[46] Most Western research taking place in the Ottoman Empire was still in the half-scholarly, half-mercenary field of biblical archaeology. At the Geographical Society, Rawson told archeologists and other scholars there that he had spent much of the previous year engaged by Rob Morris to revisit the Holy Land under the auspices of the American Holy Land Exploration Society in order to create illustrations for Morris's publications. He also ex-plained he had aided Edward Robinson's famous work some years earlier, con-necting his skill to the success of bankable and respected books and authors.

A generation after the height of Bayard Taylor's notoriety, Albert Rawson embroidered his own identity for these broad public audiences with a Middle

PLATE I.

Fig. 1 MASONIC FLAG

ABD-EL-KADER.

Fig. 2. ALBERT L. RAWSON, ORIENTAL TRAVELER AND ARTIST.

Abd El-Kader (left) with Masonic medals and Albert Rawson (right) pictured with Masonic banners for fraternal book buyers. Rob Morris, *Freemasonry in the Holy Land*, 1875, and Henry R. Coleman, *Light from the East*, 1881.

Eastern persona that branded him as "Oriental Artist" and knowledgeable traveler, often marked in publications by his Eastern-costumed portrait. Of all the illustrations he could have shown to the Geographical Society for a talk entitled "Palestine Exploration from a Practical Point of View," he chose portraits of Bedouin shaykhs to illustrate what he had discovered in the Ottoman Empire. Some of them were scoundrels, he said, but some reminded him of the biblical Abraham, and they had initiated him into Eastern fraternities of great nobility and wisdom. As brotherly quasi-Muslim mystic he sought to cross over his mysterious, potentially blasphemous initiation among Muslims in a "secret society" to Protestant scholars—who might or might not have actually had sympathy for Masonic interest in Eastern spiritualities, Rawson could not know for certain—by nonetheless capitalizing on romantic associations many had for the Bedouin as chivalrous free sons of the desert and descendents of Bible-age peoples.[47]

Rawson argued for a strengthening of biblical scholarship to these kinds of protoscholarly audiences while concurrently working for esoteric secret societies and freethinkers inimical to most Protestant belief, among them the Russian Theosophist Helena Blavatsky.[48] She had just finished her monumental work *Isis Unveiled*, a book in which she claimed to offer the one truth shared by Eastern religions and Western Freemasonry, a truth otherwise kept from the public by power-hungry clerics of established religion.[49] *Isis* was emblematic of a larger Western interest in Asian religions as a source of mystical regeneration, which went a step beyond Morris's missionizing to Eastern Masons by putting Eastern traditions at the forefront of world history, with Christians as mere humble students.[50] Rawson operated in that network of Eastern-focused entrepreneurialism and protoscholarly pursuits that sought to put capitalism and its technologies of print and travel to work in finding ancient truth in the world. This impulse gathered together people who otherwise might not agree about much: biblical archaeology scholars, Protestant clergy and their congregations, mainstream and mystical Freemasons like Rob Morris, adventure travelers, and spiritual seekers of worldly mystical truth including Theosophists like Blavatsky.

Glowingly reviewed in a number of American newspapers across the country, Anglo-Americans almost immediately sold out Helena Blavatsky's *Isis Unveiled* causing the publisher to rush a second printing the next month.[51] To publicize the book, Blavatsky made good use of the substantial media attention she was getting by promising that *Isis* explained extraordinary mysteries many readers wondered about.[52] *Isis Unveiled* did not in fact reveal Madame Blavatsky's greatest secrets since she had left certain radical truths veiled for fear they would be misunderstood.[53] Yet within the 600 pages pressed between the book's blood-red covers, curious American readers found an *Ex Oriente Lux* appeal and a claim that the mystical East was not so distant from Protestant America after all. Mysteriously she wrote, "What will, perhaps, still more astonish American readers, is the fact that, in the United States, a mystical fraternity now exists, which claims an intimate relationship with one of the oldest and most powerful of Eastern Brotherhoods. It is known as the Brotherhood of Luxor, and its faithful members have the custody of very important secrets of [spiritual] science."[54] Among the shadowy initiates of the Brotherhood of Luxor was none other than Albert Leighton Rawson. In *Isis Unveiled*, Blavatsky praised Rawson as the only Westerner to have been initiated by the Druze of Syria while developing a superlative knowledge of secret Middle Eastern sources of information "closed against the ordinary traveler."[55] Readers, whether impressed or cracked up by this passage, made sense of it because Taylor, Oscanyan, Morris, Coleman, and every other travel writer used the trope of the superficial tourist, sullied by his or her participation in the commercial travel trade and its attendant hackneyed cultural products, as a cliché of common misunderstanding to market their accounts with an *Ex Oriente Lux* appeal.

Rawson's actual relationship with Blavatsky is still shrouded in uncertainty, but apparently Rawson had been telling some people that during 1851 or 1852 they had been in Cairo together. There they disguised themselves as young Egyptian men and sought out Paulos Metamon, a Coptic Christian astrologer and magician, and had received instruction in the work of snake charming, magic, and other secret arts in his bazaar shop.[56] In Egypt, Rawson had also imparted various Freemasonic secrets to Blavatsky, after which the two had experimented with the mystical use of hashish.[57] As Rawson told it, he afterwards traveled extensively in the Middle East, Europe, and the Americas for occult purposes. He had in fact given a scaled-down Protestant-friendly version of this story to the Geographical Society of New York when he told them of his initiation by Bedouin shaykhs.

More importantly for our understanding of the satirical Eastern personae he would inspire, Rawson also played Muslim mystic with Blavatsky and other esotericists by baldly claiming to have also entered Mecca disguised as a Muslim one year before Richard Burton had done so to considerable acclaim.[58] For countless American readers who likewise imagined the desert as a magical place, the jewel in the crown of nontouristic masculine exploration was Arabia. Here was a region known for its harsh climate, with no biblical or Western touristic value, forbidden by law and tradition to non-Muslims and of interest only to those minds unconventional enough to be curious about the birthplace of Islam. Western travelers who made the trip to these Islamic holy sites— always men—wrote of possible imprisonment of intruders by local officials. Full cultural immersion in order to pass as a Muslim by way of dress, behavior, and speech were necessities in voyaging there in an age when there were no British or American populations of Muslims, and a European appearance came across in the region as condemningly Christian. Those who made the trip successfully by passing as a Muslim overseas, however, could make a living by passing as an expert on Arabia back home.[59] When Rawson began claiming to have visited Mecca and Medina after Richard Burton published his state of the art account *Personal Narrative of a Pilgrimage to Al-Madina and Meccah* (1855)—and it appears that Rawson was in jail for theft in New Jersey in the early 1850s when he was supposed to be in Arabia—many must have suspected that he borrowed this story from Burton's text.[60]

When Blavatsky's book drew attention to Rawson's mystical pursuits in the late 1870s, Rawson was in New York hard at work in a rich quasi-Muslim persona cultivating his own relationships with local Masons, both mainstream and the more esoterically minded. He told some of his more trustworthy acquaintances he had devised a mystical order in England "upon the instructions derived from an Arab in Paris, who was a member of the Occult College of Samarcand." This man, he believed, was linked somehow to Ismaili Islam and an elite group called "Guards or Keepers of the Kaaba [a holy Islamic relic in Mecca], who were a superior class of Arabs, the descendants of Ishmael, in the time of Mahommed [sic]," as the gossip went.[61] More occult in nature than Coleman's half-missionizing Oriental Order of Pilgrim Knights, Rawson's quasi-Islamic fraternity was typical of "fringe Masonry," a wing of mystical Freemasonic pursuit that dispensed with the Christian grounding to seek root knowledge in ancient Egypt, often emphasizing radical openness to feminism and left-leaning politics.[62] Now in New York, Rawson created another secret mystery school, the "Sheikhs of the Desert, Guardians of the Kaaba, Guardians of the Mystic Shrine." The well-known English Mason John Yarker later wrote that Rawson had made him a member of this fraternity, although it is not clear if or how much he paid for it. Yarker recounted that the initiation replicated symbolically the rituals of the Islamic pilgrimage ritual to Mecca and Medina, or hajj, embellished with Arabic phrases and ancient Egyptian icons.[63] As had more conventionally Christian Masons like Rob Morris, Rawson, Yarker, and other esotericists seemed to have "a compulsive need to have the Arabs endorse the antiquity of freemasonry," as Paul Rich and Guillermo De Los Reyes have discovered in reading the late nineteenth-century writings of these men, in order to add an ultranatural Eastern element to their own mystical masculinity.[64]

Rawson's work for *Harper's*, his appeal to biblical scholars, and his esoteric mystical pursuits beg the question of which performance was the real Albert Leighton Rawson, and how he could shift back and forth between a Protestant-friendly persona of Holy Land scholar and illustrator and the complex guise of brotherly Muslim mystic and confidante to chivalrous Arab warriors. Rawson presented himself to successions of different people, each in a slightly different way, more or less mystical, more or less Protestant, more or less Masonic, more or less Muslim, to serve his entrepreneurialism and the *Ex Oriente Lux* message he might need at any given moment.[65]

MAKING LIGHT OF THE MASONIC EAST:
THE SHRINERS EMERGE

In fact, many mystical travelers did not appear to take themselves too seriously in public and restricted the supremely serious business of actual esoteric work to small private groups of initiates.[66] This double life served to protect truly profound information from the ridicule of those who might profess to be Masons or seekers but who in fact might be so caged by conventional beliefs and "vulgar prejudices" that they would be too shaken by the truth to take it seriously. For instance, a colleague of Rawson's in the Theosophical Society, George Felt, had recently discovered how to reproduce what he believed were ancient Egyptian methods of creating visual manifestations of mystical intelligence. His attempts to cross this knowledge over to rank-and-file Freemasons had been disastrous, alternately drawing anger and ridicule. "Finding that only men pure in mind and body could control these appearances," he explained, "I decided that I would have to find others than my whisky-soaked and tobacco-sodden countrymen, living in an atmosphere of fraud and trickery, to act in that direction."[67]

Across town in New York, the Shriners represented just such a group of "whisky-soaked and tobacco sodden" jokers seeking to create a recreational fraternal order for thirty-second and thirty-third degree Freemasons, the upper crust within the Masonic public.[68] In the two decades after the Civil War, imaginative and ambitious men were founding ostensibly ancient fraternal orders with great regularity and increasing imagination.[69] In this crowded market, American stage actor and comedian Billy Florence and prominent New York Masonic scholar and physician Walter M. Fleming had sat down in 1872 to write a foundational history and initiation ritual for their new fraternity, the Ancient Arabic Order, Nobles of the Mystic Shrine.[70] Themed on Western readings of Islamic history and the pilgrimage to Mecca, it was to be an order adorned "with all the mysticisms of the Orient" and "a certain degree of mystery," one of their contemporaries remembered of the strangeness of the fraternity's original subculture.[71] Initially the order flagged, some of the first twelve temples becoming inactive after one meeting as the economy slumped through the decade.[72] In spite of their own creative talents, Florence and Fleming needed to revise their fraternal ritual since those that entertained, kept members paying their dues, and kept them coming back were crucial to the financial viability of an order but not easily written.[73]

From a bookshelf at New York Masonic library, Florence and Fleming may have found a copy Rob Morris's *Freemasonry in the Holy Land*, which contained the Eastern-costumed portrait of Albert Leighton Rawson as "Oriental Traveler and Artist." Rawson was just the man to provide the reputation and quality detail Florence and Fleming needed. In 1876 or 1877 Rawson actually agreed to help Florence and Fleming redesign their fraternal order, helping to create a colossally successful fraternity whose members would soon be infamous for their roast of the *Ex Oriente Lux* mode of American engagement with the Arab Middle East and just about everything Rawson stood for. There was plenty of money in fraternalism in those years, and Rawson seems to have sized up the financial opportunities in providing what Florence and Fleming needed. In fact, Rawson would continue to ask for work from the Shriners as late as 1888, by which time he came across to Mystic Shrine leadership as an opportunist "simply working a little deal of graft."[74]

Such suspicious attitudes toward Rawson were a product of the fact that as an apparently sincere student of Eastern mysticism his service to the Shriners as designer and promotional agent seemed an unlikely collaboration. It was exactly this kind of commercialization by entrepreneurial wise men of the East the Shriners critiqued. Middle-class businessmen and professionals would stock the Mystic Shrine order, and their numbers reveal how many people thought Anglo-American interest in the Muslim world was a marketing fraud that took advantage of credulous if sincere people. In New York City, these affluent men had risen up the economic ladder above the armies of clerks in American cities to become their bosses, proprietary business owners, city officials, and professionals. As a highly performative and creative order, many Shiners also emerged from the theater community. Together they were an upwardly mobile group but were building their fortunes and consequently ineligible for membership in truly elite groups like New York's Union Club. The Mystic Shrine particularly attracted those between thirty and forty-five years of age with an artistic proclivity.[75] Such men had been congregating in mumming and ball societies since at least the 1850s, Joseph Roach explains, as "an imagined kinship network founded upon mutual appreciation for one another's industry, invention, and powers of organization," with the shared experience of creative performance serving as a bond of brotherhood.[76]

Accordingly, many of the early members of the Mystic Shrine were already initiates of the notorious Sons of Malta, one of the many "Abbeys of Misrule"–type fraternities in the nation rooted in the same traditions as the New Orleans

Mardi Gras club, the Mistick Krewe of Comus, or the Veiled Prophet society of St. Louis.[77] Even before Rob Morris sent his mysterious communications to potential supporters of his Conservators' Movement, the Sons of Malta lampooned male secrecy by sending anonymous invitations to uncomprehending new recruits asking them discretely to visit an address where they would be inducted into a secret and dangerous fraternity or punished if found unacceptable. Once at the hall and blindfolded, initiates were put through various paddlings, dunkings and other well-meaning humiliations before the joke was revealed and members welcomed them into the society. Not everyone was so amused by such initiations. In 1860 a crabby, multiedition "Exposure" of the Sons in *Frank Leslie's Weekly* included "Confessions of a Chicago Victim" and complained, "The barefaced impudence of these people is so boundless, that it passes belief."[78]

Initiations and dinners were only the private component of nightly entertainment for the Sons of Malta, whose public appearances came as surreal late-night street masquerades, often with advance newspaper publicity indicating that people enjoyed watching their performances. One 1859 appearance in New York City included five hundred members "in grotesque toggery . . . Some wore crowns, some caps of red velvet; some carried swords and cimitars and one bore a mighty battle axe." Audiences of Sons of Malta street theater might also see them perform "mystic rites around the statue of the Father of [t]his country [George Washington]—whom they are said to claim as a member of their order" to roast the patriotic manhood and public sentiment of onlookers. The group employed props that spoke of centuries-old mock trials of the misrule clubs. The 1859 Sons of Malta paraders had also carried a large book, designated to the audience as "The Mystic Volume" of the order's secret wisdom. Thereafter, members "proceeded to the Malta Saloon, where they dined together. They did not go home till morning," one paper related.[79] All these street shows were reminiscent of the public satire of Revolutionary funerals for the Stamp Act or the "fantastic costumes," public drinking, and satirical rowdiness of Mardi Gras, Christmas mummery, and African American Election Days.[80]

Billy Florence and Walter Fleming would build on these performance traditions by commissioning Rawson to help them create a new ritual for their Ancient Arabic Order, Nobles of the Mystic Shrine. With Rob Morris's lectures describing Middle Eastern Masons still on the lodge circuit and Madame Blavatsky, Rawson, and others using fringe Masonic societies imitating the *hajj* to present themselves as tools of "hidden masters who sent unquestioned orders from unknown Oriental locations," American culture was rife with inspirational material with which to satirize sincerity and credulity around the persona of wise man of the East.[81]

After considerable revision, the Mystic Shrine foundational legend now related that Billy Florence had been a member of the original cast at the first performance of Verdi's *Aida* in Cairo, commissioned by Egyptian Khedive Ismail for the opening of the Suez Canal in 1869. While on tour in Europe the next year, he had been invited to a secret gentlemen's meeting held in Marseilles where he found "the British Consul at that port, another the Austrian Vice Consul, and there were dukes and counts, bankers and merchants, scholars and artists, musicians and other professionals. . . . The Illustrious Grand Potentate of the evening was the celebrated Yusef Churi Bey, [a Persian traveler] and the Temple was called Bokhara Shrine." Thereafter, Florence claimed to have experienced rituals he could not accurately recount, "[They] must have been gotten up by some one well skilled in stage scenery, for there were very well contrived dramatic effects, representing the sandy sea shore, the rough, rocky hillside, the gloomy cavern, the solemn tomb, and a transformation scene which was at first a cemetery, full of tombs and monuments inscribed with the names of the departed, . . . when in an instant, the lights having been lowered, the scene changed to a sumptuous banqueting hall, with small tables for groups of 3, 5, 7, and 9."

Florence embellished this story with an account of a later initiation into the Bektashi Sufi order in Algiers at "the Shrine of the Mogribins" among a similarly well-to-do group of local men and diplomatic personnel. Florence also claimed to have received letters from Mohammed Baki, the shaykh of this brotherhood in Algiers, a group that transcended common opinions about nationality, religion, and race. It was "indeed cosmopolitan," he said, "composed as they are of Arab, Bedawin, Moor, Mogribi, Turk, French, Italian, German, English, Austrian, Persian, Russian, Hindu, and American," that familiar spectrum of Muslim lands and European countries Anglo-American fraternalists referenced in their rituals. Dipping into contemporary politics over Asian immigration to the United States a scant three years before the Chinese Exclusion Act passed into law, Florence added to his list of cosmopolitan fraternalists, "but not as yet any Chinese."[82]

Back in the United States, the lore continued, Billy Florence, Walter Fleming, and eleven other friends (not including Rawson) made a total of thirteen and claimed to have simply proposed to found an American branch of this mysterious Eastern order, thus creating the Ancient Arabic Order, Nobles of the Mystic Shrine. This fact was in itself a joke since in those days many Americans were laughing about popular superstition over the number thirteen.[83] As hired "Representative for Eastern Countries," Albert Rawson thereafter sent to New York's "Mecca Temple" of the Mystic Shrine translations of what he asserted were Arabic-language letters from Mystic Shrine members in the Middle East. Rawson's correspondence described the Shrine rituals completed there, which employed "a carefully studied reproduction of the costumes worn by the Brothers under the early Kalifs [the first four leaders of the Muslim community after the Prophet Muhammad]." There he claimed to have dined on exotic banquet food, including "dishes of the age of Antony and Cleopatra" such as "the precious ortolan from Cyprus, a delicacy that in former times was reserved for the tables of princes," he wrote in Eastern voice, indulging in his own Oriental tale.

As he had told the Geographical Society and Madame Blavatsky of his initiation by the Druze or Bedouin Shaykhs, Rawson supplied the Shriners with news of new initiates: "Noble Brother Hassan Ibn Masteeka, professor of Chemistry and Minerology, and lecturer on Astronomy in the College of the Hassaneeyeh" and on the "pilgrims" the supposed "Alee Pasha Temple" of the Mystic Shrine in Cairo would be sending on the pilgrimage to Mecca that year.[84] The Shriners reprinted these letters in their *Annual Proceedings* after Walter Fleming read them out at meetings, creating a folklore that was carefully researched if also marked by heavy artistic license. Those Masons critical of Rob Morris's and Henry Coleman's pursuit of West Asian Masons must have found this quite funny.

The new Mystic Shrine initiation that followed was a masterpiece of satire, a campy Oriental performance art that had everything to do with why the order prospered. Inspired by earlier Masonic rites, a liberal adaptation of the initiation rituals of the Sons of Malta, and a humorous retelling of the *hajj*, these rituals were convincing because they were primarily performed, not textual, art.[85] Like Oriental tales more broadly, they communicated well-meaning advice in an entertaining guise. Yet for members of the Masonic public, a group of creative and affluent consumers, the order also provided an excuse for elaborate Orientana in stage sets, costumes, and role-playing that the more solemn and temperate fraternities would not warrant until the turn of the century.[86] That Orientana was the one thing the Mystic Shrine had that no other order would ever replicate. The fraternity provided the most well-funded public and private opportunities for playing Eastern throughout the nation's history in a superlative combination of the most extravagant ultranatural and ultra-artificial creative elements nineteenth-century Americans knew. As satirical wise men of the East, Shriners would critique the commercialization of things Eastern while engaging in it heartily themselves, a perceived authentic compromise in which affluent men could individuate themselves, not as wise men but as wiseacres of the East.

On nights when new men were invited to be initiated, candidates were put through a "weird Arabic ceremony" consisting of a series of mystifying and intimidating rituals, interrogations, and staged attacks led by Shriners with pompous titles such as "Grand Potentate," "Illustrious Chief Rabban," or "Illustrious Most High Prophet and Priest" wearing colorful robes. Photographs of these costumes appear in various Shriner-authored temple histories and exist in the archives of Library of Congress. They show men in half-Masonic and half-biblical epic stage costumes that Shriners reserved only for initiation pageants and used until at least the 1960s.[87] These men immersed the novice in elaborate faux-archaic Shriner voice, which was not the inaccurate, sparse "Indian talk" that created sacred or privileged space for members of Indian-themed fraternal societies. Rather it was that prolix Eastern voice that was the verbal manifestation of the excessive abundance and consumption Anglo-Americans associated with the Oriental tale.[88] Such pretensions to affluence, ease, and nobility defined the serious modes of the Shriner persona, and even rank-and-file members were known as "Nobles."

The New York Mystic Shrine initiation room was to resemble that of a Masonic lodge with some important innovations. At its center the ritual required a pedestal decorated with a large scimitar and adjacent to it an "Altar of Obligation," draped in black fabric, upon which was to be placed both a bible and a Qur'an, valued at $150, Shriners claimed.[89] This altar, further mimicking the Ka'aba shrine in Mecca (which is similarly draped in black fabric), also had placed on it a "Black Stone or Holy Stone of black marble, one foot square or more" in emulation of the black meteorite encased in the Ka'aba, which pilgrims venture to touch or kiss in their circumambulations of the structure. To the right was to be placed an "Altar of Incense with burning incense of myrrh, etc.," for Oriental-tale ambiance.[90]

On initiation nights, intruders were first rooted out of the temple, each proper member having to show his pass and whisper the secret word "Mecca." Thereafter followed a "Grand Hailing Salaam" (Salaam meaning "Peace" in Arabic) by the First Ceremonial Master "by facing the Orient, leaning forward as if making a low bow, arms raised and extended palms out, head thrown forward in a reverential and beseeching manner," in effect burlesquing one movement within the Muslim prayer ritual.[91] Many popular and scholarly sources provided Americans with detailed descriptions of the *salat* and its perceived "dignity," including magazine travel narratives, quintessential bestsellers like Thomson's protoarchaeological *The Land and the Book*, Oriental tales, and the *Arabian Nights*.[92] In their attention to the Muslim prayer ritual, Morris and Rawson had been typical of several generations in the United States, middle-class societies broadly permeated with and fascinated by social ritual.[93] Studying *salat* while he traveled in the Ottoman Empire, Rob Morris had proposed Masons incorporate it into Masonic ritual, but could not have predicted this. He had written, "First, the worshipper opens his hands and raises them till the thumb of each is directly under the corresponding ear, the fingers being erect." Suggesting to us the kinds of comparisons between Islamic practice, Freemasonry, and American burlesque Shriners may have been making, Morris admitted of the last gesture, "[This] is the only comical part of the proceeding. It does indeed remind me of an asinine movement in that most absurd and ludicrous of travesties, *The Sons of Malta*"(italics in original).[94]

Nobles then partially undressed and handcuffed novices, forcing them to knock on the door of the main chamber. The Oriental Guide answered, "Who dares intrude upon the ceremonies of our Mystic Shrine?" The response from the First Ceremonial Master outside: "[These] poor Sons of the Desert, who are weary of the hot sands and the burning sun of the plains and humbly crave shelter under the protecting dome of the Temple."[95] The archetype of the traveling initiate crossing the desert as a metaphorical journey for knowledge was common in upper-degree Scottish rite Masonic and Odd Fellow rituals as well as occult mystery school lore.[96] Many of these men had already undergone many a mock trial in other fraternities in which they, whether they knew it or not, played the role of outsider in the drama of the ritual. As a "traveler in the wilderness," "pilgrim in search of light," or "poor sons of the desert, who are weary of the hot sands and the burning sun of the plains," men achieved admission and protection by the end of the ceremony by passing a test.[97] The Shrine's desert metaphor also employed a romantic reference to the Arab warrior archetype, the assertive alter-ego of the brotherly Muslim mystic. Challenged by members dressed "like Arabic soldiers with large broad Cymitars," the Nobles were to create a disorienting and intimidating atmosphere that included unexpected loud noises emanating from unknown places and other tricks typical of the Sons of Malta and the more sincere blindfolded rituals of the Masons.

Interrogated as to their sincerity and "desire to promote justice and suppress wrong" as well as "due regard for female virtue," among other things, the candidates submitted to a lecture by the High Priest. Afterward, the officials of the Temple recited what appeared to be English translations of portions of the Qur'an, each verse followed by the striking of a gong and some rough music made with "Horse Fiddle and any other instrument on which a hideous noise can be produced." It is not clear whether these portions were read from an English Qur'an or recited from memory or if the initiates were initially aware that they were hearing Islamic scripture.[98] Novices further recited an "Obligation," which stated, in part, "I do hereby, upon this Bible, and on the mysterious legend of the Koran, and its dedication to the Mohammedan faith, promise and swear and vow on the faith and honor of an upright man, . . . that I will never reveal any secret part or portion whatsoever of the ceremonies I have received." Here were Protestant Anglo-Americans playing Muslim by swearing on Islamic texts to trust in "Allah" as a strange trial for the novice. The Potentate next directed initiates to perform a ritual cleansing, which referred to Muslim ritual ablutions as well as the Masonic process of spiritual rebirth that any initiate would have understood well.

Thereafter, the High Priest was to command the "Arabs," as Nobles often called one another, to unbind the candidates' hands so that they could be "one by one taken into another apartment, often stretched out on a plank to rest. While in this position a small dog or one who can imitate a dog, is caused to give a sharp yelp, just after a few drops of warm water has been squirted on the candidate's face, with the remark, 'Take that dog out, he has just pissed in the face of Mr. ——,' when a general laugh takes place and the candidate is shown the trick." Further humiliations followed wherein the candidates were to swing from a rope to unexpectedly land with a crash and to endure the "Grand Salaam," namely, a paddling on the behind emphasized by carefully-timed firecrackers.

Shriners referred to the practical jokes of initiation as "highjinks," which they enacted in "a spirit of frolic."[99] This was a man's version of what E. Anthony Rotundo has termed the "boy culture" of the mid-nineteenth century, a culture that permeated recreational fraternalism. Nineteenth-century boys formed constant clubs and alliances, sometimes organized around "mischief and secrecy," theft, or vandalism. This culture was not always kind, and

"HOLD ON TO THE ROPE"

Mystic Shrine initiation ritual imagined as Oriental tale and Sons of Malta–style satire on the seriousness of the Masonic East. George L. Root, *The Ancient Arabic Order of the Nobles of the Mystic Shrine*, 1903.

these youthful groups employed a considerable amount of "casual hostility and sociable sadism" since mutual experiences of pain helped boys to bond, ritual paddling being the classic example.[100] Adults commonly complained these boys were "wild" or "feral," describing them as "primitive savages" full of "animal spirits," like the bad boy pranksters who also inhabited popular books of the day. One adult response was an antimodernist romanticization of childhood that held that to be young at heart, boyish, and carefree was a desirable trait for adults since it represented pristine natural elements in the human spirit and an individual's true identity.[101] There is little question that the Shrine was an inheritor of this boy culture and focused around long-standing practices of secrecy, wild behavior, and ritualized but well-meaning violence cast in a manly form that corresponded with the Orientana of excessive consumption and affluence and the guise of the brotherly Muslim mystic, namely, the chivalrous Arab warrior as Arab trickster.

Finally, Shriners in trickster form told the initiate he would face a further test: "This is the place where our brethren stop to sprinkle the Devil's Pass with urine. You will contribute a few drops of urine to commemorate the time and place where all who pass here renounce the wiles and evils of the world to worship at the Shrine of Islam. Only a few drops will do. Candidate begins to obey instruction when the blinder is jerked from his eyes and he beholds before him a group disguised as women, with bonneted faces and capes showing, the rest of their bodies hid by a screen. He is allowed to escape from the room amid a roar of laughter from the on-lookers."[102] Loosely modeled on the point in the pilgrimage to Mecca at which Muslims throw stones at a notorious wall in symbolic stoning of Satan, this trick demonstrated both interest in non-Christian religions and a disregard for the sanctity of their rituals, an ingenious mixing of American fraternal practical joking and foreign content that may have gone over the heads of many participants.

A large banquet thereafter included further hoaxes and staged altercations between more senior Shriners that were designed to let newcomers in on the jokes that were the bedrock of any fraternity's common culture.[103] All of these performances further resonated with the well-meaning frauds of indoor theater, with which Billy Florence and any audience member would be well versed. For instance, Florence was a comedic expert at ethnic impersonation—German, Irish, Yankee, and more. In 1851 he had worked a typical show in which he played a fireman, or "fire laddie . . . [in] red shirt and white 'plug' hat," whose performance required him to sit amongst the audience and interrupt the show with a verbal assault on the actors. "Great commotion ensued in the theatre, and it was a long time before the audience saw the joke," one of his contemporaries remembered of the way such a staged altercation could cause mirth when audience members realized they had been fooled.[104] Similarly, the rituals of fraternal orders were a major form of evening entertainment, a kind of collective performance in which the initiate might be unaware which parts were staged, which real.[105]

By the early 1880s, Mecca Temple Shriners were planting announcements and accounts of their initiations with local newspapers, perhaps by way of a promotional agent. "The order is in a flourishing condition," one such piece said of the twenty-one temples in thirteen states. Of their activities in 1883 the *New York Times* read, "The Imperial Potentate announced the death of the Illustrious Noble El-Hadji Abd el Kader, Grand Sheik of Alee Temple, at Mecca, Arabia, which occurred at Damascus on May 26. He was the acknowledged head of the order in the Eastern Hemisphere."[106] There were few secrets here,

the hybrid identities of various participants made plain: "Walter M. Fleming, M.D., Most Illustrious Grand Potentate," or "Prof. A. L. Rawson, LL.D.,
Representative of Temples in the East."[107] Unlike the members of contemporary
parade and ball societies such as the Mistick Krewe of Comus of New Orleans's
Mardi Gras or St. Louis's Veiled Prophet Order, whose members were *never*
named by the press, these Shriners allowed themselves to be named in order to
raise the prestige of the group and show their openness to new initiates and
their fees.[108]

The Shriners crossed over their ironic treatment of the *Ex Oriente Lux* appeal
to the public in recorded print performances of their "Oriental ceremonies,"
bathed as they were in the syntax of the Sons of Malta with their roasts of
powerful authorities and half-serious threats of retribution against those who
offended members' sensibilities. For instance, just after the death of Abd el-
Kader, New York's Mecca Temple held a memorial to the popular figure, lampooning the commercialized admiration of desert warriors by Masons and the
middle-classes in general. Temple leaders issued a roasting "Imperial Death
Decree" performed in Eastern voice: "Affliction! Distress! Sorrow! Illustrious
Noble El-Hadji Abd-El-Kader, Grand Sheik of Alee Temple, Mecca, Arabia,
under the domain of the Crescent, is dead . . . [He] is officially announced
departed to the Unseen Temple."[109] A later memorial to "Ali-Mahmoud Pasha
El Falaki, Grand Shareef of Al Muhazzi of the Cairo Temple of the Ancient
Arabic Order of Nobles of the Mystic Shrine" offered humorously threatening
press notices wherein members, "all men of respectability and substance,"
promised "to execute punishment where justice was tardy."[110] Ultimately, the
secret of the Mystic Shrine was that the pomp, mystery, seriousness, and danger
of the order was a sham that mocked the reverence and credulity of the initiate
and the public towards esteemed men of all kinds.

Members would impart these early Mystic Shrine jokes and performances,
with their claims to Eastern origins and endorsements from Eastern Masons, to
initiates with a wink for decades thereafter. Along the way Shriners developed
an expensive and elaborate subculture they communicated across the country
by way of lavishly illustrated invitations and convention programs, Shriner
newsletters and magazines, newspaper publicity, and repeated performances of
the initiation ritual. Shriners used their subculture to persuade members to
finance the order by way of initiation and banquet fees, membership dues,
regalia purchases, and the rounding up of more and more initiates while aim-
ing their open-ended satire at multiple targets. Florence and Fleming's bur-

lesque of the wise man of the East would certainly remain current because it provided a chance to make fun of Freemasonry's ongoing references to the "East" and a Masonic public served by tailored cultural products like Lester's "Look to the East" or Coleman's Light from the East.[111] To be sure, plenty of men yet uninvited or too serious to join the order rightly complained that Shriners mocked Masonic tradition, even if they did so as campy roast rather than as mean-spirited attack.[112]

For others, Shriners poked fun at sincere or pretending Eastern-styled mystics like Albert Leighton Rawson or the conventionalized provocativeness of middling Protestant interest in bestselling books on Theosophy and other supposedly forbidden things. Indeed, the Mystic Shrine had broader social relevance for members and street theater audiences as a critique of Gilded Age Anglo-American pretensions and craving for novelty. William Stowe explains, "Since the vocabulary, the intellectual categories, and the rhetoric of religion pervaded thinking and writing in the nineteenth-century United States, it is not surprising that European travel [for instance] was routinely conceived in those years as a pilgrimage to sacred shrines in quest of the ineffable distinction of the initiate."[113] Thus, for example, could Americans find in the bookseller's inventory a volume of European travel called My Pilgrimage to Eastern Shrines or read Washington Irving comparing Western travelers' visits to the ruins of the Alhambra in Spain to the Muslim hajj.[114] It made sense to Shriners to play Oriental traveler to a counterfeit Mecca because they were among the age's "rollicking bad boys defying a civilization seen as feminine" even as they participated in it.[115] Manly satire was another technique of novel truth telling about old topics that had become particularly current in the years after 1880 when the Mystic Shrine began to grow exponentially.[116]

By 1892 there would be over sixty temples in the United States and Canada with a combined membership of 23,000.[117] The Mystic Shrine continued to be especially privileged in Anglo-American life because so many Americans conflated the cultures from North Africa to Persia together under the term "Oriental." In this way, people could combine Freemasonry's mystical and biblical elements with personae of natural manhood represented by the Bedouin and literary modes of playing Oriental to produce incredibly expensive and theatrical ritual and parade performances that spoke of members' critique of but success in the world of commerce. Especially as the members of competing fraternities, including Freemasonry, increased the theatricality and expense of their rituals in the latter two decades of the century, the Ancient Arabic Order,

Nobles of the Mystic Shrine would become the king of all the fraternities, to which many more men aspired than actually were invited to join. High-ranking Masons gathered there seeking a less serious venue in which to drink, smoke, and generally carry on, and Shriners soon referred to the order as the "playground of Masonry."[118]

Like Rob Morris, Bayard Taylor, Christopher Oscanyan, Albert Rawson, and other men who played wise man of the East to market their expertise, Shriners of the 1870s, 1880s, and 1890s like Billy Florence, Walter Fleming, and the rest were equally effected by the notorious volatility of the American economy and financial panics of the period. Yet they played Oriental, not to improvise a brand and career but to cement cultural relations with likeminded men as cynical about commercial use of the East as they were eager to show their wealth. Thus did they spend on membership in the Mystic Shrine, even if that membership papered over a failing business or mounting personal debt. Like so many Americans, the Shriners sought out pricey Eastern personae as a sign of success in the market yet still claimed them to be culturally authentic because they were critical of the market.

chapter 4

Arab Athleticism and the Exoticization
of the American Dream, 1870–1920

W hen and why did significant numbers of people from North Africa or
West Asia intervene in the American practice of playing Eastern? In
the mid-nineteenth century Christopher Oscanyan had done so as
an Armenian convert to Protestantism and native of Istanbul. He spent many
years talking to Anglo-Americans as best he could while making a living for
himself. Yet Oscanyan was only one voice, and his limited influence in comparison to native-born professional spokesmen like Bayard Taylor shows that it
was very difficult for anyone from overseas to come to America and participate
in public debates about the Eastern world. Indeed, why should they necessarily
want to? Most people there were probably more concerned with their own lives
than with what someone in Cincinnati or Savannah or San Francisco thought
about, say, Bedouin politics or the state of the Ottoman Empire's finances.

In fact, when a significant number of Easterners came to America they came
simply to make better lives for themselves. Some did choose to work in the
United States as public representatives of North Africa or the Middle East, but
most did not. We must resist the temptation to place on the shoulders of these
historical actors the responsibility of representing their home countries "accurately" (however we might define that), a daunting task in America with its
highly capitalized, growing entertainment and information networks in which
even native-born entrepreneurs, audiences, and artists struggled to communicate in meaningful and profitable ways. This is not to say that foreign-born
performers were not critical of the conventions of American performance and
entertainment but to acknowledge that they decided for themselves to which
parts they were resistant and when, how, and if they would attempt to bring
about change.

In fact, in the beginning, it was Arab men who in significant numbers chose
to make their migration to the United States financially viable by speaking
publicly for the Middle East. A prominent number did so by working in the tent

show trade of wild west shows and circuses, in the process displacing performers of European and African descent who had been portraying North Africa and West Asia for American audiences most of the century. Thus could they live their own version of the American success story by capitalizing on their unique connection to the Eastern world, a connection they and later immigrants, male and female, would use to move into vaudeville as well. Only in the mid-twentieth century would the American information and entertainment industries come to serve the largest, most affluent body of consumers on earth and to broadcast their cultural products out into the world. Only then would the implications of American cultural production depicting the Eastern world as a facilitating context for global military, economic, and political interests become clear and highly problematic.

In the meantime, after 1870, Arab entertainers began contributing their own expertise and energy to the arts of playing Eastern. They helped make the desert horseman and then the Arab athlete stock characters in the public options for consumer individuation. American interest in desert travel and West Asian–themed fraternal orders all the while were casting Middle Eastern lands as manly spaces of trial, rejuvenation, or spiritual realization.[1] Yet in venues like tent shows and vaudeville, which attracted family audiences from all classes, the Arab as wise man of the East was not prominent. Many of the ticket buyers at those shows had limited access to middling cultural products like *Harper's Monthly Magazine*, published books of travel, or Masonic literature that offered consumers the brotherly Muslim mystic persona. Instead, the diverse audiences at a circus or an urban playhouse might hold limited knowledge of the Arab world before seeing foreign-born entertainers there. These more democratic venues presented the Arab man in the person of the "Bedouin Horseman," a more secular, masculine free spirit and heroic villain. As wild-west shows receded after the turn of the century, many of the men who had played Arab horseman turned to earning a living in vaudevillian acrobatic acts, sometimes employing women as well. There they performed personae of Arab-American industriousness that asserted they were self-made men and women glad to live in the United States.

To understand how foreign-born people added personae of Eastern athleticism to the American repertoire after 1900, this chapter documents first the North African and Syrian men who fared best in getting over as obviously male, powerful, and exotic in American show business. The fact that these male artists later moved into mixed shows of Eastern athleticism on vaudeville is crucial to a nuanced understanding of the fact that playing Oriental was so open-ended and long-lived because it allowed foreign-born performers to reject the nativism of the late nineteenth and early twentieth centuries, especially when performing for diverse audiences of poor and working-class people, urban and rural, including the many immigrants who were flooding into the nation.

The emergence of more democratic access to the arts of playing Eastern in the last decades of the century also gives us an opportunity to really get to the bottom of what made Easterners and their cultures interesting to such diverse audiences in the United States. Academics routinely chalk up audience interest to a fascination with the "exotic." Yet we need to look a bit further and ask what, precisely, "exotic" meant to people in the bleachers. A number of scholars of performance have looked at the historical record to think about this. They argue that the acts and representations that come across to the viewer *as exotic* do so because they present something or someone that is familiar and strange at once, "both known and unknown simultaneously," Kathleen Ashley tells us. "The exotic operates as a symbol that combines cultural differences, even when they are seen as opposites [and] mediates difference."[2] People do not necessarily use the exotic to dominate the foreign but to make it comprehensible to new people who need to see their own cultural logic at work in that foreign content.

In the United States, the exotic functioned in two ways. First, it was a way for foreign-born professional entertainers, impresarios, and their ad men to cross foreign talent over as comprehensibly novel to domestic audiences, for instance, when Buffalo Bill Cody's Wild West presented Arab horsemen in cowboy terms as "Bedouin Rough Riders." By the 1880s, such performances of Eastern exotic were akin to an *Ex Oriente Lux* appeal that said "look here is something/someone interesting from far away who can be useful to you." Comprehensibly novel performances of the exotic were more appropriate for democratic modes of entertainment like circuses and wild west shows than a *Lux* appeal because they did not require a middle- or upper-class audience that was invested in the trope of "common misunderstanding," and therefore people could use them to market foreign acts and ideas to any audience in the nation regardless of income level, region, "race," or ethnicity.

Second, native-born audiences viewed performances of the exotic by foreign-born performers and modified them to their own needs of identity display. In the hands of these consumers, the exotic became a mask of incomprehensibility and a way to cross the familiar (themselves) over as slightly incomprehensible, mysterious, or even outright strange and thus more compelling than in their workaday personae. This kind of self-mystification was crucial to the evolution of Shriner street theater and alternative spirituality in the country, case studies I document in later chapters. Both modes of Eastern exotic performance speak loudly of Americans' interest in cultural difference in the years when mass consumerism emerged, and the money that could be made by catering to that interest by showing audiences that they could use their own creativity to express themselves in a market economy by globalized self-fashioning. That people so often wanted exotic performances that clearly emanated from the Eastern world reminds us that for less privileged Americans too, the consumer's Oriental tale and ultranatural manhood were ways to enact the promise of consumer capitalism.

BEDOUIN HORSEMEN IN AMERICA
AND THE BIRTH OF THE ARAB TRICKSTER

Beginning in the 1870s, men and boys from various parts of Morocco, Algeria, and the Ottoman province of Syria broke into the American circus and wild west show business, initially performing in the guise of Bedouin horseman. These artists came as part of a small but significant number of emigrants and migrant workers from those regions whose numbers would grow dramatically by the 1890s. Making travel arrangements and contracts with American circus recruiters or shipping brokers in Beirut, Izmir, or Tripoli, they traveled by sea to Marseilles or Naples and then to New York or "Nayirk" in "Merka," as it was pronounced in Arabic at the time. Most came for reasons familiar to many mobile people inside and outside the country: better economic opportunity, and freedom from military conscription, family, ethnic, or political tension.[3]

These immigrant entertainers arrived in years when impresarios like Phineas T. Barnum had created highly capitalized circuses that promised audiences parades and spectacles of "oriental and classical exotica."[4] Show producers, for instance, added "ethnological congress" features to their schedules in which ticket-buyers saw performers portray "Oriental potentates," Bedouin bandits, "Nubian" or "Soudanese" horsemen, and other Eastern characters from various time periods with imported animals in menagerie-style productions marketed with educational and fantasy qualities. Such acts became standards of the tent show business because they gave American consumers living in a swiftly globalizing nation contact with foreign peoples framed with patter and advertising that suggested multiple ways of interpreting the performers. Ticket buyers could choose either to cheer the extraordinary Easterners they saw or boo them—as audiences often did—for their cultural difference and apparent rejection of American ways.[5]

It is difficult to say how many foreign-born performers appeared in the Oriental spectacle and ethnological congress shows, and at first the circus and wild west "Bedouins" were played by costumed native-born American actors of European or African descent. Always seeking an advantage over the competition in novelty and "authenticity" of acts, in the late 1870s impresarios began using recruiters to bring talent from abroad, especially Sudanese, Moroccans, Algerians, and Syrian or Lebanese Ottoman subjects, although Turks, Indians, and Egyptians would follow in smaller numbers as well. For logistical reasons, many shows for a time employed a mixed native-born and foreign-born cast in their Eastern-styled bits, phasing in as many foreign performers as they could.

From the beginning, these performers did a large number of acts that capitalized on the circuses' roots in early hippodrome horse shows. They participated in "Moorish Caravan"–type acts featuring men on horses or camels and often advertised as "a realistic picture of the wanderings of the desert tribes" that offered performed Oriental tales and "free sons of the desert" tropes to broad audiences of consumers who might never have read an edition of the *Arabian Nights*. So did Hemmings & Cooper's Grand Consolidated Menagerie and Circus in the 1880s engage a group of Easterners, whose real identities are now lost to us, as "Hash Hamo's Troupe of Bedouin Arabs, or Children of the Desert. Ten In Number, in their unique and extraordinary Ground and Lofty Evolutions, peculiar and special with these people, and illustrating the Sports of the Children of the Sahara." The group did a caravan segment featuring acrobatic acts, feats of strength, one knife-throwing bit, and (inspired perhaps by North African or Indian market cultures) a snake-charming act, all of which contradicted the paternalism of their billing as "children" of the desert.[6]

Bedouin or Arab horsemen made particular sense to show producers because of popular clichés around the famed Arabian horse and the often-nomadic lives of desert Arabs in the Ottoman Empire and French North Africa. Living in goatskin tents in regions Ottoman and French officials struggled to control, the governing classes and town-dwelling people often perceived desert dwellers as untrustworthy. Especially in areas of American touristic activity in Egypt and the southern Levant, the Bedouin were indeed known to break deals for protection services they made with government officials, exploiting Ottoman weakness to occasionally rob villages and caravans when it served their interests as mobile political entities. Various Ottoman administrations engaged in negotiations, imprisonment of prominent Bedouin men, and periodic crackdowns that complicated but only gradually challenged Bedouin control of desert areas in the Empire.[7] To be clear, though, there had been no long-term systematic attempt in the Ottoman Empire to exterminate the Bedouin as there had been with respect to Native Americans in the American west. Nonetheless, the majority of American tourists in the Middle East initially feared the Bedouin, later explaining, however, that in person they seemed far more plain and unthreatening than imagined. Such conventionalized discovery stories of the "lessons I learned abroad" type reoccurred repeatedly—Bayard Taylor had used it himself in the 1850s—because the idea of Bedouin bandits added dramatic episodes to otherwise bland accounts of desert voyages where the real threats came in the form of fleas, heatstroke, or boredom.

In time, tent show audiences made their enthusiasm for foreign talent in acts of male sport and athleticism clear through ticket sales, and "Arabs," to use the industry term for such performers, became a standard component of the circus and wild west genres. Initially, when native-born performers of European descent began experimenting with these kinds of roles, promotional material for the shows named performers simply as generic "Arabs." By the 1880s, circus advance men and press agents might still show "An Arab" unnamed on the massive color lithograph posters with which they coated fences and buildings. Yet in the corresponding show program and press notices, agents often prominently featured their Arab performers by name and provided the public with brief biographies detailing their journeys to the United States. If injury, sickness, or sudden resignations occurred when the program promised Bedouins or Arabs, the show went on nonetheless. For instance, during the 1886 tour of a Barnum company circus, Abdellah Ben Said, the manager and head performer of the show's Arab troupe, suffered an apparently accidental gunshot wound at the hands of Orrin Hollis, a fellow performer and friend, while a group of men from the show were mucking about target shooting with a small rifle one night. While Ben Said had to stay behind in the hospital as the show traveled on, with Hollis paying his medical bills, George Carron—not of North African or West Asian descent—played Arab as an acrobatic tumbler in the troupe's subsequent performances.[8] Playing Arab for Hollis meant simply donning one of the troupe's costumes and sticking to the acrobatic demonstration Abdellah Ben Said had already choreographed. Performed at some distance from the audience, many in the stands may not have noticed the change or, in any event, took it in stride.

While Wild West promoter Bill Cody used show patter insisting his productions were "the real thing. There are no counterfeits, no 'make-ups,' no 'supers,' no tinsel,"[9] as did the circuses, most of the Arabs audiences saw presented as rough riders or Bedouin horsemen were actually, first and foremost, acrobats. Moreover, some of them did not even consider themselves "Arabs." During his early days in the industry, acrobat George Hamid contended to one promoter who referred to him as such, "I'm not Arab. I'm a Lebanese," not understanding that in the show business sense, an "Arab" was one who played desert Easterner.[10] Many of the wild west and circus employees who performed as "Arabs" were Moroccan, Algerian, and Syrian city and town dwelling people who did not necessarily consider themselves talented horsemen or "Arabs," a name many like Hamid associated with nomadic desert peoples. Entertainers of North African or Middle Eastern origin thus bore what Alberto Sandoval-Sánchez has called "the burden of representation." With respect to Cuban and Brazilian performers in the United States, he notes they were pressured by audiences, Hollywood, and Broadway to perform a generic Latinness that Americans would find comprehensible because it did not require them to consider the ethnic and national diversity across the Caribbean, Central America, and South America.[11] Easterners likewise were cast in shows where they played Oriental to represent the breadth of North Africa, West Asia, and even Persia and India, urban and rural, past and present. With ticket sales first and foremost, production designers and players drew from whatever might be on hand in Oriental tales, current events, and the existing sideshow and circus trades, picking some ideas from here, some ideas from there, in a kind of pastiche typical of the circuses, which thrived by presenting audiences with globally diverse shows that flattered consumer choice.

Consequently, by the 1880s fans already favored Eastern talent framed in accessible modes of exotic manhood that spoke to their late nineteenth-century context, offered increasingly in combinations of the ultranatural and ultra-artificial. The ultranatural came in the form of "Wild Arabs" or "Bedouins" performing in camel races, mock sword fights, or horse pageants. Crossed over in comprehensible ways as Eastern "Rough Riders"—an old cowboy term for the men who attempted to ride the most resistant unbroken horses—they flattered contemporary male interest in athletic, outdoorsy manhood.[12] The broad audiences of rich and poor who sat side-by-side in the stands at circuses and wild west shows featuring international rough riders interpreted non-Anglo-American manhoods in a cultural context in which many posited an independently masculine and free inner self that opposed, Paul Gilmore tells us, "new forces of bodily restraint associated with chastity [and] the market" that daily required hard work, thrift, and politeness from American males.[13]

In 1893, just outside the gates of the Columbian Exposition in Chicago, Buffalo Bill Cody's Wild West set up operations with a show that had a significant minority of Eastern actors playing such roles. In typical form, the program for their six-week summer run featured, "A Group of Syrian and Arabian Horsemen [who] will illustrate their style of Horsemanship, with Native Sports and Pastimes," the patter explained. Bill Cody's "military tournaments" and "Congress of Rough Riders of all Nations" packed the house with displays of staged armed combat and extraordinary horsemanship as the show adapted the long-standing interest in equine competition and endurance feats with a quarter-mile "Horse Race between a Cowboy, a Cossack, a Mexican, an Arab and an Indian, on Spanish-Mexican, Broncho, Russian, Indian and Arabian Horses," around the arena.[14] Promotional materials explained these presentations as "realism" and implied that the manly skills audiences saw were not show business creations but native to the incredible men of each nation presented. Lebanese-born acrobat and rough rider George Hamid would burst this bubble some years later when he explained that he only learned to ride a horse when he began working for Bill Cody's company.[15] In the meantime, the documentary pretenses of wild west show performances by various companies offered Eastern masculinity as a comprehensibly exotic spectacular manhood performed by actual Arab men whose Eastern origins helped them pass as the show character of expert Bedouin rider in a way native-born actors could not.[16]

Comparisons between desert Arabs and Native Americans as horsemen had emerged some years earlier, first introduced broadly in travelers' accounts in which Americans and Britons were struck by a feeling of déjà vu when they laid eyes on nomadic Bedouin families.[17] The Bedouin often unwittingly came across as lacking "civilization" in their resistance to settlement and Ottoman authority. To Americans considering the similarly complicated relations between Native Americans and the Federal government east of the Mississippi after the Civil War, romantic or cautionary comparisons between desert Arabs and Native Americans seemed obvious. Here was a way to put foreign talent into domestic terms as nomadic rebels fighting a centralizing state. As Sitting Bull and other famous Native American men would obligingly play the heroic

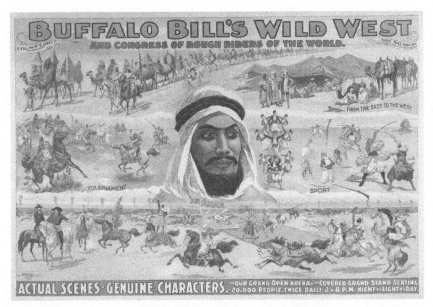

Promotional bill for the 1896 tour of Buffalo Bill Cody's Wild West and Congress of Rough Riders of the World with a rendering of Sheik Tahar and the troupe of trick riders and acrobats he managed. Collection of the John and Mable Ringling Museum of Art Tibbals Digital Collection.

villain to reap the financial rewards, so did performers like Hamid and Abdellah Ben Said play potentially admirable, liberated villains in segments themed on capture and rescue scenarios.[18]

Certainly Bill Cody and his staff attempted to control the messages of the show quite closely by way of patter and promotional materials and often sought to suggest that Anglo-American civilization would ultimately be triumphant in the world. Yet a desire to humiliate Easterners is probably not the main reason Cody and other show producers hired Arab acts. For practical issues often intervened to push Cody and his staff to keep foreign talent, with audience expectations driving them to frame that talent in particular ways. Specifically, staffing problems around getting travel documents from Federal officials for Native American actors in the show made Arab trick riders even more valuable because they could travel in Europe and beyond without complication. An international cast was a dependable godsend for these shows. It added a fresh layer of variety to productions and drew on the creativity and knowledge of foreign artists, a rule of programming the producers looking for novelty depended upon.[19]

During the 1890s, a North African group led by a man going by the professional name Sheik Hadji Tahar labored with Bill Cody's company throughout the United States and Europe and provided Americans with the most famous representations of West Asian manhood for several decades. Tahar and his men supplied the show with the "Bedouins of the Great Desert" segment and an Arab component to the Rough Riders of the World pageant in which they obscured their less glamorous identities as industrious and practical immigrant workers. In typical Cody form, the 1898 Wild West tour program featuring Tahar was shaped like the head of a buffalo. Inside it explained why Bedouin rough riders increased the excitement and comprehensiveness of a show that already presented cowboys, Indians, United States Cavalry riders, Mexican "Ruralies," trick ropers, "South American Gauchos," and European Georgians performing as "Cossack horsemen": "There is nothing that appeals more forcibly to the American sense of the heroic than the spectacle of hardy, active men astride horses . . . the general atmosphere of dare-deviltry and sudden peril, would make the blood leap in the heart of the coldest man who ever sat on a circus seat."[20]

If they hoped to keep their jobs, Tahar and his men could in no way appear passive or bored in performance but had to help Cody's company create its trademark atmosphere of action and "heroic" manhood. For audiences daily accustomed to horse-related accidents and injuries, Tahar's group rode steeds crossed over as "cat-like Arabian horses, which seem intelligent enough to anticipate their riders' wishes." Magazine and newspaper accounts regularly celebrated the famed "Arabian steeds" and Eastern equine husbandry more generally, casting Eastern men in admirable terms to many already interested in desert lands as spaces of primitive manhood and extraordinary horsemanship.[21] Naturally, Tahar did his part and posed for publicity photos wearing white robes and the flowing white headdress and black headband that was becoming a standard show business icon meaning "Arab horseman." He appeared on an equally richly decorated white horse and with his crew performed trick riding, acrobatic work (in more modest costumes), and "whirling dervish"–style spinning on the spot in adaptation of the rituals of the of famed Mevlevi Sufi mystics that defied nausea and audience belief.[22] With this kind of pastiche, Tahar and his troupe were expected by their managers and audiences to represent the whole of North Africa and the Middle East in a concise and entertaining smorgasbord-style bit.

Some scholars have speculated that late nineteenth-century circus and wild west shows offered audiences vicarious experiences of American imperialism over the world's people, particularly in globalized productions like "Buffalo Bill's Wild West and Congress of Rough Riders of the World," which began in 1893.[23] When the Battle of Wounded Knee marked the end of Indian military resistance to the U.S. government in 1890, some Anglo-Americans may have been itching for new lands south or west of the continental United States in which to expand Anglo-American political and economic power. To be sure, it is unwise to exclude any possible interpretation, and certainly the programs and announcers' patter at these productions suggested that ticket-buyers think about the shows as ethnologically authentic recreations of historical events that restaged and naturalized Anglo-American conquest of the west. Some audience members may also have made mental comparisons between the Indians and the Latin Americans in the shows to imagine Americans expanding their military or political reach to overtake all of Central and South America. Nonetheless, Louis Warren is at least equally correct when he explains that we should think about the broad audiences who brought their own histories and independent inter-pretive powers with them to these shows. To nonwhites and recent immigrants, Bill Cody's diverse "Rough Riders Of All Nations" offered a chance to think about immigration to the United States and how foreign men could make a positive place for themselves in the country by publicly embracing aspects of their heritage that Anglo-Americans valued, such as horsemanship and mili-tary bravery. Certainly this is what wild west and circus Arabs did every night on tour.[24]

Parallel public interest in global current events would also help Cody's mar-keting team boost shows for audiences who could actually choose to root for the Arab horseman. For example, in years when men of Bayard Taylor's or Rob Morris's generations were taking their sons and grandsons to these shows, many Anglo-Americans ambivalent over France and Spain's invasions of North Africa grew wistful at the thought of Arab warriors fighting valiantly yet fu-tilely against raw European power. In the mid-1890s, Americans were also nervously watching the political situation in Cuba deteriorate and debating how or if America, a benevolent "empire of liberty," should intervene by reaching across the water to challenge Spain and by extension European imperialism more generally. North African performers in Cody's shows made metaphorical strikes on the Spanish Empire in the Western hemisphere when they played Arab in the guise of "Riffian Arabs from Morocco, several of whom have lately been engaged in desperate conflicts with the Spanish at Melilia," the promotional material explained.[25] Here was the Arab warrior people had been celebrating all century yet newly current and still more chivalrous than the imperial powers he opposed.[26]

American interest in the ostensible Bedouin bandit also came to the surface in those years in the form of a colloquial American interpretation of him we can call the Arab trickster. Especially for Gilded Age urbanites and reformers, the concept of Arab trickster came out in public talk about the phenomenon of homeless children in American cities, known informally as "street Arabs." Many took them as a sign of the toll the notoriously volatile national economy was taking on American families; others took them as a sign of too-liberal immigration policies and the perceived lazy childrearing habits of newcomers to the country, which led to urban crime. New York City "swarms with a youthful horde of precocious scoundrels and incipient desperadoes," a letter to the *Times* had complained already in 1870.[27] Many perceived the thousands of homeless orphans in the city as mobile and nefariously intelligent vagabonds whose lawlessness was aggravating in its defiance.[28] Street Arabs lived by their wits, robbing or teasing respectable citizens, flitting away to hidden locations where they waited for the next mark, some said.[29] The street Arab nomenclature made sense to its users only because it was a reflection of an Arab trickster character grounded in stereotypes that associated transience and independence with a rejection of civilization and respectability.

Americans created the Arab trickster by conflating North African or Bedouin resistance to outside control with any other seemingly defiant "Arab" behavior they knew to create a generalized cliché of Arab bandit who was, in the romantic interpretation, noble in his independence, in the cautionary interpretation, untamed in his refusal to settle down to an "honest" day's work. Such a character had already grown larger than life in those traveler's accounts and Oriental tales that imagined desert caravan raids that seemed to have a commercial aspect.[30] Some of this emerged from travelers' misunderstandings of domestic politics within the Ottoman Empire. Because the Bedouin subsisted off control of desert travel routes and knowledge of the scant watering locations, they earned income by charging protection fees and taxes negotiated with each travel party, including tourist campers, between the Nile and Jerusalem. Thus, in Bedouin-style "Shaykhly" politics, wherein accepting Bedouin help brought an obligation of loyalty or later payment, Ussama Makdisi explains, "[h]ospitality was extended to foreigners—to consuls, to merchants, and to missionaries— not simply as a courtesy to strangers from distant lands but as an imperative for survival."[31] Tourists often had little conception of this paid chaperone system, and consequently described the Bedouin as swindling scoundrels who commonly exaggerated the dangers of passage to negotiate the highest fee possible.

Many people overseas figured this system of Shaykhly politics out over a period of time in the Ottoman Empire and thus reinterpreted the Bedouin from a danger into a comedic rascal who had fooled countless credulous tourists. In his sardonic *Innocents Abroad; or, the New Pilgrim's Progress* (1869), a narrative of his European and Holy Land tour, Mark Twain could not resist lampooning the stories of fearful Western encounters with desert Arabs. His take had a group of tourists hearing of rumors about a planned attack on their desert caravan in Palestine, vowing to exact the most horrible retribution on any Arab who dared molest the group. Of course, when apparent bandits appeared on horseback, all the American men panicked and ran in the opposite direction only to look over their shoulders and see their guides and the "bandits" exchange polite words and payment for passage through the region.[32] The phenomenon of urban American "street Arabs" when combined with the era's "bad-boy" humor typified by authors like Twain, brought the Arab trickster to enduring public attention as unruly and mischievous "free sons of the desert." Like the Shriners, in masculinist late nineteenth-century terms these Arabs were perpetual boys unfettered by work or family responsibility, symbolic of compelling primitive manhood untouched by the feminizing influences of "civilization" while honorable and quasi-patriotic in loyalty to their own brotherhood.

North African and West Asian men would play just such comprehensibly exotic Arab roles in the tent show business in the United States to speak to the audience's existing economies of meaning. While the Bedouin Rough Rider or bandit thus provided the ultranatural manhood audiences appreciated, circus and wild west show companies still needed the ultra-artificial component epitomized by Eastern arts. To their rescue came the story of the Eastern potentate's entertainment. It was already common in elite Oriental tales and increasingly relevant to working-class and poor Americans who examined the surreal ten-foot-high circus and wild west show broadsides on local fences and buildings. In the last decades of the century, color lithographed posters for traveling tent shows promoted the fashion for "Moorish Caravan" spectaculars and other episodes of grand performance themed on historical events that employed the entire cast, human and nonhuman. Indeed, the Oriental tale had crossed over into the circus and horse show business fairly early, before the Civil War even, since those companies' live entertainment was known for its extraordinary presentations of human and animal behavior, carefully choreographed and lavishly decorated. The post–Civil War tent show business came to epitomize centrally managed capitalist entertainment with companies competing to put on the biggest, most elaborate shows.[33] Eastern tale–style themes gave showmen the means to romanticize the expenses of a show by tapping into the consumer's Oriental tale. One 1891 Adam Forepaugh circus promotion typically trumpeted its "costly imported costumes, together with the spectacular pageant, presenting fairy-like, gorgeous view of eastern splendor recalling the historical pictures of the Arabian Nights."[34]

The caravan spectacular also came reworked as the "Sheik's Entertainments," a narrative that invited the audience to identify themselves with a leisured male Arab warrior by vicariously playing Eastern as one of his privileged guests. From a producer's standpoint, the sheik's entertainment device was a lifesaver, a way to transition from one part of a production's script to the next in ways that could make the juxtaposition of unrelated performances seem natural. In a typical example, the combined Bill Cody and Pawnee Bill Wild West and Far East Show one year included on the program a staged desert Arab raid upon a tourist caravan in the Middle East that offered the Arab rough rider and the Oriental tale in one piece. The bit certainly captured the sense of the romantic Arab trickster as bad boy and free son of the desert, dangerous but ultimately benevolent to those endeared to him. The program explained to ticket buyers: "The scene shows a camel caravan at rest in the shadow of the pyramids. They await the return of a party of tourists who come to ransom some of their numbers who have been captured and are held as hostage by the Bedouin bandits. Upon the arrival of the tourists and their payment of the ransom, the captives are released, and to commemorate the occasion the Shiek [sic] of the Bedouin tribe directs that an entertainment shall be given." The spectacular parade that followed came in an Oriental tale–style extravaganza that included far more diversity of human and animal life than any Bedouin man probably ever had at his disposal. In a continuous series of skits, the audience saw a party of four performing "musical elephants," then South Asian Indian magicians, then Japanese and Dahomian acrobats and "Australian Boomerang Throwers" followed by half a dozen other heterogeneous acts performed by men and women from across America, Asia, and Africa.[35]

As the frame tale of the *Thousand and One Nights* connected a cornucopia of different stories together in no predictable order to create a sense of the unexpected, a sheik's entertainment narrative allowed a tent show to present sword fighting Arab Rough Riders one minute, a troupe of trained Indian elephants with dancing girls the next and have it all make sense to the audience as a package. Such arrangements appealed to common show business wisdom that ticket buyers expected novel variety and comprehensible exoticism and that crossing over foreign talent in an Oriental tale frame was too dependable to resist. The Sheik's entertainments narrative was also an articulation of the older ideals of abundant choice and contented leisure American consumers had long sought out in the tales of the *Arabian Nights* and cultural practices modeled on it. Circus and wild west shows helped Americans reconcile the poles of the ultra-natural Eastern man who ostensibly resisted the market while suggesting that he—like they—was also a privileged consumer at the same time. This was how these shows flattered audiences made up of rich and poor, urban and rural, of every race and ethnicity, native-born and foreign-born as a collective society of consumers, saying to them: "As Americans, you deserve an incredible show. Sit back and enjoy."

Performances of the Eastern exotic were a phenomenon of great financial value to the tent show trade in making foreign acts from North Africa and the Middle East readable to rural and working-class ticket buyers just beginning to think about whether they could be consumers. In spite of the official scripts Bill Cody and other tent show producers used to frame their sporting shows as a story of the triumph of American civilization and progress over romantically noble people, these shows offered open-ended presentations of Arab man-hood, bravery, and independence that crossed Eastern men over as admirably familiar in athleticism, independence, and desire for leisured abundance. To poor or working-class young men, who usually found such ultranatural mas-culinity in commercial forms like dime novels and traveling shows, this charac-ter was far more accessible than the Eastern gentleman or mystical wise man of the East. Depending on the inclination of the consumer in question, the Eastern horsemen could be a despised foreigner, a chivalrous warrior, a romantic host, an Arab trickster, or a bit of each of them at once.

ENTERTAINERS AND EMIGRATION: PATRIOTIC ARAB ATHLETICISM ON STAGE

The modest flow of people headed to Ellis Island from the Ottoman Empire would surge in the 1890s as emigrants from the Middle East arrived to find that many Americans already had some idea of what the Arab world looked like or at least that there were talented horse riders there. A majority of the new emigrants were Eastern Christians, although some were Muslims who left despite Ottoman legislation banning Muslim emigration in those years. Whether intending a permanent move or not, many of them became long-term residents of the United States, with only about a third eventually taking their savings and returning East. As far as the public was aware of this immigrant group as such, it was by way of the Syrian-American community that began to develop in New York City. Their hefty remittances home to the Empire were a sizable portion of many family incomes in Ottoman Syria, persuading hundreds then thousands of others to head to the United States. Ottoman officials resented the out migration, suspicious of their self-directed subjects as " 'proletarian classes' [who] intended to become beggars in the Americas," and might cause the Empire trouble later.[36] However, Syrian immigrants could take care of themselves and included far more skilled workers and members of the commercial classes than other immigrant groups to the United States.

That so many Syrian-Ottoman immigrants became small proprietors and typically American entrepreneurs is not surprising since many of these migrants reported that missionary school teachers, emigrant letters, and popular wisdom among friends and family in Syria held that the United States was a land of great opportunity. One of them, Salom Rizk, recalled the "unbelievable things my school-master told me" about the country. That missionary had called the United States "the land of contentment . . . the land of liberty . . . the land of brotherhood . . . the land of plenty . . . where God has poured out wealth . . . where the dreams of men come true . . . where every boy and girl can learn to be what he or she wants to be."[37] Here was the American dream as celebrated by many generations of people who sought out their own personal fortunes and self-definition through education and consumer capitalism now planting new ambitions and plans in the minds of Eastern immigrants too, many with the means to make them happen.[38]

Many of these people became instant merchants, initially bringing stocks of carpets and other products to sell until they got on their feet in New York or another city. Thus was born the famous Syrian peddler, who made substantial income with a flexible, lucrative, and mobile profession. Consumers soon became accustomed to the sight of such peddlers, a trade soon known as the "fakir business" in reference to mendicant Indian miracle workers.[39] Often described in travel accounts and Oriental tales set in South Asia, the term reflected a longer history of transient salesmen selling novelties and sometimes faulty products or snake oil.[40] By 1910s many had moved beyond peddling and Syrians owned businesses of various kinds in every corner of the United States, moving fast into the commercial and professional middle classes.[41]

Syrians also spent plenty of energy comparing and discussing cultural difference between Easterners and Westerners, contrasting life in the old country with the new while determining how to individuate themselves in their new home. Those Easterners spoke of the accelerated speed of life in America, a nation whose people measured men not by family name but by their productivity. They also talked about the constant striving for money they saw among Americans, the great disparities of wealth in the nation, and the fact that women were forced to work for a living in an often-too-liberal society.[42] Eastern immigrants hashed out these debates in Arabic-language newspapers that sprang up in New York. Syrian Americans in particular used them to talk about success, business, ways of promoting Ottoman Empire imports in the United States, and how community members might best individuate themselves as Syrians, Americans, or Syrian Americans.[43] Many decided that financial autonomy by way of success in business was the best way to come across to fellow Americans as respectable citizens.

Some Americans were accepting of Syrian American communities, among them journalists looking for human interest stories. Politely excusing the preponderance of men living often-transient lives in boarding houses in Manhattan's First Ward, for instance, one reporter for the *New York Tribune* noted the community's distinctness and the beginnings of middling family life there. He was pleased by their newspaper, *Kawkab America* or "The Star of America," the many successful businesses serving the neighborhood, their sobriety, and their willingness "to learn American ways and manners, and to become citizens as soon as the law will permit . . . destined to become in the near future . . . a factor in the body politic which will make itself felt for good."[44] Such a comment was quite an endorsement since fear of foreigners "in the body politic" and the labor force had been precisely the argument behind legislation and agreements excluding Asians from the United States with the Chinese Exclusion Act of 1882 and the Gentleman's Agreement of 1906 limiting Japanese immigration. The immigration quota acts of 1921 and 1924 were not far in the future either.[45]

Some cultural alarmists in the press did attack Ottoman Empire immigrants, nonetheless. Anglo-American critics complained that their communities were insular and dominated by unattached men, which is also what they said of the Chinese, Filipino, and other migrants who sent the men ahead to find work.

Initially, the common argument was that as "Orientals," like immigrants from Asia and Latin America, they were inherently disloyal to the United States, prone to exclusivity and lack of patriotism, laziness, and violence, and paradoxically, to both poverty and greed.[46] Indeed, the 1882 Chinese Exclusion Act had specified "race" as the defining issue for immigration restriction, arguing that Asians were inherently unassimilable as Americans because of their biology, which citizens and judges evaluated by eyeballing their appearance.[47]

Nonetheless, many Middle Easterners managed to slip through since Anglo-Americans often perceived them as white, especially when dressed in Western clothing.[48] Eventually, the Quota Limit Act of 1921 would reduce immigration from the French Mandate territory of Syria to 882 persons per year by using national origin, not race, as the main criteria. In 1929, when the National Origins Act of 1924 came into effect and immigration officials further reduced that number to a mere 100, three quarters of them would nonetheless apply to become naturalized as U.S. citizens. A few would take advantage of the American legal system to challenge their racial status as "Asiatic" in the courts when they were denied naturalization.[49] Either way, race and national origin, not religion, were the key factors in restrictive legislation that threw virtually all Middle Easterners together in submitting to such quotas. In the meantime, Muslim immigrants from the Ottoman Empire and North Africa could often blend into the crowded Syrian Christian–dominated neighborhoods of New York. Since antipolygamy regulations surreptitiously yet effectively banned Muslims from naturalization as U.S. citizens between the 1890s and 1920s—Ottoman Empire quotas or not—a considerable number of Muslim migrants also passed as Armenian or Syrian Christians to avoid extra scrutiny by U.S. immigration officials.[50] Sometimes Muslim Easterners also sincerely converted to Christianity or took on names like "Johnson" to obscure their family histories.[51]

Living in one of the Arab American neighborhoods in Brooklyn in the 1890s was the North African man known as Sheik Hadji Tahar, who served as performer and manager of Buffalo Bill Cody's Wild West "Arab" acts. Indeed, the apparently Syrian neighborhoods in American cities actually brought together Christians, Jews, Muslims, former Ottoman subjects, and North Africans united by language or faith. Since the West had closed with the Battle of Wounded Knee in 1890, men like Tahar had been watching cinema and the automobile slowly kill the wild west shows of Bill Cody, Pawnee Bill, and others, while circuses monopolized the compressed market for tent shows that remained. Yet unlike Native American, Cossack, and Mexican vaqueros, for instance, because horsemanship was not in fact their main talent, men like Tahar and his troupe gave up playing Arab horsemen but continued to prosper by falling back on their original talent as acrobats. Often hankering to travel while earning a good living outside of a factory or farm setting, male acrobats from West Asia and North Africa had broken into the American tent show trade by being able to learn the horse work that made Arab shows so popular. They had done so in the 1870s and 1880s, when Chinese and Japanese acrobats were most common in American circuses and Moroccan and Algerian acrobats and vaulters tended to work in Europe. There they became famous for feats of extraordinary athleticism, dispensing with the springboards European acrobats relied upon to perform by jumping straight off the ground.[52]

In the off season, when the circuses and wild west shows were put in winter storage or a company went bust and was put up for auction, Tahar and other acrobats found more work on vaudeville stages with their feats of strength and agility.[53] With the burst of immigration from southern and eastern Europe after 1890, vaudeville ticket buyers made up an audience of working-class and upwardly mobile white-collar workers eight times larger than it had been a decade earlier.[54] Accordingly, in the winter of 1899 Hadji Tahar's men appeared at a Koster & Bial's theater where Tahar had promoted them as "Sheik Hadji Tahar and his Troupe of Royal Arabs."[55] At another booking they appeared at Huber's Fourteenth Street Museum in Manhattan. Tahar's "agile Arabs" got top billing but had to share the stage with performing seals and a woman described as "the young lady known in public life as 'the human volcano' [who] will exhibit her strange powers."[56] This work may or may not have been preferable to the exhausting schedules of constantly moving circuses and wild west shows, although audiences knew what to make of the vaudeville Arab acrobat because of the preexisting tent show trade. Nonetheless, vaudeville was a good place for acrobats, highly visual performers accessible to both native-born and non-English-speaking immigrant audiences. Moreover, Eastern acrobats' work was a family-friendly show suitable for the integrated national vaudeville circuits, whose upwardly mobile audiences sought out optimistic representations of ethnic identity and personal achievement in shows that endorsed one's engagement with the market as a worker who deserved to be a consumer.[57] When the yearly opportunities for wild west show work declined after the turn of the century, Moroccan, Algerian, and Lebanese men would lean even more heavily on circus and vaudeville work as acrobats, an act that became so famous, Lebanese performer George Hamid remembered, " 'Arab' and 'acrobat' were synonymous."[58]

As a rule, these acrobats had "Oriental managers" like Tahar or the famous Moroccan, Hassan Ben Ali. He promoted his group aggressively in trade papers such as the *New York Clipper* and *Billboard* whenever they were "at liberty," meaning they needed a booking.[59] In the late 1890s, Hassan Ben Ali's group gained national attention traveling with the Sells Brothers Circus, laying the groundwork for Eastern troupes like the Demnatis or Wazzan Troupe, who in the succeeding decades contracted with circuses, vaudeville theaters, Coney Island, and carnivals.[60] Ben Ali's troupe performed shows in which Ben Ali got top billing as producer: "Hassan Ben Ali's Moorish Caravan Arabian Nights' Entertainment Spectacular Pilgrimage to Mecca," for instance.[61] Ben Ali had been attracted to the United States during the run up to the Columbian Exposition back in 1891 and would perform and manage various troupes of comprehensibly exotic Arab athletes. Yet once the show was over, Ali was known to wear "the ordinary coat and trousers of commerce" while negotiating the next deal as the agent for "Ben Ali's Twelve Arabian Acrobats" and "Ben Ali's Bounding Bedouins" among others. He had been subject to—or the instigator of—publicity that described him as a brave explorer who had taken American consumer products to the interior of Morocco to find men to work at the Exposition, amazing them with evidence of American technology.[62] Again, men like Tahar and Ali made it clear to audiences that they were not helpless subjects of an American gaze but played Eastern in ways that showed they were also talented entrepreneurs and wily self-promoters who could style themselves in various ways for this audience or that or to refresh their performances each season.

For modern American audiences, one of the reasons these Arab acts remained relevant over time was that they became increasingly patriotic in their replication of clichéd American ideas about success and self-improvement, familiar concepts communicated by exotic people. To give their acts a comprehensible sense of Easternness drawn from the consumer's Oriental tale, Arab acrobatic performances often combined rich costumes, claims of royalty, and prolix Eastern voice with the tried-and-true demonstrations of manly athleticism audiences had loved for years. Any scholarly idea of a "feminized" Orient predominating in the minds of all Americans buckles under the weight of such evidence from the turn of the century, as it did with respect earlier decades. These acrobats inserted their own messages of triumph and self-made success into acts that defied racist hierarchies, especially with a famous bit called the pyramid in which up to ten men and boys stood in decorative formation upon the shoulders of a single man. For at least fifty years beginning in the 1880s, Arab men performed the pyramid during the main show of circus and wild west show productions, on vaudeville stages, and at carnivals and state fairs thereafter. This act was often "lustily applauded," one circus fan remembered, and certainly an Arab acrobat could "make many friends among the lady portion of the audience by his graceful tumbling," one booster noted after a "P. T. Barnum's Greatest Show On Earth" circus performance in Stevens Point, Wisconsin.[63]

Nor were these men shy when "toughs" harassed circus employees, which was a common occurrence, but defended themselves with enough bravery to be praised in the unofficial circus histories known as route books.[64] The circuses were particularly cosmopolitan communities of international performers who talked about themselves as separate from normal society and defiant of common racism and other prejudice because they lived and traveled in close proximity with their unconventional colleagues.[65] No Anglo-American acrobatic troupes ever became famous for performing pyramids in such robustly masculine Eastern personae, and it appears that North Africans and West Asians had cornered the market on the genre.[66] They would perform for mixed audiences but especially for American boys and men, who in those days were interested in seeing all kinds of extraordinary masculinity in wrestling competitions, boxing, and strongman acts. All of these bits flattered male audience members struggling mentally, as many were, with the increased power and presence of women in public and the constraints of factory or office work.[67]

George Hamid was the most successful of these "Arab" acrobats over the long term and would go on to become a circus promoter and owner of Atlantic City's Steel Pier amusement park.[68] Although for his first few years in the United States as an adolescent at the turn of the century he lived with other former Ottoman subjects in the circus speaking only Arabic, by the 1910s Hamid was as much an American as anything else. His memoir of life in show business was published in 1950 and exemplified the attitude many Arab performers worked into their acts. It was an utterly American, up-by-the-bootstraps story of a boy who had escaped poverty in the Middle East to become a preeminent American showman by the 1930s. Indeed, Hamid had left Lebanon

"Troupe of Salim Nassar Bedouin Arabs, Hassan Ben Ali, manager, 1898," posing for a
Buffalo Bill Cody's Wild West photographer. Nate Salsbury Collection of Buffalo Bill
Cody's Wild West, Western History/Genealogy Department, Denver Public Library.

at age seven and traveled to the United States on a steamer in 1906 with his
brother and a cousin, working first for Bill Cody as an acrobat and rough rider,
then for an Arab troupe managed by Hassan Ben Ali's company.

Of the famous acrobatic pyramids and other athleticism Arabs were known
for before World War II, Hamid explained that they were the product of endless practice and physical fitness as well as a "can-do" attitude that drove
these performers to constantly improvise new formations. The boys and men
who played Arab acrobat also learned tumbling, vaulting, and other dangerous
feats of agility that often resulted in injury or fist fights among the performers
when something went wrong.[69] It was an exceedingly macho world, Hamid
explained, though not in so many words, in which it was survival of the fittest
behind the scenes in order to supply the incredible show of robust masculine
power audiences would come to expect. Yet this ultranatural Arab masculinity
was hardly controversial because, as performed by Hamid and others, it flattered Anglo-American progress ideologies by its endorsement of male power in

the United States and—even if a few women took the shows this way—did not suggest that Arab men might eclipse native-born men in wooing native-born women. These men thus managed to cross over as powerful and masculine but did so in secular venues of mixed audiences, where some made light-hearted acknowledgement of their appeal to women but in which they posed no real or imagined threat to the dominant Anglo-American social order.

Others came to the United States and had to navigate between the old characters of Arab bandit, acrobat, and immigrant patriot to find something that felt right and kept them working. Dozens of Syrian performers thusly broke into show business in the 1890s and after. Their success shows us how performances of Arab athleticism had evolved from tent show trick rider and acrobatic act into a mode of playing Eastern that explicitly endorsed uncontroversial "American" values of the period such as the need for a strong work ethic and the female athleticism that circuses and vaudeville were also known for.[70] Take, for instance, the "Bayrooty Troupe," a group of apparent Maronite Christians who became famous at the turn of the century. Their manager, Barry Gray of Philadelphia, possibly recruited these performers from somewhere overseas or from within the Syrian communities in New York. The Troupe's acts included "Gun Spinning," "Sword Combats," and "Native Music," all components that spoke to the Orientana and Arab athleticism made famous in the tent shows. Barry Gray billed the woman dancer of the act " 'Marrie'—Greatest Whirling Dancer on Earth. $1000 her equal" and had publicized her with a stunt at Madison Square Garden in which she had spun on the spot for a reputed thirty-seven minutes straight. Her feat of stamina appeared in a Barry Gray production that also included "The Man with the Iron Skull," a giant, and other "freaks" that audiences used to think about the limits of the human body.[71]

Marrie's main competition the week she appeared at Madison Square Garden was "Emma Francis and her Arabian Whirlwinds" over at Keith's Theatre at 14th Street and Broadway.[72] "Handkerchief dancing" and whirling performances had appeared at the Columbian Exposition in Chicago in 1893 and were also a hit on vaudeville stages and in circus shows thereafter.[73] The Bayrooty Troupe seems to have found a way to cater to the American market, which demanded the athletic demonstrations that were so popular in the circuses and wild west shows, to make the new phenomenon of Arab musical and acrobatic troupe exotically familiar. Moreover, female performers like Marrie also came across as feminist to women spectators in vaudeville houses in their endorsement of female energy and freedom in a more respectable context than the seedy

Tradecard for the Bayrooty Troupe, a "Vaudeville Novelty of Oriental Splendor." Syrian immigrants made a respectable living on the vaudeville circuit with feats of athletic dancing framed in patriotic sentiment and a proposed Syrian-American identity. "Letterheads of Magicians and Magic Acts" Scrapbooks, Billy Rose Theatre Division, The New York Public Library for the Performing Arts, Astor, Lenox and Tilden Foundations.

carnivals and male entertainment districts that hosted suggestive "cootch" shows of Eastern-styled dancing (see Chapter 6).[74]

Athletic dancers and acrobats would make a place for Eastern Christians and Muslims on vaudeville tours across the country in a venue that embraced ethnic performance and welcomed artists and audiences from around the world in ways that cinema and television never did. In turn these entertainments helped consumers think about their own ways of being in an ethnically diverse society.[75] Thus had Marrie's promotional photos showed her holding an Ottoman flag in one hand and an American flag in the other in a way Eastern acts would cross themselves over to patriotic native-born Americans and immigrants weighing their options in a new country. Framed as performers of feats of endurance that displayed stick-to-it-iveness and ingenuity, working-class immigrants like the Bayrooty Troupe played Eastern in ways that actually asserted their hybrid identities as Syrian Arab Americans.[76] Their shows rejected the xenophobia and popular race hierarchies of the early twentieth century, which argued that Easterners were weak, undisciplined, and unsuited for citizenship while flattering other clichés about the equality of opportunity in the nation. Eastern immigrants found the practice of playing comprehensibly exotic Oriental profitable for making a living while creating personally satisfying art that spoke of their transnational life stories.

chapter 5

Making the Familiar Strange:
The Racial Politics of Eastern Exotic, 1893–1929

*T*he following three chapters all radiate out from 1890s Chicago to examine what native-born Americans did with the interventions people from North Africa, West Asia, and South Asia made into American culture. There is an important difference hereafter, though, which I must explain in regard to the previous chapter. In order to preserve the chronology of their first intervention into American culture beginning in the 1870s, Chapter 4 segregated North African and West Asian actors and the personae they suggested from audience's uses of them. That construction, while pointing out the agency of foreign-born actors in elaborating some important entertainment practices when they did, also obscures an important reality of their lives in America. The fact is, foreign-born performers and native-born Americans mingled and interacted at all times, producing competing Oriental personae that consumers found tangled together in various venues, a scenario that invited confusion. The rest of this book is designed to show how this reality made hybridity of personae, conscious acts of passing, and mistaken identity common in American life, often giving Eastern personae great utility to people seeking to remake themselves through professional or consumer individuation.

So to begin, this chapter sets the stage with a look at a particularly preeminent moment of intercultural observation and adaptation, the 1893 Columbian Exposition in Chicago. Various modes of playing Eastern became prominent there among native-born and foreign-born people who competed for press attention, income, and credibility. The official Ottoman Empire delegation to the Columbian Exposition sought to manage the Empire's public image by using the fair to cross their state over to the American public as a cosmopolitan imperial power. However, the Sultan's agents struggled mightily to be heard above the crowds of Oriental merchants, Bedouin horsemen, and others who appeared both at the exposition and around Chicago. Entertainers and entrepreneurs from North Africa and West Asia, as well as a diverse collection of native-born visitors to the exposition, would redevelop the arts of playing Eastern during that summer for purposes neither exposition planners nor the various official foreign government delegations had intended. Among the unscripted innovators who emerged on the scene were members of the Ancient Arabic Order, Nobles of the Mystic Shrine, or Shriners. Fraternalists from the local temple in Chicago used their connections with Eastern entrepreneurs at the fair to develop Shriner performances that spoke of both commercial power and the bizarre. Simultaneously, African Americans were visiting the fair and were similarly inspired by the Eastern personae they discovered. In turn, they founded the Ancient *Egyptian* Arabic Order, Nobles of the Mystic Shrine, or black Shriners, to represent the respectability of black business and social organization in ways similar to the white order. The legal battles that ensued between white and black Shriners over the right to use burlesquing Mystic Shrine personae of "Imperial Potentate" and "Oriental Noble" show how valuable playing Oriental had become.

Like the Ottoman officials at the exposition, white Shriners were conscious of how Oriental-style performance could be poached by others in ways that invited confusion and "misrepresentation." American and Ottoman elites at the fair both hoped to control the obvious democratization of Eastern personae and reserve the portrayal of the East for themselves, exposing their belief that use of exotic personae in the United States spoke of one's political, economic, or social power. Their complaints pointed out to observers that there were racial politics to playing Eastern that attempted to reserve those performances for the wealthy and powerful, in one case, a cosmopolitan Ottoman elite and in another, the Anglo-American business and professional classes. Playing Eastern became democratized despite these efforts at control because it was just as useful to native-born minorities and rural and working-class people as it had been to the Anglo-American middle and upper classes and foreign performers already.

The adaptability of Oriental personae in the United States was in part a product of the fact that the exotic functioned in two directions. Recall that it was first a way for professional entertainers and salespeople to make themselves comprehensibly novel to domestic audiences, for instance, when North African and West Asian acrobats came across as optimistic self-made men and women who endorsed "American" values. Alternately, in the hands of native-born Americans, often amateur entertainers and consumers seeking individuation, the Eastern exotic was a way to cross the familiar (themselves) over as slightly unreadable or even outright strange. Many Americans who met people from the Eastern world at the Columbian Exposition and elsewhere in those years found them "as fantastic as the *Arabian Nights*" and a fertile field of inspiration. Many used foreign-inspired objects, clothing, naming practices, and acts they gained in contact with foreign-born performers in novel and often unsettling ways to come across as mysteriously or bizarrely exotic while playing Oriental.[1] Such personae and performances were a mask of incomprehensibility that became crucial to Shriner street theater, for example. Both modes speak loudly of Americans' interest in cultural difference in these days, the profit that could be made from and the affluence displayed by catering to that interest with exotic Eastern personae that showed how human creativity could flourish in a market economy.

OPEN FOR BUSINESS AT THE COLUMBIAN EXPOSITION

The entertaining distractions of the World's Fair came at a troubled moment in American history. The United States had emerged as the world's richest industrial power yet was on the verge of financial collapse. The depression that hit that spring was the decisive economic and social event of a decade when the government would send troops out into the Pacific and Latin America to wage an imperial "struggle for markets," territory, and influence. While legislators supplied funding for the gigantic party that was the Columbian Exposition, President Cleveland would soon be negotiating with J. P. Morgan for loans to keep the government solvent as a "tsunami of liquidations, foreclosures, and bank failures," swept across the nation.[2] The United States was the preeminent capitalist power on the planet but was living beyond its means to project that image to all the other imperial governments who would similarly stage themselves at the fair, among them Russia, Britain, France, and the Ottoman Empire.

The Columbian Exposition was in its own way also a strange amplification of the labor and immigration controversies of the Gilded Age. Congress had renewed the Chinese Exclusion Act of 1882 the previous year to keep Chinese men from the labor force. Striking railway workers led by unionist Eugene Debs brought trains to a grinding halt across the Midwest, while Coxey's Army of unemployed headed to the national capital seeking federal action on joblessness. Conflict had peaked between the merchants, manufacturers, and government officials who had taken successful advantage of the capitalist integration of the economy and the nation's expanding borders and the workers who did the badly paid, often dangerous labor that made that growth possible. Accordingly, one of the greatest debates in the early days of the Columbian Exposition had been over Sunday openings, initially rejected by administrators but later permitted so that working-class Americans could attend on their single weekly day off.[3]

Meanwhile, an international group of workers and entrepreneurs inhabited the Columbian Exposition grounds producing shows, products, and services attendees would speak about warmly for decades thereafter.[4] Yet seeing the labor and consumer's history of intercultural engagement at world's fairs is not an easy thing to do. A case in point: both official souvenirs and scholarly histories of the 1893 Columbian Exposition in Chicago tend to obscure the commercial nature of the event by suggesting that foreign participants passively endorsed planners' visions of the fair.[5] The vast majority of published photographs of the Columbian Exposition show the fair drained of all signs of life in images of deserted mechanical, scientific, and architectural displays or silently posed foreigners staring solemnly into the lens.[6] It was true that American administrators, and many spectators, imagined the fair that way, as a series of pristine environments and idealized educational experiences they hoped would communicate a vision of America benignly ruled by "a corporate alliance of business, culture, and the state," as Alan Trachtenberg has summed up. In the portion of the grounds known as the White City, designers hoped to get this patriotic, procapitalist message across with a bombardment of beautiful spaces and technology.[7] The White City certainly made sense to many among the Anglo-American middle and upper classes fascinated by hierarchically categorized collections, while less developed nations appeared nearby in official state pavilions and in unpaved displays of "traditional" architecture.[8]

Yet if we view the Chicago World's Fair from the perspective of the businessman, the talent agent, the foreign performer, and the ticket buyer, the reality was that of an event premised formally on public education and compartmentalization of national groups yet financially dependent upon commercial retail and theatrical space that invited cultural exchange. Certainly some American visitors might entertain racist ideas about the people they met at the fair, but many were also fascinated by them and wanted to shop. Eastern performers there understood this clearly. Take, for instance, two of the Ottoman subjects who worked as sedan chair carriers carting around tired visitors and dignitaries. Among the various things they did to facilitate American curiosity in the

Ottoman subjects energetically played various Oriental characters to host American consumers at the Columbian Exposition. Here a sedan chair carrier calls out to a man who has unwittingly wandered into the photographer's shot. Photograph by Jos. E. Hartman, iCHi-23706, Chicago History Museum.

displays was to sit for photographs near the Turkish mosque and ice cream parlor. A strolling man in a bowler hat ruined one of the many portraits for which they posed, producing an accidental document that defies the official record of the fair. The sedan chair carriers are telling us that visitors came and stayed because of the very agency of foreign actors who created an international tourist experience right on American soil.[9] Although American tourists in the Ottoman Empire, Europe, and elsewhere might come across as unwelcome intruders to some locals, and even if foreign people at the Columbian Exposition rejected the racist premises of the exposition, every visitor was nonetheless warmly welcomed into the fantasy.

In spite of their seeming newness, the migrant workers and businessmen Americans found working at the exposition were veterans of the tourist trade in their home countries and previous expositions in Paris and Philadelphia. Although many of their shows and businesses were derived from the popular entertainments of market and festival cultures of the Eastern world, these performers had already developed products and services for the Western market; Americans just did not know it at first.[10] For instance, the dozens of artists and merchants who worked the fifty or so shops on the "Streets of Cairo" exhibit were all managed by Cairo talent agents Raphael and Banyakar, themselves represented in the United States by the talent agent Arthur H. Smythe of Columbus, Ohio.[11] One typically cynical observer, Ben Truman, exposed the bind foreign entertainers confronted in trying to please American audiences that might by turns be confused, reticent, or delighted by the artifice of the fair: "All the profuse explanations that they are here by the special permission of Sultan this and Emperor that is bosh. [For] they have not come thousands of miles merely to add a picturesque feature to this wonderful exhibit."[12] Though dismissive, Truman had a point in explaining that foreign entrepreneurs had made the trip to Chicago for their own purposes, such that their exotic self-presentation in formal dress, for example, was part of the show, not solely an expression of personal identity.[13]

Most influential in providing visitors with a chance to consider how "manifestly sincere" was the exposition and its inhabitants was the entertainment zone known as the Midway.[14] "Thought by some to be beneath the aim of the great Exposition," Fair President Thomas W. Palmer admitted, the Midway businesses were indispensable to exposition administrators' desperate work to avoid incurring unmanageable debt.[15] Humorists soon dubbed the Midway the "sideshow to the 'World's Circus'" and "A Raid on Visitors' Pocketbooks."[16] In Chicago that summer one could find 300 people providing an eclectic variety of performances and arts lining the Midway in no obvious order, much like the bric-a-brac of a contemporary Oriental cozy corner.[17] There Algerian and Turkish "villages"; the Persian theater and "Cairo Street" shared space with Irish, Javanese, Pacific Islander, Dahomian (West African), German, and Austrian displays, the hugely novel Ferris Wheel, Carl Hagenbeck's animal show, the Libby Glass Works building, and other promotional shopping displays.

A diverse group from Morocco to Persia provided the biggest contingent from the ethnically and religiously diverse Western half of the Muslim world. They offered once-daily staged Arab wedding and birthday celebrations, skits and dances, mock sword fights, costumed parades with music, various shows of dancing "girls," camel, donkey, and sedan chair rides, dervish troops, exotic cafés, artisans' workshops and souvenir stands.[18] "Cairo Street is jammed every day, and the various Asiatic natives are stared at when ever they appear on the

Walk, and are surrounded by intent groups whenever they stop to speak to an acquaintance," journalist Julian Hawthorn explained of the particular appeal of the Middle Easterners there. "We . . . are never weary of contemplating turbans, caftans, sandals, and bournouses," he continued, clothing being only the most obvious marker of identity, easily spotted and for sale in Midway shops.[19] Foreign performers wearing formal dress of Eastern countries often used friendly introductions to further endear themselves to potential customers. "It takes a pretty heartless individual to get by the café," Ben Truman agreed of the particularly importunate Egyptian salesmen at the Cairo Street tea shop.[20]

For visitors possibly unfamiliar with the artisanal lore of carpet showrooms, curio shop advertising, travel narratives, or the merchants of Damascus and Cairo bazaars, the fair presented newly accessible shopping opportunities that won over thousands of new consumers to the idea of buying a little piece of the *Arabian Nights* for themselves. On the Midway, Middle Eastern artists sold the omnipresent fez, Turkish and Moroccan slippers, brassware, carpets, pottery of their own design, and other objects imported from home.[21] So did G. Lekegian sell souvenir photographs of visitors taken in front of his shop. Lekegian advertised himself as "photographer to his Royal Highness, the Khedive" of Egypt, taking on a promotional persona of affluent cultural difference wherein his American customers could imagine themselves rubbing shoulders with a comprehensibly exotic elite.[22] "Faraway" Moses, the quintessence of picturesque but seemingly opportunistic Eastern curio peddlers, reemerged at the Columbian Exposition too, where he promoted Ottoman Empire tourism and sold souvenirs to fair visitors sympathetic to the contemporary fashion for Aladdin's lamp–style interiors.[23] Even the working-class visitors who caused so much debate over the propriety of Sunday openings could purchase "primitive indigenous handcrafts" and economical versions of the rich luxuries of the East, relatively cheap rugs, brassware, or a paper fez that might serve as emblems of worldliness or slightly incomprehensible novelties depending upon the purchaser.[24]

The marketing expertise of many of these entrepreneurs was especially obvious in the work of the Syrian dragoman Melhem Ouardy and his brother Bolossy. They made their way to Chicago to set up a promotional exhibit for Holy Land tourism displaying desert camping equipment and other representations of Syrian and Palestinian life. There they served Arab-style coffee and cigars to customers in a series of café tents they put up just outside the fair's

gates in order to avoid "the rake-off" of percentages of profits the Columbian Exposition took from concession holders. The Ouardy brothers employed
"richly dressed" assistants who entertained and talked up Middle Eastern tourism to great success by drawing on Americans' piety with respect to the Holy
Land and their romantic ideas about a consumer-friendly Middle East reminiscent of the *Arabian Nights*.[25]

In spite of his Levantine origins, Milhem Ouardy was also manager of a
Midway establishment called the Moorish Palace.[26] In so naming what was
basically a dime museum he used "Moorish" not as a national or ethnic desig-
nation but in the American sense as a commercial trade name that simply
meant "fantastic variety" and "leisured entertainment," a concept later associated with movie houses.[27] At the Moorish Palace, fair-goers could find a variety
of people and novelties worthy of a Barnum-era venture. Self-proclaimed "Chief
Attraction of Midway Plaisance," it contained a replica of the Alhambra in
Spain, a palm garden, a "Moorish Harem" display, a hall of mirrors, a café
decorated as a cave with a panorama of "Satan and His Imps," and a show of
dancing women as well as "The Guillotine that Executed Marie Antoinette."[28]
The Ouardys and their staff were certainly making their own opportunities by
shaping the specific content of their displays to westernized tastes for the
comprehensibly exotic in a "Sheikh's entertainment" mode of unpredictable
variety. In the process they came across as Oriental-tale merchants bearing gifts
from exotic places.

For these men to make such investments in the exposition required pragma-
tism and a compromise between one's own desires and the consumer's wherein
playing Eastern was a way to manage the serious financial risk in the undertaking. These conditions may explain why mostly Christian and Jewish Ottoman
entrepreneurs from major centers like Istanbul and Cairo with access to capital
and preexisting American contacts landed the concession deals at the fair rather
than immigrant Syrian American entrepreneurs without such elite American
connections or their own financing. Especially in May, when attendance was still
low, critics cast the fair's administrators who recruited such foreign entrepreneurs as opportunists who "extract enormous sums from foreigners on gilded
representations of tremendous immediate returns" through a "concession system which permits the most reprehensible features of a monopoly."[29]

As evidence of how the exorbitant fees demanded by the fair's American
organizers trickled down through the several levels of foreign entrepreneurs to
visitors, some pointed to Effendi Robert Levy, a concession holder "for all

things Turkish" on the Midway. Levy had leased out space to fellow Ottoman subjects including an Italian long resident in Istanbul, then known to Americans as Constantinople. That man had in turn gambled by bringing materials and staff over to Chicago at his own expense in order to erect and run a richly decorated Turkish café. When a *New York Times* reporter complained to the Ottoman Italian that "two pint bottles of beer and two infinitesimal caviar sandwiches cost 90 cents" in the café, this proprietor explained that he had been required to pay Levy $6000 and 15 percent of the gross profits for his spot on the Midway. He feared he would not break even on the $15,000 he had spent on the venture to that point, he said. Indeed, people had come from around the world hoping that an investment in an exposition business would make its money back, as many of them did, inspiring identical exhibits at later world's fairs and amusement parks across the country.[30] To make this work pay, these entrepreneurs came across as commercial cultural ambassadors whose ingenuity announced that the Eastern world was open for business.

OTTOMAN EMPIRE PUBLIC RELATIONS IN CHICAGO

To capitalize on the many millions of visitors to the city and the fantastic atmosphere there, theater managers and agents from all over the country converged on Chicago that year, putting on tent shows, theater productions, and sideshows of every kind.[31] These productions created a conspicuous city-wide commercial context that made the for-profit ventures of the Midway, with its Cairo Street, mock European villages, and "Moorish Palace" just the latest elaboration of an entertainment bandwagon that had left a generation earlier when the circuses first began their "Congress Of All Nations" shows. Consumers had literally dozens of options at various prices for experiencing a representation of the Eastern world. Independent Ottoman subjects and other Easterners on fair grounds and around the city presented themselves alternately as Aladdin's lamp–style merchants, friendly dragomen, fantastic horsemen, or weird sideshow acts, Turkish, Arab, Syrian, Persian, Algerian, Muslim, Christian, and Jew, "of Cairo Street" or simply Oriental, all of them worldly professionals playing Eastern to the crowds. So did the Turkish village theater inside the fair eventually mix many different groups and elements together in a presentation that featured a diverse ensemble of Ottoman subjects, "Bedouins, Druzes, Syrians, Kurds, Turks . . . Beautiful Dancing Girls of Damascus and Constantinople. Performances hourly beginning at 1 p.m."[32]

Moreover, people of various backgrounds had long erected Moorish-style buildings in or around world's fairs and charged entrance fees, often claiming to present the inside of an actual operational mosque, using Islamic architectural forms as a trademark for commerce as much as piety. Accordingly, just outside the gates in Chicago, Nestorian Christians from Syria had constructed a mosque and were charging visitors to go inside and watch people performing the Muslim prayer ritual.[33] Cairo Street also had its own mosque and occasionally let visitors into the gallery to take a look.[34]

The pay-for-a-peek mosque invited Americans to believe that Easterners liked inquisitiveness and offered their shows for cultural adaptation. Plenty of Anglo-Americans commented on these moments of subversive hybridity and cultural exchange in the "overheard on the Midway"–type anecdotes that began emanating from the exposition. One editorial cartoon depicted a Turkish man with a jug full of beer, explaining him as the "result of placing the Turkish and German Villages so close together."[35] Rumors also circulated that men from the Algerian Village enjoyed drinking parties with the Native American men employed by Buffalo Bill Cody's Wild West just outside the exposition grounds.[36] Others joked about the awkward attempts of Americans to ride the camels on Cairo street or of immigrants to comprehend people and clothing that they found there. Public interest in such gossip and humor seems to have been especially high among those sardonic observers who were bent on poking holes in the façade of ethnic separation, education, and American progress the fair ostensibly offered.[37]

Inside the gates of the Columbian Exposition, the official Ottoman government delegation struggled against this tide of commerce and performance. Ottoman Sultan Abdülhamid II sought in those years to "escape the exotic," as Selim Deringil has described it. This effort took the form of asserting publicly that the multiracial, multiethnic Empire was best represented abroad by a Europeanized Turkish elite. In their view, Western press portrayals of the Empire seemed always to focus on a connection between tyranny and the Sultanate, while within popular amusements the representations seemed to boil down to "dancing girls and dervishes," they believed, encapsulating the Empire in stale tropes of religious fanaticism, sex, and power. The Sultan's officials had long employed a special information department in Istanbul, the Foreign Ministry Foreign Press Service, and Ottoman ambassadors abroad to monitor foreign publishing and entertainment for false, humiliating, or irreverent treatment of the Sultan or Empire. Consequently, one year before the Chicago Exposition, the Sultan's office had become alarmed when their ambassador in Washington, D.C. reported a troop of Egyptians under the direction of a Syrian Christian had been busking as whirling dervishes on New York streets. Ottoman officials quickly organized the deportation of the group back to the Empire.[38]

Still, Chicago was also a powerful opportunity for the Ottoman government to communicate to the American public and try to brand the Empire internationally. To be more accurate, it was not that the Ottomans wanted to escape the exotic so much as come across with an exoticism the Sultan could control in order to be imperially exotic, a foreign but comprehensibly expansive paternal nation made familiar to the American public. Representatives of the Sultan and other members of the Ottoman elite at the exposition wished to present themselves to the world as one of the Great Powers of Europe, reform minded, forward looking, and well policed—certainly not the "sick man of Europe," as the political gossip went.

Yet who exactly should represent the Ottoman Empire? And how should they do it? Ottoman officials contracted a Turkish event company, Ilya Suhani Saadullah & Co. (which eventually went bankrupt, stranding performers in the United States), and appointed a gentleman by the name of Ibrahim Hakky Bey as Ottoman commissioner, enjoining him to present the Empire as both civilized and piously Muslim.[39] In this way they also hoped to come across as benevolent imperial caretakers of their Arab and Kurdish subjects. Like many foreign governments who participated, the Ottoman administration shared with American organizers patronizing to non-Turkish Ottoman subjects ideas about race, progress, science, and industry.[40]

Consequently, the delegation threw an informal party that June, to which they invited all sorts of world's fair dignitaries and the press. Ben Truman was on the guest list, and although he had critiqued the business savvy of those on the Midway, he did not seem to have the same analytical eye with respect to the careful Ottoman constructions of paternalistic imperial identity. He described the scene that day as Hakky Bey, "a handsome Armenian noble," and other ethnically European Turkish Ottoman officials mingling with guests while an orchestra played classical music in the background. Truman seemed especially impressed since the Ottomans presented themselves as imperial caretakers of subjects portrayed in the most picturesque form, noble but potentially dangerous people needing help and control. He wrote with some admiration that leading to the doors of the Ottoman pavilion stood a "line of soldiers from the desert in the flowing and glaring garb of the Arab" alongside two men "in the uniform of the Sultan's Guard, a bright red, bedecked with gold and silver filigree ornaments." Truman was equally impressed with the Ottoman displays of scientific and navigational technology, which he deemed "a revelation," although he explained they were "crude compared with those of American make, but they show that the Ottoman is trying to keep abreast of the times."[41] The Ottoman delegation made other attempts to compare Ottoman and American national identities by way of pairing their nationalisms; for instance, the orchestra at the Turkish theater took to playing the Ottoman and American national anthems one after the other before crowds of listeners.[42]

Near their pavilion, the Ottoman representatives erected a bazaar, a theater, and a working mosque. In choosing entertainers to work at the Ottoman buildings, the Sultan's advisers engaged Raci Bey, a businessman from the Levantine city of Acre who offered to send camels, Arabian horses, and Arab boys who would "cause much amazement" by their beauty (this including the young men), their size, grace, and calm manner. Catering to elitist Turkish sensibilities, Raci Bey proposed that the young Arab men not ride the horses in the traditional Bedouin manner, which might be too strange or noisy to Western viewers since it would involve the shooting of guns in the air and a great deal of yelling reminiscent of wild west Arab rough riders. Such a show, he argued, would only feed American clichés about Bedouin banditry in the Holy Land. Instead, Raci Bey arranged to have two Turkish soldiers in formal military uniform perform "a sort of dressage with the riders sporting Ottoman and American flags." These official displays of Eastern manhood revealed Ottoman ruling class aspirations to present Middle Eastern Arabs as picturesque primitives controlled through careful imperial guidance, which minimized the considerable antagonism among Arabs, including the Bedouin, within the Empire and their common resistance to the Sultan's government in Instanbul.[43]

The essence of the Ottoman "dressage" and other official exhibits was not to present mundane or average people from the Empire but people extraordinary either in physical beauty, costume, or behavior, presented in patriotic settings, that is, the exotically comprehensible. Before Sultan Abdülhamid II began to censor the Ottoman press in the 1880s, satirists in Turkish newspapers had regularly ridiculed such attempts, giving us reason to suspect that many Ottoman subjects might still have taken issue with the official presentations of the East as much as anything else at the fair.[44] The Ottoman officials used this language of benevolent reform of "backwards" peoples to cross the Empire over in Chicago because since the 1830s they had been centralizing the administration and infrastructure for resource, labor, and tax extraction in distant "frontier zones" and rural regions of the Empire. This process took place in a pattern akin to American resource and infrastructure development in the West although with more uneven results that had certainly not solved the Empire's cash flow problems in the same way American expansion had enriched the federal government in the United States. The male Ottoman elite, a multilingual European-educated class, were also working to marshal politically independent ethnic and religious groups to some kind of Ottoman national identity, though less successfully than in the United States, where Anglo-American nationalism was more broadly accepted.[45]

Nonetheless, as people compared the standards of Eastern horsemanship they knew to what the Ottoman delegation offered, they began to denote the Ottoman show as part of the wild west horse show genre. Inside exposition gates, visitors would soon hear Frederick Jackson Turner declare that the America's Western frontier was closed and their own Indian Wars over while Bill Cody's "Bedouin Rough Riders" packed them in almost within earshot in a massive production just outside the main gate and while the Midway shows of "Bedouins in their Encampment," also known as the "Wild East Show" were very popular.[46] Billed on fences and in the newspapers alongside Buffalo Bill's Wild West show and other brand-name circuses like Barnum and Bailey's in Chicago that summer was another "Wild East" show that played all summer at the Garfield Park Track. In "Bedouin Life in the Desert," the show's producers proffered to the public sixty Arabian horses "obtained by Special Firman of the Sultan," camels, donkeys, goats, and sheep. The animals came with a "Tribe of Over 400 Men and Women [in] Magnificent Costumes of the Desert [performing] Manners and Customs of the Desert" in a Sheikh's Entertainments narrative, in which "the Syrian women . . . will allow themselves to be daily abducted by Bedouins and daily rescued by their dusky friends."[47] In plenty of these situations, Syrian Christians seem to have been able to distinguish themselves from the Bedouins, Turks, and other Muslims from the Empire, exposing the complexity of Ottoman subjecthood. The Empire collected together many ethnic, religious, and linguistic groups, the diversity of which American audiences probably could not take in all at once but were exotically comprehensible as "Oriental splendor" or "Bedouin Life in the Desert."

Official delegation attempts at presenting the Ottoman elite as civilized imperial leaders of the Islamic world were quickly being muddled by a multitude of Ottoman subjects and other Easterners at the exposition and around the city

"Official" and for-profit ventures from North Africa and West Asia often looked alike to visitors at the Columbian Exposition. Here a mosque advertises a carpet shop. Photograph by Copelin, iCHi-20531, Chicago History Museum.

who explicitly claimed to speak either for Islam or the Empire, although many could see they were independent operators. Milhem Ouardy's Moorish Palace, the wild west and "Wild East" shows, and cover-charge mosques in and around the fair were precisely the kinds of commercialized presentations of Orientana the Ottoman delegates hoped to avoid. Concerned Ottoman officials were fighting a losing battle for control of their imperial personae as commercial imperatives took precedence over strictly nationalist ethnological performance, even in

official displays. For even the mosque at the Turkish Village—constructed under direction of the Ottoman commissioners themselves—blurred the line between culture, spirituality, and business. Some industrious person had inscribed it with advertising for a nearby shop. "GREAT FREE SHOW COME and
SEE How The NATIVES of TURKEY Make Their CARPETS This Way," the sig-
nage invited.[48] How were visitors unfamiliar with North African or Middle
Eastern life to have known if it was the Moorish Palace, the pay-for-a-peek
mosque run by Syrian Christians, or the Turkish Village Mosque that was the
for-profit show or if any of the Easterners they found at the fair were not
manipulating his or her own persona for personal gain?

SHRINERS AT THE FAIR: RETURN OF THE ARAB TRICKSTER

There were many opinions on what made cultural difference pay at the fair,
some visitors disliking the Midway altogether, some visitors seeking out idealized Oriental merchants or Arab horsemen there. Others wished for something
more incredible, even slightly incomprehensible or weird. Sol Bloom, impresario and commissioner for the Algerian Village at the exposition, had had a
revelation about how this could be. He had already gone to the Expositions
Universelles in Paris in 1889. After dutifully going to the various industrial
exhibits and racist anthropological displays, he concluded: "I found that a kind
of natural selection (though not precisely the theory enunciated by Darwin) was
governing my movements. I came to realize that a tall, skinny chap from Arabia
with a talent for swallowing swords expressed a culture which to me was on a
higher plane than the one demonstrated by a group of earnest Swiss peasants
who passed their days making cheese and milk chocolate. I acknowledged to
myself that the spiritual intensity of the performance presented by a troupe of
Bedouin acrobats exceeded the emotional power of a pre-Renaissance tapes-
try."[49] Even those who spent longer periods at the fair and rejected the common
and elite racism of the period noted that many of the Easterners they met were
intriguing because they were mysterious or even seemed strange.

Take Heber De Long, for instance. A government photographer, he worked
as a clerk for the Department of Construction at the Columbian exposition from
July 1892 to November 1893, assembling a personal scrapbook of his time at the
fair. To be sure, De Long replicated in his scrapbook the organization found in
the exposition grounds and the many official and unofficial commemorative
books and directories published at the time. In the first pages, De Long cata-

loged with pictures and postcards the American industrial and scientific displays, after which he affixed souvenirs and items from the many individual American state pavilions, followed by a similar ranking of the European nations' exhibits, followed by those of foreign governments from Asia.

Although he seems to have accepted the hierarchy of "civilized" nations suggested in the fair's layout and Gilded Age racial theory, De Long nonetheless went out of his way to develop friendships with dignitaries and workers from many Asian countries that speak of an emotional identification with them. The final pages of his scrapbook contain autographs and the business cards of Mirza L. S. Kender Khan, a Persian Commissioner, who signed his name in both English and Persian. After the death of a construction worker at on the site, De Long created a memorial page of pressed flowers, labeled "In Memory . . . from the flower-boy of Cairo Street. The White one from Joseph of Persia." De Long also asked the cast of "Oriental Wedding in Damascus, Peir Antonius Managers" and some of the Egyptian donkey drivers to give their Arabic signatures for his autograph collection, about which De Long editorialized "Queer, but they go."[50] Though he empathized with these people, he still found them strangely unreadable on some level, pointing to the difficulty of completely overcoming cultural difference and language barriers.

In fact, this unreadability was crucial to the viability of the fair and would inspire the practice of playing Eastern by native-born performers more broadly who could add novel Eastern characteristics to themselves to invite similar confusion and inquiry by observers. Members of the fraternal order known as the Ancient Arabic Order, Nobles of the Mystic Shrine were only one of the many groups of artists, writers, architects, and other creative people greatly inspired by the sensation of unreadability that could come from person-to-person contact with foreign people.[51] Shriners serve as a particularly prominent and numerous group in this story because they openly embraced the entrepreneurial ability of the Eastern performers and traders there, though in a self-interested way to be sure. Chicago Shriners would collaborate closely with Easterner traders and agents at the fair to develop bizarre performance styles that combined the guise of the comedic Arab trickster with the richest American Orientana. Shriners turned the comprehensibly exotic personae they found at the fair around to dress the familiar, namely, their Anglo-American middle-class and upper-class selves, in personae of mysteriously and bizarrely Eastern exotic. The Eastern personae the Shriners derived from the Exposition also came stamped with the apparent approval of Ottoman subjects themselves, which only added to the sense of strangeness that would be the order's public trademark.

Of all the extraordinary things that happened at the 1893 Columbian Exposition in Chicago, perhaps the most bizarre in this respect took place on April 28, just before the public grand opening. A number of Ottoman subjects with commissions at the fair had decided to dedicate the new mosque in the Turkish Village and had invited all the Muslim participants at the fair to attend the ceremony. On the appointed day, representatives of the Sultan obligingly appeared in formal dress to watch an eclectic, international parade bearing Ottoman and American flags march through the Midway to the mosque.

Somehow local Shriners had managed to insinuate themselves into the affair. While Bedouin, Persian, Turkish, and Sudanese Muslims dressed in their national costumes walked or proceeded on horseback and camel, the Shriners, all wearing rain coats (it was pouring that day) and fezzes, rode in sedan chairs or trailed along with the parade apparently making light of the situation by their presence. The *Chicago Tribune* reported that bystanders began saying "sarcastic things to the bedraggled Turks," who attempted to ignore the heckling and carry on to the mosque.[52] The *New York Times* gave its own perplexing account of the scene: "a strange mixture of Mohammedans and Americans. This motley procession moved west through the lines of wondering Javanese, Chinese, Swiss, Germans and Austrians until it reached the mosque, when Hadji Selim, who officiated as Muezzin, appeared on the portico of the minaret and welcomed the guests in the name of Allah. Then with the slow tread the faithful entered the sacred precincts of the edifice, where, behind closed doors were performed rites unknown to any save themselves." Though some papers intimated that the Shriners had been excluded from the mosque, the whole group of Shriners had "pushed in with their muddy feet and no one was there to enforce the invariable rule of taking off shoes at the doors."[53] Many of the Muslims in attendance must have been irritated and would soon be raw from accusations of profit-minded fakery that would emanate from ventures like the Nestorian faux mosque outside the gates and the Cairo Street mosque down the Midway. With respect to the Turkish Village mosque and its carpet shop advertising, the press had already been questioning "the genuineness of this Mohammedan house of worship in that paradise of fakirs and side shows, [the] Midway Plaisance," so the presence of Shriners in a building supposedly forbidden to Christians, as many Americans falsely believed, spoke of tastelessness, not godliness.[54]

People of all nations watching the affair shared at least two questions that day about whom the Shriners were and what precisely was going on at the Turkish village. Of course, the Shriners were not Muslims but Masons who had become eligible for membership in the Ancient Arabic Order, Nobles of the Mystic Shrine. The Anglo-American businessmen, civil servants, and professionals who stocked the Mystic Shrine labored long and hard to make their fortunes on the expanding resource use, commerce, and Western-directed growth transforming the country. The experience produced many men who still saw economic growth as a kind of Aladdin's lamp story and would use the ornate Orientana of the Mystic Shrine as a creative outlet, playing Eastern as "Nobles" and "Potentates" in order to represent their aspirations and success as an over-the-top Oriental tale. Their participation in the mosque dedication had been possible because first and foremost these men were publicity minded businessmen who sought out likeminded fellows among the Easterners at the fair. Effendi Robert Levy was the Istanbul entrepreneur whose Souhami Saadullah & Co. constructed and ran many of the official Ottoman exhibits. In the interest of good relations with the Chicago business community, he had invited the men from Chicago Shriner's Medinah Temple down to the event after they had recently initiated him as a Shriner. Medinah was fast becoming the largest and wealthiest Shriner temple in the nation because the city was a hub for upwardly mobile professionals and entrepreneurs poised to take advantage of the nation's capitalist expansion to the west and south.[55]

Thereafter, in the Turkish Bazaar next door, the whole group attended a banquet seemingly sponsored by the Ottoman delegation. Robert Levy made a great ceremony of giving to the Potentate (president) of Medinah Temple a large and elaborately decorated scimitar imported from Syria. The *Chicago Tribune* cynically added, "While all this was going on the Turks in the selling booths were engaged in disposing of their trophies of the Holy Land to the red fezed visitors at regular prices," referring to the trade in spurious religious relics and touristy souvenirs there.[56] Chicago's Sarkis H. Nahagian had for some time also provided Medinah Nobles with oriental rugs, lamps, and other imported objects for Shriner pageants.[57] So, too, was the Columbian Exposition an internationalized opportunity for consumption and individuation, and the shops and people there would supply the Shriners with inspiration and objects for later use in playing Eastern.

That observers found the Shriners' appearance at the mosque dedication strange is a substantial understatement. Cyrus Adler was among them. A Johns

Hopkins University Professor, traveler and entrepreneur, Adler had been hired by exposition organizers to travel to Egypt to locate talent to perform on the Midway. In spite of his worldliness, after the Shriner day procession he wondered, "It was a little difficult to understand why shy plain citizens of the United States, most of them presumably belonging to the Protestant Church, should wear baggy Turkish trousers, put a fez on their heads, the symbol of the crescent, and use the terms and passwords which are sacred to Islam."[58] This was exactly the Shriners' point. What the bystanders were witnessing was a textbook example of the Shriner performance arts of the mysteriously exotic Easterner. The creative nature of consumption allowed Shriners to take on not only a day-to-day persona represented by a respectable suit and white-collared shirt, but the possibility of temporary hybrid identities of Arab trickster and neighborhood business owner, for example. The fact that they were only barely disguised while playing Eastern and that people could see the Shriners wearing two identities at once made their performances bizarre. That unreadability conveyed a sense of mysterious power that bolstered the privileged position the Shriners would hold as affluent, politically and socially exclusive Anglo-Americans. Shriners allowed these performance traditions only to 32nd and 33rd degree Masons, who became the preeminent purveyors of a highly valuable amateur Orientana in the United States well into the twentieth century.

Shriners would help thousands of American men put what they knew of the East to work in their own creative lives to demonstrate their social position by mystifying themselves. Mystic Shrine costumes, parade performances, literary and artistic cultures, as well as their secret initiation rituals paralleled older traditions of Mardi Gras–style mumming in colorful costumes representing archetypes of incomprehensibility and the surreal, like the grim reaper, for instance, and burlesquing Oriental tales that sought gently to critique American life by way of characters who took on Eastern voice.[59] As a sort of Oriental camp, Shriner personae both celebrated and lampooned a perceived mysterious Arabia, birthplace of Islam, and a supposedly mischievous primitive manhood enacted by "free sons of the desert"-style Bedouins who roasted temperate Masonry and the powerful or overly serious.[60]

On "Shriner Day" at the fair, Adler also claimed, the Ottoman officials had watched the proceedings seemingly believing the Shriners to be actual American Muslims. He explained, "One of the Commissioners wrote a lengthy report direct to His Majesty, the Sultan of Turkey, gave a detailed description of the festivities and ended by congratulating His Majesty upon the great advances that Mohammedanism was making in the United States. He permitted me to read the report before it was sent and, not wishing to disillusion anybody, I let it go."[61] Considering that the Ottoman administration in Istanbul was usually hyperaware of any disingenuous or ridiculing treatment the Empire got overseas, it seems likely that the Ottoman delegation wished to avoid trouble by telling the Sultan's office what they would want to hear. In all probability, once left to their own devices in the United States, Robert Levy and the other Middle Eastern businessmen at the fair (many of whom were Christian or Jewish in any case) declined the burden of representing the whole of the Muslim Ottoman Empire. Instead, like Lekegian the Midway photographer, they marketed their ventures with romantic endorsements that told Americans that the Ottoman Commissioners appointed by Sultan Abdülhamid II had "kept a watchful eye on the whole [Ottoman] area" including the government building, bazaar, and mosque to ensure it went up "in excellent taste."[62]

Newspapers across the country reported on "Shriner Day" within regular daily columns chronicling the Columbian Exposition. This journalistic attention was a coded message to businessmen and professionals around the nation whose initiation fees and dues sustained the increasingly lavish spending and artistic activities of the Mystic Shrine fraternity.[63] The Shriners' endorsement of the Turkish Village, thereafter one of the most popular and profitable areas of the exposition, was further an invitation to fellow Shriners and their families to attend the fair and patronize the Turkish village, including Saadullah & Co. attractions there. Tie-ins to Shriner businesses soon followed in the local papers, one for a local soap manufacturer depicting Effendi Robert Levy leading the prayer in the Turkish Village mosque.[64] There in an amateur rendering of the mosque was the Shriner symbol of scimitar and crescent, the Turkish village mosque itself now masquerading as a Shriner fraternal temple.

Shriner Day was an apparent success among many promotional stunts the order would orchestrate, and by 1893 there were over sixty temples in the United States and Canada with a combined membership of 25,000.[65] Soon the number of men undergoing a single session of the burlesquing initiation ritual could be in the hundreds, and at especially big inductions Nobles held their initiations not in borrowed space at the local Masonic lodge but in large facilities including arenas. For example, in Sioux City, Iowa in 1893, 300 Shriners watched 100 men initiated, and in Chattanooga, Tennessee in 1914 an audience of 500 Nobles watched forty-seven candidates hazed at once.[66] Although the chance to inflict the initiation ritual on novices was a key draw for members

Ottoman subject Robert Levy in a cryptic newspaper advertisement commemorating Shriner Day at the Columbian Exposition, as well as the Shriners' penchant for combining commerce and public weirdness. In all probability, Kirk's Soap Company was owned by a Chicago Shriner. *Chicago Tribune*, 1893.

burdened with paying their pricey dues, the public performance traditions cultivated by Mystic Shrine members were even more important for recruitment. The order continued to attract men with creative leanings among the nation's professionals, business owners, and government officials like mayors and judges as well as some members of the entertainment community. In this fashion had the Shriners radiated out west and south from New York City where plenty of Masons relished the opportunity to engage in performances that grew increasingly strange with each year.

The case of Shriner Day at the Columbian Exposition showed how Shriners were taking the initiative to develop commonly shared personae and performances inherited from the original temples in New York into locally relevant forms in each new city and town. Noble James McGee of New York's Mecca Temple explained the other common component in these forms that aided the performers' ability to get a reaction from pleased onlookers. After an 1884 pilgrimage (fraternal voyage) to the new Medinah Temple in Chicago, he remembered, "At every station the platform was filled with spectators, who quaintly inquired who these fez-bedecked Arabs were. By some they were styled the Mystic Shrine Opera Company and the Mystic Shrine Baseball Club. At Valparaiso, some distance this side of Chicago, the party was increased by some twenty of Medinah Temple's Nobles, . . . With them were a dozen dusky darkies, arrayed in Arab costumes, supplied with liquid delight, which they gave to the weary and thirsty pilgrims."[67] Many Shriners found the chance to step outside their normal identities irresistible, some hoping to be gawked at much as visitors at the Columbian Exposition had done with the Easterners on the Midway. The "darkies" in McGee's story were probably Shriners in blackface supplying champagne or wine since Shriners adopted many show business standards, including minstrelsy, in their performances. Mystic Shrine performers often appeared drunk and unruly in public to lampoon frowning onlookers and point out social conventions by breaking them.

Two years later, a Shriner in Chicago had added greatly to the order's repertoire when he founded the "Arab Patrol," a drill corps tradition adopted across the order. The Arab patrols referenced the American military patrols that flourished after the Civil War in the parades and public ceremonies of all sorts of men's societies.[68] For instance, the famed Zouave troops, made famous during the Civil War and hundreds of wild west and circus shows paraded in Eastern style costume derived from French North African habits.[69] Medinah Temple members had built the Arab Patrol by first visiting local costumers, from whom they ordered "short jackets, bloomers, red shoes, fez and sashes." Fashioning scimitars from disused cutlasses, they premiered the Arab patrol unannounced at a St. Louis convention to the flabbergasted delight of passersby and fellow Nobles.[70] Thereafter a Mystic Shrine institution and favorite of parade crowds, the Arab Patrol clubs marched with serious faces and precision that contrasted with the joking of Shriners costumed as stout sultans or Bedouin bandits performing satirical *salat*, waving scimitars, and speaking mock Arabic. The notoriety that came from that first surreal parade of Chicago's Arab Patrol and the secrecy of its creation, as with so many mumming and Mardi Gras parades in the late nineteenth-century, created a lore that inspired every temple to innovate Shriner performances to their own needs.

Seven years later, in 1893, these same Chicago Shriners now had actual Arabs, Persians, and Turks at the Columbian Exposition from which to seek inspiration and their shops from which to acquire clothing and objects. Taking away an experience from the exposition that most participants and foreign commissioners could not have predicted, Medinah Shriners spoke of being particularly enchanted by the strangeness and incomprehensibility of the Eastern cultures they saw there. Earlier in the century, Americans had complained about Middle Eastern music while abroad, calling it discordant and without direction, "seem[ing] to us to be rhythmical noise, tone without harmony," Albert Rawson had said of Westerners unfamiliar with Eastern musical traditions.[71] "A grievous infliction upon the listener" and "ear-piercing and ear-stunning noise . . . intolerable to us," other travelers said of Eastern music. At the exposition too, people said Eastern music seemed "mournful, weird, plaintive and funereal by turns."[72] In Chicago Shriners were similarly struck by what one remembered as "weird music" played by "a Turk with a musette and another with a tom-tom as part of the ballyhoo in front of shows that lined the Midway."[73] In response to perplexed American listeners, those Eastern musicians insisted that their music was faithful to their homeland's traditions and entirely authentic.[74]

This was exactly the effect Shriners hoped to have on their audiences, to aggravate them with a sense of the incomprehensible, then, with feigned seriousness typical of Shriners, insist that their bizarre behavior was authentically Middle Eastern and not to be questioned. Consequently, Turkish musicians along with those who paraded daily on Cairo Street and near the Algerian Theatre inspired what Shriners hoped would be a "distinctly Arabic" Shriner genre of Middle Eastern music. A group of Medinah Shriners went shopping, acquiring some inexpensive horns, some Chinese "tom-toms," and a gong to fill out their "Oriental Band" since with no grounding in Chinese cultural heritage, many Anglo-Americans visitors also perceived East Asian musicians at the fair as notable for their "strangeness rather than their excellence."[75] Shriners incorporated this pastiche of inspiration into the first of a whole tradition of costumed musical troops called Shrine Oriental Bands. These ensembles began sprouting up around the Imperial Potentate's (Mystic Shrine's president) realms quickly and might feature prominent businessmen or politicians mumming as Nobles with "toy instruments [who] made 'music,'" as one Shriner teased with ironic quotation marks.[76] Larger groups played both marching band standards and a Shriner brand of wailing music, especially a tune they called "The Midway" that had been performed at the Columbian Exposition.[77]

In the minds of parade audiences and fellow Nobles, Mystic Shrine performances attempted to replicate that sensation of compelling unreadability Shriners themselves had experienced in 1893. It competed with the broader commercial context of Arab masculinity found in circuses and wild west shows as well as in advertising and other outlets for the consumer's Oriental tale and the Arab trickster.[78] For instance, after a dozen years of development and practice, Medinah Temple put on a huge convention in 1907 at which they paraded 1,142 initiates through the streets of the city dressed in fezzes and exotic costumes. Before being "[h]erded together in Medinah temple with full warning of the terrors they were to experience," the group was bound with ropes to elephants borrowed from a local circus and marched through downtown to the Coliseum, which was gotten up like a three-ring circus where 10,000 Shriners would watch their initiation. The parade also included the Shriners' Imperial Potentate riding a camel, Shriners performing as "wailing dervishes," an Arab Patrol, and Shrine Oriental bands. A number of floats depicting "Hot Sand" and a "Tar and Feather Factory" teased novices and unsympathetic locals with references to the imminent humiliation of Shriner initiates.[79]

Mystic Shrine performers did their bit live in parades knowing their acts would be recorded and broadcast out into the nation by way a whole genre of Shriner-authored poetry and artwork known as "Advice to the Novice." It emerged in Shriner publications and local newspapers, offering mysterious jokes and fantastic drawings of men being pierced with arrows or dipped in boiling oil. The usually sympathetic press was staffed by men who ran in the same social circles as Shriners or were Shriners, and both saw Mystic Shrine conventions and parades as boosting civic events that filled hotels and restaurants. Accordingly, Medinah's publicity committee had issued strange communications to the local newspapers that attempted to authenticate their shows of unreason and misrule by, for instance, claiming that the initiatory sand on the "Hot Sand" float had been imported all the way from the Sahara.[80] Even Effendi Robert Levy, former Ottoman Commissioner to the Columbian Exposition, helped add mysteriously exotic performances to the convention when he bestowed two gilt-embroidered tapestries depicting camels, Arabic script, and Shriner symbols to the Medinah Temple Shriners. Pictured the next day in the papers with little explanation, the donation only lent the Shriners a seeming legitimate but nonetheless bizarre endorsement in a period when Shriners were themselves debating whether to continue claiming origins in the Middle East.[81]

Chicago's Medinah Temple was the central example in the expansion of the Mystic Shrine's "Imperial" domains. Events like the huge 1907 "Imperial Session," as Shriners called their convention in Eastern voice, in the city publicized the wealth and influence of the order to men who would later rush through Masonic initiations to get to the 32nd degree and eligibility for an invitation to join. The 1907 event garnered Chicago's Medinah Temple over 1,000 new members and $54,350 in initiation fees, making Medinah the wealthiest and largest temple of the order. Five years later Medinah Nobles opened a new Moorish-style club house and theater constructed for $650,000.[82] By World War I, total male membership in the order was around 260,000 in 144 branch temples with a women's auxiliary on the rise as well, while Medinah Temple in Chicago still stood as the largest temple with over 12,000 Nobles.[83]

The bulging rolls and growing bank accounts of Medinah Temple were only one symptom of the fraternity's growth. Men across the nation would make the order the superlative fraternity in the nation by reputation and affluence. They did so as Chicago Shriners had to promote their own local economy and business networks by adapting the order's arts to their own local cultures. Thus did they add improvised content and touristic clichés to Mystic Shrine standards so that they were exotic to other members yet clearly Shrineresque in their communication of that basic incomprehensibility that made the order's performances distinctive. In a typical example, Nobles at Moslah Temple in Fort Worth, Texas became famous for parades of bound initiates, Nobles dressed as rioting Arab-styled cowboys on horseback, and goats carried in baby carriages, adding aspects of local livestock industry to Shriner Orientana. They also used the standard press notices, planted interviews, and hype before intertemple

Regional Mystic Shrine Orientana created strange juxtapositions; here patriotic Arab Patrolmen march in a 1915 Spokane, Washington, parade with Shriner cowboys and Indians from "Algeria Temple" in Montana. Montana Historical Society.

visits and "Ceremonial Sessions" (banquets and parties) to alert the community that local Shriners were up to trouble again. At one 1914 parade, Moslah Nobles sent a blindfolded novice into city traffic until the "automobiles and streetcars bump[ed] him blue," after which men in khaki uniforms pretended to shoot him with pistols, to the shock of the initiate and onlookers. Texas Shriners also drove these Novices around town for several hours, bound, costumed, and helpless in the heat of the day, to humiliate them further.[84]

One Noble encapsulated the effect he believed the Shriners' bizarre self-presentations had on audiences: "They say these men act awful, like Turks and A-rabs do,—that they wear knives and turbans, and carry pistols too. They say their feet are blistered from walking through the sand,—that riding on their camels has made them want to stand and how common the people that chance to come their way,—that Shriners get amusement from cutting up this way. . . . don't be startled, neighbour, when on the streets you see the queer, tricolored bunting [of the Mystic Shrine]. . . . Don't worry 'bout the crescents that hang about the town. . . . [Shriners] are rather kind and gentle, excepting when they're riled, and then they're apt to carve you, and eat you when you're b'iled."[85] There does not appear to be any evidence the actors who played Arab or Bedouin in the circuses or wild west shows, for example, explicitly played the villain in this way by threatening the show crowds, and it was audience interpretation that turned the Bedouin horseman into "Arab trickster." Thus had Shriners used their imaginings of the desert Arab and powerful potentate in combination with Sons of Malta traditions of roasting vigilantism to define Shriner street theater. A problematic by-product of all this was that as depicted by Shriners, the Eastern world hardly seemed approachable to many observers.

Shriners across the Imperial Potentate's domains would spend several generations taking their subculture across the continent and out into Latin America, Canada, and the Pacific by way of compelling and instantly recognizable Mystic Shrine Orientana. Their lavishly creative subculture and self-promotion made them the most ubiquitous and best funded of all performers of Eastern personae on the continent. The order provided a modern social context for men, and often their wives, to use Eastern personae in their own work of consumption and individuation, much of it put on display for the public where Shiner arts stood as an aesthetic of success and civic confidence.

SHRINERS IN COURT: THE
RACIAL POLITICS OF PLAYING EASTERN

Mystic Shrine performances, regalia, and subculture were highly valuable promotional tools Nobles guarded fiercely because they were original arrangements and creations of the members, often derived from Chicago Shriners' personal contact with actual Muslims or Ottoman subjects. Especially as similarly styled orders began emerging around the country in the 1890s, Shriners remained aware that anyone could emulate their "Moslem" personae and theatrical practices. The Dramatic Order of Knights of Khorassan, the Mystic Order of Veiled Prophets of the Enchanted Realm, the Ancient Order of Knights of the Orient, the Knights of the Ancient Essenic Order, the Mystic Order Veiled Prophets of the Enchanted Realm—there seemed to be no end to them—imitative Oriental-themed orders that challenged but would never top the Mystic Shrine's resources, publicity machine, or the elite nature of its membership.[86]

Again, the Columbian Exposition provided a central moment in the story of one of the first of these many bold replications of the Mystic Shrine. Much to the indignation of Chicago Shriners, an order called the Ancient Egyptian Arabic Order, Nobles of the Mystic Shrine appeared after African American Masons had visited the exposition during a convention of Prince Hall Masonry in Chicago that August. At the fair they purchased fezzes and other costumes. One of them, Jonathan G. Jones, subsequently said that he had been initiated by a trio of men on the Midway consisting of a Syrian, a Palestinian, and an Algerian, including a man named Roefelt Pasha.[87] As Albert Rawson and Billy Florence had claimed in the 1870s, Jones said that these men were Eastern representatives of the Mystic Shrine order in Cairo. To a black audience this language had special currency since African American popular and intellectual culture was infused with the belief that the ancient Egyptians had been black. Various theories placing American blacks' ancestors and ancient Freemasons in the ancient Holy Land, Egypt, or Ethiopia provided a noble heritage divorced from stereotyped images of the African savage.[88] Black Shriners would both claim a special link to the Middle East and play Oriental to mock it, using a half-serious burlesquing strategy typical of the era's Eastern orders.

The men at Medinah Temple were incensed by African American assertions of membership in any form of the Mystic Shrine, and a committee of three ventured out to the fairgrounds to interrogate Easterners there as to the veracity of the story. Nobles Wood, LeBough, and Thompson marched straight to the Turkish Village where they interviewed a prominent Ottoman merchant who controlled twenty of the concessions on the Midway. He assured them, the Nobles insisted, that the three Middle Eastern men Jones named were certainly not working at the fair. Next they questioned Effendi Robert Levy on Cairo Street. He surmised that any black American who claimed secret initiation at the fair had been bamboozled by scoundrels who appeared to the credulous to be wise men of the East: "The fakirs and donkey boys in the streets of Cairo, . . . for liberal 'backsheesh' will confer a degree which they call 'The Donkey Degree.' . . . This is had by payment of ten cents, when the candidate is given a slap on the back, three kicks in the posterior region, and is then hailed in Turkish as 'Brother Jackass,'" he supposedly told them.[89]

To accuse an African American of having been fooled by such a Midway trick and thusly persuaded to go about proudly presenting himself as an initiate of a prestigious Middle Eastern fraternity was a cliché practically pulled from an antebellum Zip Coon skit. Grounded in Anglo-American attitudes that cast blacks as pompous fools easily impressed by glittering but worthless things, it also spoke of the Sons of Malta's and the Shriners' early history as humiliators of credulous and self-important people. It is difficult to know from the original Mystic Shrine report of the investigation whether this is what Levy actually said or whether this was just what Shriners chose to tell one another to keep the affair lighthearted. Either way, it was true that many fraternalists believed two things: fraternal orders were rife with fraud by men who invented secret orders then accepted fees to initiate sincere initiates only to disappear soon after with the money, and many believed African American men were particularly susceptible to such fraud.[90]

The Medinah Temple dismissal of the Egyptian Shriners would be only one of a lengthy list of grievances blacks accumulated that summer after they had been summarily excluded from participation in the exposition, allowed by organizers only to hold a patronizing "Jubilee Day."[91] Even the Africans at the Dahomey Village had been able to communicate with visitors when they staffed a display (as problematic as it was since it portrayed them as the least civilized of all races at the fair) of their own arts and housing. Additionally, Arabs, Persians, and Turks at the fair got a modicum of respect due to their perceived role, and their self-presentation, as exotic visitors and merchants as well as inheritors of the arts of the ancient Middle East and the Islamic Empire. They thus existed in a perceived class above Africans, African Americans, and the Aborigines of Australia, who might find themselves described in the newspapers as "The Lowest Types of the Human Race."[92]

Conflict between the black and white Shrine orders was also a reflection of broader white failure to apply egalitarian American ideals to blacks in every aspect of social, economic, and political life.[93] Like many white institutions, white American Masons cast aside their own secret Masonic philosophies of universal brotherhood, which enjoined the initiate to defy such vulgar prejudice and to see the mystical truth in all faiths and the unity of all men, because they denied blacks initiation in their lodges.[94] Even though blacks had never been asked to join mainstream white fraternities, blacks founded their own parallel lodges of Odd Fellows, Elks, Knights of Pythias, and Freemasons, producing organizations that were as contentious among notoriously litigious Masons as the Egyptian order of Shriners would become. Of course, whites did this kind of thing all the time too. Both black and white fraternalists often used the term "unrecognized," "irregular," or "clandestine" to refer to any fraternal lodge that had not been founded with the express permission of the ruling body of a given order in a given state.[95]

As Masons attempted to limit economic competition between orders and disband rival lodges set up by renegade former members or members of another race, these fraternal turf wars were often resolved only in court. Some fraternalists went so far as to refer to the actions of competitors who founded similar lodges with terms like "theft" and "embezzlement." Much of the time there were indeed large amounts of money at stake because a successful fraternal formula was worth its weight in gold.[96] The booming rolls and swollen bank accounts of the Mystic Shrine fraternity were the greatest proof of this rule. Although individual members did not profit personally as they served in volunteer positions in administering the fraternity, the parties, ceremonies, parades, and travel opportunities of the order would pay members well for their participation and dues. All this was particularly galling to African Americans who found their fraternities subject to white accusations of being opportunistic, inauthentic copies of white orders when, as everyone really knew, all fraternal orders had shady origins either borrowed from European orders or entirely invented in the United States.[97]

Defying threats of retribution from white Shriners, Egyptian Order Shriners pressed on after the Medinah investigation, capitalizing on the entertainment value and satirical power of Shriner performance styles in their own promotion of black respectability and civic leadership. Subsequently, Egyptian Mystic Shrine temples began appearing around the nation, providing African American neighborhoods with parades in which Egyptian Shriners played Eastern as Arab tricksters. One typically droll parade in Boston included a participant calling himself "Sahara Lizzie" who "resplendent in yellow, purple, blue and orange with weird sleeve decoration . . . performed a wild dance along the route to the music of his own tambourine."[98] The local black press approvingly reported on another parade in that city, "The gaiety of 10,000 Desert Sons in 'whoopee' colors and a bedlam of noise will give the annual session of their order a real Oriental aspect . . . The Shrine Jesters . . . will sing and rejoice and give praise to 'Allah.'"[99] As with the white Shriners, for African American Shriners to be authentically "Oriental" was to be richly dressed, unruly, comic, and weird.

Surely Egyptian Shriner parades did mock the Muslim world with their caricatures of the Islamic and Arab cultures, and in this, black and white Americans were equally complicit. For instance, during World War I, when thousands of blacks joined or sympathized with Marcus Garvey's United Negro Improvement Association, Egyptian Shrine performers swaggering around in

Egyptian Order Shriners still going strong in a 1953 Denver parade, during the African American order's sixtieth year. Clarence F. Holmes Collection, Western History/Genealogy Department, Denver Public Library.

colorful outfits proclaiming themselves "Imperial Potentate" might have had an extra sting. Though he used no mock Arabs in his parades, Marcus Garvey proclaimed and dressed himself quite seriously as the "Provisional President" of Africa, complete with pseudoroyal garb. Garvey's detractors in the black business or scholarly communities perceived his romanticized African identity and colorful parades as a function of his ego. They ridiculed him accordingly as a "clown strutting around in gaudy uniforms . . . who led big parades of ignorant people down the street selling pie in the sky."[100] Grounded in old burlesquing traditions like Pinkster, Election Day, and the dark humor African Americans had developed over the centuries, black Shriner parades could also serve as a satirical poke at the absurdities of white supremacy or a cynical comment on the seriousness of black leaders.[101] Nonetheless, the black press, political bosses, and community leaders generally tolerated black Shriner performances as statements of black fraternal respectability and cultural independence from whites.

The lengths to which the first Mystic Shrine order, the nation's preeminent amateur society for the public performance of Eastern personae, went in attempting to stamp out the black order of Shriners shows what they believed was at stake. White Shriners repeatedly sued the Egyptian order, accusing them of unauthorized use of white Mystic Shrine symbols and practices.[102] For instance, in 1918 Egyptian Order Shriners lost an appeal against an injunction white Shriners had obtained in the Georgia State Supreme Court barring nonmembers from wearing fezzes, costuming, or any similar regalia in public. White Shriners had only obtained the injunction after the case had moved to a lower court in a jurisdiction outside Atlanta after it came to light that every single member of the Georgia State Supreme Court was either a Shriner or the close friend of a Shriner. In this case, Egyptian Shriners claimed to have formed their Temple in Washington, D.C., independently of the white Shriners with an Eastern initiation claim similar to the one they had used in Chicago. White Shriners countered that members of the Egyptian order were merely imitating what they had witnessed at a large white Shriner convention in Atlanta in 1914. This was exactly the manner by which Shriner performance traditions like the Arab Patrols and Oriental Bands moved from temple to temple among whites as members observed and adapted one another's creations.[103] During the heat of the legal battles, the actual racial nature of the rivalry became obvious when Egyptian Shriners won a later appeal. The national Shriner magazine The Crescent sniped, "Well, the coons win. The injunction prayed for in Atlanta, prohibiting Negroes from forming or operating as Shriners, has been dismissed after having been in the courts for a year or more. If we can't win out in Georgia there isn't much show anywhere else."[104]

The culture of segregation and racial social separation was so entrenched in the United States that there was little chance outsiders would mistake black Nobles as members of the white order or provoke "public thought that the wearers are [white order] Shriners—and their acts charged against us," as white Shriners seem to have worried.[105] One white Noble groused some years later, nonetheless, "The woods are full of organizations whose greatest claim to distinction is that they have copied some successful organization and built along the same general line—as far as many outsiders can see."[106] African Americans and other observers critical of the Mystic Shrine must have shaken their heads in disbelief when they considered these claims. White Shriners actually asserted that blacks were attempting to pass as members of the white Mystic Shrine by imitating white Nobles' impersonations of Easterners. Yet white Shriners had themselves made use of extractions of Eastern cultures hoping to be mistaken for Muslims at the Turkish Village mosque dedication in 1893 and in hundreds of parades and public appearances since then. This was after all the essence of Shriner satire, a tongue-in-cheek hybrid identity performance art in which one could be a wise man of the east, an Arab trickster, an Oriental potentate, and a successful American man all at the same time.

African Americans would nonetheless be vindicated that year. A Houston parade by black Shriners, who were previously unknown to whites in that state, prompted white Shriners to initiate another suit. The case was finally settled in United States Supreme Court in 1929 in favor of the black order. The ruling said nothing of Nobles' possible intent to ridicule Islam or Masonry but was quick to discount the claims of ancient authenticity each side used to argue for the validity of their respective fraternal orders. The court did not agree with black Shriners' claim to be the original founders of the Mystic Shrine mystery school in ancient Egypt, an argument premised on the African origins of their slavery-era ancestors. However, the court did argue that since blacks called their fraternity the Ancient Egyptian Arabic Order of Nobles of the Mystic Shrine they were not actually presenting themselves as agents of the white order.[107]

Readers of the prominent black paper the Chicago Defender found the entire transcript of the final U.S. Supreme Court judgment reprinted there. The victory must have been a matter of great pride to many blacks who saw the court's decision as proof that the judicial system might win them status as equal consumer citizens of the country, if only in small steps. The Imperial Potentate of the Egyptian Shriners, Caesar R. Blake of North Carolina, issued a "Proclamation" praising United States Supreme Court Justice Van Devanter for the verdict. "This is not only a distinct victory for our Order but for our race. Under the decree of the State of Texas, no Negro could even wear a suit of clothes to which a white man objected if he had a suit of clothes similar to his own." Blake believed the ruling was a triumph for every black institution with a white counterpart, especially the churches.[108] For African Americans, historically a consumer base with limited means, especially in rural areas of the country, consumerism on a modern scale enjoyed by whites was a recent development of the Great Migration into northern cities. For them equality meant votes, jobs, and access to the judicial system but would increasingly that century also include freedom to individuate oneself as a consumer and to be served as such equally with whites and others, something denied to blacks under Jim Crow segregation.[109]

In true Shriner tradition, Noble Blake issued his proclamation in Oriental voice, commanding members and their families to celebrate: "Every Temple under the obedience of our Imperial Council shall repair to some church at an hour convenient to the Temple and have a sermon preached and offer thanks to Allah for delivering us."[110] Thereafter, black Shriners in a number of cities held rambunctious parades in which they publicly gave "thanks to 'Allah' for delivering them from their oppressors."[111] The 1929 Texas Shriner case would portend increasingly for black religious freedom as well. By then some African Americans did wish to be perceived as actual Muslims by faith. Members of the Moorish Science Temple and later the Nation of Islam would use fezzes and other clothing some people confused with Shriner-style regalia to publicize a new African American Muslim identity and its respectability (see chapter 8). Here blacks and whites fought over the issues of cultural autonomy and the proposed equality blacks might gain as consumers and producers of highly valued Eastern personae that spoke of affluent manhood, social respectability, and equal citizenship in a nation increasingly defined by consumer capitalism.

The perceived threat from Egyptian Shriners and others came from the fact that Shriner forms could not definitively be copyrighted because improvisation was the heart of the Mystic Shrine's creative appeal. Men across the continent and beyond were able to embrace and elaborate Shriner arts because artistic license was an acknowledged part of the order's common culture that allowed so many to wear a mask of unreadability to express their power in society. African Americans who adapted playing Eastern to their own purposes as Egyptian order Shriners were expressing a desire for full citizenship. Like their white fellow citizens, they wished to play Eastern by way of the Arab trickster persona and the consumer's Oriental tale. Native-born and foreign-born performers lived in a nation in which cultural transfer was a crucial process for intercultural commerce and consumer individuation but a process no one fully controlled. The white Shriners tried to monopolize performances of Eastern personae in the bizarrely exotic mode, but like the official Ottoman Empire delegation at the Columbian Exposition, they were unprepared for the inevitable innovations that emerged.

chapter 6

Eastern Femininities for Modern
Women, 1893–1930

*I*f there was one character that defined Eastern femininity in the United States after 1893, it was the persona of the Oriental dancer. She emerged to great notoriety at the Columbian Exposition and its spin-offs in the form of actual women from North Africa and the Middle East who came to perform Eastern-style cabaret dancing as an entertaining ethnological show. As Americans took her, the Oriental dancer seemed to embody the carefree, consumerist nature of the "Golden Nineties." One wag would remember of the era, "America, definitely out of the pioneer and Indian-fighting stage, relaxed. . . . Wine, women and song became national institutions, flourishing in public. New waltz steps, gayer clothes and freer spending were other manifestations of a turn from the original grave, unbending self-discipline of the Seventies and Eighties."[1] The Eastern dancer helped Americans push away contemplation of the decade's strikes, economic depression, and war with her mischievous reputation, love of scandal, and apparent flattery of male interest in her body.

She also emerged on the scene just as crusaders for public morality became notoriously prominent in the United States. A volatile combination of reform-minded political activity and increasing consumer access to Eastern performers created a target for activists worried over the eager interest people had in Oriental dance shows, interest that seemed poised to embarrass the nation on a global level because it drove the shows' male audience members to self-destructive and raunchy behavior. These concerns were not just figments of prudish people's imaginations. As it developed in the United States, Eastern-styled dancing, also known as the *danse du ventre* or belly dance, *was* sexually suggestive because it asked new viewers to reimagine the proverbial Eastern "harem" not as a prison of helpless, exploited women but as the world turned upside down, a hedonistic space where male desire put women in control. Many American men were absorbed by the trope of the Eastern dancer and by the many native-born and foreign-born women who performed in her guise throughout the country around the turn of the century. As show producers and performers played on the controversy over the propriety of Eastern dancers to market the *danse du ventre* and its domestic imitations, known as Midway dancing or the "hootchy-kootchy," they transformed Eastern dance from racy novelty act to humorous cliché by which Americans could laugh at male desire and those who sought to contain that desire.

This chapter examines the moral panics over male spectatorship in the 1890s but only as a preface to what was really the greatest effect of the Eastern dancers in America, their influence with women. Many women flocked to these shows, and a prominent minority were inspired enough to imitate and develop Eastern dances and costumes into homegrown, suggestive, and profitable "cootch" and strip tease acts. These women were consumers turned performers, who in turn made their way through the entertainment business to burlesque houses, traveling carnivals, and amusement parks. At the same time, thousands of other American women would adopt what they saw in those women's and foreign women's performances to articulate their own identities through consumption of products and practices styled "Oriental." This consumers' Eastern persona was steeped in a sense of the ancient past, like the *Arabian Nights* but profoundly modern in its novelty and endorsement of personal cultural liberty for middle-class and working-class Americans. A whole generation of native-born and foreign-born women consumers played Eastern in ways that were highly contentious because they made Americans think about the movement of sexually aware and powerful, self-directed femininity into public.

The affluent Anglo-American women who had played Oriental by making a cozy corner in the parlor in the 1880s saw their daughters and the daughters of recent immigrants embrace feminine products and practices branded Eastern because they put women at the center of attention as creative people. Generations of women born just during or after the moral panics of the 1890s, for whom there had never been an America without Oriental dancers, were far more willing to play Eastern than their mothers had been. These American women would take from men the ultranatural East for themselves, manifested in the form of a sexually powerful woman, and combine it with ultra-artificial elements that celebrated the consumer's Oriental tale of choice and creative display. By the 1910s, they had added ancient Egyptian iconography to existing North African and Middle Eastern–styled elements to form an Easternized consumer femininity that anyone could try on by way of dance styles, cosmetics, clothing, and more.

No other mode of consumer individuation for women could provide the precise combination of self-directed sexuality and assertion of consumer power that Eastern personae did. Certainly plenty of women would choose to emulate the more chaste and polite consumption styles of elite East Asian ladies, European aristocrats, and home-grown celebrities.[2] For other women, those personae were not powerful enough statements of identity because they did not speak boldly of a modern femininity that required sexually self-aware individuation of the greatest creative freedom.

WHENCE CAME THE EASTERN DANCER AND WHY

It is not easy to tell this story in the way we can tell the stories of some of the others who played Eastern in the United States. The native-born and foreign-born women who performed as Oriental dancers in the 1890s were unwilling or unable to leave behind accounts that tell directly of their experiences. The absence of such accounts is a reflection of the balance of power in the entertainment industry more broadly because performers struggled with audiences, journalists, and their managers to control their public image at any given moment. Although consumers would gain greater power in defining themselves and displaying that identity as a modern "personality" in the years after Oriental dancers became prominent in the United States, entertainers themselves did not always have such freedom. In order to play Eastern for American audiences, these women had to keep obscured their private opinions and identities as working women and migrants so as to portray the fantasy of an entertaining retreat into a Middle Eastern café or even the clichéd harem. As a result, what we have left to document these dancers—promotional photographs, the dancers' publicity material, and newspaper accounts of their work—was shaped by managers, the press, and critics as much as the performers.

Regardless of the problems in the primary source base, the agency of these women was never in question as far as American observers were concerned. In fact, if we listen to the bulk of American comment on Eastern dancers when they became so sensational, it is difficult to miss the fact that if anything Americans exaggerated their ingenuity, portraying them as scamps who knew exactly what they were doing in exciting male interest and scandalizing Anglo-American opinion. The Eastern dancer was certainly not the clichéd odalisque in the "Ingresque formula," pictured in romantic European arts lazing half-naked on upholstered furniture. Already a stock convention of elite painting for some years, the odalisque seemingly endorsed the interpretive perspective of a presumed heterosexual male viewer by inviting him into the harem to do what he will as a metaphor for elite European ambitions for colonizing the Arab world.[3] Nor was she the tormented inmate of Mormon husbands who kept multiple wives, decried earlier in the century by Protestant critics worried over the practice of polygamy as an "exotic patriarchy" in the United States, or a helpless victim of Oriental tyranny and an all-powerful but debased male gaze.[4]

Rather, the Eastern dancer of the late nineteenth-century United States was a reflection of the beautiful and clever heroines in the *Thousand and One Nights*. Many already recast her into the alternately sentimental and humorous Oriental-tale single woman, a coquette who exasperates her suitors, and, after the 1870s, in the form of the servant girl or tempting "houri," one of the beautiful women who greets heaven-bound believers in Qur'anic discussions of the afterlife. Yet by the 1890s, many more people would also imagine her in the tradition of the *termagant*, a wanton lover who seduced men and "kissed hard," Mohja Kahf tells us.[5] Thus, the trouble for the historian is sorting out how much of the reported agency and action of actual women performers was truly theirs, how much a product of the reporter seeking to cross these women over to the listener or reader comprehensibly as a wily harem girl who tempts men to disobey overbearing wives and purity league types. This uncertainty around what Eastern women actually may have done at Eastern dance shows was as real in the 1890s as it is today and tells us that people wanted to see the Eastern dance shows for themselves to answer just these questions and to weigh in on a public debate over how or if a woman should play Eastern.

Throughout the century, North African and West Asian women had been an acknowledged fact of foreign life, but not the main focus of most Anglo-American interest, which cast the place as a field of missionizing, biblical history, and touristic consumption. Travelers to the Ottoman Empire were of course curious about local women, Eastern home life, and the privileged female spaces of the *hareem* or harem as Americans said. However, many found it difficult to get answers to their questions when they discovered the degree to which local people sought to protect their families from visitors' inquiries. Although female Westerners occasionally met local women and their families in the seclusion of middle-class and upper-class households, most travelers had only limited exposure to them by way of glances on the street or in markets, as beggars, or as the professional women dancers who welcomed tourist patrons.

Particularly in Egypt, tourists could find dancing women accompanied by male musicians at coffeehouses or public markets, where they often attracted large audiences. They appeared year round but came out especially for saints' days or for *mawalid*, the food and entertainment festivals that celebrated popular sufi shaykhs. It was also possible to invite dancing women to private houses where they might perform at evening gatherings as "learned women" who recited poetry and sang for female friends and family. Then there were the female *ghawazi*, the "celebrated voluptuous dancers of Egypt," entertainers who appeared with their faces bare for private audiences of men or in public playing for tips. The *ghawazi* emphasized their hips, hands, and midriffs with their movements and might employ candlesticks, scarves, or swords as props that added a sense of the acrobatic by extending the breadth of their movements.[6] In the early nineteenth century, travelers had taken great advantage of the services of *ghawazi* and became an important source of income to these women, who often agreed to perform on the boats Nile travelers hired. The Bostonian Edward Joy Morris found these dancers to be adept at pursuing foreign customers, saying that they waited near tourist sites hoping for *backsheesh* or cash gifts. "Our appearance among the ruins attracted a troop of dancing girls, who followed us, dancing to the sound of cymbals and Arab tambourines," he explained of a visit to the Egyptian town of Esneh. "They were attired in a rich costume, which set off their voluptuous figures with much effect, [performing] those wild Oriental dances which have more of grace than modesty in them, striking their cymbals, and throwing themselves into every variety of attitude."[7]

Writing in the early 1840s, Morris had arrived less than a decade after public outrage by the upper and middle classes in Egypt had compelled then-ruler Muhammad Ali to exile these women to Upper Egypt in 1834, a compromise wherein tourists could still find women entertainers, just not in the capital.[8] Morris correctly noted that Egyptian authorities watched closely the tourist trade in dance shows, attempting to find a balance between their own interest in the business as a source of tax revenue and the worried complaints of Egyptian observers who wished to see "marginal women" in their society out of the view of international visitors.[9] Although some found Eastern women dancers to be "disgusting" or "vulgar" in their movements, many of the middle-class and upper-class Anglo-Americans privileged enough to travel took them for what they were, describing them in matter-of-fact ways as a peculiarity of Eastern life that Americans need not find threatening. Even the biblical scholar William Thompson described female entertainers in Egypt in the 1850s who "move forward, and backward, and sidewise, now slowly, then rapidly, throwing their arms and heads about at random, and wriggling the body into various preposterous attitudes, languishing, lascivious, and sometimes indecent."[10] He also supplied readers with an illustration of such dancers in his best-selling volume, *The Land and the Book* (1859), a publication designed to provide pious insight into the Bible.

Between the 1830s and 1880s, even though some judged Eastern dancing to be inappropriate by American standards, it was no reason for any controversy right away. Middle Eastern dancing even appeared at the 1876 Centennial Exposition in Philadelphia at a Turkish coffee house concession. There audiences had seen male musicians, a woman, and a boy perform "singing, instrumental music and dancing, . . . all Turks, dressed in the costume of their country," the papers said. Some believed the women's dancing was "immodest," but the greater complaints seemed to come from the fact that no concession at the exposition was permitted to charge admission while the Ottoman subject in charge of this business had nonetheless required entrants to buy coffee at the inflated price of twenty-five cents in order to view the entertainment.[11] After the exposition, the Turkish music and dance troupe performed at another local venue to no scandal. Indeed, they closed down soon after due to lack of interest and an inability to compete with local shows of "girls kicking high in ruffled drawers" Parisian burlesque-show style, which represented the height of risqué dancing at the time.[12] Nor did a public outcry emerge some years later when P. T. Barnum included "sinuous Nautch girls," that is, Hindu women dancers in the Indian imperial court tradition, in the "Ethnological Congress" parts of his circus productions.[13]

Meanwhile, by the 1880s, the government of Egypt had permitted the *ghawazi* to return to Cairo since the tax revenues on their income were too large for the government not to help the trade, and women from across North Africa came there to work. A nominal province of the Ottoman Empire, Egypt came under British occupation that decade just as European tourists and traders in particular were becoming notorious in Cairo and Beirut for frequenting shows of dancing women, many of whom had resorted to prostitution to supplement their earnings and afford the taxes levied upon them. Pushed out of the old saint's day festivals by Middle Eastern reformers, the *ghawazi* retreated to a new performance space, the *café chantant*, which appeared in coffeehouses and hotel venues with stages where the women and their bands played for increasingly mixed Western and local audiences.[14] The *café chantant* and world's fairs in Europe put *ghawazi* and other Eastern women dancers in places where they were much more likely to get the attention of the American press.[15] Consequently, more frequent depictions of dancing Eastern women began appearing, not simply in book-length travel accounts but also in fiction and Oriental tales found in middling magazines like *Scribners*, on song sheets and stereograph cards, and eventually some of the pictorial and print souvenirs available at the Columbian Exposition's Midway.[16]

As the waft of illicit sex was drifting across the Atlantic in the 1890s, many Americans began advocating more liberal public morality, while others launched a corresponding backlash against the new commerce in sexually suggestive products and entertainment that made the decade particularly "puritanical," one observer would remember.[17] After 100 years in American life as a classic work of world literature, only then would the *Thousand and One Nights* be challenged in the courts as "obscene" literature when the John Payne translated adaptation *Tales from the Arabic* (1882–84) came under scrutiny by Anthony Comstock.[18] Public moral reform groups in New York and Massachusetts, most notably Comstock's New York Society for the Suppression of Vice, sprouted up in response to the increasing commercial availability of representations of human sexuality: birth control, racy men's magazines, nude photographs, and live entertainment of a suggestive or even sexually explicit nature.[19] Comstock was the most famous censor of all, whose earliest victory had come in 1873 when he persuaded Congress to pass what became known as the Comstock Law. The legislation banned transmission of "offensive" materials through the United States mail, lumping together any product addressing sexuality or birth control and persuading plenty of people to withdraw targeted materials or shows to avoid charges.[20]

Nonetheless, Anthony Comstock had challenged the proposed sale of Payne's *Tales from the Arabic* in New York state under the 1884 New York Penal Law, § 1141, which banned "any obscene, lewd, lascivious, filthy, indecent or disgusting book." In these kinds of cases, judges tended to bow to general public opinion of the title in question.[21] Editions of the *Arabian Nights* would survive such challenges because most Americans, including judges and the voters who elected them, argued a work was only "obscene" if produced for and consumed by innocent young people or crass readers among the "lower" classes, a logic that excluded old favorites like the *Nights*.[22] Until at least the mid-1880s, most Americans still did not speak out against the *Nights* as a "dirty book" even if they had begun reading it that way. Instead, they continued to refer to it as earlier nineteenth-century readers had, as fantastic children's literature noted for its depictions of material abundance, magic, and the surreal.[23] Indeed, Andrea Tone tells us most people disagreed with Comstock and would decide for themselves which kinds of sexual commerce they needed.[24]

Undeterred, Comstock would spearhead other court challenges that sought to restrict sale of the *Nights* and other Eastern arts thereafter because, at heart, he was also out to quash what he perceived as consumer fraud in the nation.[25] He engaged in muckraking exposés of many different kinds of risky spending: investment scams, "Bogus Mining Companies," private and state lotteries, "Quack" doctors, as well as Free Love publications from the National Liberal League (of which Albert Leighton Rawson was a member in the late 1870s).[26] In all these cases, Comstock was out to protect consumers, although he never spoke of Americans using that particular word, and to prevent people paying for a product or service that was inherently detrimental to them. He believed sexually suggestive material could lead the unwary to "perversions" like masturbation and promiscuity. The controversies over commerce and sexuality in these days were aspects of a reemergent worry that the consumer's Oriental tale had a dark side that would bring about a personal transformation in the market certainly—one that was not magical but self-destructive. For people in the business, the hype around such censorship was a boon, inspiring the "Banned in Boston" mode of book marketing, for instance, proving the old show business axiom that "nothing so advertises filth as a crusade of a purity league."[27]

New editions of the *Thousand and One Nights* also showed evidence of some Americans' loosened sexual attitudes. Many of the tales do take place in the solely female space of the Eastern household, and some had always dealt frankly with infidelity and female desire.[28] Although she had always been present in the *Arabian Nights*, it was in the 1880s and 1890s that many Americans began to talk publicly about the sexually powerful harem women, houri, or dancing girl as a character forbidden but irresistible to men. From the beginning, many Americans presumed that the audience for all such depictions of Eastern women was heterosexual and male, an assumption revealed in relatively tame ways in the person of the voyeuristic male who peeks into the privileged space of the harem. Consider "Three sisters sitting on a sofa," an illustration from a mid-1880s edition of the *Arabian Nights*. It showed Eastern women in no compromising

Late nineteenth-century editions of the *Arabian Nights* stayed current by making reference to the then-common trope of a peek into spaces of feminine sociability and autonomy, here from a McLoughlin Brothers of New York edition of *Arabian Nights' Entertainments*, ca. 1885.

position but nonetheless subject to the looks of two men who peep in through the window. The American peep show had emerged just then in spaces of for-profit recreation, where men gathered to "pay a dime to view such oddities as freaks, scantily clad women, or female genitalia preserved in glass contain-ers."[29] So did portrayals of peeking men endorse a broader stereotype of male voyeurism in spaces of female privacy that linked masculinity and consump-tion. To plenty of American women, however, the harem and modes of Eastern women's clothing resembling bloomers had long been interpreted as symbols of female privilege and friendship, an interpretation that helped give the orien-tal cozy corner feminist meaning that coexisted with the more sexualized mas-culinist interpretation. That is, a trope that many took as a sign of male power, many others took as a representation of female autonomy expressed by a collec-tive Eastern femininity that might make use of male desire.[30]

THE *DANSE DU VENTRE* SCANDAL: FROM NOVELTY TO CLICHÉ

The Columbian Exposition in Chicago provided the first opportunity for a broad segment of the American population to see an Eastern dancer for them-selves and decide whether her movements were, as a journalist functioning as art critic for the *Chicago Evening Post* suggested, "indecent or not, according as you look at it."[31] The scientific, anthropological, and imperial truth claims of the nonprofit ethnological displays and government pavilions at the exposition rubbed off on foreign visitors' use of artistic license in their commercial work.[32] Many people at the Columbian Exposition were consequently unsettled by the disjuncture between their expectations of innocent ethnological exhibits on the fairgrounds and the savvy foreigners they actually found there. Foreign entre-preneurs and performers in Chicago were not simply passive specimens wait-ing to be inspected but professionals who "began to look back and interact with the viewing public as fellow humans," Nigel Rothfels says of the 1880s and early 1890s, an improvisation that "doomed" ethnological shows that decade but would help Eastern dancers and their imitators become a genuine national sensation.[33]

At the World's Fair there was plenty of Eastern dancing to be found. Eigh-teen women from all over the Ottoman Empire danced at the Turkish Village Theatre, advertised on the façade outside as "Dancing Girls." Some performed in formal Bedouin dress consisting of heavy cloaks or in long skirts and modest blouses while waving scarves above their heads to create visual interest, a kind of dancing that required rapid spinning on the spot, a style later associated with Syrian Christian vaudevillians.[34] At the Algerian Theatre, Ouled Nail women from North Africa danced by employing their chests and hips in intentionally provocative ways that were authentic representations of their suggestive performances back home. In Algeria, Ouled Nail women had in fact worked as professional dancers and prostitutes, using their income in Algiers to marry well in their hometowns and villages in the Berber region of Algeria known as Monts des Ouled Nails. Nearby on the same section of the Midway, the Cairo Street Theatre presented customers with the famed *ghawazi* of Egypt. These women were in fact Algerian dancers who had worked in Cairo and in Chicago performed an act billed as the Cairene *danse du ventre* (as the Algerian Theatre shows were marketed), a French term for North African dancing that emerged from the tourist entertainment trade in Egypt. There they wore ankle-length skirts with a white chemise and fitted halter top, which to American eyes invited one to imagine the outfit without the chemise undershirt in ways that, like the contemporary flesh-toned tights of burlesque shows, feigned the appearance of nudity. The Cairo Theatre women danced with finger cymbals, shaking their shoulders and swiveling their hips in ways that Americans saw as highly provocative.[35]

Sol Bloom, impresario and commissioner for the Algerian Village, was a fan of all these dancers but pondered how the performers and their managers were crossing the shows over to the American market by drawing on newly sexualized clichés inspired by current interpretations of the *Arabian Nights*. He explained, "more people remember the reputation of the *danse du ventre* than the dance itself. This is very understandable. When the public learned that the literal translation was 'belly dance' they delightedly concluded that it must be salacious and immoral. The crowds poured in. I had a gold mine." Though he happily capitalized on this case of mistaken identity, he was nervous about the slippery slope of artistic license inherent in making Oriental dance comprehensible and thus financially viable and that in other people's hands the art became "debased and vulgarized . . . [with] the reputation of a crude, suggestive dance."[36]

The debate over the degree to which foreign dancers in Chicago were playing Eastern in sexual ways just to make money while exposing the vulgarity of visitors became inflamed further as the managers and performers at the Turkish Theatre began billing the women there as "Houris of the Orient" to get

The Egyptian dancer Amina worked the Midway at the Columbian Exposition wearing the chemise and halter costume that emphasized her womanly shape to American spectators. *Oriental and Occidental Northern and Southern Portrait Types of the Midway Plaisance*, 1894.

them over to Midway passersby.[37] However, the worst offender in this respect, many said, was the Persian Palace. The dance show there had switched from solemn performances of Sufi dancing to shows of women—Parisians some speculated—performing a nascent form of what came to be known as the hootchy-kootchy, a "corseted, pseudo-Oriental," half-American, half–Middle

Eastern dance unique to the Midway.[38] A "whooper-up" or "runner-in" pitch man outside the Persian Palace marketed the show as comprehensibly exotic when he proposed in the Eastern voice of Oriental tales, "Till now, you have not lived; enter, O Pilgrim, and receive the reward of your long endurance. Mahomet promised to such Musselmans as should die in defense of the Faith an eternal heaven of houris. We promise you the houris without the necessity of dying for them; coffee and refreshments furnished free gratis up-stairs; performance now commencing."[39]

Rumor had it that one Persian staff member at the Palace had become so disillusioned by his experience of these performances that he allegedly attempted to burn down the Persian Palace building.[40] Yet for visitors to the Midway dancing/*danse du ventre* performances, the shows poked fun at the elite knowledge of anthropologists and fair administrators, because the performer did not attempt paternalistically instruct the audience but celebrated the consumerist agency and preexisting knowledge of the viewer in defiance of the White City. Soon also known as "Midway dancing," the hybrid form founded in Chicago was a performance of ultranatural Eastern femininity in its hip-swinging suggestiveness and of the ultra-artificial in its rich costumes and setting.

The always-droll World's Fair edition of *Puck* magazine exposed this colloquial reality in a cartoon entitled "Human Nature." It depicted the story of the well-meaning Turkish promoter who sets up shop on the Midway before a Moorish-style doorway to wait for an expected deluge of schoolteachers and preachers for his "Life in the Holy Lands Scenes from Biblical Days!!! The Historic East as It Is and Was!!! A MORAL SHOW!!!" The days passed, and no customers filled his seats until an American "Showman" told him he had to change his program to appeal to those who would pay. The last scene of the cartoon showed top-hatted white men running, tripping, and falling in haste to pay their money and go to the new show the Turk had devised: "Life in the HAREM!! Dreamy Scenes in the ORIENT!!! Eastern Dances!!! THE SULTAN'S DIVERSIONS!"[41] Thereafter, in satire and public comment about Eastern dance shows, the image of the gaping male audience member, a distracted or bumbling husband dragged from a show by his wife, began appearing in newspaper and magazine cartoons about the controversy.

Some Chicago fairgoers had thought the Midway's *danse du ventre* and Persian Palace dances were clearly "modified to suit western taste," as one Chicago critic said.[42] Yet it was a matter of predisposition, some viewers seeing exotic art that spoke of female liberty, others seeing a crudely Eastern dance designed to bring out the worst in the men in the audience. "The national *dans du ventre* which not being understood was by many regarded as low and repulsive," F. W. Putnam, the anthropologist in charge of the Department of Ethnology at the Columbian Exposition had speculated. "What wonderful muscular movements did those dancers make, and how strange did this dance seem to us; but is it not probable that our waltz would seem equally strange to these dusky women of Egypt. What is a dance, is a question one was forced to ask after a trip through the Midway. Every nation had its own form."[43] This was precisely the question these foreign dancers put in some American minds—what is a dance?—a question that would inspire all sorts of creative people.

Those of Anthony Comstock's stripe honed right in on the Eastern dance shows, both the actual *danse du ventre* and the Midway innovation, as part of a publicity campaign that sought to get press attention due to the explosion of entertainment, some of it sexualized, across the city that summer.[44] Comstock and other reformers believed that live performance was far worse than obscene pictures or print because it was more vivid and available to anyone who could raise the admission price; one need not have a post office box or much money to see "modern indecency" performed live.[45] Comstock also said that his greatest concern was that the foreign dancers attracted audiences of "innocent girls and women" interested in ethnology who instead found themselves exposed to the "shame and humiliation" of "low minded spectators crying out to the dancers."[46] Here he invoked in his sympathizers potential disgust with the burgeoning markets for "girly" masculinist entertainment in the United States, which particularly flabbergasted middle-class and upper-class critics because they attracted men of all classes, religions, and ethnicities, who seemed to mingle together in dramatic statement of the universality of an essentialized maleness defined by risk, alcohol, and sex.[47]

The raised eyebrows over Eastern-styled dancing at the fair and the jokes about husbands sneaking away from wives to peep into a Midway "harem" became strong enough that by July Comstock had appeared in Chicago to force the fair's Board of Lady Managers to confront the shows. The Board was headed by Mrs. Potter Palmer and staffed by upper-class women permitted by exposition administration to oversee selected aspects of the fair, including the Women's Building that displayed exhibits on global women's progress. Board members were routinely ridiculed by the press, depicted as crabby old maids or the obese and mannish "Mrs. Stout," as *Frank Leslie's Weekly* lampooned an imagined member to contrast her with the ostensibly curvaceous, mischievous "girls" of the dance shows.[48] In league with Anthony Comstock, the well-meaning if officious Board attempted and failed to close down the lucrative Midway dance shows. The group also appealed directly to the dancers to leave the shows, though there is no evidence the women paid any heed to the advice they received.[49]

In fact, the scandal and the money made by Eastern dancing practically guaranteed that *danse du ventre* and Midway dancing shows would hit the road after the exposition. The productions that developed in that winter showed industry people how they could replicate the idea of scandal in a live dance performance that pitted the voices of moral purity against a sexually aware professional Eastern femininity.[50] That is, it became clear that people would pay to see some kind of dance simply to experience the scandal over art versus obscenity and over the place of Eastern content in American entertainment. Accordingly, four young Algerian women, Zelika Zimman, Zora Zimman, Fatma Mesgish, and an artist we know only as Ferida, who had demonstrated "Oriental" dancing at the Cairo Street theater, scheduled themselves into the Columbian Exposition spin-off "World's Fair Prize Winners Show" at the very epicenter of the American entertainment universe, New York City.[51] Housed at the Grand Central Palace, the act would draw capacity crowds for performances every hour, marked by a perpetual lineup at the ticket window.[52]

On the first Saturday night at the Palace, the nine o'clock show began as usual, except that there was a *New York Times* reporter planted in the crowd. The dancers and four male musicians in Turkish-looking dress made their way onto the stage. One by one, the young women appeared before the stares of a diverse crowd that included a number of "elderly men, and well-known frequenters of the Tenderloin district" who were observing the performance "with all the eagerness of their beings," the *Times* reporter sniggered.[53] In the front row there was also a stern-looking man many New Yorkers would have recognized as Police Inspector Alexander S. Williams. He was the public face of city attempts to crack down on, or appear to be cracking down on, everything from poolroom gambling to illegal garbage dumping.[54] As though on cue for the benefit of the press, Williams stood up at the finale of the show and approached the final dancer, Ferida. He ordered, "Stop That!" She ignored him. He repeated, "Stop that! There can be no more of this thing here to-night or any other night." A group of middle-aged women in the audience started for the exits as the audience's awed silence dissolved into noisy confusion.[55] Some began half-heartedly cheering Inspector Williams on, perhaps in fear of being implicated along with the "Tenderloin" gentlemen in a show Williams would call "indecent, and offen[sive to] the morals of our citizens."[56] Ferida and the others scrambled to get backstage as the crowd began pushing its way out and the show's manager attempted damage control by yelling above the ruckus that all ticket holders would be entitled to a refund.[57]

The next day, Monday, before an audience of eighteen women and thirty-two men, Zelika again performed "arrayed in red silk Turkish trousers, a blue Eton jacket, trimmed with gold, and a white gauze [sash] drawn in tight at the waist began the dance. For five minutes she wiggled and twisted, turned, cavorted, and kicked through an exhibition," in which she and the two other dancers on stage that night "wore a triumphant expression," the *Times* tattled. Arrested after the show, the papers claimed that the young women, aged only seventeen, eighteen, and twenty-two years old, "seemed to treat the whole affair as a joke, and peals of laughter could be heard coming from their dressing room" as they changed out of their costumes before leaving with the police. The three bravely went to court "[s]milingly," the papers asserted, portraying them as mischievous harem girls, where they were charged with a misdemeanor for immoral conduct. In their defense at their bail hearing, the dancers' lawyer, A. H. Hummel, addressed not the judge but the reporters in the court. He asserted that Zelika Zimman and the other two had agreed to perform knowing they might be arrested in order to provide a test case on the validity of Middle Eastern dancing in the United States.[58]

Without knowing with all certainty what the Algerian dancers believed about their labor in New York, we can know that at times they seemed to help the case their manager and lawyer made for the legitimacy of the dances as art. At trial in New York, Zelika Zimman appeared in full dress costume, and through her interpreter she defended her performances before a courtroom loaded with press and citizenry. "I am quite willing to give the dance right here," she explained. The judge declined the offer, and attempts by the arresting officers Dennis McMahon and Sergeant Daniel Archibald to imitate the exact movements that had made the dancing specifically immoral brought "a burst of laughter" in the courtroom that the judge silenced with the gavel. Here newspaper coverage of the court hearings introduced another stock component of *danse du ventre*—scandal as nascent show business gag. Staged, awkward imitations of Eastern dance by American men contrasted Eastern feminine charms with clumsy or ridiculous American manhood to reassert the power of Eastern dancers. In exposing male desire or incompetence the dancers seemed to lay bare the hidden nature of the people who ran the planet's preeminent economic power. Anthony Comstock had himself been lampooned in this way back in Chicago when a reporter for the New York World had asked him to demonstrate the acts he found offensive. Comstock's rendition of the moves of the ghawazi had been "interesting, but not at all libidinous," a New York World reporter had joked.[59]

Anthony Comstock also appeared at the New York court hearings over the Grand Palace shows, where he witnessed McMahon and Archibald's awkward attempts at replicating the movements of the Zimman sisters, Fatma Mesgish, and Ferida. He interrupted the proceedings more than once, in one exchange arguing with the judge, "I want to be heard. I am defending womanhood in this city." Justice Burke belittled Comstock by instructing him "to sit down," the papers said in a narrative that almost sounded like a vaudeville skit. In this heated context, it appears that Zelika Zimman, at the age of only eighteen, may have been a rather confident young woman. She testified in court through an interpreter that she "had been dancing in Cairo and other places for six years, and that no one had ever before charged her with any indecency. It was exactly the same dance that had been given in Cairo and Chicago. It is an artistic dance and the dance of our nation, . . . and I am sure there is nothing wrong in it or in the costumes."[60]

The day after their arrest, New York Police Department Captain Berghold had taken over the case and gone to linger around the Grand Central Palace show, taking notes and preparing evidence. He testified that the women appeared to have "toned down" the show since the initial raid, with the "offending movements" of the hips and midriff removed, thus reserving most of the dance to the movement of the arms. Except, that is, when it served the entertainment value of the production: "When the girl saw me she began her contortions [again]," Berghold told the court. In making their work comprehensible, the Algerian dancers, if correctly reported by the Times and the police, "seemed to take particular delight in coming down the stage to a place in front of Capt. Berghold" to defy his stern masculine looks.

Ultimately the dancers had their manager pay fines of $50 each, and the show stayed open for financial or contractual reasons as the dancers and their band persevered with the new choreography.[61] The profitability of even a "toned down" show exposed the dancers' ability to subtract key elements of the show in order to carry on by presenting a less sexually suggestive version of the dances still perceived as the hootchy-kootchy or "Midway dancing." The new version capitalized on the idea of an Eastern dance show as a chance for consumers to experience not just Eastern femininity that played to male audience interest but a performed version of the controversy over the *danse du ventre* itself. These and other women dancers also played clichéd harem girl to roast the audience while simultaneously deflecting public attention onto staged personae that protected their true identities.[62]

MODERN WOMEN IN EASTERN PERSONAE

While the show at the Grand Central Palace had been selling out, more than one person noted that among the audiences of "low-minded . . . Tenderloin" types were many, many women. They were there when male ticket buyers and the police witnessed the apparently sassy attitude by the Algerian dancers and had in fact been a constant presence at the shows since Chicago, some drawn by a curiosity for foreign dance, others by an interest in the controversy. Plenty must have resented censors' claims that the foreign dancers bamboozled "innocent girls and women" with an invitation to ethnological instruction that actually served to them to seedy men and the "shame and humiliation" of "low minded spectators crying out to the dancers."[63] In New York, women continued to pay to see the dancers. Some were perhaps drawn by the faked endorsement by Mrs. Potter Palmer, head of the Board of Lady Managers, that Delacroix gave to the press knowing women would respond.[64] A livid Mrs. Potter forced the papers to print a retraction in which she rejected those claims and insisted she had only seen the show in the "early in the morning" since gossip that summer had it that only men went to the shows after dark.[65] Yet even among members of the Board of Lady Commissioners, who had had to visit the shows to confirm their "lascivious" nature in Chicago, there had been admirers of the Eastern dancers. One of them, Mrs. Shepard, reportedly said of them, "I thought they were fascinating."[66] People's interest in which women went to the shows, when, and why reflected a broader debate over the New Woman in public, whether performer, reformer, or consumer and whether she might expose herself to potential male desire to portray herself as a modern person who could define her own respectability.

In the 1890s, a broadly comprehensible colloquial humor emerged to lampoon male desire for the Eastern dancer and the reformers who sought to protect American women from it. The colloquial story of the hootchy-kootchy contained two opposing casts of characters. In one corner stood the prudish,

Women were crucial consumers and imitators of Eastern dancing, here as audience members for "The Original Turkish Harem" on Coney Island, 1896. Museum of the City of New York, Byron Collection, 93.1.1.3383.

middle-aged female reformer and her "soft" male allies of preachers and Comstock-style progressives. In the opposing corner stood the randy husband or urban "low-life," unfit for marriage because of his preference for commercialized voyeurism, and the teasing dancing girl who entertained him. The joke worked because Americans believed the Easternized woman had power over men, because they knew that some women sought to regulate husbands and some men complained of marriage as an infringement on their manly liberty, a tug-of-war that seemed such a timeless fact of life that one might as well laugh about it.

Although women reformers did attack burlesque shows of sassy women playing Oriental for drinking men as well as early vaudeville acts wherein women in nude-look tights posed as naked marble statues, most female activists were out to protect children, not other adult women. They often clashed with men in the obscenity reform movements since male reformers often sought to keep women in support roles in supposed protection of their delicate sensibilities. Anthony Comstock for one would regularly insist he was out to protect the nation from "the most outrageous assault[s] on the sacred dignity of woman-hood," drawing ridicule that confounded women reformers' attempts to be taken seriously as public people.[67] In fact, for women reformers "New Woman" feminism meant freedom to attack the burlesque shows and obscene literature; for others it meant supporting dry laws, suffrage, bans on child labor, regulated prostitution, and other Progressive Era causes that sought to put women in public, just not in sexualized roles.[68]

Still, there was a generational shift occurring, and many daughters of these reforming women were attracted to womanly entertainment at the same histor-ical moment and in some of the same entertainment venues. For them the move into the public sphere was also about taking control of their own lives but as performers and consumers who defined themselves by appealing to male de-sire, not by trying to suppress it. These women also considered themselves prowoman in a colloquially-feminist way that encouraged a woman to ma-nipulate her persona to express a sense of personality.[69] They were interested in "female sensual expression," Judith Walkowitz explains, "that disrupted the Victorian conventional dichotomies of female virtue and female vice and pushed beyond such dualisms."[70] Many Americans of both sexes appreciated the shift in sensibilities as female entertainers and other women sought to make their own choices about how to present themselves in public in ways that could be self-aware and financially viable. They also put the onus on men to manage their own sexuality, not on women to be chaste in an attempt to control it. Thus, although men like Comstock claimed to protect American "woman-hood" from the men at the *danse du ventre* shows, the greater possibility was that women audience members would be most affected by the sassy women per-formers and perhaps, like Mrs. Sanders, find them "fascinating," perhaps fascinating enough to imitate them.

At first, the most obvious evidence of Eastern dancers' influence with working-class women was visible by their labor in the burgeoning exotic dance trade that blossomed after the New York shows of Midway dancing. All century, Oriental tales and the *Thousand and One Nights* had been "ransacked by compos-ers, playwrights [and] choreographers," Deborah Jowitt explains, to produce ballet and other productions in a recognizable Oriental genre, in which women bared their legs and arms but still came across as carefully choreographed and chaste in their movements.[71] Now foreign and local talent made the *danse du ventre* both exotic high art and homegrown pornography by adapting the form and taking it to every amusement park and carnival in the country. Its evolution into the burlesque act known colloquially as the "hootchy-kootchy" or "cootch show" perhaps explains the unpredictable turn of history that resulted in women who dance in gentlemen's clubs billing themselves as "exotic dancers" when they are perhaps properly described as "erotic dancers."

In any event, the most famous early woman to play Eastern dancer in this mode was a Midway dancer of Syrian extraction, Fahreda Mazhar, also known as Little Egypt. During the 1890s she would perform all over the United States until her marriage to a Greek immigrant in 1905. Photographs of her work on Coney Island between 1896 and 1898 still exist, archived in the Byron Collection at the Museum of the City of New York. In them one can see images of her posing in her modest but ornate costume before a crowd of bowler-hatted men or lying back with a water pipe in her café chantant–style theater complete with Oriental cozy corner.[72] Later, as Mrs. Spyropoulos, she performed only periodically at world's fairs while the danse du ventre was morphing into the art of striptease, much to her disgust. By 1936, she would sue the Metro Goldwyn Mayer movie company for portraying her in a film set in the 1890s as a costumed Oriental dancer with a naked midriff, arguing that the film impugned her reputation since she had never worn such revealing dress on stage. The film's projection of 1930s Eastern-styled striptease costume onto the Little Egypt legend helped to cross her over for contemporary audiences but showed how a generation after the danse scandals Americans had pressed the Eastern dancer's teasing costumes to an entirely new level.[73]

Back in the 1890s, Mazhar had inspired at least ten imitators. Among them were an American woman, Catherine Devine, and an Algerian woman going by the name Wabe. Both gained the apocryphal reputation of having appeared nude while dancing in the Eastern style and even for having emerged naked (again apocryphally) from a gigantic pie during an 1897 stag party at the Waldorf-Astoria that became legendary in entertainment circles as the "Seeley Dinner" when police intruded to arrest the party's famous guests.[74] The dinner and the police bust were fact, but the stories about what the hired entertainment had actually done there invited speculation and hyperbole that made each new audience member the butt of the joke for Easternized cootch shows that capitalized on men's willingness to pay anything to see a woman undress.[75]

Multiple performers would bill themselves as "Little Egypt" and ply the concert saloon and burlesque house trade such that it can be impossible to tell from the press notices for the shows which one featured the original Little Egypt. These venues provided highly topical, racy performances that worked through all the same issues as the Eastern dance shows around feminine desire, male voyeurism, prudishness, fun, and consumption. While the court case over the police bust was in the papers, even the Seeley's Dinner event was lampooned by a musical comedy called "Silly's Dinner" starring one of the Little Egypts.[76] This was only one of the remnants of broader entertainment industry adaptations on stage and in print inhabiting a universe of consumption that openly welcomed women and men in respectable venues. For instance, in 1896 the *New York Journal* would publish a songsheet called "Ootchy-cootchy Baby" from "Lost, Strayed or Stolen," a musical comedy capitalizing on the scandal.[77] Even Mae West would eventually perform a version of the bit.[78]

Why did so many women choose to play Eastern for a living in those days in spite of the real disrespectability of the act? The proliferation of the *danse du ventre* and domestic hootchy-kootchy was proof that a successful act will always produce countless imitators looking for a sure thing. Many women played Oriental dancing girl to great profit knowing the show business truism that producers and bookers seldom humored failure. Press agent and striptease promoter Bernard Sobel remembered, "with actor, agent, booker and manager all hanging on the lifeline of the performer's acceptance by a fickle public, the test of any act's position on a bill came after the first performance; for in spite of contractual arrangements, if the act didn't go over, the manager put it in the spot he thought suitable. Or threw it out."[79] Since most of the original foreign-born performers of the *danse* had been Arab, just about any woman could do the bit, which required no blackface makeup or other complicated act of passing but merely dark hair, the right costume, and a show business "harem girls" backdrop to "go over," as Sobel put it. In the mid-1890s, dozens of carnivals and amusement parks thusly installed bankable "Streets of Cairo," "Turkish Harem," "Singing Girls of Baghdad," "Oriental Dancing Girls" attractions, though they might or might not employ performers of Eastern extraction.[80]

In his memoirs, Bernard Sobel recalled how around 1895 the proliferation of the cootch show as a comedic performance of gendered scandal had become an amusement park sensation. As a boy, he desperately sought to see the *danse du ventre* at the local county fair and "learn the mysteries of life at once." This was a randy show promising something exotic that turned out to be a parody of male desire performed by local women:

> Suddenly, a reedy instrument announced the opening of the hootchy-kootchy show; whereupon I rushed forward madly, quite ignorant of

what I was going to see. There was a crowd already in front of the tent and everyone pushed and shoved when the barker shouted out, "Gather in closely." Then six girls appeared, all heavily painted and wearing kimonos that gave the shocking impression that they had just come out of the bedroom. . . .

The barker was a young man, likable and expert. I listened to his spiel until I knew it by heart: "On the left, we have Mme. Zoo-Zoo from Paris. When she dances, every fibre, every tissue in her entire anatomy shakes like a jar of jelly from your grandmother's Thanksgiving dinner. Now, gentlemen, I don't say that she's hot, but I say she's as hot as a red-hot stove down in Jacksonville County on the Fourth of July."

Once inside the show, Sobel found that

a crowd of men was already standing in front of the small stage, making wisecracks and shouting to the girls to hurry. After what seemed centuries, the curtains parted and the barker stepped out to act as master of ceremonies. . . .

The show itself consisted of living pictures: girls in pink tights who acted out anecdotes about the traveling salesman and the farmer's daughter. . . . The double-entendres were numerous, but the whole performance was pretty tame until the last number when a girl did the hootchy-kootchy. She wore a thin chemise, voluminous skirts, harem slippers and a sash that made her stomach prominent. She wiggled her hips so violently and with such dexterity that she actually reached the floor, dusting it off with her wriggling belly.[81]

In 1895, Sobel's main concerns at the county fair were about infiltrating an adult entertainment and studying the interaction of "girls" and men in a show that was only vaguely about foreign lands anymore, with Little Egypt replaced by "Mme. Zoo-Zoo" in a type of Oriental costume quickly becoming a standard in the industry.

Sobel explained that the people who paid to see the shows knew they were seeing a commercial gag that lampooned audience expectation as an interpretive dance in which a woman played Eastern to perform the *danse du ventre* scandal itself. He said one popular song ribbed, "Oh I once knew the gal that's known to you / As 'Little Egypt,' as 'Little Egypt' / They say she came from Cairo, maybe Cairo, Illinois."[82] The success of cootch show and its musical derivatives also proved (if anyone even doubted it anymore) that upwardly mobile white-collar workers and working-class Americans had a taste for international-style acts presented baldly as entertainment, not as education, because they were crossed over to flatter their viewers as wily consumers, newly individuated through things Eastern that had previously been monopolized by middle-class and upper-class consumers.[83]

When an Eastern dancer appeared on the front of the National Police Gazette to capitalize on some later shows of the danse du ventre on Coney Island, the connection between Eastern femininity and perceived womanly pleasure in male spectatorship must only have been more appealing to some men and the danger of the dances only confirmed to critics.[84] Publications like the National Police Gazette represented the worst of American culture, some said. A pioneer of tabloid journalism and "guilty pleasure," many read the Gazette because it was perceived as tasteless with its large, vivid illustrations, its tales of sex, crime, and male athleticism. In its pages "pink tight"–clad burlesque dancing girls described as "Favorite of the Baldheads" or "Pride of the Dudes" appeared with images of other women caught unawares with calves bared or in candid poses in theater dressing rooms. All of them were sexually aware women whose ingenuity made them interesting and would appear in the iconography of main-stream magazines within a decade.[85]

When the scandals over Eastern dance hit the United States, the Gazette was at its peak as a mediator of "modernity and consumerism that turned sex into a commodity," David Reel tells us. The magazine already featured warm, some-times almost feminist coverage of female entertainers, women who seemed to invite and enjoy male desire in contrast to supposedly asexual church ladies and suffragists who seemed to demand restraint.[86] The Gazette's main contribution to the cootch show as performance of the Eastern dance scandal came in 1896 when the paper printed a half-fictional account of the Brooklyn shows with a front cover illustration of an Eastern dancer performing with apparent wild abandon in the common chemise, skirt, and halter jacket costume before an audience of gaping and grinning men, beers and cigars in hand. A packed house, the paper sensationalized, had watched "Fatima" perform a series of dances, each one in increasing states of undress until finally the show's barker announced she would perform "as she was dressed on the day she was born," namely, wearing nothing but a pair of black stockings![87] The story was untrue in the details, readers probably guessed, but was spot on in its amplified perfor-mance of the ways women played Eastern to satirize male desire.

The Brooklyn venue for the story was no accident either as Coney Island was a place known for female agency and the presence of women as performers and consumers, even if the *Gazette*'s depiction of Fatima's dance did not admit this. "Many Americans perceived Coney Island as a 'naughty' place . . . where women and men might be more forward with one another," Jon Sterngass explains, famous for horse racing and beaches to be sure but also for seedier businesses: concert saloons and brothels where one could find liquor and gambling. "No wonder that the actress known as Little Egypt chose Coney Island as the venue in which to set up shop in 1895," he observes.[88] The *National Police Gazette* account of Fatima reflected Coney Island's commercialized, liminal spaces where women saw male desire with their own eyes. In the district's concert saloons and bars some young women, "amateur-prostitutes," were known to walk the fine line between worker and customer by inviting dates and sex with men who bought them drinks.[89]

Women were fast appropriating male consumer interest in feminine sexuality, a process that between 1893 and 1910 would transform the act of playing Eastern by women into an icon of colloquially feminist consumerism. After the Chicago and New York scandals, amusement park and world's fair cootch shows would make a newly modern, Easternized femininity accessible through dance to working-class and middle-class women working out how to individuate themselves as modern. Many of the new commercial entertainments of the era that observers suspected catered to male desire actually appealed to and were designed for women. In nickelodeons and early cinema shorts, dancing and jumping women were prominent subjects of a new technology unique for its ability to capture intriguing movement.[90] Nickelodeon shorts additionally employed risqué "take-a-peek" narratives of women disrobing or of burlesque dancers and chorus girls.[91] In elaborating the peep show mode that brought people's private sexual identities into the view, "motion pictures demonstrated a surprising recognition of female desire and sexual availability, [even] aggressive female sexuality," Sharon Ullman explains.[92] For instance, a Boston dancer calling herself Ella Lola moved her feet and wiggled her pelvis in provocative "Oriental" ways in an early Edison film short from 1898 that showed how the *danse du ventre* was morphing into something more homegrown.[93] Many such voyeuristic films of the period in the spirit of burlesque, the *National Police Gazette*, and the cootch shows acknowledged a competing female subjectivity that toyed with men and their embarrassing desires.[94]

In dance halls, too, young women and men began in those years to engage in other liberal amusements that implied women's sexuality could be visible in public. For instance, a fad for "rough dancing" encouraged bodily contact and parodied the stiff and chaste dance styles of earlier generations.[95] Especially among working-class women at commercial dance halls, amusement parks, and department stores, where one could see and be seen spending, styles emerged in 1890s, 1900s, and the overtly feminist 1910s that, Carolyn Kitch tells us, "enabled a shedding of restraint, figuratively through the illusion of class mobility ("slumming") and literally through physical mobility. It also required a shedding of clothing and a transformation in dress styles. Women's fashions became less constraining, more revealing, yet also more girlish."[96]

There was a sharp public consciousness of that feminine consumer perspective projected onto the many young women making their way in the nation at the turn of the century. One tune that emanated from the phenomenon of Eastern dance as scandal was called "Streets of Cairo." It told the story of an innocent country "maiden" who ventured to Chicago to make her mark in life and ended up performing a raunchy dance show: "To appear each night in abbreviated clothes. All the dudes were in a flurry, for to catch her they did hurry." The chorus of the piece explained that she was tricked into working the show because "She never saw the streets of Cairo, On the Midway she had never strayed, She never saw the kutchy-kutchy, Poor little country maid."[97] The meaning of this song rested on a stereotype that defined worldly female knowledge by spectatorship of Eastern dancers and by knowledge of male desire. Like the carnival or concert saloon cootch show, early cinema accordingly offered content that encouraged people to think about sex with its depictions of randy girls who submitted to the audience's gaze. In contrast critics used clichéd characters like "The Old Maid" or the asexual wife to poke fun at political women, women of an older generation, and married women who rejected Easternized sexuality.[98]

For these diverse audiences, feminine performance and consumption of the Eastern dance in the form of cootch shows carried on in vaudeville, musical comedies, and amusement parks. Female audience members became performers like Princess Rajah, who worked the St. Louis Exposition in 1904 and eventually an amusement park at Venice Beach, California. She claimed birth in Tehran but performed a Midway-style Oriental dance that employed not just candlesticks or scarves but a chair that she balanced on her head during the act to give a further acrobatic element. To stay current, by 1910 she had redeveloped her act into a "Cleopatra Dance" that tapped into the increasing feminine interest in things Oriental by way of ancient Egyptian iconography. She also stepped the suggestiveness up a notch by phallic reference to the animal that had killed the historical Egyptian queen. Hammerstein's vaudeville house would welcome her to their stage in 1909 to perform the dance as "Princess Rajah in her Oriental Creation THE CLEOPATRA DANCE with a Real LIVE SNAKE."[99]

The burlesque dancers of the day would also combine existing Orientana with commercial Egyptomania elements, turning the *danse du ventre* artist of the 1890s into the substantially nude "Oriental Dancer" of the 1910s. Down at the amusement park and in red-light districts, women combined the cootchy-Eastern dances with older burlesque traditions that became more and more suggestive of sex after World War I. Interwar striptease and *Arabian Nights* show dancers on stage and screen displayed not just the movement of the hips and torso with feet stationary but "bumps, a quick thrust forward of the abdomen, the grind, a rotating motion of the hips, and the muscle kick." These were the movements of women whose costumes were shrinking by the 1920s, "discarding harem pantaloons, chemise and veil, she limits her costume to a bejeweled G-string and brassiere," Bernard Sobel said, with no slippers or stockings.[100]

In fact, there was a generational moment just after the turn of the century when consumption and creativity were very obviously in symbiosis. Often women sought personal and professional individuation in the same moment of playing Eastern. They help us see how American consumers actually used the Oriental tale as artistic practice to live vicariously through commercial Orientana that invited consumer experimentation. At least one of these moments of inspiration was captured by a crucial founder of American modern dance, Ruth St. Denis. In 1904, when the Eastern-styled dance was still a rage in amusement parks, carnivals, and theaters, St. Denis was working as a leg-baring skirt dancer in vaudeville. Seeking better opportunities, she landed a contract with the Broadway-based Belasco Company and began touring the United States with them. One day she went to lunch at a drug store in Buffalo, an accident of history that changed the direction of American dance forever. "We were laughing as usual over some joke, and sipping our sodas, when my eyes lifted above the fountain and I saw a cigarette poster of Egyptian Deities," she remembered.

> It must have contained a potent magic for me. I stopped with my soda half consumed and stared and stared. . . . This seated image of Isis, a superficial, commercial drawing for a cigarette company, opened up to

> me in that moment the whole story of Egypt. . . . Lying on my bed, look-
> ing at this strange instrument of fate, I *identified myself in a flash with the*
> *figure of Isis.* She became the expression of all the somber mystery and
> beauty of Egypt, and I knew that my destiny as a dancer had sprung alive
> in that moment. . . . I wanted to become this seated figure who sym-
> bolized the whole nation of Egypt. . . . I had glimpsed in the history, reli-
> gion, and art of Egypt the symbol of man's eternal search for the beauty
> and grandeur of life. . . . By the time we reached San Francisco I had
> blocked out in detail the various episodes of the dance *Egypta* (emphasis
> added).[101]

The commercial image of Isis triggered for St. Denis a stereotype of feminine power and expression that inspired her first major work as a dancer/
choreographer, *Egypta*, and dozens she would produce and perform into the
1960s. By playing Eastern professionally, she suggested to her audiences how to
make use of the East in their own ways.

Even though St. Denis wished to capture Eastern cultures and to celebrate
them through dance, she still had a context to cope with. She studiously avoided
explicitly copying cootch-style North African–inspired dances as Princess Rajah, Fatima, Little Egypt, and other women had because their work spoke of the
humorous seediness of Coney Island or the *National Police Gazette*'s coverage
of the *danse du ventre* as scandal. Instead, St. Denis's Eastern-styled creations
showed her immersion in the broad commercial Orientana of the period, to be
sure, but also careful choices that allowed her to be of the East ultranaturally and
ultra-artificially in sincere performances in which she employed perceived primitive artistic themes as well as rich sets and costumes. These personae kept her
distant enough from Midway dancing that she could cross herself over to her
patrons as a serious artist. She performed first as Cleopatra in *Egypta*, a production that without question inspired Princess Rajah to switch from Midway to
"Cleopatra"-style dancing in 1910. Then St. Denis devised a performance in the
guise of Indian nautch dancer, an influential production she called *Radha*.

Her partner and colleague, Ted Shawn, explained how they had developed
Eastern-styled modern dance in an era when the competition consisted, he said,
of "the balletic art of Anna Pavlova at one extreme and hootchy kootchy at the
other." Shawn and St. Denis founded the Denishawn school of dance, where
they sought to connect the two poles, "to combine ballet professionalism with
modern freedom; to make the dance respectable and the audiences respectful,"

Quick, Henry, the sneeze-powder!

Airplane view of Muscle Shoals.

This lady and Fred Allen's whoopoo bird fly backward. They don't care where they're going—they want to see where they've been.

Believe it or not, an Oriental dancer.

Burlesque dancers combined elements from modern artists like Ruth St. Denis, the Orientana of contemporary advertising, and the cootch acts to play Eastern as various kinds of "Oriental" dancers. Bernard Sobel, *Burleycue*, 1931.

Shawn said.[102] That is, they sought to create modern dance as art, which thus had to be apparently sexually benign, but also had to be well researched, even if it was inspired by the commercial art of a cigarette advertisement and obvious artistic license.[103]

Modern advertising men also seem to have been aware that broad groups of American women were similarly using the Eastern world and its depictions in the United States to think about consumption and individuation and that many women wanted more feminine Eastern personae from which to choose. "Consumer capitalism produced a culture," William Leach explains, "that first appeared as an alternative culture—or as one moving largely against the grain of earlier traditions of republicanism and Christian virtue—and then unfolded to become the reigning culture of the United States . . . the heart of American life."[104] Indeed, the hedonism in dance and commercial leisure that seemed so controversial in the 1890s was utterly mainstream by Ruth St. Denis's day. A younger generation of American women would play Eastern as ad hoc Cleopatras, Little Egypts, and more by way of homegrown and imported consumer products.

Meanwhile, mail-order catalogs and department stores allowed more people than ever to buy imported Middle Eastern items, piles of cushions, overstuffed upholstered furniture, and Asian and Middle Eastern–inspired fashions that became signifiers of feminist self-discovery in every mode of entertainment and home décor.[105] They all drew up a modern interpretation of Oriental tale styles that required colorful design, modern personal liberty, and unrestrained self-expression. A slew of well-illustrated art and design books and magazines served as Oriental tale how-to manuals, featuring patterns inspired by Islamic art and actual reproductions of the art itself. They circulated among professional artists, writers, and production designers from the medicine show to department stores to advertising agencies to the Broadway stage.[106] Contemporary marketing and advertising pastiche similarly drew from the whole of North Africa and Asia, past and present, especially merging Egyptomania with Eastern dance and self-presentation as a kind of modern Orientalness that women could use to voice their consumer power.[107]

Prominently, cosmetic companies encouraged shoppers to develop unique personalities with ad copy that instructed, "Find Yourself," and marketing materials that offered suggested personae like the "exotic type" or "Sheba type" to readers. Ad men employed such Easternized appeals to communicate with Anglo-American women to be sure but also with other consumer bases seldom invited to play Eastern before: Hispanics, African Americans, or southern European immigrants whose dark hair and skin made a Cleopatra or Eastern desert princess personae appealingly accessible. Companies also used images of Little Egypt and "Moorish"-styled branding to promote cosmetics and hair products while, Kathy Peiss tells us, "Cleopatra was virtually a cult figure."[108] The made-up woman, like the Eastern dancer, had been disreputable a generation earlier, but by World War I a new batch of young women would embrace her and the consumer arts of playing Oriental as a sign of modern femininity voiced through spending, sharing her mischievous attitude as a personality attribute coded Eastern.

Nor was it extraordinary that Ruth St. Denis had found her inspiration for artistic individuation in an advertisement for cigarettes. The quintessentially modern product for women—the cigarette—was routinely branded in Eastern modes since tobacco had so long been associated with the Ottoman Empire and produced there for the American market. The most enduring, Camel brand, appeared in 1912, after R. J. Reynold's executives had auditioned a number of simple Easternized names for the new brand, among them Aga, Kismet and Osman, that in league with contemporary advertising theory provided an uncomplicated, consumer-oriented guise for the product. Camel brand was only the most famous example of many similar products marketed as Helmar, Mecca, and Fatima, for instance.[109] Jackson Lears tells us these products modernized the consumer's Oriental tale for new consumers, including women, by offering "the promise of magical self-transformation through the ritual of purchase."[110] Ad men would continue to use commercial Orientana that worked in symbiosis with cinema and other commercialized leisure as well as the century-old consumer's Oriental tale to hide the mundane means of production and less-than-glamorous origins and ingredients behind an Easternized narrative of satisfaction, self-expression, and abundance. Certainly this is how Ruth St. Denis had interpreted that Egyptian deity's cigarette poster at that Buffalo drug store.

Moreover, such Eastern-branded products made sense as vehicles of ease, plenty, and identity because the consumer's Oriental tale was still widely relevant. All century Oriental tales had been making their way through multiple venues of fashion, theater, advertising, stage and costume design, circuses, and more, all of it culminating in elaborate high-budget theater productions like Robert Hichens's desert romance *Garden of Allah* (1904), which moved quickly into cinema.[111] The Oriental spectacular, a prominent form in early feature films, was loaded with endorsements of the consumer's Oriental tale that replicated the "situations of fulfillment" ad men were using to "sell satisfactions" by contextualizing products with images of success and social power.[112] Movie magazines further offered serialized fiction in which American women went abroad and passed as Turkish or Arab women, inviting readers to play Oriental like the starlets posed in movie magazines as "nautch girl," Cleopatra, turban-wearing vamp, or richly-attired harem woman who flirts with a desert Sheik.[113]

A LOGICAL CONCLUSION: THE DESERT ROMANCE

Long gone was the progressive-era woman who went to see the *danse du ventre* out of embarrassed curiosity or a sense of outrage. Could she ever have imagined that many women of her daughter's generation would themselves become Eastern girls of a sort? The act of playing Eastern by women had undergone a dramatic shift since the Columbian Exposition in Chicago, passing from ethnological show, to controversy over male desire and obscenity, to comedic bit that poked fun at the prudish but liberal 1890s, to stock personae of modern strip tease, international dance, and consumer individuation. All the while, the women in the audiences and on stage at these various shows found suggested modes of playing Eastern in all sorts of media content and live performance directed at modern women.[114]

Followed to its logical conclusion, or feared consequence, the Easternization of modern women's consumption, many believed, invited women seek out an Eastern man, at least imaginatively. In 1928, Morris Bishop commented on this phenomenon and the dismissive uneasiness around Easternized femininity by way of a limerick: "There's a vapourish maiden in Harrison/Who longed for the love of a Saracen/But she had to confine her/Intent to a Shriner/Who suffers, I fear, by comparison."[115] Certainly modern Shriners believed they were charming to American women and that, to the public, they appeared as "a lot [of] men looking like 'cigarette signs,'"[116] disclosing a consciousness of how the consumer arts of playing Oriental worked hand in hand with Orientana promoting cigarettes and other products aimed at women. For people like Bishop, the Shriner was a ridiculous Babbitt, a character inspired by Sinclair Lewis's 1922 novel of the same name, a "small-minded masculine booster" who joins any social organization, no matter how pointless, in order to deny the reality of business failures and meaningless pursuit of "success" in America.[117] He was no Eastern Valentino but a bad copy more likely to be seen ogling the girls at a carnival harem show than bounding across the desert on a steed.

Undeniably, many women who would dabble in Oriental romance in the 1910s and 1920s did not do so by flirting with Shriners. Rather, they did so as consumers of fictional desert romances set in North Africa or the Middle East. The most famous sign of this vogue was Rudolph Valentino. The Italian actor was famous for his portrayals of aggressive, sexually potent desert Arabs in films like *The Sheik*. He was also famous for his ability to speak to modern feminine subjectivities, a skill evidenced by the legions female filmgoers who deluged him with fan mail and the desperate crowds at the New York City funeral that marked his untimely death in 1926.[118] Valentino and other actors of the age played "foreigners, tanned, robust, vibrant . . . a character of aggressive physicality and smoldering passion, unfettered by the restraints of 'civilization,'" Gaylyn Studlar observes.[119] Indeed, one of his fans confided to a woman journalist around 1921 that she had come to see Valentino for herself at the movies after her parents had argued: "My mother's always telling me about him. My mother used to have a Valentino scrapbook. My father made her throw everything away."[120] The Valentino phenomenon was created by women who constructed what Gaylyn Studlar calls "woman-made masculinity" by projecting fantasies of romances with Eastern men onto the actor, fantasies that reflected back an extraordinary identity for a woman as subject of an mysteriously exotic man's desire.[121]

Valentino's Arab roles emanated from a number of classic desert romances including Edith M. Hull's *The Sheik* (1919), published first in London, and its sequel, *Sons of the Sheik* (1925), which inspired the Valentino screen adaptations. All these vehicles told stories of independent young women who defied family or society to find themselves in a foreign land, only to be abducted out of a desert caravan and raped then eventually falling in love with her hypermasculine Arab captor. Moreover, in *Sons of the Sheik* female audiences were invited to play Oriental imaginatively since the heroine is a "high-born English girl whose parents disappeared on a trip in North Africa" compelled by her Arab captor to dance in cafes and bazaars in the style of a *ghawazi* until her eventual liberation. There was no ultimate danger of "race mixing" since, Osman Benchérif explains, in "The Sheik" the Arab captor in time revealed his true identity: "Under the floating robes and the desert tan, Ahmed Ben Hassan is actually a Scottish nobleman, the Earl of Glencarry, who had been abandoned in the Sahara as a baby."[122] So had British diplomat T. E. Lawrence become famous in 1919 and was crossed over to American theater audiences as "Lawrence of Arabia" by journalist and impresario Lowell Thomas. His tritely commercial musical slide show toured the nation presenting images of Lawrence apparently playing Eastern in Arabia, "lands of history, mystery, and romance," Thomas said.[123]

To female consumers, Rudolph Valentino's sheik movies and other modern desert romances were about individual expression, romantic love, and an imagined life that edited out crying babies, factory work, ringing telephones, and other sources of labor and anxiety. To others, the desert romance fad also pointed out a nexus of consumption and individuation in the nation that both encouraged and lampooned women's growing colloquial feminism in capitalism as workers and spenders.[124] The Eastern "girl" was no pushover but self-directed with her own money to spend. Most dangerously, she asserted that one's persona was entirely open to manipulation by way of dress, naming practices, body language, and every kind of consumption. The following chapter goes out after these women to see what happened when some of them rejected Shriners and other work-a-day native-born men to seek out actual men from the Eastern world in the United States.

chapter 7

Turbans and Capitalism, 1893–1930

What happened to the persona of the wise man of the East with the rise of modern mass consumerism among the middle and working classes? Once he had been a fixture of American fraternal orders and a standing joke among Shriners critical of the Gilded Age commercialization of masculine mysticism. Yet by the turn of the century, he became newly relevant to female consumers, and he made American men very nervous. Women already had limited access to actual men from the Eastern world as immigrants and traveling entrepreneurs. Yet between 1893 and the 1930s these men would be joined by a group of highly controversial Hindu and Sufi emissaries, Indian nationalists and university students, and plenty of native-born and foreign-born imitators, all of whom would crowd together in the domestic marketplaces for entertainment and spirituality. A new generation of urban women consumers sought these men out in order to gain worldly, modern experiences of spiritual Eastern masculinity in the flesh. This chapter is about why and how that happened and how Americans commented on the phenomenon in order to talk about the relationship between manhood and economic failure in the years leading up to the Great Depression.

We must begin when Indian religious leaders first arrived in the United States when the Columbian Exposition in Chicago hosted the World's Parliament of Religion in 1893. In the preceding years, American media coverage of South Asia had been limited since the region was not a major American tourist destination nor did it figure into American cultural history like the Middle East as Holy Land, so most people knew far less about India than Egypt or Palestine.[1] South Asian Hindus, Buddhists, and others attended the parliament, the only meeting of its kind in world history, in order to speak about Eastern spiritual traditions to an audience of mostly affluent Anglo-Americans, some of whom took up the Eastern philosophies of the visiting swamis and yogis themselves. This process of adaptation was complicated when predominantly male Indian migrant workers began arriving on the west coast in significant numbers in the early 1910s, inflaming xenophobic feeling among some observers. Thereafter, two constituencies of native-born and foreign-born men created a proliferation of domestic wise men of the East in the country: South Asian migrants who worked as swamis and yogis in the United States and home-grown mediums and carnival fortune-tellers who Easternized themselves in order to pass as wise men of the East, be they saints or scoundrels. The early twentieth-century newspaper "Swami" might employ a persona drawn from any part of the Eastern world, sometimes in eccentric combination, creating a colloquially "Hindoo" or "Oriental" wise man of the East who was not specifi-cally Muslim, Hindu, or Buddhist. Yet like the actual spiritual emissaries of the 1890s, he also attracted an overwhelmingly female audience.

A decade later, when the desert romance fad began overflowing from Ameri-can theaters, newspapers, and movie magazines, many people would conflate the Indian migrant and the desert sheik into a more sexualized, generically Eastern man who particularly sought out white women. This development reshaped and bolstered the idea that the Indian turban would replace the white headdress of Valentino's "Sheik," as far as many Americans were concerned, as the marker of a newly predatory and opportunistic Eastern masculinity that threatened to break up marriages, empty bank accounts, and upset the social order. Critics worried that it was not Eastern religions that were so persuasive to American women but the masculine Eastern persona symbolized by the turban-clad swami.

A unique alliance of men including clergy, police, the press, some sincere Eastern spiritual leaders, professional stage magicians (many of whom per-formed a type of magical Eastern manhood themselves), as well as perplexed husbands together decried the turban-wearing man as a ne'er-do-well. All American men found themselves in the difficult position of needing to achieve "success" because the United States had always been a highly competitive place, Scott Sandage tells us, "a commercial democracy, [in which] commodity and identity melded." Native-born and foreign-born men struggled to navigate a cultural contrast Americans internalized between "the 'couldn't-do-it' and the 'can-do-it' men" that left those men who stumbled in their careers at risk of coming across as inconsequential failures.[2] The disreputable swami was a person unable to succeed in the world of Anglo-American business, critics said, who resorted to performances of spiritual Eastern masculinity in private spaces like hotel rooms in order to subsist immorally off the most credulous American consumers, namely, women.

Exempted from this economy of judgment were those who came across as masculine and Oriental to be sure but did so in secular performances that women usually attended chaperoned by their families: parading Shriners, professional stage magicians, and Arab Americans who performed feats of athleticism in circuses and vaudeville shows. By contrast, it was spiritual South Asian man that Anglo-Americans would speak about using feminine-gendered language that they similarly directed at India as a whole. South Asians of any religion or level of wealth were "spiritual, impulsive, and even irrational," Andrew Rotter explains of a broad American opinion. Thus, people perceived the Indian man and his turbaned imitator to be failures, paradoxically lazy, effeminate, and sexually predatory toward white women entranced by the idea of the "Mystic East."[3]

First-person accounts of the cosmopolitan relationships between American women and turban-wearing men, native-born and foreign-born, between 1893 and the 1930s have gone largely unrecorded, and we know much more about how critics responded than about what actually took place. Yet the financial viability of the wise man of the East and the persistence of his persona tells us that many individuals found meaning in their relationships with the turban-wearing spiritual man. He engaged in up-close live performance crafted for women who sought to defy the overwhelming racism and xenophobia of the early twentieth century through worldly spiritual experience, even if he politely asked for money at the end of the encounter. The story of how and why the turban became a sign of failure to so many Americans is important to our examination of why playing Eastern mattered because it shows how difficult it could be for South Asians to intervene in American life and how American women nonetheless helped make that intervention possible. The Eastern swami came bearing an antimaterialist critique of the United States, and many Anglo-American women saw in it a rebuke of white male power and American modernity premised upon it.

THE MODERN SWAMI'S ANTIMATERIALIST CRITIQUE

Once again, to understand how this all got started we need to go back to Chicago in 1893 and the World's Parliament of Religions. Alongside the carnival of information, experience, and commerce that was the Columbian Exposition, actual spiritual emissaries came to the Parliament to speak directly to Americans, bypassing native-born speakers like Albert Rawson and the Theosophists who had spread foreign wisdom in the country earlier that century. Visitors like Paramahansa Yogananda, Swami Vivekanda, and Swami Prabhavananada were only the most famous of various representatives of Hinduism, Buddhism, Roman Catholicism, Judaism, Islam, Protestantism, and Theosophy who sought Americans' attention. Many Anglo-American Protestants at the Parliament were taken aback by how assertive foreign religious speakers were in Chicago, how they criticized United States foreign policy, Americans' lack of cultural relativism, and especially their nerve in sending missionaries to Asia.[4] Just as importantly, the attention generated by the meetings demonstrated to foreign and domestic observers that there was a large audience of paying customers eager to see performances of Eastern spirituality.[5] Thereafter, a number of these messengers used professional booking agents to take traveling lectures and courses on Asian spiritualities to every major American city. "Something savoring of ancient oriental wisdom, yet refreshingly new!" one sympathetic observer said of the comprehensible Ex Oriente Lux message these speakers would offer the middle and upper classes by comparing life in the West to that in the East.[6]

South Asians became so prominent in these years because Muslims and Eastern Christians had only limited ability to participate in the debate at the Parliament of Religions and for at least two decades thereafter. The Ottoman Sultan, Abdülhamid II, had refused to permit any Ottoman subjects to speak at the event, even though the Sultan was technically the inheritor of the Islamic Caliphate and the highest representative of Muslims in the world. Nor were the North Africans and former Ottoman subjects in the United States privileged enough to be invited to speak for their respective faiths. Instead an American convert and diplomat, Alexander Mohammed Russell Webb, filled the void as a lone voice for Islam at the meetings. Defying the Protestant missionaries there who presented unsympathetic papers on the faith, Webb announced he would begin his own missionary work in New York City.[7] Webb's novelty got him some polite journalistic interest in places like Frank Leslie's Weekly, where he was pictured in a suit and white turban to signify his conversion. In these venues and his public lectures, Webb used the classic Lux appeal, admonishing middling readers that "Mohammed is the most thoroughly misrepresented and misunderstood character in history." He also argued that the essential tenets of the Prophet Muhammad's message were the same as that of Moses, Abraham, and Jesus, although his defense of polygamy got him lampooning coverage in the local press, pictured in a fez and Turkish slippers being attacked by a woman with an umbrella. Like many at the Parliament of Religions that fall, Webb would attempt to make his beliefs comprehensible by crossing them over in comprehensible terms that hopefully flattered listeners as an informed, open-minded public.[8]

Other Eastern messengers, especially Hindus, would have a much greater impact than Webb or any voice for Islam in the United States between the Parliament and the mid-1920s. Many of them would offer similar Lux appeals, yet their overarching modus operandi was to cast Western materialism as inauthentic and spiritually empty. They invited listeners to individuate themselves outside the market, to define their identities not by earning and spending but through study and contemplation of ancient Eastern philosophies. In a nation wracked by labor troubles, regular economic panics, and red scares, this critique was a revelation to some among the privileged upper class who were critical of their nation. To others, the swamis' antimaterialist critique was a sign of weakness in the speaker, who made a living by entertaining an uncritical segment of the American elite, especially society ladies. The tension between the two perspectives would set the tone of debate over South Asians in America and of the turban for more than a generation.

To get a sense of how most Americans unable to attend the Parliament of Religions discovered this unsolicited foreign advice, consider Swami Vivekananda. An Indian Hindu, he is best remembered today for introducing yoga to the United States and for founding the Vedanta Society in California. He spent the middle part of the 1890s lecturing his way around the country, attracting considerable interest and positive press notice before heading to Britain. Vivekananda was a trail blazer in the spirit of Christopher Oscanyan, concerned enough about Westerners to live among them to try to win them over, if not as converts to his beliefs, at least as respectful observers of Hindu civilizations. A sympathetic if hackneyed reminiscence of Swami Vivekananda's first days in the United States by a follower replicates the spirit of his antimaterialism as his own self-staging and followers' interpretation of him came together to make him comprehensibly Eastern with his advanced spiritual knowledge but naïvete in business affairs. "Unused to handling money," one retelling of the story went, "the Swami was robbed and imposed upon at every stage of his journey, when he finally reached Chicago, he was nearly penniless." Alone in the city, "crowds, attracted by his quaint dress, followed him on the streets, hooting at him. His situation was desperate." Clearly, the street was not Vivekananda's venue, something that became abundantly clear soon after when a kind-hearted socialite befriended him during a train ride, put him up in her home and introduced him to a different audience: a Harvard professor and other elite Bostonian seekers of wisdom who would finance his travels.[9] One cynical observer of Vivekananda described famous swamis' representation of their beliefs in America as "export Hinduism," which played to American stereotypes about the mystic East and crass, capitalist West.[10] He had a point in that the interpretation of Hinduism that those turn-of-the-century emissaries would develop for Western audiences came to hold great authority for decades thereafter.[11]

As more and more upper-class Americans sought out these Indian visitors after the turn of the century, they were able to make their way through well-to-do private homes and lecture halls collecting donations and speaking honoraria. They did indeed attract a predominantly female audience, a pattern that helped to portray the swami not as sincere messenger but as pampered guest of wealthy white women, especially, some said, "New Woman" feminists. These were women seeking spiritual individuation, self-discovery, and feminism through yoga, Eastern mysticism, and, sometimes, communal living with Indian spiritual emissaries. This fact caused consternation among these women's friends and families, especially since many of these seekers had already unnerved loved ones by having previously investigated Christian Scientist, New Thought, or Theosophical beliefs.[12]

Clergy and journalists were the loudest initial detractors of the potential Easternization of elite American spirituality as an invasion by foreign ne'er-do-wells. Protestant missionaries were some of the most vocal complainers, particularly shaken by the phenomenon of Eastern men offering exotic spiritualities to American women, which held an unsettling irony then as it had in 1893. "The churches of America are appending annually more than $20,000,000 for foreign missions; but from the very fields where all this money is garnered, the Eastern religions, against which these efforts are made, are gathering their harvest also," the *Literary Digest* advised in 1912. "Is it any wonder that missionaries on the foreign field, hearing of these strange facts, are sending to their home offices in New York and Boston the peremptory inquiry, 'What do women of Christian America *mean*?'" (italics in original).[13] Such attacks on foreign teachers denied the fact that practicing women outnumbered men in most religions and congregations in the United States, as Ann Braude has pointed out. The regular warnings from the clergy about declining church attendance or the secularization of society were often mostly a function of the woman-

centered nature of American religious practice and the clergy's financial depen-
dence on communities of believers that could and sometimes did look elsewhere for meaning.[14]

Still, an announced crisis could be put to use to sensationalize dwindling
cash flow by giving readers a role in solving the proposed problem. For instance, in 1912, popular writer and commentator on women's issues, Mabel
Potter Daggett, worried in a missionary periodical that, "the danger to American women, . . . lies not so much in the worship of images such as little brown
buddhas and little jade Krishnas—although that is bad enough—but in the
worship of men, their Hindu gurus, or swamis. After a certain swami has
finished his devotions, his female devotees bow eagerly to kiss his sandaled
feet."[15] Here was blasphemy with sexual overtones, Daggett implied of imagined physical contact between Anglo-American women and "brown" men. She
further raised the alarm over the "descent from Christianity to heathenism"
that made former society women "unbalanced," "a physical wreck," or, in one
alleged case, "incarcerated as a raving maniac in an Illinois asylum" by their
contact with Indian men.[16]

That year, during a sermon at the First Methodist Church in Chicago, Bishop
Frank W. Warne also publicly decried such women as "credulous." He was
outspoken about the moral panic over Indian men "who cannot make a living in
India. They are outcasts with no standing, yet they come to this country and
with glittering turbans, oriental costumes and mystical phrases get thousands
from women who are silly enough to believe them."[17] This was the consumer's
Oriental tale at work selling Eastern religion, it seemed. Warne particularly
castigated Swami Vivekananda with the language of fraud and Eastern deca-
dence, calling him a "charlatan" who had collected enough money from American women to live in a "magnificent palace" in India to which he "brought
three women from the Pacific Coast as inmates of his establishment."

As Gaylyn Studlar has summarized it, there was considerable concern in the
1910s and 1920s over foreign men, who represented a "stereotype of sexualized
and greedy masculinity, at his most dangerous he was darkly foreign, an immigrant who was ready to make his way in the New World by living off women and
their restless desires."[18] Warne summed up his diatribe by accusing American
women who funded or visited Indian spiritual emissaries of embarrassing the
United States before British colonial authorities in order to preface his own "im-
passioned plea for contributions," which raised $1,000 on the spot, or so the

papers reported in a story provocatively headlined "Scores Women Cult Victims."[19] Indeed, Warne shared with the spiritual emissaries he critiqued the need to survive financially while appearing to be immune from financial matters.

Much of this kind of public activity on the part of missionaries lumped together celebrity emissaries like Swami Vivekananda and Swami Abhednanada with new groups of Sikh migrant workers in the country. The conflation was a function of media panic over a supposed "Hindu Movement" that emerged up and down the west coast and in the national press between 1910 and 1914, when restrictive legislation limiting Indian entry to the United States came to the attention of Congress.[20] Hundreds of Sikh men from the Punjab had come to work in the United States, many of them in timber, mining, and agriculture. They caused particular alarm among some Anglo-Americans worried about competition over jobs and religion, as had the arrival of new migrants from Ireland, Germany, China, and Japan before.[21] More than one person would now argue that since their numbers had been limited by restrictive legislation in 1882 and 1905, the once-despised Chinese had settled into peaceful lives as domestic servants and the Japanese Americans as business owners and productive farmers. Meanwhile, since they were British subjects, there were no controls on Sikhs or any other Indians entering the United States that might give anxious whites a sense of control.

With respect to Indian migrant workers, some Anglo-Americans explained that Indians were "the same ancient Aryan stock" as Anglo-Americans and thus white for all intents and purposes. Yet, the logic went, South Asians were still unable to assimilate as Americans because of the profound cultural differences they carried with them. "It is not, indeed, a question of the yellow and the white, but of the Oriental and the Occidental," one nativist explained.[22] That is, the same argument of Eastern whiteness that saw Arab Americans cross themselves over as patriotic immigrants, especially Syrian Christians, was of little use to Hindus from south Asia whose religious beliefs were too unsettling to many and whose cultural difference was being explained by famous swamis who contrasted East and West on publicity-seeking speaking tours. Journalists consequently vented popular and elite antiimmigration sentiment in sensational talk of "the Hindoo invasion . . . even more menacing than the Chinese or Japanese invasion" and "A TIDE OF TURBANS" materializing from the Pacific.[23] Because Sikh men did wear turbans as a matter of culture and religion, even though many of the South Asian spiritual teachers appeared bareheaded, many Anglo-Americans projected the Sikh turban onto all South Asian men as an icon of an opportunistic manhood put to use by scoundrels who railed against modernity and capitalism in the West to drum up donations from the elite.

How did the celebrity Eastern emissaries cope with this? We do have some first-hand accounts that show how they attempted to control their own publicity as spiritual educators and wise men of the East. Sufi philosopher Pir O-Murshid Inayat Khan was among the most well-known public representatives of the Muslim world in the United States in these years, although most probably just took him as "Hindoo." Indeed, most American accounts of South Asia took the region as almost completely Hindu, with Muslim, Buddhist, Christian, Sikh, and other religions seldom mentioned.[24] A Muslim from Baroda, India, Khan espoused not formal Islamic teachings but Sufism, the esoteric, mystical part of Islamic tradition that encompasses a diverse collection of practices and schools of thought united largely only in name. Khan's teachings described Sufism as the essence of all religions (as some Hindu teachers said of their philosophies also) expressed most effectively through artistic expression. For Khan, the true Sufi mystic was a seeker, male or female, of the one truth that will inevitably "rise above the boundaries of creed, race, caste and nation," he said.[25] The autobiographical account of his experiences in spreading this message in the United States tells us much about what some Americans wanted from Eastern men and how the press would capitalize on this interest to recast the meaning of the turban as a comment on capitalism, race, and gender.

Beginning in 1910, Inayat Khan began lecturing, counseling, small talking, and fundraising his way around the country. Khan's Ex Oriente Lux appeal shared the romanticism about the "Mystical East" that earlier emissaries from India and their American patrons had often contrasted with America as spiritually barren and materialistic. Like many Eastern men and some American liberals, Inayat Khan also blamed Christian missionaries and clergy for what he called "the wrong impression [of Islam] spread in the West."[26] He accused them of creating a sense of emergency to fill the church pews and donation plates, a practice that undermined his work to win people over to the mystical unity of humankind. Khan played Oriental in his own way by replicating certain expectations in order to be recognized as wise man of the East when criticizing Anglo-American culture.[27] With his students he came across as endlessly patient, slow to anger, exuding indefatigable positive attitude, and unconcerned with possessions or wealth. Exotic visitors like Swami Vivekananda and Inayat Khan, as Emily Brown puts it, were men whose "very Indian-ness gave him an entrée into intellectual circles which he might not otherwise have had and to this end he was willing to accentuate what Westerners considered the eccentricities of his cultural background."[28]

Khan was also owner of an unlimited supply of stories about his life back in India that all had a fabled, Oriental-tale quality about them. Many consisted of maxims that taught love, patience, and humility in yarns liberally sprinkled with camel drivers, elephant rides, visits to the homes of Maharajas, leisured father-son pontifications on the mystical meaning of life, and even miraculous events of healing and mind reading. On first arriving in New York, he wrote of being "transported by destiny from the world of lyric and poetry to the world of industry and commerce." Still his uncle had earlier cautioned him, "life in the West is difficult for an Eastern person. To make a living is still more difficult."[29] The contrasts Khan encountered between rural India and New York City may have convinced him of these truisms. Yet whether he believed them or not, they helped him cross over more challenging content to American patrons anxious to escape the modern American drive for success and accumulation. Khan could have cut his hair and donned a suit and briefcase, but he would not have been nearly so successful in communicating his messages of spiritual universalism and the divine to his often-wealthy American supporters.[30] Instead, he lectured with uncovered shoulder-length hair and often through universities in order to preserve the nonprofit, middle-class respectability of his presentation of Sufism. Like South Asian teachers, Khan used the swami's Lux appeal to contrast an idealized, essential Indianness with modern Anglo-American personhood in order to take power in a conversation with Americans by arguing that his cultural difference was a valuable cultural capital he controlled and could dole out to followers and benefactors.[31]

Khan insisted that his mystical ideas were best communicated by way of a student's contemplation of his music and poetry, but he also had bills to pay; to make ends meet, at one point he had accepted an invitation to work and travel with the then-up-and-coming American dancer Ruth St. Denis. He later lamented that he felt he had compromised his music's spiritual essence by performing with St. Denis's international troupe of Indian-inspired dancers. American audiences consequently perceived his art as "an amusement for them, [which was] painful for us," he said.[32] Yet in other venues more to his purpose, sincere American seekers interrupted his musical performances and talks wanting "to know all in plain words, which makes the idea cut and dry, taking away the beauty of its curve. . . . No sooner does a student read something than he is eager to discuss it, he is ready to judge before pondering upon the subject by himself," as Khan essentialized a proposed American get-rich-quick approach to spiritual growth.[33] Such stories he would use to define his Sufi persona by inviting followers to join in his evaluation of American ways that similarly essentialized a diverse group of people.

Like others, he struggled with the ambivalent opportunity presented by the press, which seemed to often determine which performers of spiritual Eastern manhood would be taken seriously and which not. Journalists were crucial for communication with the public and often an entirely unmanageable, self-interested third party themselves working to keep afloat financially by predicting audience demand for information and entertainment. In those years such men inspired Walter Lippmann to redefine the term stereotype to talk about how journalists framed content to flatter existing audience perceptions. Likewise, Khan explained, "Newspaper reporters in the United States used to come and would speak with me on different subjects and would be very much impressed by the ideas, and the next day a very ugly article would appear in the paper."[34] Lippmann would have warned him, "this is the underlying reason for the existence of the press agent. The enormous discretion as to what facts and what impressions shall be reported is steadily convincing every organized group of people that whether it wishes to secure publicity or avoid it, the exercise of discretion cannot be left to the reporter."[35] After repeated questions from Khan, one reporter in fact admitted that his editor thought little of American newspaper readers, Khan revealed to his supporters, and only wanted stories that catered to the perceptions of "every man on the lowest level."[36]

Despite the efforts of men like Inayat Khan, during the first three decades of the twentieth century plenty of Anglo-Americans expressed deep resentment against poor South Asian immigrants, to be sure, but especially against a group one crabby xenophobe ridiculed as "the Swamis, poets and fakirs who come over here to talk to pink teas and tell us of our inferiority and materialism."[37] Celebrity South Asians had been very assertive in gaining access to the United States, many of them relying on the well-to-do "pink tea" types who had the luxury of complaining about capitalism from the top of the economic ladder. Beyond the famous swamis and Sikh laborers, even more South Asian men had access to the United States: playwrights, novelists, diplomats, educators, and professional lecturers were willing and able to visit and to meet with journalists, politicians, and academics to talk about world politics, religion, cultural differences between East and West, and more.

Swami Abhedananda got typically cynical press treatment, here by way of sensational illustrations implying a predatory gaze on his part, belatedly added by editors to a sympathetic piece documenting the swami's ideas. *New York World*, 1906. Billy Rose Theatre Division, The New York Public Library for the Performing Arts, Astor, Lenox and Tilden Foundations.

Around then, the soon-to-be famous dancer Ruth St. Denis had sought out some of the Eastern men she found in American cities in her own search for artistic inspiration. "They would sit on the floor and answer in a chorus the questions that I flung at them," she remembered. Even someone as sympathetic to foreign performers as St. Denis saw that some of these young men were unsettled, still finding their way in the world, and certainly not celebrity visitors or wealthy diplomats. "They were of all varieties—Hindus, Moslems, Buddhists," she said. "Some were clerks from shops, some were students at Columbia, and one or two were unmistakable ne'er-do-wells."[38] The trope of Indian man as ne'er-do-well was a persistent one since just enough men fit the profile to give a grain of truth to a cliché that could be broadcast onto the whole group. Har Dayal, an Indian nationalist resident in the United States who was regularly attacked by the press and government as a foreign radical, specifically complained of Indian migrants and immigrants who had little formal spiritual training but capitalized on their knowledge of Indian cultures and languages to play swami. Men like "Super Akasha Yogi Wassan," Dayal accused, took on an Americanized Hinduness emanating from the interactions of these foreigners' real selves with market demand to coax "credulous middle-aged ladies out of their dollars."[39]

It is difficult to say how many Indian students and migrant laborers rejected low-paying factories or resource-industry labor in favor of providing performances of spiritual Eastern manhood as ad hoc yoga teachers or "Hindoo" advisers, yet however many there were, they drew plenty of attention through their self promotion. Inayat Khan for one had vowed to avoid confusion with all the turbaned and costumed pseudoswamis now working the country. Still people came to him demanding lessons in yoga. By the late 1920s, American investigations of yoga and meditation had drawn many serious American practitioners. "In America everybody knew the name of Yoga and began to search for it as one does for every drug or herb, seeking if they can buy it somewhere," Khan complained.[40] So was Professor Rao just then advertising yoga instruction patent medicine–style: "No more divorces. No more drunkenness—only happy homes and happy souls. No more sorrow; no more moonshine—only sunshine."[41] Inayat Khan's attempts to publicly clarify the subtleties of Sufism from Eastern-derived mind-over-matter techniques of breathing, and to get across the fact that he was not even Hindu at all, were further complicated by a wider show business context of press images and circus acts of lean, turbaned Indian men "sleeping" on beds of nails or withstanding other physical dangers.

So many men took up the ad hoc swami trade because after the 1910s, the possibility of presenting oneself as Eastern became much more powerful since most Americans knew there were actual people from North Africa, West Asia, and South Asia in the United States and might expect to encounter one of them. In an age before color television or large-scale immigration from those regions, Americans often had a difficult time telling an actual swami or sufi missionary from others who might dress the part, put on some kind of unusual accent, and go about the cities advertising themselves as carriers of Eastern wisdom. Streetwise yogis and fortune-tellers of various origins plied a trade in spiritual advising by using mysterious personae to embellish the perceived authority of their secret powers or "Oriental" wisdom with a degree of incomprehensibility.

White women fortune-tellers might use a French or Gypsy-sounding name, and African American women drew from these and from African and Middle Eastern personae. However—and crucially for our analysis—men of all complexions drew almost exclusively from West Asian and South Asian identities, although some would of course come across as Native American healers as well. An especially popular persona many used was "Hindoo." As a trade term, religious entrepreneurs often juxtaposed "Hindoo" with ancient Egyptian, Islamic, East Asian, or black folk medicinal symbols and words in eccentric combination, such that "Hindoo" came to mean simply "of the East." In general parlance in the United States, to avoid confusion with Native Americans who were of course also known as Indians, the term "Hindoo" persisted to describe someone of any faith who came from the Indian subcontinent.[42] This usage could result in odd contemporary statements about the "Hindoo type of Islam" or "Sikh Hindoos" in the United States as the national and religious terms got tangled.[43]

The construction of such mysterious Eastern personae between the 1890s and 1930s tells us what terms like "Moslem," "Hindoo," or "Oriental" actually meant to large urban segments of the population with no authorial access to Anglo-American publications. If one was in the business of coming across as modern wise man of the East, there were a number of necessary components that would make it work, the more the better: an exotic-sounding name, colorful costume with turban if possible, a foreign accent, romantic Oriental tale–style patter, a meeting space with elements of Oriental décor, and last, an apparent non-Anglo-Saxon racial or ethnic identity, which might only be implied by the previous components.

These practitioners played Eastern to offer a kind of want-ad spirituality, available to new consumers through the papers and the bustling urban neighborhoods of rural migrants and foreign immigrants. In San Francisco in 1906, one could obtain readings from those who employed Muslim-style personae, such as the mystifying psychic "Miss Zemdar" or someone called "Ottoman Zar-Adusht Hannish." So did "Ismar" advertise himself as an "Egyptian Clairvoyant and Palmist" and give private counsel "from 10:00 am to 5:00 pm daily; three questions answered for $1.00, a full life reading for $5.00."[44] Plenty of these seemingly Indian or Middle Eastern practitioners offered lessons in Hindu-based or Muslim-based mystical systems, lessons in self-healing, the secrets of Tibetan monks, "Hindoo psychology," and yoga, among other topics. Yogi Ramacharaka (William Walker Atkinson) even went so far as to found the Yogi Publishing Society, through which he offered books and pamphlets for sale through newspaper announcements—the exact spot in which the unemployed sought work, cynics noted.[45]

TURBANS AND MALE FAILURE

It is impossible to sort out among these performers who was native-born or foreign-born, who a saint or a scoundrel, who a sincere Indian swami, an Eastern-styled fortune-teller, or—even more confounding—a professional stage magician. The messiness of this period was flagrantly revealed by a group of fringe magicians who converged with the economy of wise men of the East in American cities. These performers were not sincerely spiritual but were professional illusionists, some of them not entirely disreputable but not successful enough to headline a vaudeville booking either. All these individuals had a similar story of mystical travel in the "East," meaning North Africa, the Middle East, Persia, India, and often Tibet, wherein they had survived some sort of spiritual or magical test. Like the foreign swamis and streetwise mystics, they came across as messengers bringing to the West secrets that would set Americans free, a story that would be especially appealing into the 1920s and 1930s. They were also some of the most vocal, well-financed critics of Indian teachers in the United States, especially because many Americans could not tell the two types of exotically Eastern men—professional magician and swami adviser—apart.

Take, for instance, a man calling himself the White Mahatma. Employing a classic magus story in 1903 and 1904, he performed in a persona verging on satire, telling audiences he was "General Inspector of the Supreme Esoteric council of Thibet" and a "Hindoo prince," son of Indian and French nobility. The character of the Eastern magus is an old archetype in human history and was current among all sorts of esotericists and seekers from Helena Blavatsky to the Masons to those inspired by the swamis at the World's Parliament of Religions in Chicago.[46] The modern magi of urban America carried a spiritual Ex Oriente Lux message in both for-profit and nonprofit contexts to audiences who might come to believe themselves as insiders privy to secret knowledge through which to make out their own identities. The White Mahatma explained that he had "been sent by the Masters or Mahatmas into the West to propagate their doctrines in America." The White Mahatma was actually a man known alternately as Count de Sarak and Samri S. Baldwin, a professional entertainer and sincere occultist. Dressed in Catholic robes, Sarak and his young female assistants gave performances of fortune-telling and mind-reading at the Waldorf-Astoria and the Fulton Street Theatre in Brooklyn. So did his Theosophist wife hold séances in New York city theaters.[47] If the White Mahatma was not convincing enough in his demonstration of mystical powers to skeptical modern Americans, there were others who might win them over. "Prince P. Ishmael Hindoo Magician" performed adorned with a biblical name, a fez, and a costume native to India. Then there was "Hewes, the White Yogi," his original identity lost to history, a man who invited misidentification just after the turn of the century by performing various magical illusions of Indian origin.[48]

Such personae were a product of a kind of religious and show business pastiche that created hybrid Eastern manhoods many thought were ridiculous put-ons, to be sure, but never attracted the kind of racist vitriol the Sikh migrant, celebrity swami, or Indian-student yoga teacher did.[49] Professional stage magicians were the show business arm of the larger network of criticism and moral panic surrounding Eastern spiritualities and Eastern men in the United States that reveals how white men thought about people's attempts to celebrate the sincere wise man of the East. They, of all people, knew how precarious was the business of playing Eastern man for profit because they did it every day. As magician-debunkers they often tried publicly, as a career move, to expose the work-a-day identities of Eastern-styled streetwise mystics, psychics, and healing artists who made spiritual truth claims and denied that their work was a performance or illusion.[50] From their perspective, the streetwise adviser who manipulated his or her persona for profit did so as part of a larger fraud. According to the magicians' code of ethics, a "modern magician" might play Oriental on stage and in promotional material for a commercial show. Every customer who paid the money and walked in the door understood that in spite of what their eyes saw, the magician would always insist: "This is just an illusion." Indeed, intercultural cross-dressing was the stock-in-trade of theater, often serving to reassert social distinctions and Waspy norms in venues like vaudeville where audiences expected the magician to "play with his identity," as Marjorie Garber has said of all actors. They argued that for a man to represent himself as of another race, ethnicity, or nationality for profit was only acceptable in jest on stage where every observer understood a performance would take place.[51] Modern magicians and their supporters in the press and church argued that all the swamis and streetwise mystics who performed illusions of spirituality and identity did so in venues like the want ads or hotel rooms, where the fact of performance and illusion were not necessarily understood by the usually female viewer.

By the 1910s, there almost 2,000 professional magicians and an estimated 10,000 amateurs working in the country.[52] Most native-born magicians were young Anglo-American men who had started out in their late teens or early twenties doing coin and card tricks at parties or the local opera house. The most talented performers built life-long careers by devising truly original illusions, including mind reading acts that mimicked the costuming and apparent psychic abilities of streetwise yogis and celebrity swamis. Like the best performers in every part of the entertainment industry, American stage magicians made the most of whatever content and inspiration the Eastern world had to offer, whether of Hindu, Muslim, or some other derivation, including magi-style personae with richly elaborate costumes that included satin or jewel-encrusted turbans. They pooled this professional wisdom in Eastern-styled magicians' trade journals like *Mahatma*, *Magic Wand*, and *The Sphinx*. "Magic means 'the east,'" one vaudevillian reminded his fellow magicians.[53]

Plenty of these artists blended together masculinist elements from across North Africa, West Asia, and South Asia, combining a mysteriously exotic persona with patter spoken in Eastern voice and *Arabian Nights*–style props. For instance, Howard Thurston, also known as The Great Thurston, won favorable reviews early in his career for creating "a subtle atmosphere of mysticism" at his shows by appearing before audiences in "the garb of a Persian Prince." Thurston employed a turbaned black child actor as a "Morocco boy" who swallowed eggs whole, which then appeared to emerge from his naked chest. He also had white women performing on stage as "Circassian princesses [who] came in and out with censors, emitting incense fumes."[54] Frequently the "Oriental sumptuousness in the architecture of the auditorium," as one reviewer called contemporary Moorish theater styles, helped such performers wishing to create a show "reminiscent of the Arabian Nights," as Thurston did.[55] Playing Eastern by his costume, show name, stage decoration, and patter provided the misdirection that persuaded the viewer to perceive a performance mentally *as a magical illusion*, not just a man in a turban sawing a box with a woman protruding from one end, fake legs from the other.[56]

The degree to which the magician played a role was even more obvious because Anglo-American magicians competed directly with a group of international magicians from India, Egypt, Japan, and China who also performed in Eastern guise in American circuses, medicine shows, vaudeville, and carnivals. These foreign magicians promptly reproduced existing standards on vaudeville, many of which were derived from foreign magical traditions in any event. An Indian Muslim working under the name Mohammad Ali Alexander, for example, did a show with various Indian assistants that he promoted Oriental-

tale style as previously enjoyed by "Rajahs, Begums, and other turbaned potentates" overseas before Alexander had arrived in the United States "in his cloud
of Oriental mystery," as one journalist put it.[57]

Just after the turn of the century, most white magicians were quick to defend
foreign colleagues who injected new material into a business that required
endless novelty to keep the audience's attention. In part this acceptance also
came from the fact that foreign-born magicians joined their native-born colleagues in debunking the migrant yogis and swamis in a long-term publicity
crusade to make stage magic and some Eastern personae a respectable public
service. So did Egyptian slight-of-hand artist Mohammed Hanafi adopt the
mode of modern magician to cross himself over as a gentleman exposer of
superstition. At the St. Louis World's Fair, he had surveyed the culture of stage
magic in the United States, and told visitors he was out to debunk "THE
FRAUDS OF NECROMANCY." Hanafi said to audiences that he had "established
the mysterious art of legerdemain [sleight of hand] on a purely scientific ba-
sis."[58] Thus did Hanafi gain some sympathetic press coverage as a modern
performer while offering visitors a secular vision of the Middle East that might
counter the ahistorical religious overtones of the biblical Jerusalem Exhibit
nearby.[59]

When both native-born and foreign-born stage magicians looked at the
perceived miracles and psychic powers of want-ad advisers and hotel swamis,
they perceived the same illusions that they performed on the vaudeville circuit
every night. "Ninety-eight per cent of the professional 'mediums' are imposters, gouging dollars out of the public through an elaborate system of psycho-
logical deception, apparatus, and conjuring," one typically accused.[60] Harry
Houdini would be the most famous of these entertaining activists out to promote themselves by claiming to protect consumers, though he was only one of
hundreds less famous today. "Adrian Plate Magical Entertainer" went so far as
to list on his business card "Anti-Spiritualism" along with other specialties like
"Conjuring" and "Mnemonics."[61]

Professional stage magicians attempted to present illusions (not "tricks") as
exposé. They reproduced fraudulent magic and spiritual miracles to instruct the
audience, making sure "that it was clearly and publicly identified as a deception
and properly rationalized as a tool for increasing 'useful knowledge,'" as James
Cook tells us.[62] Stage magicians could make no spiritual truth claims if they
hoped to keep their honor with their colleagues. Accordingly, by the turn of the
century, as proposed gentlemen scholars plenty of stage magicians had begun

wearing tuxedos with their turbans rather than Eastern-styled satin or velvet robes to signify their modern aspirations to newly respectable status in a world where men were increasingly judged by their "success" in business or in the progressive development of society.[63] Moreover, in spite of their own employment of female assistants and the mysterious powers they appeared to exercise over them in performances, professional stage magicians seldom found themselves accused of being Eastern-style predators of women.

Plenty of observers noticed that the lines dividing follower-sponsored spiritual teaching by sincere foreign teachers, mystical-style entertainment by the homegrown yogi, and the modern magic of the fringe or vaudevillian magician was incredibly thin. When the Rudolph Valentino Sheik phenomenon struck the United States after World War I, Eastern men seemed to be testing Anglo-American manhood all the more. A fan of the actor described the Valentino persona in terms of his partial incomprehensibility, which flattered common female stereotypes that associated more knowable Anglo-American men with household labor or boredom: "It's not just that he's good-looking, but his personality! . . . Such a different appeal. He's sultry. Mysterious. The type that appeals to women."[64] In his Sheik guise, Valentino had a slightly unreadable, exotic Eastern masculinity. Thus did the moral panics over pseudoswamis meet up with the newly critical character of the "Sheik." The name of Valentino's most famous role became a humorously pejorative colloquial term describing the young male hustler or Romeo. Parents, the press, police, and clergy would describe him as a sexual predator who offered women self-indulgence and freedom from family and marital duties. The women attracted by the sheikh type also boldly discarded the xenophobia of the decade, which rejected immigrants from nations outside northern Europe as well as intermarriage between Anglo-Saxons and others in fear of creating a "degenerate" or "mongrel" majority in the United States.[65]

That woman-made masculinity resided not just on the movie screen in the early 1920s, but in real-life interactions between American women and foreign men, at first in pay tea parlors and other public locations of commercialized close dancing and amusement in the 1910s and early 1920s.[66] As women gained broader access to the consumer arts of self-fashioning, Eastern men also became more and more accessible to them in cryptic newspaper advertisements for urban yoga schools, exotic advisers in medicine shows, carnivals, and amusement parks. Arab acrobats in the United States appear to have escaped conflation with the turban-wearing Eastern man or the Sheik, characters who became enmeshed and bore the brunt of resentment against women's desires for exotic men, which was considerable.[67] Thus by the 1920s, people were using a gendered, market-based language of fraud to complain that female desire of him marked the turbaned swami as a sign of manly failure and sexual predation who might expose Anglo-American men's failure to protect and control their women.

Suspicious authorities made little distinction between Hindu, Muslim, Sikh, or other Easterners, spiritual or secular, in their accusations of fraud when targeting someone with an apparently sincere Eastern persona. Authorities branded such men "charlatans" and "cult leaders" who "duped" "credulous" American women out of money and/or sex by flattering them with exotic costumes and Orientalized pseudofeminist talk of self-discovery and contentment. Journalists and police especially pointed out that these men often operated out of exotically decorated store fronts, medicine shows, circus midways, newspaper mail-order operations, or—more shady still—hotel rooms, a venue that implied fraud, mobility, and of course, illicit sex.[68] Police who arrested such men due to complaints from customers or their husbands usually asserted that upon arrest the perpetrator had been found to have on his person large quantities of cash and to be in the company a woman not his wife.

The papers vilified such men and their female clienteles in ways some saw as evidence of the stupidity of the modern consumer and others took as a cynical comment on the lengths to which papers would go to increase circulation by boiling up crime and scandal news as front-page moral panic. The press regularly ridiculed these native-born and foreign-born American men who put on a turban and exotic accent to cater to women desiring a mysterious foreign confidante, while their work became criminalized as police hauled them into court under various charges, commonly, practicing medicine without a license, fortune-telling, fraud, imposture, bigamy, and violation of the Mann Act.[69] Actor Rudolph Valentino of Sheik movie fame had likewise been charged with bigamy before his death, giving the idea of a turbaned or Easternized man with a "harem" of multiple women companions an informal satirical bite.

The press, police, stage magicians, and concerned citizens certainly knew the unwritten rules they would use to govern when it was acceptable for a man to play Eastern, when not, and by whom, a rubric that became a minefield for actual spiritual ambassadors from Eastern countries. In the 1920s, a substantial minority of urban Americans of various classes still wished to talk with Eastern teachers like Inayat Khan and, even more, Swami Paramahansa Yogananda. An

Indian Hindu from Uttar Pradesh state, Yogananda was born in 1893, the same year as many Americans first encountered Indian spiritual emissaries in their midst at the World's Parliament of Religions. Swami Yogananda had grown up in India hearing about "the materialistic West," or so he said in his autobiography for Western readers. India was a land very different from the United States, he insisted, a place "steeped in the centuried aura of saints" and inherently spiritual. Determined to spread his ideas about Hinduism and yoga, Yogananda later recalled that he had "go[ne] forth to discover America, like Columbus." By 1920 he had founded the Self-Realization Fellowship in California to provide a base for his work. This permanency pushed the perception of him past quaint visitor to migrant, not as obviously industrious as men like George Hamid or Hadji Tahar but more reminiscent to Americans of the Indian migrant turned yoga teacher of the 1910s.

In 1928 he set out for Miami on another of many speaking tours offering to make his Eastern philosophies relevant to modern American living. This affair was a complete disaster, not that Yogananda was really to blame. He was a veteran speaker by then, yet it appears that several women took Yogananda's teachings by their own interpretation. Some seemed to see him as a kind of miracle worker, or at least the men in their lives thought that was what was going on. One "irate husband" threatened to kill Yogananda if he appeared in Miami since he could not convince his wife to stay away from the lectures.[70] Another man claimed his mother had attempted to walk on the Miami River after hearing Yogananda speak. Even a letter of recommendation from a former California Congressman was not enough to clear up the misunderstandings and sensational news reports flowing to papers around the country.

When police ordered Yogananda and his supporters out of Miami, newspapers ran sardonically inflammatory pieces, for instance, referring to his Self-Realization Fellowship and its multiple properties in California as Yogananda's "love cult" in Los Angeles. They charged Yogananda with having "influenced more than 200 Miami women to pay him $35 each for lessons in sex consciousness," misspelling his name in one article as Yoganando.[71] Thereafter, a court injunction against Yogananda's public lectures forced him to leave town when a Miami Circuit Court judge sided with police, who claimed to have received complaints from local residents about the Indian's "mystic cult" and feared the Swami's life might be in danger. Yogananda disputed the public description of his teachings, the reported $35 price, the accusation of having doled out "private lessons," and any implication that his teachings had sent one woman to hospital. Earlier he had gone so far as to publish tracts with titles like "Yellow Journalism versus the Truth" defending his teachings from the all too frequent press attacks.[72]

Yogananda's humiliated retreat from Miami was also a result of journalists looking for higher ad revenue and of two further facts of life for South Asian emissaries in the country. First, as had swamis and male fortune-tellers before World War I, they did still attract many more female than male students.[73] The women they attracted were often looking for self-fulfillment and did leave husbands and children to seek spiritual awareness and independence.[74] Second, and even worse, some thought, these Asian men often spoke out publicly on the treatment of women in the West. Swami Yogananda's supposed lessons in "sex consciousness" were actually an invitation for women to consider their femininity in a spiritual way as a kind of mystical Eastern feminism. Endorsements from wealthy male students like horticulturalist Luther Burbank probably only made matters worse. The interest of elite Americans hardly eliminated the seeming challenge Eastern men like Yogananda, with their critiques of the masculinist materialism of American life, seemed to point at middle-class and working-class American white men.[75]

The episode in Miami was also part of a larger argument, beginning in the 1910s, that asserted exotic "cults" fueled by greed and immoral desires were on the rise in the nation, especially in California.[76] Still, even in places like New York City one might also find Yogananda's talks promoted on the religion page of the paper next to press notices for Theosophy, Spiritualists, New Thought and other self-help advice, traditional preachers, turbaned hotel-room swamis, and someone called "A. K. Mozumdar—Messianic World Message—World Famous Healer."[77] As it turns out, Mozumdar was the name of an actual Indian spiritual leader who had appeared at the World's Parliament of Religions in 1893, but how was the average person to tell if this was the same the foreign-born adviser or a scoundrel making use of a famous name?[78] For-profit and nonprofit spiritual teachers playing Oriental were more numerous than ever in the universe of want-ad spirituality and other marketplaces of wisdom that lumped together the sincere foreign-born emissary, the stage magician, and other turban-wearing men.

The mysterious personae and potential for mistaken identity that made the want-ad spirituality appealing to working and middle class seekers also had meaning because it was useful and current. In the 1920s, when religion seemed more commercial and this-worldly than ever with Sister Aimee's radio ministry

On the eve of the Great Depression, the urban religious marketplace offered traditional churches, sufism, Theosophy, and turban-clad hotel advisers packed together, all offering paths to spiritual and financial success. *San Francisco Examiner*, 1929.

broadcasting from Los Angeles and Bruce Barton's portrayal of Jesus as an advertising man, *The Man Nobody Knows: A Discovery of the Real Jesus* (1924), selling out, Swami Yogananda saw that for some urbanites traditional churches had lost influence to media-savvy religious leaders and the secular, mind-over-matter philosophies of Babbitt-style "success" and popular psychology.[79] Before leaving India, Yogananda's spiritual teacher had warned him "don't adopt all the ways of the Americans."[80] Nonetheless, Yogananda took this advice with a grain of salt and had been sending a secretary ahead to cities before speaking engagements to plaster billboards and place ads in local newspapers in a very practical attempt to spread the word and attempt to shape his public image independently of the press. He particularly admired the techniques of Christian Scientist and New Thought organizations in the United States and adopted similar self-help terminology to describe his teachings on Hindu mysticism, for example, lecturing in 1925 at the Buffalo Rotary Club on "How to Recharge Your Business Battery Out of the Cosmos."[81] By such ventures Yogananda came across to many people as just another peddler of get-happy-quick schemes that drew up that stereotype of the turbaned man as opportunist, whether he endorsed capitalism and the drive for success or offered an anti-materialist critique.

While the turban had emerged as a sign of male failure, thousands of men wore one in order to avoid going broke. Various men donned an Eastern persona in order to be useful to some audience or other, playing Eastern as a sort of professional self-fashioning that had existed since the mid-nineteenth century but was aimed at a broadly democratic consumer America now. The overlap between all the Easternized men in the United States caused friction but gave the upper hand to native-born whites among them, men who tended to have the ear and sympathy of white men in the media, police departments, and churches as well as an Anglo-American middle-class and upper-class public driven by extraordinary nativism. These men fought mightily to carve out an exclusive right to Eastern personae, even against actual South Asian men.

The competition over these guises was stiff. Inayat Khan for one in May 1926 discovered his cerebral lecture series on Sufism listed on the "Amusements" page of the *New York Times* across from local Shriners billing themselves as "Moslems" from "Mecca Temple" in a show at their lodge entitled "Harem-Scarems." That day he was also upstaged on the very same page by an Italian vaudevillian performing as "Rahman Bey—Fakir—Hypnotist," who puffed himself as "NOT a Magician, NOT a Faker, NOT a Fraud BUT A Genuine Egyptian Miracle Man."[82]

Indeed, professional stage magicians were still trying to make a go of it in Eastern personae. Their shift from older forms of more disreputable showmanship to secular modern magic had in fact facilitated their arrival into respectable venues of middle-class entertainment lasting into the 1930s. As vaudeville began to wind down in those years, many agreed that the public profile of their work must make it crystal clear to audiences and critics that modern illusions still had a place in American life so that, one explained, "the long hours of study, thought and practice may be adequately rewarded."[83] Modern stage magicians had long since crossed over as self-designated, chivalrous guardians of "the ignorant and the innocent"—namely, women—ostensibly providing a "service to the race."[84] It was not just modernity that stage magicians celebrated but the modernity of Anglo-American men who earned a living by a kind of turbaned white-collar work.

By the Great Depression, after decades of defending the foreign magicians and traditions that had laid the groundwork for their professional knowledge, white American stage magicians began discrediting the idea that the East was a source of magical knowledge: "To speak truth, there never have been such magicians as are in the Occident today . . . and all this stuff about the marvels of the East is vastly exaggerated" decided John Mulholland in 1933. Known himself for pulling rabbits from hats, he elaborated, "A man will explain that some bit of his magic is known only to the Yogis or Swamis and himself. This is pure bunk. . . . The East Indian mystic . . . is better in fiction than in real life."[85] Magician Charles Carter agreed, "The sorcerers of the Orient nowadays even here borrow from the skill and devices of the Occident, aping their western colleagues down to the minor details of dress and deportment." That is, he said, all the events of apparent mind-reading or miracles were illusions to be unpacked by the modern Anglo-American magician who need not give credit to nonwhites any longer.[86]

The sense that men were competing for the credibility to make use of Eastern personae in hard times was undeniable after 1929 but all the more appealing to people struggling to make a living. Many white magicians paradoxically believed they had discredited the turban as a sign of male failure and laziness or a predatory sexuality while putting it to good use themselves as a prop that exoticized their tuxedos. Yet far more people remained genuinely intrigued with the Eastern man and the promises he made, which, like the genie in the lamp, still said that anyone might find the American Dream of autonomy and affluence through consumption of spirituality and politics styled Eastern.

chapter 8

Sign of Promise: African Americans and Eastern Personae in the Great Depression

hen the economic system began to crumble in the late 1920s, performers of spiritual Eastern manhood would have a more difficult time playing Oriental as a way of prospering in the market, although many turned to playing Eastern as a way to cope with the worst fiscal crisis the nation had ever seen. A "crescendo of credit criticism" from moral watchdogs had for several years already acknowledged the growing opinion that consumers were an important measure of the strength of the economy but that many consumers made irresponsible choices. Plenty of people in the middle classes and working classes were living beyond their means since many had internalized what Lendol Calder calls a "psychology of affluence" premised on consumer credit. The "Aladdin's Lamp" of installment plans and other credit available from manufacturers and retailers, he explains, had grown astronomically from $500,000 in 1910 to $7 billion in 1929.[1] The inability of actual consumer incomes to absorb the nation's productive bounty was only one ingredient leading the nation to economic disaster along with an overvalued stock market, weak banking regulation, and similar downturns around the globe, among other factors. When the crash came that October, many finally had to recognize the larger structural problems within American consumer capitalism that ruined individuals no matter how intelligent or hard working but kept them always hoping for more.[2]

Along with the stories of homelessness, bread lines, and suicides by men who perceived themselves as failures when they lost jobs, investments, and their marriages came word-of-mouth and press accounts of a national debate over how the economic crisis could be fixed, some useful, some not, much of it grounded in a democratic national public culture. Many citizens wrote to their elected officials with various schemes and solutions. For instance, Michigan Senator Arthur Vandenberg received a letter that suggested the government create work by hiring men to move the Rocky Mountains.[3] At the same time,

Swami-style mind reader in dress tie and exotic cloak, crystal ball in hand, Louisiana State Fair, Donaldson, Louisiana, 1938. Note costumed portrait on right. LC-USF33-011769-M4, Russell Lee Photograph Collection, Library of Congress.

and perhaps just as ineffectually, books and movies continued to celebrate gangsters like Al Capone as self-made men who shrugged off economic downturns, while the peddlers of "success" manuals and other commercial "folklores of capitalism," as Charles McGovern calls them, such as Dale Carnegie, author of the iconic *How to Win Friends and Influence People* (1931) made a living offering lessons for unlimited personal achievement.[4]

Then, in 1933, at the depths of the crisis, Hollywood offered to the public *The Mind Reader*, a cinematic cautionary tale about the dangers of failure for men and the contrast between who Americans hoped they could become in a liberal capitalist country and who they really were. The movie implied that perhaps many men were secretly suffering from imposter syndrome in a romantic drama played out in the story of a failed door-to-door salesman who resorts to the business of fortune-telling to preserve his role as breadwinner at home. "He elects to be known as Chandra the Great and to impress his clients he wears Oriental headgear and talks in sepulchral tones," a contemporary review of the film recounted.[5] The plot of the film had Chandra and his sidekick Frank cavorting with society women and underage girls while his innocent wife believes him to be earning an honest living, briefcase in hand.

The promotional poster for *The Mind Reader* depicted a nude woman barely obscured in sheer fabric laying draped over a giant crystal ball, within which was framed the devious face of a magician wearing a pencil-thin mustache. The obvious moral of the story was that only weak men would stoop so low as to earn a living in a turban, even in the depths of the Great Depression. The modern persona of wise man of the East was also symbolic of American men's own struggle to materialize great wealth in a precarious capitalist system in which the consumer's Oriental tale seemed increasingly like a magician's illusion.

Although the turban was a sign of emasculation to some and had been partly discredited by prominent whites, Americans had absorbed that new Asian content into established mystical performance practices to serve not just the middle-class and upper-class women the missionary and press critics worried about but also the working class and the poor. The homegrown fortune-teller trade increased the currency of the turban as a metaphor for failure since critics perceived these religious services as a "racket" that fleeced not the wealthy with its antimaterialist message but the foolish and desperate with promises of quick fortune. Bearing an *Ex Oriente Lux* appeal, the modern homegrown swami did in fact attract those marginalized by the economy, especially African Americans, because he was a sign of promise for the future and an example of how to amplify one's own identity and make it visible to others.

The wise man of the East appeared in the black neighborhoods of a number of American cities to communicate with people suffering from every kind of discrimination, economic, political, cultural, and social but carrying a newly globalized outlook.[6] He offered ways of being that put believers in charge of their lives as worldly consumers, as entrepreneurs, and as enactors of spiritually and racially autonomous ideas that put blacks at the center of world history. Believers would represent that identity by way of Eastern-styled personae that were often misunderstood by outsiders. Yet to many southern African Americans an Eastern persona allowed them to take the consumer's Oriental tale for themselves for the first time and to express *Ex Oriente Lux* messages that had been publicly monopolized by whites and Asians for decades.

Thus, this chapter also serves as a kind of conclusion. It brings us to the point at which the nation was at its greatest economic crisis while at the same time the practices of playing Eastern became accessible to the majority of urban African Americans, a segment of the population long dismissed by white-owned retailers, advertisers, banks, and economists as spendthrifts and non-spenders.[7] The phenomenon of the black uses of the arts of playing Eastern sincerely and in jest was really part of the publicity around the consolidation of a black market segment in American cities, where people sought to make the most of what they found, just as the Anglo-American elite always had and white and Asian working-class consumers had since the 1890s. Between 1925 and 1935, there was a cascade of new religious movements that emerged espousing Eastern-inspired philosophies by and for African Americans and critical of the interlocking networks of racism, poverty, and political powerlessness that burdened black history. Members made their ideas public in various forms, some claiming links to Judaism, Islam, Buddhism, Christianity, black spiritualism, and philosophies that defied characterization. Yet they all had three things in common: an implicit or explicit economic critique, their members' insistence on communicating by way of Eastern personae, and the timing of their emergence just before and during the Great Depression.

Playing Oriental as a practice had been available for a century by then, while African Americans had also been debating alternative black histories and race theories for generations. So it was not that African Americans had not had reason to speak of their identities in globalized terms or to speak of themselves as descendents of Africa but that they had only recently acquired the means to articulate those ideas with Easternized personae. This is why causation and context are so important in explaining the broad phenomenon of playing Eastern in the United States in order to understand when and why people presented themselves as representations of the Eastern world when they did. The simultaneous events of black urbanization and economic crisis inspired people to produce spiritual Easternized African American identities after 1925 because they appealed to urban blacks living with increasing economic instability in an intellectually cosmopolitan setting. That is, the new religions welcomed members who might not be able or willing to run for political office or go to university but who daily experienced life as workers and consumers. Led by men who came in the guise of the wise man of the East, these new modes of self-fashioning and expression offered critiques in language that made sense to people struggling with poverty and thinking about the links between race and capitalism.

IDENTIFYING THE BLACK URBAN CONSUMER

Who was this market segment? More diverse than the black Masons and Shriners of the turn of the century, they were made up of northern blacks and plentiful southern migrants. In the years following the rush of the Great Migration, thousands of southern blacks had taken charge of their destinies by forming new cultural, economic, and political networks in northern cities. Forsaking the older ideal of landed independence, blacks sought the twentieth-century interpretation of the American Dream in the city. This conception of "freedom" did not mean blind emulation of whites or northern African Americans but the freedom to live proudly as blacks while still being considered full American citizens.[8] The face of urban America was irrevocably altered as black communities situated amidst ambivalent or hostile white neighborhoods became densely populated, resulting in mutual resentment, increased segregation, and occasional riots.

Initially, cautionary tales developed among whites and blacks long resident in the north that imagined southern African Americans suddenly dropping their hoes in the fields at the urging of labor agents who directed them to idling north-bound trains. Once in Chicago or Harlem these men and women, supposedly too unsophisticated to comprehend the massive cities they found, became bewildered and lonely, resorting to escapist religious and political movements or a life of unemployment and crime. Many proceeded from the patronizing assumption that southern blacks were simple people best suited to rural living. Regardless of the critics, the urban north soon became home to the most intellectually diverse black communities in the nation, where former southerners encountered every kind of political, religious, or social idea, not to mention products that facilitated self-expression: cosmetics, music, and periodicals that presented blacks to themselves as a community of consumers.[9]

The bulk of the new black residents in cities like Chicago, New York, and Detroit were southern migrants, who for the first time found steady work in the north during World War I in factories, businesses, and inevitably domestic and other service work. As the 1920s had progressed, these migrants were the first to lose their jobs. Consequently, the black neighborhoods of American cities had early been rife with rumors that an economic crisis might be afoot well before most Americans had any inkling. It was precisely when the economy was at a moment of incredible decline that so many American blacks sought to demonstrate inborn identity and talent by way of exotic personae that recast the meaning of being black in the United States, that redefined "race" and by extension the interconnection of their lives as believers, as voters, as workers, and as consumers in line with the consumer's Oriental tale.

In 1929, a year after Swami Yogananda was driven from Miami, another Easternized man was also in the headlines. He was a product of this burgeoning market base, a consumer turned performer who called himself Jovedah de Rajah. In January of 1929, in a profound if unintentional statement of the Oriental tale as metaphor for American capitalism, he had appeared in a New York City court room to face charges wearing a business suit and purple turban. A radio swami of some celebrity, de Rajah, a.k.a. Joe Downing, with his wife had become relatively well known on the vaudeville stage after World War I. There Downing played an Oriental-style mystic adviser, "Jovedah de Raja," with his wife performing as his glamorous courtesan and assistant "Princess Olga." Together they did a mind-reading act whereby they secretly communicated to one another information provided by audience members but got the act across as evidence of de Rajah's claimed powers of telepathy. By 1926, the year Rudolph Valentino died at the young age of thirty-one to great public anguish, Downing had secured a number of contracts to broadcast advice over the radio through at least three stations in and around New York City.[10] People loved his show, and his mostly female listeners were reputed to have sent him tens of thousands of "yearning letters" each year. In return he moonlighted by providing them with telepathic access to dead relatives and personal advice by mail or in person at $50 for a package of three readings.[11]

For middling, working-class, and rural Americans, such Eastern wisdom came particularly frequently and persuasively from the speaker in the household radio. Wireless communication had became a dramatic consumer phenomenon in the early 1920s as sales of radio sets, radio parts, and periodicals documenting broadcasting grew exponentially into the later parts of the decade. Scholar of radio communication Susan Douglas has since suggested that for listeners the sound of the human voice, whether in a Presidential message, live news report, religious broadcast, or personal advice show, carried more convincing performances and sense of reality than any other mode of print or electronic communication available at the time.[12]

Radio was also the most mysterious mode of communication Americans had ever encountered. The idea of invisible radio waves traveling through the dark of night for hundreds of miles to emerge as a disembodied voice simultaneously in every home carried an otherworldly sense that inspired many to speculate that aliens beings might use the waves to conduct surveillance on humans or that radio might prove the existence of psychic phenomena and other invisible modes of communication. "You look at the cold stars overhead, at the infinite void around you. It is almost incredible that all this emptiness is vibrant with human thought and emotion," one man typically speculated.[13]

"The most occult goings-on are about us. Man has his fingers on the trigger of the universe. He doesn't understand all he is doing. He can turn strange energies loose," journalist Joseph K. Hart agreed.[14]

The mysterious but appealing character of radio made it a perfect vehicle for spiritual content. Listeners believed they experienced close relationships with people on the air because the sound of their voices and the informal, talkative mode they used persuaded the listener he or she was part of nationwide community of believers.[15] Thus could de Rajah get his persona across invisibly and from a distance to people for whom a modern "culture of personality" had emerged that made some preoccupied with "success" and business prowess. With his optimistic, encouraging shows, Jovedah de Rajah was a Dale Carnegie in a turban. His ability to win friends and influence women with his kind and flattering words, along with his Eastern-styled name and mysteriously radio-borne voice, had announced to police and the press that he required investigation.[16]

It had not taken long for troubling accusations to emerge, accusations de Rajah would face in court. Among de Rajah's many fans was Wilhemina Halliday, wife and mother of three from New Brunswick, New Jersey. She had apparently paid de Rajah money and visited him in New York and Chicago for spiritual advice. Her husband quickly sued for divorce. Thereafter, Halliday claimed that Downing, as de Rajah, had initiated an adulterous affair with her soon after their first meeting. As evidence for these claims she pointed out that she was carrying a child, whom she later named Jovedah de Rajah Jr. to emphasize her point. In Chicago she charged de Rajah with "bastardy" for abandoning her and the baby and sued him for $25,000 for breach of promise, arguing that he had backed out of an alleged engagement.[17] De Rajah responded in court that the woman had been stalking him and produced letters from Halliday to him in which she called de Rajah "her soulmate," proving, he said, her "mad infatuation" with him.[18] Contemporary newspaper readers would have recognized Halliday's fan mail and her deep identification with de Rajah's mysterious Eastern personality as the telltale signs of celebrity at work. Powerfully attractive celebrities—film stars most commonly—were known to drive women to distraction when they experienced emotional identification with men they saw on screen, read about in print, or heard on the radio.[19]

The scandal was significant because Downing/de Rajah was also probably an African American. Although the papers never said so explicitly, many appear to have taken him that way, including the editorial staff at the prominent black newspaper, the *Chicago Defender*. The paper gave the de Rajah saga considerable coverage and never followed his name with its common race marker for Anglo-Americans, for instance: "Arthur Smith (white)." The issue of race was an important one since critics would note the potential for miscegenation in the radio swami's relationships. To African Americans Downing demonstrated that perhaps "race" was a matter of culture not biology and exposed the common but seldom-discussed phenomenon of fair African Americans who passed for and lived as whites or Asians without discovery.

Soon after the public learned of Halliday's case, it came out that a year earlier Jovedah de Rajah had gotten himself into similar trouble with another white woman, Olive Fink, a "45-year-old divorcee" who also considered herself de Rajah's fiancé. Olive Fink gave up her story to police after she and Downing were arrested for failure to pay a saleswoman who had been marketing their lessons in mystical psychology on commission. De Rajah explained, "[Mrs. Fink] told me once that through her medium she was informed that she and I would be together forever, but I interpret this to mean in our work. I never spoke of love to her."[20] At least two interpretations were possible here: de Rajah as pseudoswami womanizer versus de Rajah as helpless subject of female irrationality. Either way, de Rajah got to the crux of it when he told the police, "I'm afraid that Mrs. Fink has confused a spiritual union with a physical one." Such confusion enraged many American men who saw the turban as the sign of a sexualized con game, and it may have been in these days that the hackneyed story of the fortune-teller who advises women customers, "I see a tall dark man in your future," was born.

Men such as Downing/de Rajah nonetheless served as a promise of a new identity in a market economy by connection to Oriental wisdom. The mystic could be antimodern since he flattered not technology, rationalism, science, or xenophobia but crossed over seemingly ancient ways of being to people who sought to dissent from modernity as spiritual consumers, even if only temporarily.

Sincere or not, de Rajah was not persuasive with customers because he could predict the future but because he told people things he should have had no way of knowing about his client's present life.[21] Many other black men similarly worked in the spiritual end of show business to considerable success by catering to the black community. The mysterious voice of "Rajah Raboid, Mind Reader" filled the airwaves on Friday nights from WMCA in New York City, sandwiched in between the news and the Mobil Oil Orchestra show.[22] In Chicago, the turbaned and bearded "Prince Ali, the world's greatest prophet" performed on stage and answered questions in the *Chicago Defender*.

Clients came seeking advice from these radio swamis on family matters or deceased relatives, of course. Yet much of what they wanted was access to Eastern spirituality as a tool for navigating the market as citizens with extremely limited options due to racial segregation, legal and customary. Prince Ali regularly got questions regarding business, "Q. Will the Pullman porters get a raise in salary?" and lost personal possessions, "Q. I would like to know where my diamond ring is.—Mrs. L. F. J. A. I am sorry to say and hope you will use good judgment when I tell you, your son took the ring and pawned it in a pawn shop at North Clark and Grand Ave."[23] For such patrons, an adviser's connection of the economy and the spiritual world was no sign of fraud but the sign of a mystical teacher firmly grounded in the daily reality of the community he served. Indeed, he gained spiritual authority by embracing the market and suggesting that believers would also prosper if they held the right beliefs.

In 1925, scholar and social commentator Winthrop D. Lane cynically wrote of these acts of passing as jobs that paid well, explaining, "Black art flourishes. . . . Egyptian seers uncover hidden knowledge, Indian fortune-tellers reveal the future, sorcerers perform their mysteries. . . . A towel for turban and a smart manner are enough to transform any Harlem colored man into a dispenser of magic to his profit."[24] Yet he was really getting at the way that African Americans, constrained by great poverty whites believed was marked on their bodies by their race, had for generations lived with the idea that they were judged by their appearances far more than any other Americans. Many who played Eastern professionally or sincerely as an expression of a transformed spirituality argued against this history when they donned a turban.

The key example of this popular tradition of Easternized cultural criticism was black spiritualism, a highly cosmopolitan brand of American belief and practice that was the soil from which the Nation of Islam, the Moorish Science Temple, and other Eastern-styled faiths would sprout. It collected together international religious texts and philosophies by drawing from Catholicism, Protestantism, hoodoo (African American folk magic), white Spiritualism, Islamic and Jewish elements, an interest in mystery schools like Freemasonry, Christian Science, and New Thought, and often black nationalism. Based on their understanding of the transcendent truth of God's spirit in each person, many black spiritualists spoke to their clients of humankind's ability to understand the "science" of the spiritual workings of the universe and to undergo mental transformation, for a chosen few, even into a divine form.[25]

To express the racially specific nature of these powers rooted in centuries of African American magical practice, many of the hoodoo practitioners and black spiritualists represented their expertise and products with exotic-sounding magi personae such as "Professor Abdullah," "Professor Uriah Konje," or the classic Eastern magi, "Three Wise Men."[26] Black spiritualists could be men or women and often operated out of newspaper advertisements, private homes, or storefronts in black neighborhoods. The language of fraud was common as critics, the black middle class among them, voiced their belief that poor blacks were foolish spendthrifts prone to exotic persuaders' appeals and flattery. However, the growth of such globalized urban spiritual services was really a sign of the growing power of a black consumer market base.

Like the radio swami who predicted how long the Pullman Porter strike might last, these practitioners spoke directly to the economic status of their African American clients. Their personal appearance and places of ministry also endorsed the common wisdom that because economic autonomy and respectability were closely related to black critiques of capitalism, creative consumption was crucial to those blacks seeking to discover and display personalities and identities of their own devising. Black spiritualists in particular often came across in Eastern personae, which made sense to clients because they were the most rich and costly personae and evoked the consumer's Oriental tale much as the Shriners, cozy corner builders, and theater people had for decades. Such personae were also connected to popular histories that argued the original inhabitants of the Holy Land, Arabia, and East Africa had been black. Thus did the exotically costumed wise man—or often woman—of the East endorse black beliefs in the inborn respectability and regal heritage of people of African descent.

Interwar spiritualist churches held performance-style services that included displays of magical or mystical powers by a "Moslem" or "Hindu" adept known to conduct services while wearing turbans or veils and long robes that served as visual evidence of the teacher's true mystical self that would be hidden by conventional dress.[27] Often they operated in lavishly decorated apartments meant to evoke the romanticized scenes of luxury and abundance in the *Arabian Nights* in "an obvious attempt to affect an Oriental atmosphere—soft, thick rugs, semi-darkness, burning candles, and incense all contribute to this end," as one visitor explained.[28]

As with white customers, black customers probably appreciated this expensive décor as considerable evidence of the solvency of the medium and thus veracity of the information he or she supplied. For blacks whose neighborhoods hosted the informal economies of urban gambling shared by risk-takers of every race, Eastern-styled spiritualists carried considerable influence since they also served actively as lucky number advisers, policy gambling bankers, and booking agents for networks that boomed during the Great Depression's early years.[29] That is, they endorsed the informal economies of chance tied to the daily stock market numbers that many blacks used to supplement their incomes while making a sharp comment on the unstable, speculative nature of the ostensibly respectable Anglo-American world of business represented by the New York Stock Exchange. Thus did these practitioners go by stage names reminiscent of the various foreign-born teachers touring the country. In the case of Detroit, advisers like the generically Oriental "Ishmael the Mighty, Rajah Abdullah, Prince Yogi" practiced alongside more traditional hoodoo experts like "Dr. Wizard" or "Prof. J. Herbert Psychotie."[30]

The proliferation of these individuals and their many clients tell us that plenty of blacks were open to alternative religions that endorsed their experiences with self-directed uplift messages and implied critiques of Anglo-American domination of social and economic power. American black spiritualist and magical works such as the *The Mystic Test Book of the "Hindu Occult Chambers"* argued that mystical knowledge and ability was the preserve of nonwhites, women, and the poor. "The true Clairvoyant is very seldom Saxon," the volume had explained, endorsing more colloquially spiritual race pride that led African Americans to seek out black cunning women and men in their own neighborhoods, while still attending a more mainstream churches on Sunday.[31]

These urban black communities were known for their cultivation of innovative ideas and debate, even outside the United States. Consequently, while Swami Yogananda and Inayat Khan made their way on speaking tours to middle-class and upper-class Anglo-American venues, missionaries from the Ahmadi branch of Islam had arrived in the United States in 1920 specifically to speak with African Americans.[32] One of these emissaries, Muhammad Sadiq, also set up shop near the heart of Chicago's black community. There he published a small apologetic proselytizing newspaper that crossed Islam over to local people with an *Ex Oriente Lux* appeal by flattering common perceptions of the faith as a religion native to Africa that engendered racial equality among believers. Sociologist Charles Braden explained at the time, "There are no false statements, but only the brighter aspects of things are mentioned."[33] By 1926, Sadiq's successor, Mohammed Yusuf Khan, was pursuing African Americans by purchasing announcements on the religion page of the *Chicago Defender*. In them he encouraged blacks to come to his Sunday services and learn about the religion "of your forefathers."[34] Sadiq had sized up the local religious market very quickly, speaking at white spiritualist churches *and* actively engaging inquisitive African Americans. In the early 1930s, his successor Sufi M. Bengalee, probably a local African American convert, gave lectures at various churches and the University of Chicago, possibly in Eastern garb. He advertised his lectures, crafted to cater to the local audience's interests in opportunities for individuation, inter-racial understanding, "success," and self-fulfillment through alternative spirituality, with enterprising talks like "The Object of Life: Spiritual Progress and the Means of Accomplishing It" and " 'The Supreme Success in Life.' This spiritually informative lecture is an outline which the speaker is prepared to elaborate into a study course."[35]

EASTERN PERSONAE AND RACIAL EQUALITY

All the while, the turban and suit combination shared by mind-readers, urban hotel swamis, and even Muslim missionaries had been fast becoming to non-believers a metaphor for the pressures capitalism put on modern men to materialize wealth for wives and children, Aladdin-like, merely by talking their way to success as salesmen, stockbrokers, accountants, or business owners. The affluence, or apparent affluence, of the turbaned adviser among American blacks was more than this, though, he was also a representation of the promise of equal consumer rights. Consumption and civil rights had always been connected for African Americans.[36] The long struggles of the Ancient Egyptian Arabic Order, Nobles of the Mystic Shrine or black Shriners, demonstrated how hard people would fight to gain the right to Mystic Shrine costumes and performances or for the right to adapt and innovate those practices and personae for themselves. By extension, they were working for equal opportunity as consumers, an idea that would in time be a prominent plank in the platforms of postwar civil rights movements but was grounded in black political consumer activism of the interwar period.[37] Certainly since the turn of the century whites and other Americans had seen consumption as a service to the economy and a right of citizenship.[38]

Thus would American blacks make their own attempts to demonstrate spiritual and political beliefs as well as personal autonomy displayed on their bodies, often in ways that asserted the inborn abilities and mystical nature of nonwhites. Among these new articulations of identity through Eastern personae were some dozen groups that appeared similarly innovative at the time. Some of these groups were sincere, and some were led by scoundrels whose followers were sincere, such that the saint/scoundrel paradox was still relevant for neighbors, police, journalists, and members of the African American community wondering what to think about these spiritual organizations. Nonetheless, scholars of religion, "race," and African American reform in the United States have long considered these various groups important, in particular, the Moorish Science Temple and the Nation of Islam, for the groundwork they laid in associating race pride and activism with Easternized self-presentation and the name of Islam. In the 1950s and 1960s, some of these scholars interpreted the Nation of Islam, made prominent in the post–World War II era of civil rights reform by speakers like Malcolm X, as the lamentable reaction of angry and poor African Americans to the heritage of racism in the United States.[39] Scholars of religion have more recently placed these groups in a broader history of global engagement by those of African descent that seeks to express identities linking black agency, redemption, and Islam marked on the body through naming practices, clothing, and deportment.[40]

All these explanations are pieces of the story, but they underemphasize one critical component that helps us see how very American these people were in their articulation of their spiritual beliefs and political assessment of the United States by arguing, if not for integration, for black inclusion in the promises of consumer capitalism. Since the late eighteenth century, broader and broader groups of consumers had taken the act of playing Muslim or Eastern for themselves. Members of the Moorish Science Temple, the Nation of Islam, and others linked social uplift and Eastern personae as a way to claim the consumer's Oriental tale that had so long functioned among Americans as a sign of social and economic power. They were also grounded in the ideal of an ultranatural Easternness that was not primitive or debased but, in their interpretation, offered authentic manhood and womanhood to blacks so long denied social equality and respectability by American whites.

In the meantime, African Americans tried on Eastern personae—many quite sincerely to be sure—in ways that led many observers to misread them as merely doing so in the interest of fraudulent activity. While we need not pass judgment on the spiritual claims of people who used Eastern personae, we should look closely at how and why the language of the market seemed useful to them in voicing spiritual and political calls for reform just when capitalism was most broken down. These new religious groups were forced to compete in cities in which for-profit modes of communication and entertainment created an inescapable context of depictions of the Muslim world and its peoples that could both help and hinder the cause.

Most of the religious experiments and nascent movements blacks produced in those days were earnest, while some were earnest at first but fell into disarray over time. The frequent disintegration of and power struggles within these groups caused many observers to misconstrue their Eastern personae as evidence of a "cult." Virtually all of them would at some point suffer public attacks such as Jovedah de Rajah and Swami Yogananda had, instigated by cultural authorities within both the black and white communities when people grew critical of the intersection between playing Eastern and intergroup conflict or controversial activity. The media scandals around these new religions took the same form, linking persuasion, sex, greed, and Eastern manhood to attempt to discredit them in seemingly the same way time and time again, in ways that still can obscure the intentions of members.

The problem of misrecognition dogged many of these religious groups because of the commercial context of Oriental-style performance around them. The black middle classes were exceptionally critical at times, especially African American journalists and intellectuals who wrote sometimes patronizing books and articles on black "folk" life. The black press was staffed by men as anxious to humiliate those who threatened to embarrass the African American community as they were to sell papers with sensational headlines. They were determined that it was critical to disavow any association of the black community with those who broke the law and drew the criticism of whites since everyone knew the actions of a few people would reflect badly on all African Americans. Moreover, blacks were barely represented in interwar urban police forces and often were targeted unfairly by officers whose attention tarnished the reputation of the black community as a whole. So were sociologists quick to frame these religious entrepreneurs as for-profit "cultists" and interwar evidence of black urban pathology.[41] This was a somewhat scholarly version of the old canard that rural southern people were impressionable and easily tempted into crime, radical politics, or social deviance by the crowded diversity of life in cities.

Nonetheless, the most innovative spiritualities of the period all came with an economic program that showed their practicality and were delivered by a man in Eastern garb. Consider two groups who came to public attention in the late 1920s: the Kaaba Alif and the Moorish Science Temple. Both groups represented larger African American interest in the Muslim world and ways of rejecting poverty as the defining element of African American identity. Both would eventually suffer the "harem" scandal treatment by black and white papers around 1930. Master Hazrat Ismet Ali, possibly a black West Indian immigrant, founded the "Kaaba Alif" group (the Arabic terms referring to the sacred building at the center of the Great Mosque at Mecca, and the number "one," respectively). It appears that the organization flourished in New York, Buffalo, and Detroit, where Ismet Ali catered to those curious about what the papers called "Hinduism." Recall that this term could serve as a catchall for any stripe of Eastern spirituality. When Ali and his white wife appeared in Chicago in 1935, police charged and convicted them for operating a confidence game.[42] Spread to multiple cities, the organization certainly carried the appearance of a for-profit "success" course got over in Oriental form, with the poverty of members often discrediting the practitioners who served them.

Indeed, among northern cities, Chicago's south and west sides, Detroit, and Harlem were centers of African American new religions that identified their economic and political critiques with Eastern personae. Radiating out from one of these communities to the others, members would often set up new temples, recruit, and then send a new messenger to the next city to begin the process again. This evangelical approach brought the Moorish Science Temple to broad public attention in the late 1920s. The Moors had a more clearly articulated economic plan than the Kaaba Alif but were similarly led by a man carrying a wise man of the East persona, namely Noble Drew Ali. He said he had traveled in Egypt and created sacred texts explaining that he believed American blacks had originated in Morocco and were thus Moorish American.[43]

The Moors' articulations of a hybrid Moorish American identity were very similar to those being used by Syrian Americans at the time, immigrants who often came across as industrious and prosperous. Like Syrian Americans who appeared at celebrations bearing Ottoman and American flags, the Moors appeared in parades carrying the stars and stripes as well as the Moroccan flag with its star and crescent to come across as the descendants of respectable people from the East. In the 1920s and 1930s, scholars had openly begun questioning the biological reality of "race," substituting the idea of ethnicity to admit cultural difference but argue against means of identifying racial characteristics.[44] Indeed, in consciously articulating Moorish American identity, the Moors were ahead of their time with respect to common sentiment in pointing out that perhaps one's ethnicity needed to be consciously articulated in obvious ways in order to be visible to observers. They also noted that the melting pot, which had never accommodated African Americans, might be forced open to allow blacks in as ethnic Americans, "Asiatics," as Noble Drew Ali said, referring to blacks as West Asians of a sort.[45] Noble Drew Ali had always held that the Moors' public face should be in the form of business enterprises, and from day one the group linked its ethnicity with race pride and entrepreneurialism. The Moors also ran their own newspaper, the *Moorish Guide*, and a patent medicine business. Advertised in the *Guide*, Ali's Moorish healing compounds and tonics, regardless of their efficacy, were in fact central to the Moor's messages of inclusion and spiritual realization by way of economic uplift. Through cooperation with the city's political establishment and black-owned businesses, the Moors spread the word with parades, public appearances, packaging of Moorish products, and decorations featuring crescents and stars.[46]

Until 1929, with the black press and several thousand members, the Moorish Science Temple prospered as an entrepreneurial uplift group of sincere if innovative "Moslems." After Noble Drew Ali's untimely death that year, remaining members fought for control, eventually drawing the Chicago police into a violent confrontation. Diligent journalists consulted a private detective, the African American Sheridan A. Bruseaux, who told a *Chicago Tribune* reporter that the group's recently deceased prophet, Noble Drew Ali, had "posed as a Moor, born in Europe. [But, h]e was born in the south. He was a negro" in order to run the " 'Moor Temple' Racket," selling allegedly "Fake Moslem Teaching [to] fool his ignorant dupes" and to collect a "harem" of women.[47] Once it was on the wrong side of the law, the press and influential members of the black community abandoned the group, crossing it over as a turbaned cult in a way eminently familiar to readers by then.

Black aspirations to respectability and spiritual peace nonetheless still required self-help. Of both the Moors and the Nation of Islam Ernest Allen explains, "African-Americans had to take the initiative in attending to their material condition—such as, for example, maintaining orderly families and proper eating habits, adopting frugal practices, observing appropriate behavior in public, and engaging in gainful employment."[48] Indeed, one's material condition was precisely the point of many Eastern-styled religions, especially one born of the consumer's Oriental tale like the Nation of Islam, perhaps the most important of all the African American new religions bearing an Ex Oriente Lux message to emerge in this period. In the early days, before they burst onto the national scene in 1959 represented by the spokesman Malcolm X, the group was no less controversial than they would become in the 1960s. The Nation never suffered the accusations of immorality and "harem" keeping that other eastern-style religions endured. Conservative gender relations dictated segregation in the Temple and the necessity that young women of the Nation go in public chaperoned by a brother or their father, especially since so many men had joined the movement.[49] The Nation of Islam became a collection point for former Moors, black spiritualists, and other politically active spiritual people, many of whom would participate in public demonstrations for economic reform that decade during the demonstrations and job boycotts in black neighborhoods.[50]

The Nation of Islam began sometime in 1930 when Wallace Fard, an apparent Syrian peddler, arrived at the Detroit home of Mrs. Lawrence Adams selling raincoats and other clothing. Once inside, he showed her beautiful silk garments and told her that he had come from the land of her forefathers in the East, a land where everyone wore such lovely and delicate clothing. She recalled, "So we all asked him to tell us about our own country." Adams was intrigued to hear Fard say further that he had come to tell American blacks of their true identities as Muslims, the descendents of a holy race of people from Mecca in Arabia. He asked them to make that identity visible through honorable and correct consumption, which meant avoiding traditional black southern foods, one follower explained: "If we asked him to eat with us, he would eat whatever we had on the table, but after the meal he began to talk: 'Now don't eat this food. It is poison for you. The people in your own country do not eat it. Since they eat the right kind of food they have the best health all the time. If you would live just like the people in your home country, you would never be sick any more.' So we all wanted him to tell us more about ourselves and about our home country and about how we could be free of rheumatism, aches and pains."[51]

Soon groups of believers were gathering in local houses to hear Fard speak, perhaps as healer, perhaps as prophet, and he converted many to his ideas. One man explained, "Up to that day I always went to the Baptist church. After I heard that sermon from the prophet, I was turned around completely. When I went home and heard that dinner was ready, I said: 'I don't want to eat dinner. I just want to go back to the meetings.'"[52] Apparently something close to 8,000 blacks joined Fard's movement, the Nation of Islam, most of them migrants from the south.[53]

Like many mystical teachers before him, Fard gave his students new Arabic names to represent their return to their true identities.[54] He himself came to be known by some of his students as "Wali" Fard, some surmising this was short for Wallace.[55] The term *wali* is also a North African title used for Sufi saints. Though this may be a coincidence, it is also possible Fard gave himself this name to mark his role as spiritual teacher. Either way, members of the Nation of Islam used their new names in all situations, even in their contact with the government. Social workers and county clerks, one paper recounted, "struggled with Negroes who insisted upon being registered by weird Arabian names." Administrators in Detroit soon issued "a notice forbidding the clerks to countenance signatures such as Mohammed, or Ali, or Bey," in attempts to discover these mysterious believers' previous names.[56]

The group initially came to the attention of police and other black community leaders when members established their own school and refused to send their children to state schools. A later scandal emerged when one overzealous member killed another.[57] In an interrogation with Detroit police thereafter, Fard allegedly admitted that the Nation of Islam was a "racket" designed to accumulate money. It is not clear, as Claude Clegg points out, whether this admission was "the ugly truth," merely a story Fard fed to police in order to escape worse prosecution, or a tale the police invented themselves in order to discredit the group in a familiar way.[58] In any event, Wallace Fard left Detroit the next day, while believers speculated he had gone back to Mecca or some other part of the East from whence he had come. In fact, he had spent time behind bars in California before appearing in Detroit, his mug shots leaving a familiar record of many such messengers from the East in the eyes of the police and plenty of white observers. It seems he was of Pacific Islander and English descent and may not have spent any time in the Middle East at all.[59]

Still bolstered by Fard's words and their own militant attitudes, the Nation of Islam continued with a local man, Elijah Wood, now Elijah Muhammad, at the helm. Members began founding businesses and speaking in public as the movement spread to other cities. In each place, the group united Elijah Muhammad's teachings about discipline, respectability, and pride with a vigorous work ethic and serious public profile that many respected. Regardless, it seems these movements always had encounters with the police that demonstrated perhaps the challenging nature of their behavior and beliefs. By 1935, there were dozens of people joining the Nation's Chicago temple. After an altercation on a streetcar between Nation of Islam members Zack and Rosetta Hassan and a white rider, Mrs. Athenasia Christopolous, the three members of the Nation were instructed to appear in court on charges of causing a disturbance. Fifty showed up, the men wearing fezzes decorated with crescents (seemingly similar to Shriner-style fezzes), some yelling "Freedom and Justice!" in the courtroom, linking their Eastern costumes and names with defiance of white power. Soon after, a fracas broke out in which dozens were injured, someone shot a bailiff in the chest, and a police captain had a heart attack and died due to the "excitement and the assault of several cultists," the papers accused.[60] Thereafter, someone in the court room shot two young members of the Nation, King Shah and Allah Shah. Investigators could find no gun on any of the citizens in court that day, though several police officers and bailiffs were seen with their guns drawn while the disturbance was under way.

Various members identified themselves to the courts that day with new Muslim names, which "puzzled the police." Some were also dressed in turbans and crimson robes, and at least a few could be seen wearing elaborate Cleopatra-style eye make up when photographed for a police lineup.[61] In an attempt to humiliate the group and condemn their "uppity" actions, the Chicago Tribune reported that most of the members of the Nation were on social assistance and that the "fezzes and red robes, which the cultists also wore, apparently were rented."[62] Again, such attacks showed a misunderstanding of what members of the Nation were getting at, that their faith and economic organization was a sign of promise for the future as much as a claim of achievement. Their Eastern costumes and names invited others to symbolically join in remaking themselves and achieve in reality what members believed to be true about the abilities of blacks as autonomous citizens but were struggling to make material.

Within the Nation of Islam, Eastern-style clothing, name changes, and religious identification were designed to signal that believers had rediscovered their true identities, which were simply made obvious to viewers through proper self-fashioning in Eastern mode. Members of the Nation of Islam believed that blacks in America who dressed in common American modes were merely deceiving themselves since the white man's "civilization" was not for those of African descent. Elijah Muhammad grounded his interpretation of black identity in creation myths that focused on the Middle East and Africa, positing that

[TRIBUNE Photo.]

COLORED CULTISTS ARE HELD FOR INQUIRY AFTER COURT RIOT SCENE.
Left to right: Lennie Ali, Lennel Cushman, Georgia Jordan, Anna Belle Pasha, Hattie Majie,
Mary Gold, and Mary Ali, who are among the 43 women and men arrested and facing possible
murder charges.   *(Story on page 1.)*

Early women members of the Nation of Islam bearing names like "Ali" and "Pasha,"
photographed by police in turbans and Cleopatra-style make up after a court disturbance.
Chicago Tribune, 1935.

African Americans would only return to their former more developed state, as
Wallace Fard had originally told those ladies buying his silk, when they rediscovered their inborn identities as African Muslims. Indeed, in the early days
the group called themselves the Lost and Found Nation of Islam as a way to
signal that members had rejected instrumentalist arguments made by black
elites that it was poor blacks' subculture, not race itself, that caused whites to
discriminate against them.[63] They also asserted that persona manipulation could
make real on the body one's internal landscape and ancestry, so that one would
no longer inadvertently pass as a poor southern black person when he or she was
really a descendent of Muslims crucial to world history. Exercising freedom as
consumers individuating themselves as Eastern men and women was the easiest
way to communicate this, each member of the Nation serving as a public
representation of their philosophies and the promises of self-transformation
and self-reliance the group offered to Depression-era Americans.

All these men and women who took on foreign names and dressed as Easterners for political and spiritual purposes closely resembled the black spiritualists and hoodoo practitioners, plenty of people noted. These entrepreneurs were known to be "partial to oriental vestments, either Hindu or Persian, Arabian or Egyptian," as one early observer described them.[64] In fact, members of the black spiritualist community would continue to offer market-based critiques of race in Eastern garb while indigenous Islamic movements were emerging from the same streets. The overlap between the mystical entrepreneur, the sincere seeker, and the political activist in the name of consumer equality was exemplified by Sufi Abdul Hamid. An African American man, he had spent some time studying with the Ahmadi Muslim missionaries on Chicago's South Side in the late 1920s, he said, who inspired him to reject constructions of blackness that associated race with poverty. In 1930, as the Depression was draining jobs from black neighborhoods everywhere, he came to prominence as the leader of boycotts of white-owned businesses that refused to employ blacks. He soon left for Harlem to organize more.[65]

Hamid attacked merchants who refused to employ blacks in their shops and brought renewed energy to the ongoing "Don't Buy Where You Can't Work!" boycotts of the decade that sought to bring about reform through consumer-based protests and would set the bar for later boycotts and sit-ins after World War II.[66] Hamid suggested ways of reforming the economy by asserting the power of blacks as consumers—not spendthrifts or bankrupts as many whites believed. His reforms were part of a broader pattern of challenges to capitalism supported by black political and religious organizations in the early 1930s, when the economic crisis had turned many otherwise indifferent people to public talk about protecting blacks from opportunistic business interests, especially in Harlem, some said, where department stores like Blumstein's happily accepted black customers' money but employed only whites.[67] Hamid's Eastern persona was a novelty, as one man explained, that brought Hamid attention in neighborhoods stocked with jackleg preachers and sidewalk political speakers of great energy and often-radical ideas. "It was odd to listen to him all tricked out in his Oriental toggery," he remembered.[68]

To some black shoppers and workers, Hamid appeared as wise man of the East offering to link black consumption with black authenticity in ways many whites resented as they complained about black poverty while paradoxically dismissing black economic achievement as the product of greed. Dressed in "turban, green velvet blouse, Sam Browne belt, riding habit, patent leather boots, and wearing a black crimson-lined cape carelessly around his shoulders," journalist Roi Ottley remembered, Hamid hired "a slick Negro press agent named Ace Parker" to promote his work. He grounded his economic and political ideas in verses from the Qur'an or the poetry of Omar Khayyam, among other foreign sources. His organization, the Negro Industrial and Clerical Alliance, engaged in street-corner speeches and demonstrations with great frequency. Roi Ottley described Hamid's supporters as "hoodlums, idlers, relief recipients, and a discouraged fringe of high-school and college graduates, not to mention the numbers who ordinarily lived by their wits and hoped to enrich themselves at the expense of the gullible."[69] While dismissive, Ottley was really noting the radical levels of underemployment among African Americans, even those with considerable education, great intelligence, and worldly experience, who seldom found employment outside service work. They used Hamid's boycotts and other activities to challenge the disjuncture between their abilities and aspirations and their achievements.

Sufi Abdul Hamid's especially vehement attacks on Harlem merchants (many of whom were Jewish) led some merchants to name him "Harlem Hitler" and perpetrate rumors that he had had amiable meetings with Nazi agents. Various newspapers including the *New York Times*, the communist Harlem *Liberator*, and two Jewish dailies jumped on the situation, engaging in a smear campaign aimed at ending the Negro Industrial and Clerical Alliance pickets and marches, which were doing serious damage to white-owned businesses in the neighborhood. Hamid's Eastern-style persona, reminiscent of the Arab world as it was, only exacerbated attacks by prominent Jewish groups who saw in him the same anti-Semitism they saw in Germany and some regions of the Arab Middle East in those years.[70]

After a trial for stirring up anti-Semitic hatred, Hamid eschewed further political action and transformed himself into a more familiarly exotic character, the wise man of the East. As "His Holiness Bishop Amiru Al-Mu-Minin Sufi A. Hamid" he became the leader of his Universal Holy Temple of Tranquility, a storefront religious congregation and lucky-number/fortune-teller service he founded in Harlem.[71] Hamid's transforming individuations from black spiritualist to apparent Muslim political activist and back to spiritualist again showed the flexibility of personal experience and expression available to African Americans, who were, to be sure, engaging with the world in increasingly confident ways. In fact, before his career in New York, Hamid had already presented himself to Chicago's South Side as "Bishop Conshankin, a Buddhist missionary and a devotee of Oriental magic."[72] Locals in Harlem sardonically took to calling him "Snoofi," and police revealed that Bishop Amiru Al-Mu-Minin Sufi A. Hamid was previously Eugene Brown from Philadelphia.[73]

In spite of those critical of African Americans who played Eastern in a process of self-definition and civil rights work, all these people voiced an important critique of the inequalities of opportunity for defining oneself in the United States, a consumer capitalist nation that would soon be defined by the globally relevant cliché of self-definition and satisfaction for individuals through the "American Dream." Tellingly, black popular culture contained numerous stories of foreign-born blacks escaping racial discrimination in the United States because of their exotic appearance, especially in the story of the traveling Moor. For instance, in his influential work of uplift ideology, Up From Slavery, Booker T. Washington remarked favorably upon an 1879 incident whereby a black man was refused service in a white-owned hotel in a southern town. Because he spoke English, the man in question was assumed to be African American. However, after he managed to prove his Moroccan citizenship, hotel staff apologized and granted him service.[74] Many blacks recognized in the old story of the Moorish traveler not so many truths about Morocco but the fact that Americans had constructed blackness such that it had specifically to do with being both black and American, particularly if one was also from the south. This blackness many Americans associated with uppity antiwhite radicalism or with laziness, greed, and immorality, yet it could be overcome by simply wrapping one's head in a turban and putting on an exotic accent.[75]

Postwar spokesman for the Nation of Islam Malcolm X would recognize the irony of the resulting black African privilege in the United States in years when consumption and civil rights were being debated anew. He explained how an Eastern persona paired with civil rights action spoke of a desire for cultural autonomy, for blacks to decide for themselves and tell others who they were, not be defined by segregation and poverty. Speaking of its continuing relevance in the twentieth century, he said: "A friend of mine who's very dark put a turban on his head and went into a restaurant in Atlanta before they called themselves desegregated. He went into a white restaurant, he sat down, they served him, and he said, 'What would happen if a Negro came in here?' And there he's sitting, black as night, but because he had his head wrapped up the waitress looked back at him and says, 'Why, there wouldn't no nigger dare come in here.'"[76] In the intervening period between Booker T. Washington's and Malcolm X's presentations of the connection between the American construction of race and persona, the validity of manipulating one's identity in the work of civil rights advocacy had flourished. Indeed, to take on Eastern guise had long been a way for many Americans of all backgrounds to argue they too would partake of the Aladdin's-lamp promises of equality of opportunity, comfort, and abundance many believed American consumer capitalism offered.

In ending the story of Eastern personae in the United States with the rise of groups like the Nation of Islam and the Oriental-styled consumer boycotts led by Sufi Abdul Hamid up to 1935, I seek to follow American performers and consumers from the early national marketplace to the worst economic crisis in the nation's history to see how different groups and generations shared the experience of playing Eastern to talk about, cope with, or even capitalize upon the ambivalent opportunities of a market economy. There were many characters at hand: Oriental merchant, wise man of the East, Imperial Potentate, Arab trickster, Arab athlete, modernist dancing girl, and finally, turbaned swami critic of American capitalism. All of the people who took on these guises and played Eastern sought familiar things: inclusion and self-fulfillment in a nation that seemed to offer contentment and plenty to every citizen. It is ironic perhaps that so many people would use the consumer's Oriental tale and the ultranatural and ultra-artificial modes of expression contained within it to cross themselves over to others as Eastern and thus quintessentially American at the same time.

The Depression would prove to be a critical period in which the state restructured its relationship to citizens to enable more people to engage in consumer capitalism and experience the democratic egalitarianism the political system could not always deliver.[77] Additionally, for many, the nation's greatest economic crisis did make obsolete the naïvely optimistic consumer's Oriental tale by which so many had imagined the promise of consumer individuation and opportunity in the market. The decade spelled the beginning of the end at least for the Eastern male persona. Certainly the Shriners would press on through jesting parades, but they earned respectability through hospitals and other charity work. Actors, novelists, cartoonists, filmmakers, and others would continue with *Arabian Nights* extravaganzas and desert rescue narratives but only in fictional modes. Only African Americans would sincerely wear exotic Oriental personae into the postwar period, crossing over as Easternized self-made men and women determined to redefine race in the United States and to create a more egalitarian America for themselves.

notes

ABBREVIATIONS

The following abbreviations are used throughout the notes.

AAONMS   Ancient Arabic Order, Nobles of the Mystic Shrine

CHM   Miscellaneous Pamphlets, Chicago History Museum,
         Chicago, Ill.

JMP   Joseph T. McCaddon Papers, Rare Books and Special
         Collections, Princeton University Library, Princeton, N.J.

NIP   "Negro in Illinois" Papers, Vivian G. Harsh Research Collection
         of Afro-American History and Literature, Carter C. Woodson Regional
         Library, Chicago Public Library, Chicago, Ill.

SRES   Saram R. Ellison Scrapbooks, Humanities Microfilms, Theater
         Collection, Visual and Performing Arts Division, New York Public
         Library, New York, N.Y.

INTRODUCTION

1. Both Marr and McAlister rightly explain American depictions of the Muslim world as products of Americans' context and thinking about the interrelation of global issues and domestic subjectivities. Yet neither account in any theoretical way for the role of capitalism in determining how these sources were produced, distributed, and consumed, for the practical realities of the creative process in a market economy, or for the communications between author and audience that determined to which representations and performances people gave cultural authority by paying for them. Marr, *Cultural Roots*; McAlister, *Epic Encounters*.

2. The classic texts here are, of course, Said, *Orientalism*; Said, *Culture and Imperialism*.

3. On the political and intellectual context of Said's scholarship, see Aruri and Shuraydi, *Revising Culture*; Ashcroft and Ahulwalia, *Edward Said*; Lockman, *Contending Visions*, 148–214. The recent abundance of syntheses on postcolonial and Saidian theory intended for undergraduates attests to the fact that scholarly analysis in this mode has become utterly conventional. This literature is far too large to discuss at length here, so see, for instance, Gandhi, *Postcolonial Theory*; Catherine Hall, *Cultures of Empire*; Valerie

Kennedy, *Edward Said*; Macfie, *Orientalism*; Moore-Gilbert, *Postcolonial Theory*; Schwarz and Ray, *Companion to Post-Colonial Studies*.

4. This field is also impossibly large, so see, for example, Ackerman, "Gérôme's Oriental Paintings"; Beaulieu and Roberts, eds., *Orientalism's Interlocutors*; Behdad, *Belated Travelers*; Bhabha, "Of Mimicry and Man"; Codell and Macleod, *Orientalism Transposed*; Dunch, "Beyond Cultural Imperialism"; King, *Orientalism and Religion*; Reina Lewis, *Rethinking Orientalism*; Lowe, *Critical Terrains*; MacKenzie, *Orientalism*; McClintock, *Imperial Leather*; Said, "Orientalism Reconsidered," 89–107; Warraq, *Defending the West*.

5. Numerous authors are guilty of this, but for some prominent examples of this construction, see, for instance, Christison, *Perceptions of Palestine*, 16; Little, *American Orientalism*, 9; Suleiman, *Arabs in the Mind of America*.

6. See, for instance, Bernstein and Studlar, *Visions of the East*; Holly Edwards, *Noble Dreams*; Hammons, "American Images of Arabs"; Jacobson, *Barbarian Virtues*, 107–21; Obeidat, *American Literature and Orientalism*, 19, 23–24; Obenzinger, *American Palestine*; Porterfield, "Baghdad on the Hoosic"; Schueller, *U.S. Orientalisms*; Steet, *Veils and Daggers*; Sweetman, *Oriental Obsession*; Tchen, *New York before Chinatown*.

7. Initially inspired by the spirit the second Great Awakening, 100 or so young Yankees traveled to the Middle East between 1819 and 1900 primarily to convert Eastern Christians to Protestantism. The few Eastern Christians who did convert did so at some personal risk, and during their first thirty-five years in Greater Syria, the total number of conversions for American missions was less than sixty-five. By 1900 there were in fact fewer Christians in the region than there had been in 1800 due to emigration. Daniel, "American Influences," 77–78; Finnie, *Pioneers East*, 108, 123–24, 134; Khalaf, *Cultural Resistance*, 107–41, 177–85; Makdisi, "Reclaiming the Land of the Bible," 690–97; Obenzinger, "Holy Land Narrative," 241–67; Tibawi, *American Interests in Syria*. On American academic interest, see Lockman, *Contending Visions*. Historians who study Americans abroad have shown that local populations often made their own self-interested use of missionaries, tourists, or diplomats or rejected them altogether, restricting American influence abroad greatly in spite of any confident statements to the contrary Americans made at the time. Dunch, "Beyond Cultural Imperialism," 301–25; Makdisi, *Artillery of Heaven*, 140–213; Nance, "Facilitated Access," 1056–78; Reid, *Whose Pharaohs*.

8. [Crosby], *Lands of the Moslem*, 17–18.

9. Silbey, *Storm Over Texas*.

10. There are too many examples to list here, but for examples drawn from the last thirty years and various disciplines, see Brody, "Fantasy Realized," 10–19; Hammons, "American Images of Arabs," iii; Porterfield, "Baghdad on the Hoosic," 113–14; Said, *Culture and Imperialism*, 341–408; Shamir, " 'Our Jerusalem,' " 31.

11. David Hall, *Cultures of Print*, 180. Of the textual bias that drives most cultural analysis, Claire Sponsler notes that since at least the 1980s theorists like Bourdieu and de Certeau have been critical of "the way that practices tend to disappear in object-oriented

analyses, especially since [they see] practice as essentially a nondiscursive domain, a domain that analysis tries (often unsuccessfully) to submit to discourse. Practice, de Certeau insists, always has to be seen as ambiguous—as both beyond discourse and produced by it." Sponsler, "Introduction," 12 (n. 4). See also de Certeau, *Practice of Everyday Life*, 165–76.

12. I. C. Campbell, "Culture of Culture Contact," 63. See also Fluck, "The Modernity of America," 348–50.

13. For instance, James Cook has argued forcefully for the importance of context in any historical understanding of clearly dated artistic forms: "Sweeping retroactive assertions of prejudice or vague ahistorical generalizations about exoticized others on stage hardly even begin to explain the cacophony of voices and competing theories of difference set in motion by the showman's open-ended promotional maneuvers." Cook, *Arts of Deception*, 121; Lears, *Fables of Abundance*, 124; McAlister, *Epic Encounters*, 1–23.

14. The academic temptation to essentialize different kinds of American cultural production and activity with respect to Eastern people and lands over broad spans of time under the blanket rubric of Orientalism probably also emanates from the authority created by scholars' repeated, facile citation of a key passage, namely, Edward Said in *Orientalism*: "Orientalism can be discussed and analyzed as the corporate institution for dealing with the Orient—dealing with it by making statements about it, authorizing views of it, describing it, by teaching it, settling it, ruling over it; in short, Orientalism is a Western style for dominating, restructuring, and having authority over the Orient." Said, *Orientalism*, 3. From the beginning, Said conflates people who make statements, people who authorize views, people who describe, people who teach, people who aspire to settle, and people who actually rule Eastern lands, seemingly taking their professions of omnipotence at face value.

15. Sharafuddin, *Islam and Romantic Orientalism*, xviii.

16. Among political thinkers, journalists, and media scholars, he is still regarded as one of the most important early theorists of human communication. Carey, *Communication as Culture*, 75; Luskin, *Lippmann*, 51–52; Schlesinger, "Walter Lippmann," 202; Steel, *Walter Lippmann*, 183.

17. Luskin, *Lippmann*, 40–45.

18. Lippmann, *Public Opinion*, 64–69; see also Kitch, *Girl on the Magazine Cover*, 5.

19. Lippmann, *Public Opinion*, 224; see also 53–56; Luskin, *Lippmann*, 15.

20. Perhaps influenced by Lippmann's pessimistic view of interwar journalism and public culture, many authors have tended to strip the term of its analytical complexity in using it to document American depictions of the Muslim world. Especially after the nadirs of intercultural suspicion and misunderstanding that followed the oil crises of the 1970s and the Gulf War, people understandably sought to catalog categories of "negative stereotypes" of Arabs and Muslims throughout United States history (however a given author defined "negative"). These they juxtaposed with polling information or

political cartoons as an explanation for public support for American foreign policy. With little obvious theory of audience reception with which to contextualize their sources, these authors assert that stereotypes carried predetermined, unchanging meanings, even over the course of centuries according to some. For scholarship in this genre, see, for instance, Ghareeb, *Split Vision*; Hajji, "Arab in American Silent Cinema"; Hammons, "American Images of Arabs"; Kamalipour, *U.S. Media and the Middle East*; Karim, *Islamic Peril*; Kearney, "American Images of the Middle East"; Obeidat, *American Literature and Orientalism*; Shaheen, *Reel Bad Arabs*; Shaheen, *The TV Arab*; Simon, *Middle East in Crime Fiction*; Stockton, "Ethnic Archetypes and the Arab Image"; Suleiman, *Arabs in the Mind of America*; Terry, *Mistaken Identity*.

21. Lippmann, *Public Opinion*, 264; see also 8, 91, 204–23.

22. In modern parlance, a crossover act is any artist who manages to gain popularity outside his or her own niche and communicate in the mainstream market, usually by adapting to more conventional styles of performance and thus appealing to a broader audience. Hence, taking the music industry as an example, for the Spanish-language act who records an English-language album that sells many copies or the country or rap artist who crosses over to have a number-one hit on the pop music charts, a crossover album or song can be a substantial triumph personally and professionally, applauded by the industry and new fans alike. For older fans and critical fellow entertainers, such an event can be the sign of an artist who made unjustifiable creative compromises to abandon the old fan base in a search for greater earnings or fame.

23. Diamond, *Performance and Cultural Politics*, 1.

24. Janet Davis, *Circus Age*, 27. See also, for instance, Desmond, "Dancing Out the Difference," 28–49; Diamond, *Performance and Cultural Politics*, 1–8; Roach, "Kinship, Intelligence, and Memory," 219–38; Rothfels, *Savages and Beasts*, 12.

25. Although ideally I would have liked to use foreign language sources to try to fill in some of the resulting gaps in the historical record, what may exist in archives and private households would come in a half-dozen languages—Arabic, Turkish, Persian, Urdu, Hindi, and Punjabi. It is my hope that scholars who know those languages better than I will continue to add to this analysis.

26. Weeks, "About Face," 46–47, 55. A number of authors have asked us to consider the agency of foreign peoples in subverting and challenging Western "discourses," a relatively new focus in the literature, for instance, Beaulieu and Roberts, *Orientalism's Interlocutors*; Çelik, *Displaying the Orient*; Codell and MacLeod, *Orientalism Transposed*; Deringil, *Well-Protected Domains*; Dirlik, "Chinese History and the Question of Orientalism," 96–118.

27. In using Lippmann's ideas to help us see the connections between artist, audience, medium, and market, I am using them in a new way since I am considering not solely commercial mass media like newspapers or movies but the creative process of consumption and individuation more broadly in a commercial context. Lippmann's ideas are still

useful in the original sense with respect to print communication since many of the live performances of Eastern personae I examine were known to their audiences only by recorded means such as newspaper reports, fraternal newsletters, or advertising. Indeed, scholars of performance argue that "as an art form, performance lacks a distinctive medium" and is experienced by audiences in multiple ways, live and recorded, so that recorded communications serve as "the repository and medium of transmission of performative tropes." Carroll, "Performance," 78. See also Roach, "Kinship, Intelligence, and Memory," 218.

28. Emile Boutmy quoted in Cronon, *Nature's Metropolis*, 53–54.

29. Wollen, "Fashion/Orientalism/The Body," 8. See also Studlar, *This Mad Masquerade*, 186.

30. I refer to these depictions and performances with the term Orientana, which I derive from similar words like Americana and Canadiana in order to discuss the objects, ideas, and practices Americans understood to be of the "Orient" in some way, whether actually originating overseas or created in the United States. I avoid the terms "Orientalism" and "Orientalist" as properly understood in the late-twentieth-century sense, as defined by Edward Said and other postcolonial scholars, since my sources do not provide evidence for the theories of subconscious discursive power they describe.

31. Lee, *Orientals*, 3.

32. Jacobson, *Barbarian Virtues*, 24–26, 73–97, 180–89.

33. Neil Harris, *Cultural Excursions*, 176–81.

34. Browder, *Slippery Characters*, 3; Neil Harris, *Cultural Excursions*, 181.

35. Judith Butler, *Gender Trouble*, xxviii; see also 171–80; Judith Butler, "Performative Acts," 519–28.

36. Zakim, *Ready-Made Democracy*, 17.

37. Goffman, *Presentation of Self*, 71–74.

38. Ewen, *Captains of Consciousness*, 47; Lears, *No Place of Grace*, 55. Various scholars of ethnicity, "race," gender, nationality, region, and more have theorized the invention and performance of identity through behavior and consumption. See, for instance, Browder, *Slippery Characters*, 5–6; Judith Butler, *Gender Trouble*, 22–24; Cornell and Hartmann, *Ethnicity and Race*; Garber, *Vested Interests*; Gleason, "Identifying Identity," 913–15; Hebdige, *Subculture*.

39. A. L. Rowse, "Foreword," in Steadman, *Myth of Asia*, 11.

40. Majaj, "Arab-Americans and the Meaning of Race," 320–24; James Lewis, "Savages of the Seas," 82; MacKenzie, *Orientalism*, 53; McAlister, *Epic Encounters*, 37–38; Naff, *Becoming American*, 320.

41. Boskin, *Sambo*, 10–11; Hodin, "Disavowal of Ethnicity," 211–26; Holmes, "All the World's a Stage," 1295–97; Levine, *Highbrow/Lowbrow*, 69–82; Moon, *Yellowface*, 1–9.

42. Diamond, *Performance and Cultural Politics*, 4–5; Leach, *Land of Desire*, 105–7; Lears, *Fables of Abundance*, 126.

CHAPTER I

1. Breen, *Marketplace of Revolution*; Zakim, *Ready-Made Democracy*.

2. Napier, "Some Book Sales in Dumfries," 443, 445.

3. Jacob Abbott, "Memoir of Damascus," *Harper's New Monthly Magazine* 7, no. 41 (October 1853): 597. For some typical examples, see W. E. Henley, "Arabian Nights' Entertainments," *Scribner's Magazine* 14, no. 1 (July 1893): 56; "Notices of New Books," *United States Democratic Review* 22, no. 119 (May 1848): 480; G. W. P., "The Thousand and One Nights," *American Whig Review* 6, no. 6 (December 1847): 611.

4. Bond, "Civilization Comes to the Old Northwest," 20; Isani, "Oriental Tale," 87; Mott, *Golden Multitudes*, 305.

5. Halttunen, *Confidence Men*; Marr, *Cultural Roots*.

6. Neil Harris, *Cultural Excursions*, 181; Leach, *Land of Desire*, 6; Zakim, *Ready-Made Democracy*, 7–9.

7. Trentmann, "Knowing Consumers," 4.

8. Colin Campbell, *Romantic Ethic*, 2–9; Leach, *Land of Desire*, xiii; Lears, *Fables of Abundance*, 17–74.

9. Yamanaka and Nishio, *Arabian Nights and Orientalism*, 4.

10. Various authors have critiqued the scholarly notion of pristine and helpless foreign cultures contaminated by contact with Westerners. See, for instance, Richter, *Facing East*, 3–47; Thomas, *Entangled Objects*, 3.

11. Irwin, *Arabian Nights*; Schacker-Mill, "Otherness and Otherworldliness," 167.

12. Luedtke, *Nathaniel Hawthorne*, xvii–xix; Matar, *Turks, Moors and Englishmen*, 3; Schwab, *Oriental Renaissance*, 6–10; Said, *Orientalism*, 12–18.

13. Royall Tyler quoted in David Hall, *Cultures of Print*, 156, 158, 164; Isani, "Oriental Tale," 74–76.

14. See, for instance, Allibone, *Critical Dictionary of English Literature*, 616; G. W. P., "The Thousand and One Nights," *American Whig Review* 6, no. 6 (December 1847): 601–18.

15. David Hall, *Worlds of Wonder*, 21–69; David Hall, *Cultures of Print*, 172–73; Isani, "Oriental Tale," 88–97; Zboray, *A Fictive People*, 36.

16. Richard Brown, "From Cohesion to Competition," 301.

17. Lane, *Thousand and One Nights*.

18. Allibone, *Critical Dictionary of English Literature*, 616; Irwin, *Arabian Nights*, 16–18; Toy, "The Thousand and One Nights," 756; Richardson, *Three Oriental Tales*, 4.

19. Schacker-Mill, "Otherness and Otherworldliness," 164–67, 170.

20. Toy, "The Thousand and One Nights," 757; Allibone, *Critical Dictionary of English Literature*, 616.

21. "Critical Notes," *American Whig Review* 8, no. 6 (December 1848): 649.

22. Edward Forster, *The Thousand and One Nights; or, The Arabian Nights' Entertainments* (Boston: J. H. Francis, 1847); Lane, *Manners and Customs of the Modern Egyptians*; Moussa-

Mahmoud, "English Travellers and the 'Arabian Nights,'" 102. See also Schacker-Mill, "Otherness and Otherworldliness," 164–84.

23. Bell, Culture, 79; Charvat, Literary Publishing, 68–80; Davidson, Revolution and the Word, 37–40.

24. Caracciolo, "Such a Store House of Ingenious Fiction," 6; Isani, "Oriental Tale," 87.

25. Charvat, Literary Publishing, 72.

26. Alderson, "Scheherazade in the Nursery," 87–92. See also Sharafuddin, Islam and Romantic Orientalism, xxvii, xxxi, 120, 135.

27. Schacker-Mill, "Otherness and Otherworldliness," 167.

28. Neil Harris, Cultural Excursions, 338–39.

29. Hanley, Caliphs and Sultans, v–vi.

30. "Critical Notices," American Whig Review 6, no. 5 (November 1847): 548. Alderson finds European children similarly had access to many inexpensive editions of the Nights, which often had openly educational purposes in communicating moral messages. Alderson, "Scheherazade in the Nursery," 82–84; MacLeod, American Childhood, 120–21.

31. "Notices of New Books," United States Democratic Review 23, no. 126 (December 1848): 570.

32. Isani, "Oriental Tale," 85–86; Sale, Koran; Sharafuddin, Islam and Romantic Orientalism, xxx, 135; Sweetman, Oriental Obsession, 3, 267 (n. 50).

33. Isani, "Oriental Tale," 85–86; Sweetman, Oriental Obsession, 3, 267 (n. 50). The Persian poet Maulana Jalauddin Rumi is still the best-selling poet of any period or nationality in the United States. "Rumi Madness," Wall Street Journal, 2 March 2001, W15.

34. Levine, Highbrow/Lowbrow, 13–16.

35. Conant, Oriental Tale, vii–xxiv.

36. Allison, Crescent Obscured, 39, 68, 72, 95; Isani, "Oriental Tale," 87–97, 111–13; Richardson, Three Oriental Tales, 1–20; Said, Orientalism, 2–10; Sharafuddin, Islam and Romantic Orientalism, 120, 215–16.

37. Allison, Crescent Obscured, 39, 68, 72, 95; Conant, Oriental Tale, xxvi; Isani, "Oriental Tale."

38. Gifra-Adroher, Between History and Romance, 153; Isani, "Oriental Tale," 36, 98, 108–9.

39. Richard Brown, "From Cohesion to Competition," 306; Richardson, Three Oriental Tales, 5–6.

40. Isani, "Oriental Tale," 97.

41. Allison, Crescent Obscured, 68.

42. Newly independent and thus without British protection on the seas, American ships were regularly captured and held for ransom by North Africans who patrolled the Atlantic and Mediterranean. Allison, Crescent Obscured, 79–82, 91–93; Benchérif, Image of Algeria, 2–35; Cray, "Remembering the USS Chesapeake," 445–74; James Lewis, "Savages

of the Seas," 75–84; Montgomery, "White Captives, African Slaves," 615–30; Schueller, *U.S. Orientalisms*, 45–74.

43. Allibone, *Critical Dictionary of English Literature*, 616; Christy, "Orientalism of Whittier," 247–57; Christy, "Orientalism in New England," 372–92; Fields, *Whittier*, 96, 99; Richardson, *Three Oriental Tales*, 4.

44. "Lalla Rookh," *Graham's* 40 (June 1852): 599, quoted in Isani, "Oriental Tale," 90.

45. Gifra-Adroher, *Between History and Romance*, 145; Irving, *The Alhambra*, 103; Sharafuddin, *Islam and Romantic Orientalism*, 3, 49–50.

46. Toy, "The Thousand and One Nights," 762.

47. Isani, "Oriental Tale," 38, 42–46.

48. Gill, *Lords of Misrule*, 48.

49. Irving, *Alhambra*, 103; Isani, "Oriental Tale," 38, 42–46; Gifra-Adroher, *Between History and Romance*, 145; Sharafuddin, *Islam and Romantic Orientalism*, 3, 8–22, 49–62, 87–92.

50. "Orientalism," *Knickerbocker* 41, no. 6 (June 1853): 32–33.

51. Sharafuddin, *Islam and Romantic Orientalism*, 135.

52. Steiner, "Authenticity, Repetition, and the Aesthetics of Seriality," 92–101. Miles Orvell makes a comparable point in *Real Thing*, xvi–xix.

53. "Books of the Day," *Appleton's Journal* 7, no. 6 (December 1879): 570; Hawthorne quoted in Woodberry, *Nathaniel Hawthorne*, 54.

54. Isani, "Oriental Tale," 12.

55. "Poetry of the Orient," *The Nation* 1, no. 17 (October 26, 1865): 535–36.

56. "The Oriental Merchant," *Harper's New Monthly Magazine* 9 (June–November 1854): 680–82.

57. Richardson, *Three Oriental Tales*, 4.

58. Olin, *Travels in Egypt*, 1:viii–ix; see also Richardson, *Three Oriental Tales*, 6, 238–42.

59. Neil Harris, *Cultural Excursions*, 178–79.

60. Sandage, *Born Losers*, 26–27; Robert Sobel, *Machines and Morality*; Stokes and Conway, *Market Revolution in America*, 1–21; Zakim, *Ready-Made Democracy*, 38, 73.

61. "Wonders of California," *New York Times*, November 3, 1851.

62. Barth, *City People*, 122–27; Neil Harris, *Cultural Excursions*, 170–83; Zakim, *Ready-Made Democracy*, 98–99.

63. "New York Daguerreotyped," *Putnam's Monthly Magazine* 1, no. 2 (February 1853): 121–24.

64. MacKenzie, *Orientalism*, 52; see also Nance, "Facilitated Access," 1056–78; Stowe, *Going Abroad*, 3.

65. Finnie, *Pioneers East*, 165–66; Steinbrink, "Why the Innocents Went Abroad," 278–79; Wegelin, "Rise of the International Novel," 307.

66. Allison, *Crescent Obscured*, 187–206; John Davis, *Landscape of Belief*, 10–50; Nance, "Ottoman Empire." The scholarship on the business and cultures of American travel writing is far too extensive to discuss here. See, for instance, Metwalli, "Americans

Abroad," 68–82; Obenzinger, *American Palestine*; Schueller, *U.S. Orientalisms*, 29–33; Spiller, "Pilgrim's Return," 827–42; Walker, *Irreverent Pilgrims*; Ziff, *Return Passages*.

67. John Davis, *Landscape of Belief*, 13–26; Finnie, *Pioneers East*, 112–14; David Hall, *Cultures of Print*, 162–63; Obenzinger, *American Palestine*, 12–13; Vogel, *To See a Promised Land*, 15–19.

68. Conant, *Oriental Tale*, xvi.

69. Walker, *Irreverent Pilgrims*, 3, 82.

70. "Tokina," *Harper's New Monthly Magazine* 6 (December 1852–May 1853): 635–36.

71. Buzard, *The Beaten Track*, 1–17.

72. "Ethiopian Nights' Entertainments," *Putnam's Monthly Magazine*, 4, no. 20 (August 1854); William Perry Fogg, "The Land of the 'Arabian Nights,'" *Scribner's Monthly* 14, no. 5 (September 1877): 600–607.

73. "Notices of New Books," *United States Gazette and Democratic Review* 22, no. 119 (May 1848): 480. See also Ahmed, *Edward W. Lane*, 153–57; Schacker-Mill, "Otherness and Otherworldliness," 168.

74. Toy, "The Thousand and One Nights," 758, 762. See also Caracciolo, "Such a Store House of Ingenious Fiction," 4–5; Isani, "Oriental Tale," 86–90, 120–22; Moussa-Mahmoud, "English Travellers and the *Arabian Nights*," 95–110.

75. M. A. Edwards, *Philip in Palestine*, vii, 79; "Five Years in Damascus," *North American Review* 83, no. 172 (July 1856): 42; Lucy Gordon, *Letters from Egypt*, 127; Moussa-Mahmoud, "English Travellers and the 'Arabian Nights,'" 102; Prime, *Boat Life*, 154–55.

76. Eames, *Another Budget*, 192–93.

77. Fetridge, *American Travelers' Guides*, 923, 976.

78. "Five Years in Damascus," *North American Review* 83, no. 172 (July 1856): 40–44.

79. Bayard Taylor, *Lands of the Saracen*, 149–51.

80. Prime, *Boat Life*, 160–61, 183.

81. Spencer, *Egypt and the Holy Land*, 71–73, 77.

82. Jacobson, *Barbarian Virtues*, 131; MacKenzie, *Orientalism*, 62–63.

83. Leach, *Land of Desire*, 105.

84. Hilton, *Smoking in British Popular Culture*, 19–24, 55–56; Martin and Koda, *Orientalism*, 45; Walton, *Faber Book of Smoking*, 68.

85. Prime, *Boat Life*, 169.

86. "Five Years in Damascus," *North American Review* 83, no. 172 (July 1856): 43.

87. Eames, *Another Budget*, 43, 104.

88. Nance, "Facilitated Access."

89. Dorr, *Notes of Travel*, 38–41, 133; Fetridge, *American Travellers' Guides*, 923.

90. Doumani, *Rediscovering Palestine*, 54–232; Owen, *Middle East in the World Economy*, 45–82; Quataert, *Consumption Studies and the Ottoman Empire*.

91. Lynch, *Narrative*, 88–89.

92. Bayard Taylor, *Lands of the Saracen*, 122–23, 131.

93. Wilson, "Studio and Soirée," 235–36; Silverman, "Tourist Art," 62.

94. Nance, "Ottoman Empire Tourism."

95. "Editor's Easy Chair," *Harper's New Monthly Magazine* 8, no. 43 (December 1853): 276.

96. Burns, "Price of Beauty," 214.

97. Zakim, *Ready-Made Democracy*, 98.

98. Batkin, "Tourism is Overrated"; Neil Harris, *Cultural Excursions*, 178–79; Leach, *Land of Desire*, 20; Ownby, *American Dreams*, 82–97; Stearns, *Consumerism in World History*, 49.

99. Hoganson, *Consumers' Imperium*, 22.

100. Lee, *Orientals*, 28–29; Sweetman, *Oriental Obsession*, 163.

101. McAlister, *Epic Encounters*, 37–38; Naff, *Becoming American*, 320.

102. *Fargo City Directory*, 1898; Khater, *Inventing Home*, 72–82; Naff, *Becoming American*, 105–46.

103. Khater, *Inventing Home*, 67.

104. Twain, *Innocents Abroad*, 381; "Trouble of 'Faraway Moses,'" *New York Times*, November 6, 1877.

105. Colin Campbell, *Romantic Ethic*, 8, 54; Neil Harris, *Cultural Excursions*, 179–80; MacKenzie, *Orientalism*, 43.

106. Neil Harris, *Cultural Excursions*, 179–80; Hoganson, *Consumers' Imperium*, 13, 32, 43.

107. Leach, *Land of Desire*, 9; Lears, *Fables of Abundance*, 149.

108. Hoganson, *Consumers' Imperium*, 14.

109. Sweetman, *Oriental Obsession*, 60, 189–90, 196. See also Brody, "Fantasy Realized," 42–43; Burns, "Price of Beauty," 209–38; Hilton, *Smoking in British Popular Culture*, 34; Hoganson, "Cosmopolitan Domesticity," 72; Martin and Koda, *Orientalism*, 45; MacKenzie, *Orientalism*, 62.

110. Zakim, *Ready-Made Democracy*, 38.

111. E. M. Butler, *Myth of the Magus*, 181; Sweetman, *Oriental Obsession*, 68–69.

112. Lears, *Fables of Abundance*, 149.

113. "On Furnishing," *New York Times*, February 25, 1872; Sweetman, *Oriental Obsession*, 178–81, 201–3, 226–27, 230–32.

114. "On Furnishing," *New York Times*, February 25, 1872.

115. Sweetman, *Oriental Obsession*, 230–32.

116. Burns, "Price of Beauty," 209–38; Phillips and Steiner, "Art, Authenticity, and the Baggage of Cultural Encounter," 15–16; Sweetman, *Oriental Obsession*, 178–81, 201–3, 226–27.

117. Hoganson, "Cosmopolitan Domesticity," 69–70; Spooner, "Weavers and Dealers," 197–98.

118. Brettell, "Nineteenth Century Travelers' Accounts," 164; Deloria, *Playing Indian*; Jacobson, *Barbarian Virtues*, 24–26, 73–97, 180–89; Lee, *Orientals*, 3.

119. Batkin, "Tourism is Overrated," 291–92. See also Cohodas, "Elizabeth Hickox and Karuk Basketry," 122–40.

120. "Eastern Rugs in New York," *New York Times*, February 5, 1899.

121. "Carpets from the East," *New York Times*, August 28, 1876. See also Ella Rodman Church, "How to Furnish a House," *Appleton's Journal* 2, no. 2 (February 1877): 152–62.

122. Macleod, "Cross-Cultural Cross-Dressing," 63–64; Reina Lewis, *Gendering Orientalism*, 126–88; Schueller, *U.S. Orientalisms*, 118–19.

123. Hoganson, *Consumers' Imperium*, 24–26

124. Brendon, *Thomas Cook*, 120–35.

125. William Perry Fogg, "The Land of the 'Arabian Nights,'" *Scribner's Monthly* 14, no. 5 (September 1877): 605.

126. Frank Chaffee, "Bachelor Bits," *The Home-Maker* (February 1899): 355.

127. Hoganson, "Cosmopolitan Domesticity," 63–68. See also Macleod, "Cross-Cultural Cross-Dressing," 63–85.

128. Dirlik, "Chinese History and the Question of Orientalism," 102 (n. 17).

129. Hoganson, *Consumers' Imperium*, 8.

130. "On Furnishing," *New York Times*, February 25, 1872.

131. "The Age of Bric-a-Brac," *New York Times*, January 2, 1879.

132. Howells, *Hazard of New Fortunes*, 49–50.

133. Hoganson, *Consumers' Imperium*, 14.

134. Alice Maynor, "Pretty Corners," *The Ladies Home Journal* 15, no. 10 (September 1898): 15.

135. De Certeau, *Practice of Everyday Life*, xii.

136. Howells, *Hazard of New Fortunes*, part VII.

CHAPTER 2

1. "Poetry of the Orient," *The Nation* 1, no. 17 (26 October, 1865): 535–36.

2. Christy, *Orient in American Transcendentalism*, 2–8.

3. Henkin, *City Reading*, 3–7; Ryan, *Civic Wars*, 5–9; Scott, "Popular Lecture," 791–809.

4. Marr, *Cultural Roots of American Islamicism*, 20–133.

5. Rothenberg, *From Market-Places to Market Economy*, 4; Zakim, *Ready-Made Democracy*, 8, 55.

6. Sandage, *Born Losers*, 5.

7. Charvat, *Literary Publishing in America*, 72; Michael Gilmore, *American Romanticism*, 2–6.

8. Scott, "Print and the Public Lecture System," 292.

9. Bell, *Culture*, 73.

10. Brown, "From Cohesion to Competition," 307; Cullen, *Art of Democracy*, 9–86; David Hall, *Cultures of Print*, 154, 165; Scott, "Print and the Public Lecture System," 284–89; Tucher, *Froth and Scum*.

11. Conroy, *Muse in the Machine*, 5.

12. "The Popular Lecture," *Atlantic Monthly* 15, no. 89 (March 1865): 364.

13. Cayton, "Making of an American Prophet," 608–11; Conroy, *Muse in the Machine*, 7.

14. "Latest Missionary Intelligence," *New York Evangelist*, December 17, 1846.

15. See, for instance, "Lectures on Constantinople," *Boston Recorder*, January 18, 1838; "Lectures on Constantinople," *Christian Watchman* (Atlanta), December 7, 1838.

16. Austin, *African Muslims*, 51–84; Younis, "Arabs Who Followed Columbus," 13–14. The story of the Arab in the West nostalgic for the desert is an old one in American popular culture and may be a product as much of romantic American ideas about the silence, beauty, and freedom of Middle Eastern deserts as actual communication with Eastern travelers. See, for instance, "Selim of Virginia," *Graham's Magazine* 51 (November 1857): 433–37; Eilts, "Ahmad bin Na'aman's Mission to the United States," 219–77; Fields, *Whittier*, 54–55; Parkes, "New England in the Seventeen-Thirties," 403.

17. Finnie, *Pioneers East*, 11.

18. John Davis, *Landscape of Belief*, 19–34; Marr, *Cultural Roots*, 69–71; Obenzinger, "Holy Land Narrative," 241–63.

19. "Lectures on Constantinople," *Christian Watchman* 19, no. 49 (December 7, 1838): 95.

20. Hatch, *Democratization of American Christianity*.

21. "Lectures on Constantinople," *Boston Recorder*, January 18, 1838.

22. Ibid.

23. See, for example, "A Turkish Revolution," *Harper's New Monthly Magazine* 9, no. 52 (September 1854): 516; "Editor's Easy Chair," *Harper's New Monthly Magazine* 8, no. 43 (December 1853): 276; Murray M. Ballou, *The Turkish Slave; or, The Mahometan and His Harem* (1850), quoted in James Lewis, "Savages of the Seas," 81; [Crosby], *Land of the Moslem*, 23, 167; Lynch, *Narrative of the United States Expedition*, 54, 88–89, 132, 167; Morris, *Notes of a Tour*, 160; Bayard Taylor, *Lands of the Saracen*, 337; Toy, "The Thousand and One Nights," 763.

24. Barnum, *Struggles and Triumphs*, 581.

25. Marr, *Cultural Roots of American Islamicism*, 74–78, 169.

26. Halttunen, *Confidence Men*, 170–85.

27. Lehuu, *Carnival on the Page*, 108–20.

28. "At the Boston Lyceum," *Journal of Education* 1, no. 5 (July 1838): 39.

29. "Marriages," *Christian Register and Boston Observer*, December 14, 1839; "Ten Years in a Public Library," *The Galaxy* 8, no. 4 (Oct 1869): 533.

30. "Mr. Oscanyan's Turkish Khave," *The Independent* (New York), January 17, 1856.

31. See, for instance, "A Turk Lecturing on Turkey," *New York Times*, October 20, 1855; "Lectures," *New York Observer and Chronicle*, March 26, 1863.

32. "A Turk Lecturing on Turkey," *New York Times*, October 20, 1855.

33. Albert L. Rawson, "A Bygone Bohemia," *Frank Leslie's Popular Monthly* (1896): 96–107; "Christopher Oscanyan," <http://digital.lib.lehigh.edu/pfaffs/people/individuals/85/htm>.

34. "The Sultan and His People," *The Independent* 9, no. 436 (April 9, 1857): 8.

35. Oscanyan, *Sultan and His People*, 10.

36. Bailey, "Ottomans and the Bedouin Tribes," 324–31; Quataert, *Ottoman Empire*, 101–3; Rabinowitz, "Themes in the Economy of the Bedouin," 219–20; Rogan, *Frontiers of the State*, 7, 46; Schölch, *Palestine in Transformation*, 206–9, 254.

37. MacKenzie, *Orientalism*, 55–59.

38. "Editorial Notes," *Putnam's Monthly Magazine* 9, no. 53 (May 1857): 550.

39. "Literary Notices," *Harper's New Monthly Magazine* 15, no. 85 (June 1857): 120.

40. "Editor's Easy Chair," *Harper's New Monthly Magazine* 25, no. 146 (July 1862): 274.

41. "General Sherman in Europe and the East," *Harper's New Monthly Magazine* 47, no. 280 (September 1873): 485; "How They Manage Their Lectures in England," *Putnam's Monthly Magazine* 13, no. 13 (January 1869): 102–3.

42. Smyth, *Bayard Taylor*, 26.

43. Wermuth, *Bayard Taylor*, 35–41.

44. "Talmage, Friday Evening Lecture," *Liberty Weekly Tribune* (Missouri), March 18, 1879.

45. Wermuth, *Bayard Taylor*, 37–41.

46. Bayard Taylor, *Lands of the Saracen*, vi.

47. "Editorial Notes," *Putnam's Magazine* 4 (December 1854): 668.

48. Bayard Taylor, *Lands of the Saracen*, 310.

49. Taylor quoted in Smyth, *Bayard Taylor*, 89–90; R. H. Stoddard, "Reminiscences of Bayard Taylor," *Atlantic Monthly* 43, no. 256 (February 1879): 247.

50. Dorr, *Notes of Travel*, 143.

51. Bayard Taylor, *Lands of the Saracen*, 40, 345.

52. Ibid., 139–40. Many Western dabblers in mysticism used drugs such as hashish to facilitate visions and other unusual spiritual experiences in the nineteenth century. Godwin, *Theosophical Enlightenment*, 173, 287.

53. Wermuth, *Selected Letters of Bayard Taylor*, 114.

54. John Davis, *Landscape of Belief*; Richard Hall, "Wilder Shores of Art," 194–201; Leed, *Mind of the Traveler*, 42; Sweetman, *Oriental Obsession*, 77, 83, 131, 233–36; Wermuth, *Bayard Taylor*, 96, 98, 99.

55. Bayard Taylor, *Lands of the Saracen*, 310–11. Romantic poets strove to glorify the natural, the beautiful, and the primitive as a foil to the unmanly "fetters" of a rigid society that denied self-expression and self-discovery. Colin Campbell, *Romantic Ethic*, 2–9; Sweetman, *Oriental Obsession*, 117.

56. Bayard Taylor, *Lands of the Saracen*, 359.

57. Bayard Taylor, *Poetical Works*, 38.

58. Ibid., 41. *Poems of the Orient* was in fact Taylor's most popular book of poetry, selling several thousand copies, to be successful if not a blockbuster, probably riding the crest of his own notoriety, dependable interest in Eastern-style tales, and general interest in Ottoman Empire politics during the Crimean war. Fields, *Whittier*, 96, 99; Isani, "Oriental Tale," 111–13; Wermuth, *Bayard Taylor*, 112–21.

59. Brown, "From Cohesion to Competition," 307–8; Cayton, "Making of an American Prophet," 597–620.

60. "The Popular Lecture," *Atlantic Monthly* 15, no. 89 (March 1865): 369. See also "Lectures and Lecturers," *Putnam's Monthly Magazine* 9, no. 51 (March 1857): 317–22.

61. Cayton, "Making of an American Prophet," 613.

62. Mead, *Yankee Eloquence*, 114–18.

63. Harvey, *American Geographics*, 27–60; Mead, *Yankee Eloquence*, 20–22; Scott, "Popular Lecture," 803.

64. For instance, Bayard Taylor, *Journey to Central Africa*, 15, 59–61; Bayard Taylor, *Lands of the Saracen*, 60–61, 80–82, 131–32, 345.

65. Ibid., 24, 76.

66. "Mechanics' Society Lectures," *New York Times*, January 21, 1854.

67. Harvey, *American Geographics*, 55. See also Lears, *Fables of Abundance*, 56–64, 142–46.

68. "Mechanics' Society Lectures," *New York Times*, January 21, 1854.

69. Samuel Goodrich, *Peter Parley's Tales about Africa* (1830) quoted in Harvey, *American Geographics*, 47–57; see also Allison, *Crescent Obscured*, 210–24.

70. Finnie, *Pioneers East*, 5–6; Ziff, *Return Passages*, 36–50.

71. Hansen-Taylor and Scudder, *Life and Letters*, 1:276.

72. Bayard Taylor, *Lands of the Saracen*, 114.

73. Conwell, *Life*, 171–72.

74. Denning, *Mechanic Accents*, 29–30, 171–203; Kimmel, *Manhood in America*, 120–45; Swiencicki, "Consuming Brotherhood," 791–92.

75. Melville, *Redburn*, 5; Twain, *Innocents Abroad*, 227–28.

76. Wermuth, *Selected Letters*, 112.

77. Smyth, *Bayard Taylor*, 103.

78. Hansen-Taylor and Scudder, *Life and Letters*, 1:294.

79. Bell, *Culture*, 78, 138–42, 184–85; Charvat, *Profession of Authorship*, 305–6; "Lectures and Lecturers," *Putnam's Monthly Magazine* 9, no. 51 (March 1857): 321; Zboray, *Fictive People*, 80–81.

80. Hansen-Taylor and Scudder, *Life and Letters*, 1:227, 276; "New York City—Bayard Taylor," *New York Times*, November 16, 1855. See also Charvat, *Profession of Authorship*, 315; Mead, *Yankee Eloquence*, 118–23; Wermuth, *Selected Letters*, 95, 120, 112.

81. Hansen-Taylor and Scudder, *Life and Letters*, 1:276. See also "The Bayard Taylor Sensation," *New York Times*, April 20, 1859; Smyth, *Bayard Taylor*, 87.

82. Conroy, *Muse in the Machine*, 6.

83. Wermuth, *Selected Letters*, 111.

84. Paul Gilmore, *Genuine Article*, 7–15; see also Marr, *Cultural Roots*, 268.

85. Smyth, *Bayard Taylor*, 87–88.

86. "Fanny Fern's Portraits," *Liberty Weekly Tribune* (Missouri), April 18, 1856. As late as 1878, during an interview for the *Whig* of Troy, New York, Taylor's interviewer still perceived an Oriental affectation: "In the most natural manner possible, Mr. Taylor slid

off, as it were, from the sofa on which he had been sitting, and assuming the position of a Turk on the rug before the sofa, remained there for ten or fifteen minutes, playing with the delighted Tom [the house cat] in the most buoyant manner, still continuing his conversation." Hansen-Taylor and Scudder, *Life and Letters*, 1:270.

87. Whittier, *Poetical Works*, 2:125, 141, 231. See also Christy, "Orientalism of Whittier," 247–48; Fields, *Whittier*, 41, 83.

88. Whittier quoted in Christy, "Orientalism of Whittier," 249.

89. Wermuth, *Bayard Taylor*, 21–28.

90. "Putnam's Monthly Portraits," *Putnam's Magazine*, 4 (August 1854): i.

91. On the conventions and examples of portraits of well-traveled Western men in Eastern dress, see the images in Finnie, *Pioneers East*; Marr, *Cultural Roots*; Sweetman, *Oriental Obsession*.

92. "Chewing Hasheesh in Egypt," *Brooklyn Daily Eagle*, October 6, 1852; Mills, *Cannabis Britannica*, 79.

93. Bode, *American Lyceum*, 217. See also Cary, *Genteel Circle*, 16; John Davis, *Landscape of Belief*, 41–42; Marr, *Cultural Roots of American Islamicism*, 270; Schueller, *U. S. Orientalisms*, 217.

94. Thomas Hicks, "Portrait of Bayard Taylor," 1855, <http://www.npg.si.edu/cexh/brush/index/portraits/taylor.htm>. While some have interpreted this painting as an example of the "magisterial gaze" of the Westerner at work and stark evidence of American imperial interest in the Middle East, this was arguably not a common interpretation at the time. Boime, *Magisterial Gaze*, 101–5; John Davis, *Landscape of Belief*, 41–42; Holly Edwards, "Portrait of an Orientalist," 120–23.

95. For instance, in the 1850s, biblical scholar and theologian Horatio Hackett cited 2 Samuel 11:2; Daniel 4:30; 2 Samuel 9:25–26. Hackett, *Illustrations of Scripture*, 71–72.

96. Bergmann, "Panoramas of New York," 119–37; Orvell, *Real Thing*, 21; Sweetman, *Oriental Obsession*, 218–19.

97. Cary, *Genteel Circle*, 17.

98. Warnock, "Unpublished Lectures of Bayard Taylor," 125–26.

99. Hansen-Taylor and Scudder, *Life and Letters*, 2:419, 714–15, 723.

100. Wermuth, *Selected Letters*, 161–62.

101. "Editor's Easy Chair," *Harper's Monthly Magazine* 58, no. 346 (March 1879): 622.

CHAPTER 3

1. Deloria, *Playing Indian*, 40–68; Lears, *No Place of Grace*, 142–71.

2. Lears, *No Place of Grace*, 234–37; Rotter, "Gender Relations," 518–42.

3. Plenty of scholars have made too much of the argument that Westerners sought to gender the Middle East feminine, passive and helpless against Western "penetration"— political, economic, or cultural. Indeed, the concept that Americans engaged in a process of "negative self-definition" that required "Othering" Easterners is fundamental to

Saidian theory and its application, even though history shows this formulation to be often inaccurate. Ashcroft et al., *Key Concepts in Post-Colonial Studies*, 167–73; Mason, *Deconstructing America*, 43; Said, *Orientalism*, 1–18.

4. Lott, *Love and Theft*, 53, 157. See also Deloria, *Playing Indian*, 34–36; Paul Gilmore, *Genuine Article*, 1–20.

5. Clawson, *Constructing Brotherhood*, 7; W. S. Harwood, "Secret Societies in America," *North American Review* 164, no. 485 (April 1897): 620.

6. W. S. Harwood, "Secret Societies in America," 622; B. H. Meyer, "Fraternal Beneficiary Societies," 649.

7. Carnes, "Middle-Class Men," 51–52; Clawson, *Constructing Brotherhood*, 123–25; Lears, *No Place of Grace*, 176.

8. W. S. Harwood, "Secret Societies in America," 617–24; B. H. Meyer, "Fraternal Beneficiary Societies," 656; Swiencicki, "Consuming Brotherhood," 776.

9. Dumenil, *Freemasonry and American Culture*, 13–23, 113–15; Swiencicki, "Consuming Brotherhood," 784–86.

10. Clawson, *Constructing Brotherhood*, 213–21; Swiencicki, "Consuming Brotherhood," 773–808.

11. Morris, *Freemasonry in the Holy Land*, 5.

12. Scott, "Popular Lecture," 795–96.

13. Morris, *Faithful Slave*; Morris, *Youthful Explorers in Bible Lands*.

14. "Obituary" for Rob Morris ca. 31 July 1888, unidentified Chicago newspaper, Charles Harpell Scrapbooks, 65, Chicago Historical Society, Chicago, IL. See also "Honors to a Masonic Author," *New York Times*, February 16, 1883; "A Successor to Robert Burns," *New York Times*, December 18, 1884.

15. Austen, *Well-Spent Life*; Denslow, *Masonic Conservators*; Rule, *Pioneering in Masonry*, 47–90; George Smith, "Strong Band Circular," 560.

16. Friedman, *Birth of a Salesman*, 34–55.

17. Morris Relief Fund, *An Appeal to Generous Masons*, 10.

18. John Davis, *Landscape of Belief*, 49–50; Morris, *Freemasonry in the Holy Land*, 13–14.

19. Dumenil, *Freemasonry and American Culture*, 31–71, 148–84.

20. Braude, "Women's History," 96–97; Carnes, *Secret Ritual and Manhood*, 5, 9–10, 50, 61–62, 72–79; Gamm and Putnam, "Growth of Voluntary Associations," 514.

21. Clawson, *Constructing Brotherhood*, 212.

22. Pike, *Morals and Dogma*, 287.

23. Wilmshurst, *Meaning of Masonry*, 19, 29, 48, 93. Mackey's entry under "Orient" also explains that sometimes Masons and other fraternalists used this term instead of "East." Mackey, *Encyclopaedia of Freemasonry*, 1:226–27, 2:537.

24. Harrison Harris, *Harris' Masonic Text-book*, 10.

25. Lester, *Lester's "Look to the East."*

26. John Davis, *Landscape of Belief*, 45–48; Kuklick, *Puritans in Babylon*, 22–23.

27. Rawson, "Palestine Exploration," 106; Daly, "Palestine Exploration," 166–68. See also John Davis, *Landscape of Belief*, 49–50.

28. Morris, *Freemasonry in the Holy Land*, 14–15.

29. Ibid., 3–4, 8; Khalaf, *Cultural Resistance*, 153.

30. Godwin, *Theosophical Enlightenment*, 80, 87–89, 97.

31. Hitti, "America and the Arab Heritage," 9–10; Sharafuddin, *Islam and Romantic Orientalism*, 160.

32. Algar, *Religion and the State*, 185–96.

33. "Death of Abd-El-Kader," *New York Times*, November 12, 1879.

34. "Abd-el-Kader," *New York Times*, November 28, 1873; "Death of Abd-El-Kader," *New York Times*, November 12, 1879; Benchérif, *Image of Algeria*, 163–80.

35. Makdisi, *Culture of Sectarianism*, 1–5.

36. Benchérif, *Image of Algeria*, 75–89; Morris, *Freemasonry in the Holy Land*, 574–78.

37. Morris, *Freemasonry in the Holy Land*, 571–79.

38. D'Ohsson, *Oriental Antiquities*. D'Ohsson (1740–1807) grew up in the Ottoman Empire as the son of an American consul for Sweden there. Sweetman, *Oriental Obsession*, 82.

39. Godwin, *Theosophical Enlightenment*, 303. See, for example, "Kaaba," "Order of Kadiri," "Koran," in Mackey, *Encyclopaedia of Freemasonry*, 375, 378, 417; Mackey, *History of Freemasonry*, 233–243; Harrison Harris, *Harris' Masonic Text-book*, 10–11; Pike, *Morals and Dogma*, 29, 35, 38, 53, 78–82; Wilmshurst, *Meaning of Masonry*, 40, 64, 179–80.

40. Morris, *Freemasonry in the Holy Land*, 14, 17.

41. Coleman, *Light from the East*, 5, 8.

42. Ibid., 10.

43. E. M. Butler, *Myth of the Magus*, 219; Godwin, *Theosophical Enlightenment*, 98–101; Mackey, *Encyclopaedia of Freemasonry*, 1:127–8.

44. E. M. Butler, *Myth of the Magus*, 78, 242; Friedman, *Birth of a Salesman*, 23, 42; Laird, *Advertising Progress*, 19–23; Lears, *Fables of Abundance*, 40–74; McNamara, *Step Right Up*, 164.

45. Rawson et al., *What the World Believes*; Rawson, "Palestine Exploration," 101–13; "Senator Douglas Lying in State," *Harper's Weekly*, June 22, 1861; Paul Johnson, "Albert Leighton Rawson," 231, 236.

46. Lockman, *Contending Visions*, 68; Reid, *Whose Pharaohs*, 130–33. In spite of their self-designation as the American Oriental Society, these scholars only studied Hebrew, Assyrian and Aramaic, languages associated with the Bible but not ostensibly "Oriental" in spirit. Conant, *Oriental Tale*, vii–xxiv; Hitti, "America and the Arab Heritage," 13.

47. Rawson, "Palestine Exploration," 101–13.

48. Ibid., 109–12.

49. "A Lamasery in New York," *New York World*, March 26, 1877.

50. Lears, *Fables of Abundance*, 109; Lears, *No Place of Grace*, 176–77.

51. Gomes, *Dawning of the Theosophical Movement*, 141–42; "Buddhism in America," "Catechizing a Buddhist," and "Various Slanders Refuted," *New York Sun*, May 6, 1877.

52. "A Lamasery in New York," *New York World*, 26 March 1877.

53. Gomes, *Dawning of the Theosophical Movement*, 141–42.

54. Blavatsky, *Isis Unveiled*, 2:308; Godwin, *Theosophical Enlightenment*, 283.

55. Blavatsky, *Isis Unveiled*, 1:38; Godwin, *Theosophical Enlightenment*, 280; Paul Johnson, *Masters Revealed*, 5, 31–32, 83, 232–39; Albert Leighton Rawson, "Mme. Blavatský: A Theosophical Occult Apology," *Frank Leslie's Popular Monthly* (February 1892): 199–208.

56. Godwin, *Theosophical Enlightenment*, 279.

57. Blavatsky, *Isis Unveiled*, 2:308; Godwin, *Theosophical Enlightenment*, 280, 283; Paul Johnson, *Masters Revealed*, 28, 31–32; Albert Leighton Rawson, "Mme. Blavatsky: A Theosophical Occult Apology," *Frank Leslie's Popular Monthly* (February 1892): 199–208.

58. Burton, *Personal Narrative*; Paul Johnson, *Masters Revealed*, 66.

59. These men usually took on the identity of a visiting Muslim traveler, which included local clothing (often unwittingly inappropriate), a long beard, and a new name. "European Literature," *Putnam's Monthly Magazine* 7, no. 40 (April 1856): 443; Burckhardt, *Travels in Arabia*, 101; Burton, *Personal Narrative*, 2:172, 230, 263–64, 267; Finnie, *Pioneers East*, 54, 143–45, 210–14; [Keane], *Six Months in Mecca*, 2–3, 17; Bayard Taylor, *Travels in Arabia*, 78.

60. Deveney, "Travels of H. P. Blavatsky," 10; Paul Johnson, *Masters Revealed*, 66.

61. Paul Johnson, "Albert Leighton Rawson," 232–33; Deveney, "Nobles of the Secret Mosque."

62. Godwin, *Theosophical Enlightenment*, 281, 292. Rawson also entertained atheism and became secretary of a Freethinkers' organization known as the National Liberal League in the late 1870s. *Proceedings of the Freethinkers Convention*, 12.

63. Gomes, *Dawning of the Theosophical Movement*, 156–57; Paul Johnson, *Masters Revealed*, 80–89, 232–33.

64. Rich and De Los Reyes, "Nobles of the Shrine," 18.

65. Scott, "Popular Lecture," 795.

66. Paul Johnson, *Masters Revealed*, 5–8.

67. George Felt quoted in Godwin, *Theosophical Enlightenment*, 286.

68. Freemasonry in the United States is composed of two main branches: the Scottish rite imported from Britain, the highest rank being 32nd degree (with an honorary 33rd degree for a few men), and the American York rite, the highest rank being Knight Templar. The two branch off from the first three degrees, called "Blue Lodge" degrees (Entered Apprentice, Fellowcraft, Master Mason), shared by both York and Scottish rite Masonry. Initiates proceed from degree to degree through study of Freemasonic secrets and initiation at each level in one branch or the other or occasionally in both. For a summary of Masonic degrees, see Brockman, *Theatre of the Fraternity*, 13–15.

69. Carnes, *Secret Ritual and Manhood*, 98–99; Clawson, *Constructing Brotherhood*, 123–24; Deloria, *Playing Indian*, 62–68; 212 (n. 30).

70. "William Jermyn Florence," *New York Times*, November 20, 1891; Ueland, *William Jermyn Florence*, 26.

71. Noble James McGee quoted in Melish, *History of the Imperial Council*, 12–13.

72. AAONMS, *Annual Proceedings*.

73. Carnes, "Middle-Class Men," 40; Carnes, *Secret Ritual and Manhood*, 4–5; Dumenil, *Freemasonry and American Culture*, 32–42.

74. Melish, *History of the Imperial Council*, 30. Debate is still ongoing over these events, and some see Florence and Fleming as sincere mystical seekers who took Rawson's claims seriously. Thereafter, this argument goes, later Mystic Shrine leadership rejected the serious mystical work of early founders and only in the 1880s began to disavow their connection to secret societies in the Middle East. Deveney, "Nobles of the Secret Mosque," 254–55.

75. Melish, *History of the Imperial Council*, 17; "Chatter of the Clubs," *New York Times*, September 27, 1903.

76. Roach, "Kinship," 226.

77. "Mystic Societies of Gulf Cities," *Appleton's Journal* 7, no. 145 (January 6, 1872): 6; "National Convention of the Sons of Malta," *New York Times*, July 20, 1858; Burke, *Popular Culture*, 183–85; Clawson, *Constructing Brotherhood*, 30–32; Natalie Davis, *Society and Culture*, 98–123; Susan Davis, *Parades and Power*, 161; Gill, *Lords of Misrule*, 43–48, 50; Roach, "Kinship," 222–23.

78. "Grand Exposure of the Ceremonies of the Sons of Malta by an Eye-Witness," *Frank Leslie's Illustrated Weekly*, February 25, 1860.

79. "Masquerade of the Sons of Malta," *New York Times*, October 12, 1859.

80. "Mystic Societies of Gulf Cities," *Appleton's Journal* 7, no 145 (January 6, 1872): 6–9; Aimes, "African Institutions in America," 15–32; Susan Davis, *Parades and Power*, 100–111; Shane White, "Pinkster," 68–75.

81. Paul Johnson, *Masters Revealed*, 8.

82. AAONMS, *Annual Proceedings*, 51–53.

83. Barnum, *Struggles and Triumphs*, chapter 44.

84. AAONMS, *Annual Proceedings*, 5, 56.

85. Clawson, *Constructing Brotherhood*, 239; B. H. Meyer, "Fraternal Beneficiary Societies," 648. Though original copies of this ritual exist in the libraries of Masonic lodges and Shrine temples, they are officially private and not open to scrutiny by nonmembers. During the nineteenth century, those suspicious of fraternal orders occasionally published these rituals and other Masonic texts nonetheless in order to "expose" the ostensibly dangerous nature of secret societies. One reprint introduced the ritual of the Shrine by explaining that the order served as a vigilante group to exact vengeance on wayward Masons and to police the community at large. AAONMS, *Mystic Shrine Illustrated*, 3. In this chapter I cite a later reprint, *Mystic Shrine: An Illustrated Ritual*, which appears to agree completely in detail with original rituals. This volume cites Albert Mackey's *En-*

cyclopaedia of Freemasonry to explain that reprints intended to publicly expose secret orders were often used by fraternalists unable to find the scarce originals.

86. B. H. Meyer, "Fraternal Beneficiary Societies," 658. Only after the Mystic Shrine had become famous would Scottish Rite Masonic Lodges likewise make use of "the full theatrical trappings of the popular-entertainment stage," to boost membership. Brockman, *Theatre of the Fraternity*, 13; Ames, "Lure of the Spectacular," 21.

87. "Posed group of officers of Mecca Temple of the Ancient Arabic Order of Nobles of the Mystic Shrine of New York," <http://lcweb2.loc.gov/cgi-bin/query/h?pp/PPALL: ffeld(NUMBER+@1(cph+3b11295))>.

88. Deloria, *Playing Indian*, 65; Lipsitz, *Time Passages*, 244.

89. "Ruin by Fire and Water," *New York Times*, December 2, 1883.

90. AAONMS, *Mystic Shrine: An Illustrated Ritual*, 11–12.

91. Ibid., 12–14.

92. Eames, *Another Budget*, 32, 64. See also Thomson, *Land and the Book*, 128; John Davis, *Landscape of Belief*, 45–48.

93. Halttunen, *Confidence Men*, 188–90.

94. Morris, *Freemasonry in the Holy Land*, 564.

95. AAONMS, *Mystic Shrine: An Illustrated Ritual*, 15.

96. My thanks go to Mark Carnes on this point. See also E. M. Butler, *Myth of the Magus*, 179–80.

97. Gist, "Culture Patterning in Secret Society Ceremonials," 499–500.

98. AAONMS, *Mystic Shrine: An Illustrated Ritual*, 12, 17–20.

99. Ibid., 7.

100. Rotundo, "Boy Culture," 15–36.

101. Kidd, *Making American Boys*, 5; Lears, *No Place of Grace*, 144–49; MacLeod, *American Childhood*, 120.

102. AAONMS, *Mystic Shrine: An Illustrated Ritual*, 22–28.

103. AAONMS, *Mystic Shrine Illustrated*, 3. See also Fleming and Paterson, *Mecca Temple*, 4.

104. "William Jermyn Florence," *New York Times*, November 20, 1891.

105. Clawson, *Constructing Brotherhood*, 228–39.

106. "Abd El Kader's Masonic Friends," *New York Times*, June 7, 1883.

107. "A New Temple of the Mystic Shrine," *New York Times*, October 25, 1884.

108. "Mystic Progenitors of the Veiled Prophets," *Missouri Republican*, October 6, 1878; Parsons, "Midnight Rangers," 811–36; Spencer, *St. Louis Veiled Prophet Celebration*, 19.

109. Root, *Ancient Arabic Order*, 42.

110. "A Great Mystic Shrine Ceremony," *New York Times*, January 5, 1886.

111. Lester, *Lester's "Look to the East."*

112. Carnes, *Secret Ritual and Manhood*, 17–21, 152; Dumenil, *Freemasonry and American Culture*, 150–51, 204–6; Root, *Ancient Arabic Order*, 60.

113. Stowe, *Going Abroad*, 19.

114. Sweetman, *Oriental Obsession*, 120.

115. Stowe, *Going Abroad*, 139–43.

116. Budd, *Our Mark Twain*, 39–41; Burns, "Price of Beauty," 226–27; Carnes, "Middle-Class Men," 48; Ann Douglas, *Feminization of American Culture*, 4–19; Halttunen, *Confidence Men*, 153–90; Kidd, *Making American Boys*, 77–79; Lears, *Fables of Abundance*, 72, 348.

117. AAONMS, *Annual Proceedings*, 1879, 1880, 1881; Melish, *History of the Imperial Council*, 47, 53–56, 70.

118. Melish, *History of the Imperial Council*, 11.

CHAPTER 4

1. Benchérif, *Image of Algeria*, 163–80.

2. Ashley, " 'Strange and Exotic,' " 84–87; Stephen Foster, "Exotic as a Symbolic System," 21–30.

3. Karpat, "Ottoman Emigration," 180–84; Naff, "New York: The Mother Colony," 3–10; Suleiman, "Impressions of New York City," 29.

4. Glassberg, *American Historical Pageantry*, 27.

5. Adams, *E Pluribus Barnum*, 164–92; Rothfels, *Savages and Beasts*, 81–141; Saxon, *Enter Foot and Horse*, 48.

6. "Barnum's Latest Additions: A Squad of Genuine Bedouins," *New York Times*, March 29, 1888; "Last Two Weeks of Barnum," *New York Times*, April 7, 1889; "Hemmings & Cooper's Grand Consolidated Menagerie and Circus," n.d., box 48, JMP.

7. Bailey, "Ottomans and the Bedouin Tribes," 324–31; Peters, "Prisons and Marginalization," 40; Quataert, *Ottoman Empire*, 101–3; Rabinowitz, "Themes in the Economy of the Bedouin," 219–20; Rogan, *Frontiers of the State*, 7, 17–20, 42–46; Schölch, *Palestine in Transformation*, 206–16, 231, 254.

8. Morris H. Warner, *The Barnum Budget or Tent Topics, An Original Route Book* (1886), box 47, JMP.

9. "Buffalo Bill's Wild West and Congress of Rough Riders of the World 1898," box 2, folder 3, Buffalo Bill Collection, American Heritage Center, University of Wyoming.

10. Hamid, *Circus*, 67.

11. Sandoval-Sánchez, *José Can You See*, 31–61.

12. Bederman, *Manliness and Civilization*, 170–239; Conklin, *Ways of the Circus*, 146–48; Russell, *Lives and Legends of Buffalo Bill*, 370.

13. Paul Gilmore, *Genuine Article*, 8. See also Benchérif, *The Image of Algeria*, 163–80; Jacobson, *Barbarian Virtues*, 127–33; John Kasson, *Houdini*, 5–20.

14. Blackstone, *Buckskins, Bullets and Business*, 56; Rosa and May, *Buffalo Bill*, 158, 187; Russell, *Lives and Legends of Buffalo Bill*, 376.

15. Hamid, *Circus*, 23.

16. "Rough Riders of the World," *New York Times*, May 6, 1894; "Buffalo Bill," *Littleton Independent* (Colorado), September 2, 1898; "Buffalo Bill's Wild West," *Greeley Tribune* (Colorado), July 31, 1902.

17. For instance, John Lloyd Stephens had explained to his readers already in the 1840s, "The Bedouin roams over [the desert] like the Indian on our native prairies." Stephens, *Incidents of Travel in Egypt*, 284. See also Lewis, "Savages of the Seas," 81; Twain, *Innocents Abroad*, 222–23; Vogel, *To See a Promised Land*, 77–78.

18. L. G. Moses, *Wild West Shows*, 22–28.

19. Russell, *Lives and Legends of Buffalo Bill*, 370.

20. "The Cossack in the United States," *Frank Leslie's Illustrated Weekly* (April 20, 1893): 247; "Wild West Georgians," <http://www.georgians.ge/all.htm>.

21. There was a constant stream of this kind of material, with a peak in the 1890s. See, for instance, the extensive series on horsemen of North Africa and Asia by T. A. Dodge that appeared in *Harper's New Monthly Magazine* from July to November, 1893.

22. "Buffalo Bill's Wild West and Congress of Rough Riders of the World 1898," box 2, folder 3, Buffalo Bill Collection, American Heritage Center, University of Wyoming.

23. Joy Kasson, *Buffalo Bill's Wild West*, 112; Slotkin, "Buffalo Bill's Wild West," 172–74.

24. Warren, *Buffalo Bill's America*, 421–22.

25. "Rough Riders of the World," *New York Times*, May 6, 1894; *Buffalo Bill's Wild West and Congress of Rough Riders of the World 1897, Historical Sketches and Programme*, box 50, folder 2, JMP.

26. Benchérif, *Image of Algeria*, 83; see also 75–89; Deloria, *Playing Indian*, 1–3; Janet Davis, *Circus Age*, 144–48, 186–89.

27. "Little Street Arabs," *New York Times*, March 27, 1869; "Our Street Arabs," *New York Times*, November 20, 1870.

28. Brands, *Reckless Decade*, 94; Kidd, *Making American Boys*, 93, 100, 105; Jacobson, *Barbarian Virtues*, 126.

29. Kidd, *Making American Boys*, 94, 207.

30. Readers found stories of Middle Eastern desert raiders not just in guidebooks and narratives of travel but also within trusted classics such as translations of the *Arabian Nights* and Oriental tales. From there, casual references to attacks of "hostile Arabs" filtered onto the stage, into newspapers, and into oral tradition. Perhaps equally influential were Bible accounts describing travelers robbed by bandits, for instance, in the parable of the Good Samaritan. Some Americans believed that Bedouin nomads were descendants of such Bible-age brigands. Makdisi, "Reclaiming the Land of the Bible," 690–91; Reid, *Whose Pharaohs?*, 34.

31. Makdisi, *Culture of Sectarianism*, 76. Obenzinger, *American Palestine*, 191–97; Rabinowitz, "Themes in the Economy of the Bedouin," 218–19, 222; Rogan, *Frontiers of the State*, 25, 38–41; Schölch, *Palestine in Transformation*, 163–64, 218.

32. Twain, *Innocents Abroad*, 545–49.

33. Janet Davis, *Circus Age*, 39–50.

34. "Official Route Book of the Adam Forepaugh Shows, Season of 1891," "Miscellaneous Materials: Route Books," box 46, JMP.

35. "Buffalo Bill's Wild West combined with Pawnee Bill's Great Far East. Magazine of Wonders & Daily Review, ca. 1910," Buffalo Bill Collection, box 2, folder 4, American Heritage Center, University of Wyoming.

36. Karpat, "Ottoman Emigration," 180, 186–88.

37. Salom Rizk quoted in Suleiman, "Impressions of New York City," 29–31.

38. Naff, *Becoming American*, 118–27.

39. Naff, "New York: The Mother Colony," 4–7.

40. Guy T. Viskniskki, "A Newsboy Started the Fakir Business," *Atlanta Constitution*, January 25, 1903; Friedman, *Birth of a Salesman*, 23–44; McNamara, *Step Right Up*, 48.

41. DiNapoli, "Syrian-Lebanese Community," 20; Naff, "New York: The Mother Colony," 7–10.

42. Suleiman, "Impressions of New York," 29–44; see also Khater, *Inventing Home*, 88–90.

43. Debate in the Syrian-American press, sometimes heated, saw men argue for or against Syrian-American identity, support for Syrian-Arab nationalism. By the 1920s a new identity had emerged in "Phoenicianism," which emphasized the attitudes of the Maronite Christian commercial classes. All these groups favored group identities tied to the East but distinct from Ottoman or French colonial subjecthood. "Lively War between Syrians," *New York Times*, January 13, 1899; "Syrian Editor Not Un-American," *New York Times*, January 19, 1899; "The Syrian Revolutionists," *New York Times*, March 18, 1900; Ismaeal, "Creating an Imagined Community," 7–13.

44. "A Picturesque Colony," *New York Tribune*, October 2, 1892.

45. Jacobson, *Barbarian Virtues*, 202–33.

46. Kearney, "American Images," 308–65.

47. Pascoe, "Miscegenation Law," 52–59.

48. Daniels, *Guarding the Golden Door*, 12–13.

49. DiNapoli, "Syrian-Lebanese Community," 16, 19; Majaj, "Arab-Americans and the Meaning of Race," 320–24; James Lewis, "Savages of the Seas," 82; McAlister, *Epic Encounters*, 37–38; Naff, *Becoming American*, 320.

50. Kearney, "American Images," 300–303.

51. Karpat, "Ottoman Emigration," 182.

52. Frost, *Circus Life and Circus Celebrities*, 145–46.

53. Alvaro Betancourt [Stewart], comp., *My Diary or Route Book of the P. T. Barnum's Greatest Show on Earth and Great London Circus for the Season 1882* (1882), 40, "Miscellaneous Materials: Route Books," box 47, JMP.

54. McLean, *American Vaudeville*, 40–42.

55. "Grand Opera House," *New York Times*, October 23, 1894; "Huber's Fourteenth

Street Museum," *New York Times*, January 24, 1897; "Koster & Bial's," *New York Times*, February 21, 1899.

56. "Huber's Fourteenth Street Museum," *New York Times*, January 24, 1897.

57. John Kasson, *Houdini*, 14; Laurie, *Vaudeville*, 17–22; McLean, *American Vaudeville*, 1–80; Robert Snyder, *Voice of the City*, 5–40, 130–60.

58. Hamid, *Circus*, 9.

59. "Keith's Continuous Performance," *New York Times*, December 26, 1898;

60. Employment Cards, Ringling Brothers, Barnum & Bailey Circus Collection, Robert L. Parkinson Library and Research Center, Circus World Museum, Baraboo, Wisconsin; "Luna Park," *New York Times*, May 11, 1904; "Song Bill Tonight by Judy Garland," *New York Times*, September 26, 1956; "Theatre: Judy Garland," *New York Times*, September 27, 1956.

61. "Barnum to Draw from Algiers," *New York Times*, November 20, 1887; "Koster & Bial's To-Night," *New York Times*, October 29, 1894; "Keith's," *New York Times*, December 31, 1898; Fox, *American Circus Posters*, 31.

62. "What an African Will Do," *New York Times*, November 22, 1891; "Notes of the Week," *New York Times*, October 18, 1896.

63. Morris H. Warner, *The Barnum Budget or Tent Topics, An Original Route Book* (1886), 36, "Miscellaneous Materials: Route Books," box 47, JMP.

64. Alvaro Betancourt [Stewart], comp., *My Diary or Route Book of the P. T. Barnum's Greatest Show on Earth and Great London Circus for the Season 1882* (1882), 30, 36, "Miscellaneous Materials: Route Books," box 47, JMP.

65. Cochran, *Showman Looks On*, 29; Janet Davis, *Circus Age*, 34.

66. Hamid, *Circus*, 9.

67. John Kasson, *Houdini*, 2–15; Kevin White, *First Sexual Revolution*, 8–12.

68. "Vaudeville Gossip," *National Police Gazette*, July 5, 1902; Laurie, *Vaudeville*, 22.

69. Hamid, *Circus*, 30–32.

70. Kibler, *Rank Ladies*, 140–72.

71. "Letterheads of Magicians and Magic Acts," scrapbooks, Theatre Collection, Visual and Performing Arts Division, New York Public Library, New York, New York; "Dizzy Record Broken by a Syrian Whirler," *New York Times*, April 2, 1906; "Girl Dancer Whirls for 37 Minutes," *New York World*, April 2, 1906.

72. "Keith's," *New York Times*, April 1, 1906.

73. "Ali Bendib Troupe," Photographs-Exotica," box 1, JMP; Carlton, *Looking for Little Egypt*, 26–29; Heber De Long scrapbooks, Newberry Library, Chicago, Illinois; Handy, *Official Catalogue of the Exhibits*.

74. McLean, *American Vaudeville*, 42; Ullman, *Sex Seen*, 12–13.

75. Laurie, *Vaudeville*, 79.

76. "Girl Dancer Whirls for 37 Minutes," *New York World*, April 2, 1906.

CHAPTER 5

1. Hebdige, *Subculture*, 100–127.

2. Brands, *Reckless Decade*, 202; see also 38–40, 63, 73–79

3. Ibid., 298; Jacobson, *Barbarian Virtues*, 59–98, 193–209; Rydell, *All the World's a Fair*, 40.

4. Cronon, *Nature's Metropolis*, 348–50; Lee, *Orientals*, 3.

5. Because most scholars argue that such spectacles turned visitors into modern—meaning passive—audiences, they overstate the influence of the elites who staged the displays hoping to popularize scientific racism and anthropological theory that ranked the world's peoples, placing the United States at the top. Greenhalgh, *Ephemeral Vistas*, 2; Hinsley, "The World as Marketplace"; Rydell, *All the World's a Fair*, 1–8; Rydell and Gwinn, *Fair Representations*.

6. See, for instance, *Oriental and Occidental Northern and Southern Portrait Types*; *World's Columbian Exposition Portfolio*; Handy, *Official Catalogue of the Exhibits*; John McGovern, *Halligan's Illustrated World*.

7. Trachtenberg, *Incorporation of America*, 217–19. See also 209, 231.

8. Rebecca Edwards, *New Spirits*, 155–57; Rydell, *All the World's a Fair*, 38–52.

9. Hawthorn, *Humors of the Fair*, 138. See also Truman, *History of the World's Fair*, 551.

10. Van Nieuwkerk, "A Trade Like Any Other," 23.

11. Truman, *History of the World's Fair*, 553–54.

12. Ibid., 550–54.

13. Raibmon, "Theatres of Contact," 157–60.

14. W. C. Brownell, "The Paris Exposition: Notes and Impressions," *Scribner's Magazine* 7, no. 1 (January 1890): 27.

15. Thomas W. Palmer, "Introductory," in Truman, *History of the World's Fair*, 19–20. See also Brands, *Reckless Decade*, 45; Greenhalgh, *Ephemeral Vistas*, 82–109; Rydell, *All the World's a Fair*, 56, 94.

16. Julian Ralph, *Chicago and the World's Fair* (1893), quoted in "The Midway Plaisance," *Harper's Weekly*, 37 (13 May 1893): 442; Truman, *History of the World's Fair*, 550. See also "Side Shows of the Great Fair," *New York Times*, April 30, 1893; "A Raid on Visitors' Pocketbooks," *New York Times*, May 4, 1893; "Extortion to be Stopped," *New York Times*, May 6, 1893; "World's Fair Annoyances," *New York Times*, May 22, 1893. American circuses routinely used the word "midway" to describe the long rows of attractions and displays arranged to lead audiences into the main big top tent. Circus midways were notorious for their perceived tasteless side shows with sword swallowers, tattooed women, "freaks," imported animals, and the pickpockets who robbed distracted circus goers. Stoddart, *Rings of Desire*, 24–25.

17. Hoganson, *Consumers' Imperium*, 49.

18. "A Novel Procession at the Fair," *Harper's Weekly*, July 1, 1893, 629–30; "Shows

Many Customs," *Chicago Tribune*, April 30, 1893; *Oriental and Occidental Northern and Southern Portrait Types*, 67, 97, 113; Ira Robinson, *Selected Letters of Cyrus Adler*, 1:20, 29–38.

19. Hawthorn, *Humors of the Fair*, 35.

20. Truman, *History of the World's Fair*, 550, 552–53.

21. "In a Tunisian Bazaar," *Chicago Daily News*, March 16, 1893; Phillips and Steiner, "Art, Authenticity, and the Baggage of Cultural Encounter," 11–12, 19; Wilson, "Studio and Soirée," 230–36.

22. "C. Lekegian & Co. Photographers," ICHi-22843, Ready Prints, Chicago History Museum, Chicago, Illinois.

23. F. Huntington Smith, "The Picturesque Side," *Scribner's Magazine* 14, no. 5 (November 1893): 601–11.

24. Batkin, "Tourism Is Overrated," 282–300; Hoganson, "Cosmopolitan Domesticity," 65–68; Rydell, *All the World's a Fair*, 94.

25. "Dinner a la Syria," *Chicago Evening Post*, May 29, 1893.

26. *Oriental and Occidental Northern and Southern Portrait Types*, 83, 101.

27. Conner, *Oriental Architecture*, 174; Lears, *Fables of Abundance*, 52; MacKenzie, *Orientalism*, 89–90, 204; Sweetman, *Oriental Obsession*, 220–30.

28. *Moorish Palace and Its Startling Wonders*; *Oriental and Occidental Northern and Southern Portrait Types*, 83, 101; Truman, *History of the World's Fair*, 559; "Moorish Palace Opened," *Chicago Evening Post*, June 3, 1893.

29. "World's Fair Annoyances," *New York Times*, May 22, 1893.

30. Çelik, *Displaying the Orient*, 17–49, 95–180; Deringil, *Well-Protected Domains*, 135–65; Grigsby, *Extremities*, 124, 131, 162; L. G. Moses, *Wild West Shows*; Rabinovitz, *For the Love of Pleasure*, 47–67; Raibmon, "Theatres of Contact," 157–90.

31. "Bedouin Life in the Desert," "Buffalo Bill's Wild West," and "Seventh Extravaganza Season, Ali Baba," *Chicago Evening Post*, May 26, 1893; "Diversion in Plenty," *Chicago Tribune*, April 30, 1893; *Oriental and Occidental Northern and Southern Portrait Types*, 11, 21; Russell, *Lives and Legends of Buffalo Bill*, 374; Truman, *History of the World's Fair*, 551–52.

32. "Try Our Turkish Refreshments," Events and Exhibitions, Midway II, World Columbian Exhibition 1893, Ready Prints Photograph Collection, Chicago History Museum, Chicago, Illinois; "In a Tunisian Bazaar," *Chicago Daily News*, March 16, 1893; "Cairo on Dress Parade," *Chicago Evening Post*, May 27, 1893; "The Turkish Theatre—Midway Plaisance," *Chicago Evening Post*, May 28, 1893.

33. Deringil, *Well-Protected Domains*, 154–55, 161

34. "Shriners Dedicate the Temple," *Chicago Tribune*, April 29, 1893; Hawthorn, *Humors of the Fair*, 77.

35. *World's Fair Puck*, no. 4 (May 29, 1893): 40.

36. Bloom, *Autobiography*, 136–37.

37. Hawthorn, *Humors of the Fair*, 17. There are too many examples to cite here, so see, for example, "Mohamed Noor Was Drunk," *Chicago Evening Post*, June 3, 1893; "Johnson Family on the Midway Plaisance," *Harper's Weekly*, August 5, 1893, 743.

38. Deringil, *Well-Protected Domains*, 150–51. See also Mitchell, *Colonizing Egypt*, 4–13.

39. Çelik, *Displaying the Orient*, 10, 12, 23; Deringil, *Well-Protected Domains*, 159–61.

40. The Canadian and Mexican governments, for instance, also sought to portray their states as modern industrial nations caring for backward indigenous peoples. Heaman, *Inglorious Arts of Peace*, 234–56; Raibmon, *Theatres of Contact*, 157–190; Tenorio-Trillo, *Mexico at the World's Fairs*, 184–88.

41. Truman, *History of the World's Fair*, 537–38.

42. Handy, *Official Catalogue of the Exhibits*.

43. Deringil, *Well-Protected Domains*, 157, 170; Makdisi, "Ottoman Orientalism," 768–96.

44. Çelik, *Displaying the Orient*, 49.

45. Rogan, *Frontiers of the State*, 6; see also 12–15, 48–55; Makdisi, *Culture of Sectarianism*, 59–60; Schölch, *Palestine in Transformation*, 253–54.

46. Deringil, *Well-Protected Domains*, 157; Trachtenberg, *Incorporation of America*, 13–15.

47. "A Living Oriental Exhibit," *New York Times*, April 26, 1893; "Bedouin Life in the Desert," "Buffalo Bill's Wild West," and "Seventh Extravaganza Season, Ali Baba," *Chicago Evening Post*, May 26, 1893.

48. "Mosque in Turkish Village, Photograph by Copelin," Events and Exhibitions, Midway II, World Columbian Exhibition 1893, Ready Prints Photograph Collection, Chicago History Museum, Chicago, Illinois.

49. Bloom, *Autobiography*, 106.

50. Heber De Long scrapbooks, Newberry Library, Chicago, Illinois.

51. Trenorio-Trillo, *Mexico at the World's Fairs*, 185–88.

52. "Shriners Dedicate the Temple," *Chicago Tribune*, April 29, 1893.

53. "Men of the Desert, A Strange Procession in the World's Fair," *Atlanta Constitution*, April 29, 1893; "All but Exhibitors Barred," *New York Times*, April 29, 1893.

54. Truman, *History of the World's Fair*, 556–58.

55. Cronon, *Nature's Metropolis*, 349; Robert Sobel, *Machines and Morality*, 49–50.

56. "Shriners Dedicate the Temple," *Chicago Tribune*, April 29, 1893.

57. A.A.O.N.M.S., *Whence Came the Oriental Band*.

58. Adler, *I Have Considered the Days*, 176–77.

59. Glassberg, *American Historical Pageantry*, 27–28; Roach, "Kinship, Intelligence, and Memory," 220–24.

60. Here I do admit to using the term "camp" anachronistically. Moe Meyer defines the phenomenon of Camp as "a specifically queer cultural critique" and elaborates that "camp (with a lowercase *c*) is what results when 'Camp' is appropriated by the 'unqueer,'" although this kind of celebratory ridicule—also known as a roast—must be as old as humanity. Moe Meyer, "Reclaiming the Discourse of Camp," 1.

61. Adler, *I Have Considered the Days*, 176–77.

62. Ira Robinson, *Selected Letters of Cyrus Adler*, 1:38.

63. "Men of the Desert: A Strange Procession in the World's Fair Grounds," *Atlanta*

Constitution, April 29, 1893; "Preparing for the Fair," *Los Angeles Times*, April 29, 1893; "All but Exhibitors Barred," *New York Times*, April 29, 1893; "Work in Bad Weather," *San Francisco Chronicle*, April 29, 1893; "Rain Cannot Hinder Work," *San Francisco Examiner*, April 29, 1893.

64. "Kirk's American Family Soap," *Chicago Tribune*, April 29, 1893.

65. AAONMS, *Annual Proceedings*; Melish, *History of the Imperial Council*, 47, 53–56, 70; "The Nobles of the Mystic Shrine," *Harper's Weekly* 37 (June 24, 1893): 607; Carnes, *Secret Ritual and Manhood*, 4–5; Dumenil, *Freemasonry and American Culture*, 32–42.

66. "Iowa Shriners Hold a Conclave," *Chicago Tribune*, April 29, 1893; "Alhambra at It Again," *The Crescent* 5, no. 8 (October 1914): 28; "It Was Some Parade," *The Crescent* 5, no. 4 (June 1918): 48.

67. Fleming and Paterson, *Mecca Temple*, 37–38.

68. Clawson, *Constructing Brotherhood*, 233–35.

69. Russell, *Lives and Legends of Buffalo Bill*, 381; Spann, *Gotham at War*, 22–23.

70. "Shriners in Midnight Ceremonial," *Chicago Record-Herald*, October 22, 1911.

71. Rawson, "Palestine Exploration," 111.

72. Bevan, *Sand and Canvas*, 36; Nathaniel Burt, *Far East*, 142; Bloom, *Autobiography*, 135–37. See also Carlton, *Looking For Little Egypt*, 56; Charles Kennedy, "When Cairo Met Main Street," 275–76; Salvador-Daniel, *Music and Musical Instruments of the Arab*, 4–16; Truman, *History of the World's Fair*, 558.

73. A.A.O.N.M.S., *Whence Came the Oriental Band*, 4–12; A.A.O.N.M.S., *100 Years of Love*, 11–12.

74. "Theatres in Midway," *Chicago Evening Post*, May 25, 1893; "Theatres in Midway, Chinese, Turkish, Algerian and Soudanese Play Actors," *Chicago Evening Post*, May 25, 1893.

75. "Theatres in Midway, Chinese, Turkish, Algerian and Soudanese Play Actors," *Chicago Evening Post*, May 25, 1893.

76. "The Mystic Shrine," *Helena Daily Herald*, July 31, 1890.

77. A.A.O.N.M.S., *100 Years of Love*, 11–12.

78. The Cody's Wild West productions similarly inspired African Americans in Louisiana to develop the Mardi Gras Indians parade and burlesque troupes around the same time, in their case, to communicate community cohesion and resistance to white power. Lipsitz, *Time Passages*, 233–55.

79. "1,100 'Cross Sands' to Holy Shrine," *Chicago Tribune*, September 28, 1907; "Shriners Will Parade with Camel and Elephant Tonight, Thousands Being in Line in Uniform," *Chicago Daily Journal*, September 27, 1907; "Rameses' Natal Day, Say Mystic Shriners," *Chicago Daily News*, September 27, 1907.

80. "March through Rain to Sands of Desert," *Chicago Record-Herald*, September 28, 1907.

81. "Rameses' Natal Day, Say Mystic Shriners," *Chicago Daily News*, September 27, 1907. The strange photographs of Levy and the banner are available online through the Library

of Congress: "Shriner Robert Levy, standing with silk curtains that he presented to the Medinah Temple," 1907, and "Robert Levy, a Shriner, standing outdoors," <http://mem ory.loc.gov/ammem/ndlpcoop/ichihtml/cdnhome.html>. On the debate over Shriner authenticity and foreign origins, see, for instance, Cochrane, *Shriners Book*; Senter, *Pictorial History of Al Malaikah Temple*, 2.

82. "Shriners to Pay Honor to Chief," *Chicago Tribune*, September 27, 1907; "Shriners Open $650,000 Mosque," *Chicago Tribune*, October 31, 1912.

83. "Standing of the Order," *The Crescent* 9, no. 1 (March 1918): 3–5.

84. "And Now They're Off, Big Doings at the Institution of Moslah Temple, July 4," *The Crescent* 5, no. 6 (August 1914): 38–40.

85. "Just Advice," *The Crescent* 5, no. 8 (October 1914): 20.

86. Carnes, *Secret Ritual and Manhood*, 152; Clawson, *Constructing Brotherhood*, 232–33; National Court, Royal Order of Jesters, *59th Annual Meeting*, July 5, 1976, and Grottoes of North America, Supreme Council, Mystic Order of Veiled Prophets of the Enchanted Realm, 21 September 1978 to William Klesow, Fraternal Pamphlets Collection, Grand Lodge F. & A.M. of California, Institute for Masonic Studies, Grand Lodge of California, San Francisco, California; Rich and De Los Reyes, "Nobles of the Shrine," 9.

87. Walkes, *History of the Shrine*, 14–16.

88. Bay, *White Image in the Black Mind*, 121–23; Hickey and Wylie, *Enchanting Darkness*, 271; Trafton, *Egypt Land*, 69–74.

89. "Report of Committee Appointed to Investigate the Alleged Conferring of the Degree of the Nobles of the Mystic Shrine, by Rofelt Pasha and Others," Harry A. Williamson Masonic Papers, Manuscripts and Rare Books Division, Schomburg Center for Research in Black Culture, New York Public Library, New York.

90. Palmer, "Negro Secret Societies," 211.

91. Lorini, *Rituals of Race*, 33–75; Reed, "All the World Is Here!" 3–36, 143–71.

92. "Men from the Antipodes," *Chicago Daily News*, March 17, 1893; see also "Darkies' Day at the Fair," *World's Fair Puck*, no. 13 (July 31, 1893): 186–87. See also the cartoon series, "The Johnson Family on the Midway Plaisance," *Harper's Weekly*, 37 (August 5, 1893); 37 (August 19, 1893), etc.

93. Crawford, *Prince Hall and His Followers*, 94; Palmer, "Negro Secret Societies," 209.

94. Grimshaw, *Official History of Freemasonry*, 67–95, 102–7; Harrison Harris, *Harris' Masonic Text-book*, 130–32. The founders of Prince Hall Masonry and the African Grand Lodge in Boston had in fact come to the conclusion in 1791 that they had no other recourse but to seek independent authority for their own lodges from a Grand Lodge in Britain. White Masons in the United States almost unanimously rejected Prince Hall Lodges' legitimacy nonetheless. Black Masons were split over whether to strive for integration into white Masonic organizations, the majority preferring their own orders over which they had full political and financial control. Clawson, *Constructing Brotherhood*, 131–35; Crawford, *Prince Hall and His Followers*, 15–18; Voorhis, *Negro Masonry*, 7–22.

95. Gist, "Structure and Process in Secret Societies," 352; Palmer, "Negro Secret Societies," 207–12.

96. Calvin Burt, *Egyptian Masonic History*, 203.

97. Crawford, *Prince Hall and His Followers*, 32–34; Walkes, *History of the Shrine*.

98. "Shriners End Fine Session in Bean City," *Chicago Defender*, September 4, 1926; "100,000 View Pythians in Big Parade," *Chicago Defender*, August 20, 1927; "Masons Will Hear Leaders Discuss Fraternal Issues," *Chicago Defender*, January 12, 1929.

99. "Shriners to Get Welcome in Big Style," *Chicago Defender*, June 29, 1929.

100. Levine, "Marcus Garvey," 121; Watkins-Owens, *Blood Relations*, 116–19.

101. Aimes, "African Institutions in America," 15–32; Shane White, "Pinkster," 68–75.

102. Gist, "Structure and Process in Secret Societies," 352; Guy Johnson, "Some Factors in the Development," 333–34.

103. "Negro Imitators Lose," *The Crescent* 5, no. 12 (February 1915): 24; "Won on the Appeal," *The Crescent* 9, no. 7 (September 1918): 36; Walkes, *History of the Shrine*, 87–98.

104. "Well, the Coons Win," *The Crescent* 5, no. 10 (December 1914): 11.

105. Jose H. Sherwood, deposition, D. W. Michaux et al. vs. A. H. Burrill et al., 55th District Court of Harris County, Texas, 1922, Harry A. Williamson Masonic Papers, Schomburg Center for Studies in Black Culture, New York Public Library, New York, New York.

106. "Good Stuff," *The Crescent* 5, no. 8 (October 1914): 9.

107. The 1920s had been particularly active time for fraternal court cases with white Masons, Shriners and Pythians challenging their black counterparts in a dozen states. "Texas Lodge Case to Get Final Airing," *Chicago Defender*, January 21, 1928; "The Text of United States Supreme Court Decision in Shrine Case," *Chicago Defender*, August 17, 1929; Williams, *Black Freemasonry*, 87.

108. Caesar R. Blake Jr., "Proclamation, no. 4," Harry A. Williamson Masonic Papers.

109. Cohen, *Consumer's Republic*, 41–53; Weems, *Desegregating the Dollar*, 1–4.

110. Caesar R. Blake, "Proclamation, no. 4."

111. "Secret Order Elated over Court Fight," *Chicago Defender*, June 22, 1929.

CHAPTER 6

1. Meyer Berger, "Step Right This Way and See the —," *New York Times*, April 16, 1939.

2. Barbas, *Movie Crazy*, 21–48; Hoganson, *Consumers' Imperium*, 48–50; Yoshihara, *Embracing the East*, 15–44.

3. Çelik and Kinney, "Ethnography and Exhibitionism," 41; see also Carlton, *Looking For Little Egypt*, 24; Reina Lewis, *Rethinking Orientalism*, 12–18; Richardson, *Three Oriental Tales*, 3.

4. Robert Allen, *Horrible Prettiness*, 46–48, 227–36; Marr, *Cultural Roots*, 185–218.

5. Kahf, *Western Representations*, 4–7, 172.

6. Carlton, *Looking for Little Egypt*, 40–44; Van Nieuwkerk, *A Trade Like Any Other*, 26–27.

7. Morris, *Notes of a Tour*, 193.

8. Fahmy, "Prostitution in Egypt," 79–81, 89–93; Morris, *Notes of a Tour*, 230–31.

9. Fahmy, "Prostitution in Egypt," 78–91; Van Nieuwkerk, *A Trade Like Any Other*, 29–32.

10. Thomson, *Land and the Book*, 2:346, 445.

11. "An Immoral Coffee-House," *New York Times*, June 15, 1876; see also Norton, *Frank Leslie's Historical Register*, 118–20.

12. Gilbert, *American Vaudeville*, 16.

13. Poignant, *Professional Savages*, 109; Smith and Litton, *Musical Comedy*, 45–46.

14. Hanssen, "Public Morality," 187–96; Van Nieuwkerk, *A Trade Like Any Other*, 38–39.

15. Van Nieuwkerk, *A Trade Like Any Other*, 41.

16. See, for instance, "Arab Dancing Girl, Upper Egypt," card 20033671184, Underwood & Underwood Stereographic Cards, Prints and Photographs Division, Library of Congress, Washington, D.C.; "At Dinner with a Persian Prince," *Living Age* 171, no. 2217 (December 18, 1886): 705–68; "Irene the Missionary," *Atlantic Monthly* 43, no. 259 (May 1879): 587–601; Flinn, *Official Guide to the Midway Plaisance*; Knox, *Adventures of Two Youths*, 230; Norton, *Frank Leslie's Historical Register*, 118–20; Clinton Scoliard, "The Shêkh Abdallah," *Scribner's Magazine* 8, no. 3 (September 1890): 358–59; Charles Dudley Warner, "The Golden Home: A Novel," *Harper's New Monthly Magazine* 89, no. 530 (July 1894): 165–81

17. Gilbert, *American Vaudeville*, 16.

18. "Evidence: Judicial Note," 156–57; Jenkins, "Laisser-Faire Theory of Artistic Censorship," 73–75.

19. Alpert, "Judicial Censorship," 53–54; Horowitz, *Rereading Sex*, 369; McLaren, *Trials of Masculinity*, 29–31; Tone, "Black Market Birth Control," 439–40.

20. Trumbull, *Anthony Comstock*, 239. See also Alpert, "Judicial Censorship," 57, 65–66; "Enforcement of Laws," 955; Tone, "Black Market Birth Control," 438–39, 442.

21. Alpert, "Judicial Censorship," 64; "Enforcement of Laws," 952.

22. "Enforcement of Laws," 57–90; "Evidence: Judicial Note," 156–57; Alpert, "Judicial Censorship," 54; Jenkins, "Laisser-Faire Theory of Artistic Censorship," 73–75.

23. Alderson argues the same for European readers who as children had access to many inexpensive editions of the *Nights*, which often had openly educational purposes in communicating moral lessons. Alderson, "Scheherazade in the Nursery," 83–84.

24. Tone, "Black Market Birth Control," 440.

25. Annam, "Arabian Nights in Victorian Literature," 41.

26. Comstock, *Frauds Exposed*.

27. Cook, *Arts of Deception*, 177.

28. Conant, *Oriental Tale*, xxv.

29. Swiencicki, "Consuming Brotherhood," 791; see also Lears, *Fables of Abundance*, 140–52.

30. Hoganson, *Consumers' Imperium*, 31; Reina Lewis, *Gendering Orientalism*, 126–88;

Macleod, "Cross-Cultural Cross-Dressing," 63–85; Roberts, "Contested Terrains," 179–203.

31. "Theatres in the Midway," *Chicago Evening Post*, May 25, 1893.

32. Çelik, *Displaying the Orient*, 2, 18–24.

33. Rothfels, *Savages and Beasts*, 12; see also Janet Davis, *Circus Age*, 186; Rabinovitz, *For the Love of Pleasure*, 64–65.

34. Truman, *History of the World's Fair*, 558. See also "Theatres in Midway," *Chicago Evening Post*, May 25, 1893.

35. Carlton, *Looking for Little Egypt*, 27–44; Van Nieuwkerk, *Trade Like Any Other*, 26–27.

36. Bloom, *Autobiography*, 135. Americans adapted the term from the French burlesque-dance term meaning "shake your tail." Carlton, *Looking for Little Egypt*, 58.

37. Truman, *History of the World's Fair*, 558. See also "Theatres in Midway," *Chicago Evening Post*, May 25, 1893.

38. "It's Got to Stop," *St. Louis Post-Dispatch*, August 6, 1893; Carlton, *Looking for Little Egypt*, 50; Charles Kennedy, "When Cairo Met Main Street," 275; John McGovern, *Halligan's Illustrated World*, 307–10.

39. Hawthorne, *Humors of the Fair*, 140–41.

40. John McGovern, *Halligan's Illustrated World*, 308.

41. "Human Nature," *World's Fair Puck* 14 (August 7, 1893): 210–11.

42. "Theatres in the Midway," *Chicago Evening Post*, May 25, 1893.

43. F. W. Putnam, "Introduction," in *Oriental and Occidental Northern and Southern Portrait Types*, 2.

44. Brands, *Reckless Decade*, 44–45.

45. "Enforcement of Laws," 954.

46. "It's Got to Stop," *St. Louis Post-Dispatch*, August 6, 1893; Carlton, *Looking For Little Egypt*, 50; John McGovern, *Halligan's Illustrated World*, 307–10.

47. Swiencicki, "Consuming Brotherhood," 790–92; see also Erenberg, *Steppin' Out*, 18–21.

48. "World's Columbian Exposition," *Frank Leslie's Illustrated Weekly*, October 26, 1893, 264; Broun and Leech, *Anthony Comstock*, 206.

49. "Want Midway Dances Stopped," *Chicago Tribune*, August 4, 1893; "Is Gone Dance Crazy," *Chicago Tribune*, August 6, 1893; "The Midway Plaisance," *St. Louis-Post Dispatch*, August 4, 1893; "No More Midway Dancing," *New York Times*, December 7, 1893; Carlton, *Looking for Little Egypt*, 52.

50. "Getting Ready for the World's Fair Show," *New York Times*, Nov. 15, 1893; "World's Fair in Miniature," *New York Times*, Nov. 24, 1893.

51. "Getting Ready for the World's Fair Show," *New York Times*, November 15, 1893; "Police and Law Defied," *New York Times*, December 5, 1893; "World's Fair in Miniature," *New York Times*, November 24, 1893; "Exposition by Prize Winners," *New York Times*, November 30, 1893.

52. "Too Oriental for Williams," *New York Times*, December 3, 1893.

53. Ibid.

54. See, for example, "Minden Was a Sacrifice," New York Times, March 21, 1891; "A Poolroom Cursed City," New York Times, March 22, 1891; "The Dumping of Garbage," New York Times, August 15, 1880.

55. "Too Oriental for Williams," New York Times, December 3, 1893.

56. "No More Midway Dancing," New York Times, December 7, 1893. See also "Inspector Williams Stops the Dance," New York Tribune, December 3, 1893; "Concert at the Prize-Winners' Show," New York Tribune, December 4, 1983.

57. "Too Oriental for Williams," New York Times, December 3, 1893.

58. "Police and Law Defied," New York Times, December 5, 1893.

59. New York World, August 5, 1893, quoted in Broun and Leech, Anthony Comstock, 227.

60. "No More Midway Dancing," New York Times, December 7, 1893; "The Midway Dancers Fined," New York Tribune, December 7, 1893.

61. "No More Midway Dancing," New York Times, December 7, 1893; "Police and Law Defied," New York Times, December 5, 1893.

62. Alloula, Colonial Harem, 5; Carlton, Looking for Little Egypt, 19.

63. "It's Got to Stop," St. Louis Post-Dispatch, August 6, 1893; Carlton, Looking For Little Egypt, 50; John McGovern, Halligan's Illustrated World, 307–10.

64. "Too Oriental for Williams," New York Times, December 3, 1893; "Police and Law Defied," New York Times, December 5, 1893.

65. "Mrs. Palmer Misrepresented," New York Times, December 6, 1893.

66. Broun and Leech, Anthony Comstock, 227.

67. Ibid., 218–28.

68. Wheeler, Against Obscenity, 27–32.

69. Barbas, Movie Crazy, 29–31.

70. Walkowitz, " 'Vision of Solome,'" 337–76. See also Garber, Vested Interests, 312–31; Macleod, "Cross-Cultural Cross-Dressing," 63–85; Studlar, This Mad Masquerade, 154–57; Wollen, "Fashion/Orientalism/The Body," 8.

71. Jowitt, Time and the Dancing Image, 50–51.

72. Truman, History of the World's Fair, 552; Van Nieuwkerk, A Trade Like Any Other, 38. These photographs are available online, for instance, "View of a woman gipsy/dancer posing outside at Coney Island," <http://museumofnyc.doetech.net/Detlobjps. cfm?ObjectID=17362&rec_num=12&From=obj_key.cfm#42>; and "View of a woman gipsy/dancer seated in her side-show theatre at Coney Island," <http://museumofnyc.doetech.net/Detlobjps.cfm?ObjectID=46953&rec_num=48&From=obj_key.cfm>.

73. Robert Cross, "The Real Little Egypt Exposed at Last," Chicago Tribune, February 2, 1983.

74. " 'Little Egypt' at Sherry's," St. Louis Post-Dispatch, January 2, 1897; Robert Cross, "The Real Little Egypt Exposed at Last," Chicago Tribune, February 2, 1983; Laurie, Vaudeville, 40–41.

75. Bloom, Autobiography, 135; Ramsaye, Million and One Nights, 334–34.

76. "Olympia Music Hall and Winter Garden," *New York Times*, January 6, 1897; "Chapman Hearing Begins," *New York Times*, January 8, 1897; "Shame: Doings at Seeley's Orgy," *New York World*, January 10, 1897; "Little Egypt to Testify," *New York World*, January 12, 1897; "Little Egypt's Story," *New York World*, January 13, 1897; "Chapman on the Stand," *New York Times*, January 13, 1897.

77. Graziano, "Music in William Randolph Hearst's *New York Journal*," 400–401; Charles Kennedy, "When Cairo Met Main Street," 277–78.

78. Alexander, *Strip Tease*, 6; Bernard Sobel, "Historic Hootchy-Kootchy," 13–15, 46; Bernard Sobel, *Burleycue*, 16, 31, 54. See also Robert Allen, *Horrible Prettiness*, 46–48, 227–36; Janet Davis, *Circus Age*, 127–28.

79. Bernard Sobel, *A Pictorial History*, 55.

80. McKennon, *American Carnival*, 48, 52, 55, 62, 133.

81. Bernard Sobel, *Broadway Heartbeat*, 21–22.

82. Bernard Sobel, "Historic Hootchy-Kootchy," 13. See also Charles Kennedy, "When Cairo Met Main Street," 277.

83. Register, *Kid of Coney Island*, 47.

84. "Fatima Dance in Flatbush," *Brooklyn Daily Eagle*, March 9, 1894; "Fatima in Brooklyn Again," *Brooklyn Daily Eagle*, March 22, 1894; "Fatima Was an Attraction," *Brooklyn Daily Eagle*, August 23, 1894; "No More Fatima Dances," *Brooklyn Daily Eagle*, August 23, 1894.

85. "Masks and Faces," *National Police Gazette*, September 9, 1893; Kitch, *Girl on the Magazine Cover*, 56–74.

86. John Beynon, *Masculinities and Culture*, 46; Reel, *National Police Gazette*, 3–6, 146.

87. "Danse du Ventre in Brooklyn, N.Y.," *National Police Gazette*, March 31, 1894.

88. Sterngass, *First Resorts*, 229–41, 252–54.

89. Erenberg, *Steppin' Out*, 22.

90. Laurie, *Vaudeville*, 40; Peiss, *Cheap Amusements*, 56–89; Ramsaye, *Million and One Nights*, 114–19. Experimental film technology had appeared at the Columbian Exposition in the form of Edison's Kinetoscope but had been upstaged by live dancers and other attractions on the Midway then. Brands, *The Reckless Decade*, 52–53.

91. Nead, "Strip," 135–50; Peiss, *Cheap Amusements*, 157.

92. Ullman, *Sex Seen*, 19, 75, 114–15.

93. "Turkish Dance, Ella Lola," 1898, <http://memory.loc.gov/cgi-bin/query/D?var stg:2:./temp/ammem_2IAe::@@@MDb=mcc>. To get a sense of how the *danse du ventre* was transformed into Midway dancing and the hootchy-kootchy, compare in chronological order the "Egyptian Dance," 1895, with "Turkish Dance, Ella Lola," 1898, and "Princess Rajah Dance," 1904, in the Library of Congress online cinema collections.

94. Rabinovitz, *For the Love of Pleasure*, 82–83.

95. Lears, *Fables of Abundance*, 109, 115–16; Peiss, *Cheap Amusements*, 101–04; Rabinovitz, *For the Love of Pleasure*, 74–78.

96. Kitch, *Girl on the Magazine Cover*, 59.

97. Charles Kennedy, "When Cairo Met Main Street," 277; Sobel, "Historic Hootchy-Kootchy," 13.

98. Peiss, *Cheap Amusements*, 148–49; Ullman, *Sex Seen*, 22–23.

99. "The Merry Life on the Trail at the Portland Fair," *Washington Post*, July 23, 1905; "Shake Heads at Princess Rajah," *Los Angeles Times*, May 29, 1906; "Hammerstein's," *New York Tribune*, January 17, 1909; "Musical Comedy Poised on Dance Toes," *New York Times*, August 21, 1910; Laurie, *Vaudeville*, 40–41; "Princess Rajah Dance," 1904, <http://mem ory.loc.gov/cgi-bin/query/D?varstg:28:./temp/ammem_ Vwun::@@@MDb=manz,eaa>.

100. Bernard Sobel, "Historic Hootch-Kootchy," 46; Bernard Sobel, "History of the 'Hootch,'" *New York Times*, March 24, 1946.

101. St. Denis, *Ruth St. Denis*, 48–51.

102. Ted Shawn quoted in Schlundt, *Professional Appearances*, 5; see also McKenzie, *Orientalism*, 89–90, 194–200.

103. Jowitt, *Time and the Dancing Image*, 87.

104. Leach, *Land of Desire*, xiii.

105. Ibid., 106; Yoshihara, *Embracing the East*, 16–43.

106. Leach, *Land of Desire*, 105–10. See also Jowitt, *Time and the Dancing Image*, 50–51; Sweetman, *Oriental Obsession*, 232.

107. Lant, "Curse of the Pharaoh," 87–112.

108. Peiss, *Hope in a Jar*, 146–49.

109. Hower, *History of an Advertising Agency*, 91–93; Laird, *Advertising Progress*, 271; Tilley, *R. J. Reynolds*, 204–16; Smith, *Smoke Signals*, 20.

110. Lears, *Fables of Abundance*, 139.

111. McKenzie, *Orientalism*, 89–90, 194–200.

112. Marchand, *Advertising the American Dream*, 22–24; see also Miriam Hansen, *Babel and Babylon*, 176–77.

113. Studlar, "'Out-Salomeing Salome,'" 109–11.

114. Garber, *Vested Interests*, 312–31; Studlar, "'Out-Salomeing Salome,'" 99–129; Studlar, *This Mad Masquerade*, 154–57; Wollen, "Fashion/Orientalism/The Body," 8.

115. Bishop, *Best of Bishop*, 188. My thanks go to Tim Portious for bringing this poem to my attention.

116. "Shriners Seize Child's Lunch," *Algeria* 4, no. 1 (January 1921): 3–4.

117. Kimmel, *Manhood in America*, 214–46; see also Dumenil, *Freemasonry in American Culture*, 73–74, 92–93.

118. Barbas, *Movie Crazy*, 225.

119. Ann Douglas, *Terrible Honesty*, 78; Studlar, *This Mad Masquerade*, 10–89. See also Garber, *Vested Interests*, 309–11, 359–63; Hodson, *Lawrence of Arabia*.

120. Unmarked newspaper clipping, "Valentino, Rudolph" clippings file, Dance Collection, New Your Public Library for the Performing Arts, New York, N.Y.

121. Ann Douglas, *Terrible Honesty*, 78; Studlar, *This Mad Masquerade*, 10–89. See also Garber, *Vested Interests*, 309–11, 359–63;

122. Benchérif, *Image of Algeria*, 180–85.

123. Hodson, *Lawrence of Arabia*, 30.

124. Ian Gordon, *Comic Strips and Consumer Culture*, 120; Miriam Hansen, *Babel and Babylon*, 122.

CHAPTER 7

1. Stern, "American Views of India," ii–v.

2. Sandage, *Born Losers*, 116, 255.

3. Rotter, "Gender Relations," 523; see also King, *Orientalism and Religion*, 7–14; Rotter, "In Retrospect," 177–88.

4. Rebecca Edwards, *New Spirits*, 172; Stern, "American Views of India," 163–65.

5. Burke, *Swami Vivekananda*, 198–249; Engh, "Practically Every Religion," 211; Ferguson, *Confusion of Tongues*, 297–320; Lancaster, *Incredible World's Parliament of Religions*, 8–25; Moore, *Gurdjieff, A Biography*, 197–210; 230–41; Mullick, "Protap Chandra Majumdar and Swami Vivekananda," 219–34; Seager, *World's Parliament of Religion*, 63–122.

6. Thomas, *Hinduism Invades America*, 77.

7. Rebecca Edwards, *New Spirits*, 172; Seager, *Dawn of Religious Pluralism*, 247–81.

8. Born in Hudson, New York, Webb was a journalist, former owner of the *Missouri Republican*, Theosophist, and recent ambassador to the Philippines. He had converted to Islam overseas, where he spoke with Muslims about the possibility of proselytizing in the United States. L. Grebsonel, "The Mohammedan Propagandist," *Frank Leslie's Illustrated Weekly*, March 30, 1893, 204–5; Seager, *Dawn of Religious Pluralism*, 284.

9. J. V. Nash, "The Message and Influence of Vivekananda," *Open Court* 39, no. 12 (December 1925): 747–48; see also "Marie Louise a Monk," *New York Times*, March 20, 1896.

10. John Fenton, "Hinduism," 2:692; see also Prashad, *Karma of Brown Folk*, 40–43.

11. King, *Orientalism and Religion*, 5, 97–111.

12. Thomas, *Hinduism Invades America*, 80, 117.

13. "Strange Gods of American Women," *Literary Digest* 45, no. 1 (July 6, 1912).

14. Braude, "Women's History Is American Religious History," 87–107.

15. Mabel Potter Daggett quoted in Thomas, *Hinduism Invades America*, 120.

16. Carl Jackson, *Vedanta for the West*.

17. "Scores Women Cult Victims," *Los Angeles Times*, August 12, 1912.

18. Studlar, *This Mad Masquerade*, 151.

19. Warne was himself only visiting the United States since he was in fact stationed in Calcutta as the head of Methodist missionizing in India. "Scores Women Cult Victims," *Los Angeles Times*, August 12, 1912.

20. Gould, *Sikhs, Students, Swamis and Spies*, 98–130. After extraordinary lobbying,

Americans of Indian descent would win the right of naturalization only in 1946, after years of work by members of the Indian community in the United States in winning over politicians and the press. Daniels, *Guarding the Golden Door*, 97–99.

21. "Secretary Would Raise Immigration Standard," *Atlanta Constitution*, January 24, 1914.

22. Herman Scheffauer, "The Tide of Turbans," *Forum* (June 1910): 616.

23. "The Perils of Immigration Impose on Congress a New Issue," *Current Opinion*, March 1, 1914; Herman Scheffauer, "The Tide of Turbans," *Forum* (June 1910): 616.

24. Stern, "American Views of India," 164.

25. Khan, *Biography*, 9, 250.

26. Ibid., 221–22; 231–32.

27. Browder, *Slippery Characters*, 2–5.

28. Emily Brown, *Har Dayal*, 125; Prashad, *Karma of Brown Folk*, 143.

29. Khan, *Biography*, 50–51, 112, 121; Thomas, *Hinduism Invades America*, 104–5.

30. Van Stolk, *Memories of a Sufi Sage*, 27, 42.

31. Dirlik, "Chinese History and the Question of Orientalism," 103–5, 111.

32. Khan, *Biography*, 124.

33. Ibid., 241–48.

34. Ibid., 246.

35. Lippmann, *Public Opinion*, 217.

36. Khan, *Biography*, 246.

37. Scrutator, "Asiatics Busy Buying, If Not Entering United States," *Chicago Daily Tribune*, May 12, 1924.

38. St. Denis, *Ruth St. Denis*, 56.

39. Har Dayal quoted in Emily Brown, *Har Dayal*, 87; Thomas, *Hinduism Invades America*, 217–18. Dayal had himself been arrested by American immigration officials and targeted by journalists as a dangerous radical whom they claimed advocated support for some old bogeymen of disorder: anarchism, Socialism, and the Industrial Workers of the World. Dayal had in fact advocated violent resistance to the British in India but had also won over well-to-do Anglo-Americans who were sympathetic to the cause of Indian independence. "Hindu Reformer Arrested," *New York Times*, March 27, 1914; "Indian Quotes Bryan," *Washington Post*, March 30, 1914; "Will Go If an Anarchist," *Washington Post*, April 5, 1914.

40. Khan, *Biography*, 221–22, 231–32.

41. "Yoga—The Yoke of Health and Happiness," *Chicago Defender*, April 23, 1927; "Yoga—The Herb Tonic Supreme—Prof. Rao," *Chicago Defender*, June 4, 1927.

42. Emily Brown, *Har Dayal*, 7, 88.

43. Thomas, *Hinduism Invades America*, 225.

44. "Miss Zemdar" and "Ismar, The Egyptian Clairvoyant and Palmist," *San Francisco Daily Morning Call*, April 21, 1906.

45. Thomas, *Hinduism Invades America*, 177–85, 223–24.

46. E. M. Butler, *Myth of the Magus*, 2–3. See also Godwin, *Theosophical Enlightenment*, 296–99, 289, 405.

47. "Mystic from India Does Queer Feats," *New York World*, November 17, 1903; " 'White Mahatma' Reads Minds of His Auditors," *Brooklyn Eagle*, January 12, 1904, vol. O, SRES; Stern, "American Views of India," 104.

48. "Proctor's," *New York Times*, April 21, 1901; *Prince P. Ishmael Hindoo Magician*, "Letterheads of Magicians and Magic Acts," scrapbooks; "The World of Magic: Magicians' Doings, News, Views and Comment about Conjurers and Illusionists in all Parts of the Globe," *The Sphinx* 9, no. 2 (April 1910): 32.

49. "Thurston Really a Great Magician," *Morning Telegraph*, June 16, 1903, vol. S, SRES.

50. Cook, *Arts of Deception*, 163–213.

51. Garber, *Vested Interests*, 34–40.

52. Nina Carter Marbourg, "Learning the Black Art of Magic," *Frank Leslie's Weekly Magazine*, May 11, 1905.

53. Charles J. Carter, "Secrets of Oriental Magic," *Detroit Free Press*, November 27, 1932.

54. "Thurston Really a Great Magician," *Morning Telegraph*, June 16, 1903, vol. S, SRES.

55. "This Is 'The Great Thurston' at Keith's," *New York World*, July 5, 1903; "Palace Theatre—'The Great Thurston,'" *Sydney Morning Herald*, July 24, 1905; "Thurston World's Master Magician," promotional flyer, vol. S, SRES.

56. "The Magic Racket," *New York Times*, May 15, 1927.

57. "Marvels of Hindoo Magic," *New York World*, January 15, 1905, vol. O, SRES; "Our Magic As Good As India's," *The Sun*, March 17, 1907, vol. R, SRES.

58. "Mohammed Hanafi," *St. Louis Post-Dispatch*, December 21, 1904, vol. O, SRES.

59. Vogel, "Staying Home for the Sights," 251–67.

60. Will Irvin, "The Medium Game: Behind the Scenes with Spiritualism, Part I," *Collier's*, September 14, 1908, vol. Q, SRES.

61. *Adrian Plate Magical Entertainer*, vol. R, SRES; Houdini, *Miracle Mongers and Their Methods*.

62. Cook, *Arts of Deception*, 118, 166–77, 200–201.

63. Henry Ridgely Evans, "Robert-Houdin: Conjuror, Author, and Ambassador," *Open Court* 17, no. 12 (December 1903): 720, vol. P, SRES; Cook, *Arts of Deception*, 179.

64. Unmarked newspaper clipping, "Valentino, Rudolph" clippings file, Dance Collection, Visual and Performing Arts Division, New York Public Library, New York.

65. Studlar, *This Mad Masquerade*, 150–54.

66. Ibid., 150–98.

67. Miriam Hansen, *Babel and Babylon*, 170–78.

68. On the point that mobility implies fraud, see McNamara, *Step Right Up*, 20.

69. Long, *Spiritual Merchants*, 53; McNamara, *Step Right Up*, 177. Also known as the "White Slave Traffic Act," the Mann Act "represented an attempt to regulate prostitution by prohibiting the transportation of women across state lines for immoral purposes." Mumford, *Interzones*, 11.

70. "Swami Returns from East," *Los Angeles Times*, January 15, 1928; "Miami Police Order Love Cult's Leader to Get Out of Town," *Chicago Tribune*, February 3, 1928; "Women Cheer Hindu Mystic Ousted by Court," *Atlanta Constitution*, February 3, 1928; "Swami's Lectures to Women Face Ban as Miami Official Foresees Violence," *New York Times*, February 4, 1928; "Injunction Denied Swami," *New York Times*, February 7, 1928; "Swami Quitting Miami," *New York Times*, February 11, 1928.

71. "East Indian Mystic Sets Miami Astir," *Chicago Defender*, February 11, 1928.

72. Thomas, *Hinduism Invades America*, 162–63, 219.

73. Hazrat Khalifatul-Masih II, "Muhammad—The Liberator of Women," *Moslem Sunrise* 3, no. 3 (July 1930): 5–10, 20; Addison, "Ahmadiya Movement," 28–29; Emily Brown, *Har Dayal*, 95–96, 104–6, 110, 115; Thomas, *Hinduism Invades America*, 76, 80, 117, 138.

74. Ferguson, *Confusion of Tongues*, 300–301; Inayat Khan, *Biography*, 10–11, 126; Thomas, *Hinduism Invades America*, 120.

75. Yogananda, *Autobiography of a Yogi*, 412–17.

76. Braden, "Why Are the Cults Growing?" 45–47; Ferguson, *Confusion of Tongues*, 1–14; Carey McWilliams, "The Cults of California," *Atlantic Monthly* 177 (March 1946): 105–10.

77. "Religion," *New York Times*, April 10, 1926.

78. Stern, "American Views of India," 163.

79. Dumenil, *Modern Temper*, 160–61.

80. Yogananda, *Autobiography of a Yogi*, 400–403.

81. Yogananda's "Church of All Religions" further combined Christian and Hindu practices and met on Sunday mornings to suit the beliefs and schedules of believers, as did the Vedanta Society and Inayat Khan's Sufi movement. Thomas, *Hinduism Invades America*, 96, 132, 145–49, 170–71; Van Stolk, *Memories of a Sufi Sage*, 35–36; Yogananda, *Autobiography of a Yogi*, 415.

82. "Inayat Khan," *New York Times*, May 18, 1926; "Rahman Bey Arrives," *New York Times*, May 18, 1926; "Loew's State," *New York Times*, July 18, 1926.

83. *Prospectus of the Brotherhood of Magicians*, in SRES, vol. O.

84. Fred A. Chappell, to G. F. Schulte, October 28, 1926, George Frederick Schulte Papers, CHM.

85. John Mulholland, "The Hand Is Not Quicker Than the Eye," *New York Times*, October 8, 1933.

86. Charles J. Carter, "Secrets of Oriental Magic," *Detroit Free Press*, 27 November 1932.

CHAPTER 8

1. Calder, *Financing the American Dream*, 156–217.

2. Cohen, *Making a New Deal*, 213–50; Ellis, *Nation in Torment*, 98–124.

3. Ellis, *Nation in Torment*, 96–97, 207–8.

4. Charles McGovern, *Sold American*, 261–300; Dumenil, *Modern Temper*, 87–88; Ellis, *Nation in Torment*, 536–38; Ruth, *Inventing the Public Enemy*, 132.

5. Mordaunt Hall, "The Screen: Clairvoyant Racket Shown," *New York Times*, April 7, 1933.

6. Calder, *Financing the American Dream*, 218; Ownby, *American Dreams*, 111.

7. Mehaffy, "Advertising Race," 131–74; Olney, "When Your Word Is Not Enough," 408–31; Ownby, *American Dreams*, 111; Weems, *Desegregating the Dollar*, 1–2.

8. Grossman, *Land of Hope*, 17, 42–47; Drake and Cayton, *Black Metropolis*, 58–62; Sernett, *Bound for the Promised Land*, 40–43; Foner, "Meaning of Freedom," 458–60.

9. Cohen, *Making a New Deal*, 147–49; Peiss, *Hope in a Jar*; Weems, *Desegregating the Dollar*, 7–30.

10. "Shubert Vaudeville," *New York Times*, November 20, 1921; "44th St. Theatre," *New York Times*, November 23, 1921; "Celebrated Century Concert To-Night," *New York Times*, January 22, 1922; "Winter Garden," *New York Times*, March 19, 1922. Regarding the radio show "Jovedah de Rajah, Oriental Mystic," see, for instance, "WFBH, New York—273," *New York Times*, March 10, 1925.

11. Thomas, *Hinduism Invades America*, 219–20; "Indian Prince Tells His Side of Love Suit," *Chicago Defender*, January 12, 1929.

12. Susan Douglas, *Inventing American Broadcasting*, 300–317.

13. Ibid., 304.

14. Joseph K. Hart quoted in Susan Douglas, *Inventing American Broadcasting*, 304.

15. Hangen, *Redeeming the Dial*, 20–29.

16. Dumenil, *Modern Temper*, 87–88, 183; Kimmel, *Manhood in America*, 200; Sandage, *Born Losers*, 260.

17. "Joveddah Is Baby's Dad Court Finds," *Chicago Defender*, February 2, 1929.

18. "Indian Prince Tells His Side of Love Suit," *Chicago Defender*, January 12, 1929.

19. Barbas, *Movie Crazy*, 225.

20. "Three Seized in Ad Case," *New York Times*, January 13, 1928; "Acquitted of Ad Fraud," *New York Times*, February 7, 1928; "White Widow Aims to Wed Cult Leader," *Chicago Defender*, February 18, 1928.

21. McNamara, *Step Right Up*, 164; Will Irvin, "The Medium Game: Behind the Scenes with Spiritualism, Part II," *Collier's*, 21 September 1908, vol. Q, SRES.

22. "Today on the Radio," *New York Times*, May 14, 1930.

23. "Prince Ali, The World's Greatest Prophet," *Chicago Defender*, October 20, 1928; "Prince Ali Answers Questions," *Chicago Defender*, October 27, 1928.

24. Winthrop D. Lane, "Ambushed in the City: The Grim Side of Harlem," *The Survey* 53, no. 11 (1 March 1925): 692–93.

25. Baer, *Black Spiritual Movement*, 10, 26, 40, 92, 110–39.

26. Carlson, "Number Gambling," 116; Chireau, *Black Magic*, 142–44; Fabian, *Card Sharps*, 144–50; McKay, *Harlem*, 106.

27. Baer, *Black Spiritual Movement*, 21–22, 85–89; Sutherland, "Analysis of Negro

Churches," 38–40; Hickey and Wylie, *Enchanting Darkness*, 27–33; Howe, *Afrocentrism*, 42–50, 66–76; Wilson Moses, *Afrotopia*; Wolcott, "Culture of the Informal Economy," 58–61.

28. Carlson, "Number Gambling," 92. See also Baer, *Black Spiritual Movement*, 21–22.

29. Wolcott, "Culture of the Informal Economy," 46–75; Wolcott, "Mediums, Messages, and Lucky Numbers," 287–89.

30. Carlson, "Numbers Gambling," 93.

31. De Laurence, *Mystic Test Book*, 114. See also de Laurence, *Great Book of Magical Art*, 45–51.

32. The Ahmadiyya are a heretical Muslim sect whose own leader, Mirza Ghulam Ahmad, proclaimed himself prophet in 1880. Persecution from other Muslims, plus the group's experiences as subjects of assertive Christian missionary work in Northern India, encouraged a number of them to leave Asia in the early twentieth century and proselytize in Europe, West Africa, Australia, and the United States. In these countries, Ahmadiyya spokesmen strategically adopted British missionaries' information and publicity tactics and initially pursued white converts among the middle and upper classes, just as Inayat Khan or Swami Yogananda did. Friedmann, *Prophecy Continuous*, 30–31, 117, 132–35; H. D. Griswold, "Ahmadiya Movement," 373–79; Walter, *Ahmadiya Movement*; Walter, "Ahmadiya Movement To-Day," 66–78.

33. Braden, "Islam in America," 311. See also Bousquet, "Moslem Religious Influences," 42; Hoffert, "Moslem Propaganda," 140, 167; Turner, "Ahmadiyya Mission," 50, 53, 56–61.

34. "Islam or Mohammedism Means the Religion of Peace," *Chicago Defender*, October 23, 1926; "From a Moslem," *Chicago Defender*, June 4, 1927; "East Indian Tells of Native Religion," *Chicago Defender*, August 31, 1929; Braden, "Moslem Missionaries in America," 338–39; Haddad and Smith, *Mission to America*, 58–64; Turner, *Islam in the African-American Experience*, 126–30.

35. Sufi M. Bengalee, "What Would Muhammad Say to Chicago?" *Moslem Sunrise* 3, no. 3 (July 1930): 18. See also "Activities of the American Ahmadiyya Moslem Mission," *Moslem Sunrise* 3, no. 3 (July 1930): 12.

36. Mullins, "Race and the Genteel Consumer," 22–38.

37. Cohen, *Consumer's Republic*, 41–54, 166–93.

38. McGovern, *Sold American*, 1–22.

39. Essien-Udom, *Black Nationalism*; Lincoln, *Black Muslims*; Joseph Washington, *Black Religion*, 114–15, 120–21; Wilmore, *Black Religion and Black Radicalism*.

40. Ernest Allen, "Identity and Destiny," 163–96; Curtis, "African-American Islamization," 659–84; Curtis, "Islamicizing the Black Body," 167–96.

41. Erdmann Beynon, "Voodoo Cult," 894–907; Bontemps and Conroy, *Anyplace But Here*, 206; Fauset, *Black Gods of the Metropolis*, 41–51, 115–16; Frazier, *Negro in the United States*, 74–75.

42. "Ali's Mysticism Didn't Foretell Prison Term," *Chicago Defender*, January 18, 1930.

43. Nance, "Respectability and Representation," 623–59.

44. Conzen et al., "Invention of Ethnicity," 3–41; Steve Fenton, *Ethnicity*, 55–60.

45. Higham, "Integrating America," 7–25.

46. Nance, "Respectability and Representation," 627–29.

47. "Cult Leader Dies; Was in Murder Case," *Chicago Defender*, July 27, 1929; "6 Held to Grand Jury for Cult Battle Murders," *Chicago Tribune*, September 28, 1929. See also "Seize 60 after So. Side Cult Tragedy," *Chicago Tribune*, September 26, 1929; Nance, "Respectability and Representation," 623–59; Illinois Writers Project, "I Your Prophet," NIP.

48. Ernest Allen, "Identity and Destiny," 166.

49. Illinois Writers Project, "Lost Found Nation of Islam," NIP.

50. Erdmann Beynon, "Voodoo Cult," 898; Bontemps and Conroy, *Anyplace But Here*, 161, 167; Frazier, *Negro Family*, 81; Martin, *Race First*, 74–76; Turner, "Ahmadiyya Mission," 59–61; Vincent, *Black Power*, 222.

51. Sister Denke Majied (Mrs. Lawrence Adams) quoted in Erdmann Beynon, "Voodoo Cult," 895, 900–901.

52. Challar Sharrieff, (Mr. Charles Peoples) quoted in Erdmann Beynon, "Voodoo Cult," 896.

53. Erdmann Beynon, "Voodoo Cult," 897.

54. Ibid.," 910–12.

55. Al-Mahdi, *Who Was Noble Drew Ali?* 50.

56. "New Human Sacrifice with a Boy as Victim Is Averted by Inquiry," *Detroit Free Press*, November 26, 1932.

57. "500 Join March to Ask Voodoo Kings' Freedom," *Detroit Free Press*, November 25, 1932; "New Human Sacrifice with a Boy as Victim Is Averted by Inquiry," *Detroit Free Press*, November 26, 1932; "Intended Voodoo Victims' Number Still Mounting," *Detroit Free Press*, November 27, 1932; "Pastors Decry Growth of Cult Practices Here, Negro Leaders Pledge Support to Wipe Out Voodooism," *Detroit Free Press*, November 28, 1932; Illinois Writers Project, "Lost Found Nation of Islam," NIP; Erdmann Beynon, "Voodoo Cult," 894–907; Clegg, *An Original Man*, 31–34.

58. Ibid., 34.

59. Ibid., 20–21.

60. "Cultists Riot in Court; One Death, 41 Hurt," *Chicago Tribune*, March 6, 1935; "Capt. Palczynski a Chicago Policeman for Fifty Years," *Chicago Tribune*, March 6, 1935.

61. "Colored Cultists Are Held for Inquiry after Court Riot Scene," *Chicago Tribune*, March 6, 1935; "Cultists Riot in Court; One Death, 41 Hurt," *Chicago Tribune*, March 6, 1935; "Cultists 'Guilty'; 32 Given Jail Sentences," *Chicago Defender*, October 10, 1942.

62. "Cultists Riot in Court; One Death, 41 Hurt," *Chicago Tribune*, March 6, 1935.

63. Illinois Writers Project, "Lost Found Nation of Islam," NIP.

64. McKay, *Harlem*, 76–77.

65. Wilbur Young, "Activities of Bishop Amiru Al-Mu-Minin Sufi A. Hamid," n.d., "Negroes of New York," box 1, Works Progress Administration Papers, Federal Writers'

Program, Schomburg Center for Studies in Black Culture, New York Public Library, New York.

66. Cohen, *Consumer's Republic*, 166–90.

67. Greenberg, "Or Does It Explode?" 114–39.

68. McKay, *Harlem*, 205, 210.

69. Ottley, *New World A-Coming*, 116–17.

70. McKay, *Harlem*, 197–203.

71. Wilbur Young, "Activities of Bishop Amiru Al-Mu-Minin Sufi A. Hamid," n.d., "Negroes of New York," and Henry Lee Moon, "Policy Queen, St. Clair, Stephanie," n.d. "Negroes of New York," box 1, Works Progress Administration Papers, Federal Writers' Program, Schomburg Center for Studies in Black Culture, New York Public Library, New York; Raymond Jones, "Comparative Study of Religious Cult Behavior," 121–23; McKay, *Harlem*, 205.

72. Ottley, *New World A-Coming*, 118–19. See also Crowder, " 'Don't Buy Where You Can't Work,'" 7–44.

73. "Plane Crash Fatal to 'Harlem Hitler,'" *New York Times*, August 1, 1938; Wilbur Young, "Activities of Bishop Amiru Al-Mu-Minin Sufi A. Hamid," n.d., "Negroes of New York," and Dorothy West, "Outline by Dorothy West for a Portrait of Sufi, for 'Portraits of New York,'" n.d., "Negroes of New York," box 1, Works Progress Administration Papers, Federal Writers' Program, Schomburg Center for Studies in Black Culture, New York Public Library, New York; McKay, *Harlem*, 190.

74. Booker T. Washington, *Up From Slavery*, 60.

75. Austin, *African Muslims*, 51–61, 67–72; Nance, "Respectability and Representation," 630–31.

76. Malcolm X, "Ballot or the Bullet," 36; see also Sherman Jackson, *Islam and the Blackamerican*, 3–5; Romano, "No Diplomatic Immunity," 546–79.

77. Cohen, *Making a New Deal*, 251; Cross, *All-Consuming Century*, 68–90; Ian Gordon, *Comic Strips and Consumer Culture*, 163–65.

bibliography

ARCHIVES AND MANUSCRIPT COLLECTIONS

American Heritage Center, University of Wyoming, Laramie, Wyo.
    Buffalo Bill Collection
Carter C. Woodson Regional Library, Chicago Public Library, Chicago, Ill.
    Illinois Writers Project, "Negro in Illinois" Papers, Vivian G. Harsh Research
        Collection of Afro-American History and Literature
Chicago History Museum, Chicago, Ill.
    Ancient Arabic Order, Nobles of the Mystic Shrine, Miscellaneous Pamphlets
    Chicago Daily News Collection
    Ready Prints Collection
    George Frederick Schulte Papers
Denver Public Library, Denver, Colo.
    Salsbury Collection of Buffalo Bill's Wild West Show
Institute for Masonic Studies, Grand Lodge, F. & A. M. of California, San Francisco,
    Calif.
    Fraternal Pamphlets Collection
John and Mable Ringling Museum of Art, Sarasota, Fla.
    Tibbals Circus Poster Collection
Library of Congress, Washington, D.C.
    Russell Lee Photographs, Farm Security Administration/Office of War Information
        Photograph Collection
    Underwood & Underwood Stereographic Cards, Prints and Photographs Division
Museum of the City of New York, New York, N.Y.
    Byron Collection of Coney Island Photographs
Newberry Library, Chicago, Ill.
    Heber De Long Scrapbooks
New York Public Library for the Performing Arts, New York, N.Y.
    Theatre Collection
        Saram R. Ellison Magic Collection
        Saram R. Ellison Scrapbooks, Humanities Microfilms
        Letterheads of Magicians and Magic Acts, Theatre Scrapbooks
    Dance Collection
        "Valentino, Rudolph," Clippings File

Princeton University Library, Rare Books and Special Collections, Princeton, N.J.
  Joseph T. McCaddon Papers
Robert L. Parkinson Library and Research Center, Circus World Museum, Baraboo,
    Wis.
  Ringling Brothers, Barnum & Bailey Circus Collection
San Francisco Public Library, San Francisco, Calif.
  Schmulowitz Collection of Wit and Humor
Schomburg Center for Research in Black Culture, Manuscripts, Archives, and Rare
    Books Division, New York Public Library, New York, N.Y.
  Moorish Science Temple of America Collection
  Harry A. Williamson Masonic Papers
  Works Progress Administration Papers

PERIODICALS

Algeria (Helena, Mont.)
American Whig Review
Appleton's Journal
Aspen (Colo.) Weekly Times
Atlanta Constitution
Atlantic Monthly
Billboard Advertising
Boston Recorder
Brooklyn Daily Eagle
Castle Rock (Colo.) Journal
Catholic World
Chicago Daily News
Chicago Defender
Chicago Evening Post
Chicago Record-Herald
Chicago Tribune
Christian Register and Boston Observer
Christian Watchman (Atlanta, Ga.)
Collier's
Colorado Transcript (Golden, Colo.)
The Crescent
Current Opinion
Detroit Free Press
Fort Collins (Colo.) Courier
Forum
Frank Leslie's Illustrated Weekly

Frank Leslie's Popular Monthly
The Galaxy
Graham's Magazine
Greeley (Colo.) Tribune
Harper's New Monthly Magazine
Harper's Weekly
Helena Daily Herald
The Home-Maker
The Independent (New York, N.Y.)
Journal of Education
The Knickerbocker
The Ladies Home Journal
Ladies' Repository
Liberty (Mo.) Weekly Tribune
Literary Digest
Littleton (Colo.) Independent
Living Age
Los Angeles Times
McClure's Magazine
The Meccan (New York, N.Y.)
Missouri Republican
Moslem Sunrise
M.S.U. Independent (Columbia, Mo.)
The Nation
National Police Gazette
New Castle (Colo.) News

New York Evangelist
New York Herald
New York Morning Journal
New York Observer and Chronicle
New York Sun
New York Times
New York Tribune
New York World
North American Review
Open Court
Putnam's Monthly Magazine
The Riverside Magazine for Young People
San Francisco Chronicle
San Francisco Daily Morning Call
San Francisco Examiner

Saturday Evening Post
Scribner's Magazine
Silverton (Colo.) Standard
Southern Literary Messenger
The Sphinx
St. Louis Post-Dispatch
The Survey
Trestle Board
United States Gazette and Democratic Review
Vancouver Sun
Wall Street Journal
Washington Post
World's Fair Puck
Youth's Companion

PUBLISHED PRIMARY SOURCES

Adler, Cyrus. *I Have Considered the Days.* Philadelphia: Jewish Publication Society, 1941.

Allibone, Samuel Austen. *A Critical Dictionary of English Literature and British and American Authors.* Philadelphia: J. B. Lippincott & Co., 1859–71.

Ancient Arabic Order, Nobles of the Mystic Shrine. *100 Years of Love, 1883–1983: A Centennial Commemorative.* Chicago: Medinah Temple, 1984.

——. *Whence Came the Oriental Band and Why.* Chicago: Medinah Temple, 1954.

——. *The Mystic Shrine: An Illustrated Ritual,* rev. ed. 1921. Reprint, Chicago: Ezra Cook, 1950.

——. *Annual Proceedings of the Imperial Council, 1876–1881.* New York: Ancient Arabic Order, Nobles of the Mystic Shrine, 1889.

——. *The Mystic Shrine Illustrated.* n.d. Reprint, Kila, Montana: Kessinger Publishing, n.d.

Arabian Nights Entertainments. New York: McLaughlin Brothers, 188–.

Austen, Thomas R. *The Well-Spent Life: A Brotherly Testimonial to the Masonic Career of Robert Morris, LL.D.* Louisville, Kentucky: n.p., 1878.

Barnum, Phineas Taylor. *Struggles and Triumphs: Or, Forty Years' Recollections of P. T. Barnum, written by himself.* Buffalo, N.Y.: Warren, Johnson & Co., 1873.

Bevan, Samuel. *Sand and Canvas: Narrative of Adventures in Egypt, with a sojourn among the artists in Rome.* London: Charles Gilpin, 1849.

Bishop, Morris. *The Best of Bishop: Light Verse from the New Yorker and Elsewhere.* Edited by Charlotte Putnam Reppert. Ithaca and London: Cornell University Press, 1980.

Blavatsky, Helena Petrova. *Isis Unveiled: A Master-Key to the Mysteries of Ancient and Modern Science and Theology,* 2 vols. New York: J. W. Bouton, 1877.

Bloom, Sol. *The Autobiography of Sol Bloom.* New York: G. P. Putnam's Sons, 1948.

Brown, John P. *The Dervishes: Or, Oriental Spiritualism.* Philadelphia: J. B. Lippincott and Co., 1868.

Browne, J. Ross. *Yusef; or, The Journey of the Frangi.* New York: Harper & Brothers, 1855.

Bryant, William Cullen. *Letters*, 6 vols. Edited by William Cullen Bryant II and Thomas G. Voss. New York: Fordham University Press, 1975–81.

Burckhardt, John Lewis. *Travels in Arabia.* 1829. Reprint, London: Frank Cass & Co., 1968.

Burt, Calvin C. *Egyptian Masonic History of the Original and Unabridged Ancient and Ninety-six Degree Rite of Memphis.* 1879. Reprint, Kila, Mont.: Kessinger Publishing, n.d.

Burt, Nathaniel Clark. *The Far East; or, Letters from Egypt, Palestine, and Other Lands of the Orient.* Cincinnati: R. W. Carroll, 1868.

Burton, Richard F. *Personal Narrative of a Pilgrimage to Al-Madina and Meccah*, 2 vols. 1855. Reprint, New York: Dover Publications, 1964.

Cielo, Astra. *Signs, Omens and Superstitions.* 1918. Reprint, Kila, Mont.: Kessinger Publishing, n.d.

Cochran, Charles B. *Showman Looks On.* London: J. M. Dent and Sons, 1946.

Cochrane, Harry Hayman. *The Shriners' Book: Following the Fez.* Chicago: n.p., 1920.

Coleman, Henry R. *Light from the East: Travels and Researches in Bible Lands in Pursuit of More Light in Masonry.* Louisville: Henry R. Coleman, 1881.

Comstock, Anthony. *Frauds Exposed; or, How the People are Deceived and Robbed, and Youth Corrupted.* New York: J. Howard Brown, 1880.

Conklin, George. *Ways of the Circus; Being the Memories and Adventures of George Conklin, Tamer of Lions.* New York: Harper, 1921.

Conwell, Russell H. *The Life, Travels and Literary Career of Bayard Taylor.* Boston: B. B. Russell & Co., 1879.

Crawford, George W. *Prince Hall and His Followers: Being a Monograph on the Legitimacy of Negro Masonry.* New York: The Crisis, 1914.

[Crosby, Howard] El-Mukattem. *Lands of the Moslem: A Narrative of Oriental Travel.* New York: Robert Carter & Brothers, 1851.

Curtis, George William. *The Howadji in Syria.* New York: Harper, 1856.

———. *Nile Notes of a Howadji.* New York: Harper & Brothers, 1851.

Daly, Charles P. "Palestine Exploration." *Journal of the American Geographical Society of New York* 5 (1874): 166–68.

Dawood, N. J., comp. and trans. *Tales from the Thousand and One Nights.* New York: Penguin Books, 1973.

de Laurence, L. W. *The Mystic Test Book of the "Hindu Occult Chambers."* Chicago: De Laurence, 1909.

———. *The Great Book of Magical Art, Hindu Magic, and East Indian Occultism and the Book of Secret Hindu, Ceremonial, and Talismanic Magic.* Chicago: de Laurence, n.d.

Denslow, Ray V. *Masonic Conservators.* St. Louis: Grand Lodge, Ancient Free and Accepted Masons of the State of Missouri, 1931.

Doerflinger, William. *The Magic Catalogue.* New York: E. P. Dutton, 1977.

D'Ohsson, Ignatius Mouradgea. *Oriental Antiquities and General View of the Othoman Customs, Laws, and Ceremonies.* Philadelphia: Select Committee and Grand Lodge of Enquiry, 1788.

Dorr, Benjamin. *Notes of Travel in Egypt, the Holy Land, Turkey, and Greece.* Philadelphia: J. B. Lippincott, 1856.

Eames, Jane A. *Another Budget; or, Things which I Saw in the East.* Boston: Ticknor & Fields, 1855.

Edwards, M. A. *Philip in Palestine.* Philadelphia: J. S. Claxton, 1865.

Fargo City Directory, 1904. Fargo, N.D.: n.p., 1904.

Fargo City Directory, 1898. Fargo, N.D.: n.p., 1898.

Fields, Mrs. James T. *Whittier: Notes of His Life and of His Friendships.* New York: Harper, 1893.

Fetridge, William Pembroke. *The American Travellers' Guides: Hand-Books for Travellers in Europe and the East.* New York: Fetridge & Co., 186–.Fleming, Walter M. and William S. Paterson, comp. *Mecca Temple: Its History and Pleasures, together with the Origin and History of the Order.* New York: Andrew H. Kellogg, 1894.

Flinn, John J. *The Official Guide to the Midway Plaisance: The Authorized Official Guide to the Columbian Exposition.* Chicago: Columbian Guide Company, 1893.

Forster, Edward, ed. and comp. *The Thousand and One Nights; or, The Arabian Nights' Entertainments.* Boston: J. H. Francis, 1847.

Frost, Thomas. *Circus Life and Circus Celebrities.* London: Chatto and Windus, 1881.

Galland, Antoine, comp. and trans. *The Arabian Nights Entertainments: Consisting of a Collection of Stories Told by the Sultanness of the Indies . . . Translated into French from the Arabian MSS. by Mr. Galland, and now into English, from the Paris Edition.* New York: Evert Duyckinck, 1815.

Gordon, Lucy Duff. *Letters from Egypt. 1862–69.* Reprint, New York: Praeger, 1969.

Grimshaw, William H. *Official History of Freemasonry among the Colored People in North America.* Washington, D.C.: n.p., 1902.

Hackett, Horatio B. *Illustrations of Scripture; Suggested by a Tour Through the Holy Land.* Boston: Heath and Graves, 1855.

Hamid, George A. *Circus, as Told to His Son, George A. Hamid, Jr.* New York: Sterling Publishing Co., 1950.

Handy, M. P., ed. *Official Catalogue of the Exhibits on the Midway Plaisance.* Chicago: W. B. Conkey, 1893.

Hanley, Sylvanus, trans. and ed. *Caliphs and Sultans: Being Tales Omitted in the Usual Editions of the Arabian Nights Entertainments.* London: L. Reeve and Company, 1868.

Hansen-Taylor, Marie, and Horace E. Scudder, eds. *Life and Letters of Bayard Taylor,* 2 vols. Boston: Houghton Mifflin and Company, 1884.

Harris, Harrison L. *Harris' Masonic Text-book: A Concise Historical Sketch of Masonry, and the*

Organization of the Masonic Grand Lodges, and especially of Masonry among Colored Men in America. Petersburg, Va.: Masonic Visitor Company, 1902.

Hawthorn, Julian. *Humors of the Fair.* Chicago: E. A. Weeks, 1893.

Houdini, Harry. *Miracle Mongers and Their Methods.* New York: E. P. Dutton & Company, 1920.

Howells, William Dean. *A Hazard of New Fortunes; A Novel.* 1890. Reprint, Oxford: Oxford University Press, 1965.

Irving, Washington. *The Alhambra.* 1832. Reprint, London: MacMillan & Co, 1898.

Irvine, Jack. *Prominent Shriners in Caricature.* San Francisco: Islam Temple, 1929.

[Keane, T. F.] Hajj Mohammed Amin. *Six Months in Meccah: An Account of the Mohammedan Pilgrimage to Meccah.* London: Tinsley Brothers, 1881.

Khan, Inayat. *Biography of Pir-o-Murshid Inayat Khan.* London: East-West Publications, 1979.

Knox, Thomas W. *Adventures of Two Youths in a Journey to Egypt and the Holy Land.* New York: Harper & Brothers, 1882.

Lane, Edward W. *An Account of the Manners and Customs of the Modern Egyptians.* London: C. Knight and Co., 1842.

——, comp. and trans. *The Thousand and One Nights, Commonly Called, in England, The Arabian Nights' Entertainments. A New Translation from the Arabic, with Copious Notes,* 3 vols. 1839–41. Reprint, London: Chatto and Windus, 1858.

Lester, Ralph P. *Lester's "Look to the East."* Chicago: Ezra A. Cook, n.d.

Lynch, William Francis. *Commerce and the Holy Land.* Philadelphia: King & Baird, 1860.

——. *Official Report of the United States Expedition to Explore the Dead Sea and River Jordan.* Baltimore: John Murphy & Co., 1852.

——. *Narrative of the United States Expedition to the River Jordan and the Dead Sea.* Philadelphia: Lea and Blanchard, 1849.

Mackey, Albert G. *An Encyclopaedia of Freemasonry and Its Kindred Sciences,* 2 vols. 1873. Reprint, Chicago: Masonic History Company, 1921.

——. *The History of Freemasonry: Its Legendary Origins.* 1881. Reprint, New York: Gramercy Books, 1996.

McGovern, John, ed., *Halligan's Illustrated World: A Portfolio of Views of the World's Columbian Exposition.* New York: Jewell N. Halligan Company, 1894.

McKay, Claude. *Harlem: Negro Metropolis.* New York: E. P. Dutton, 1940.

Medinah Temple. *100 Years of Love: 1883–1983, A Centennial Commemorative.* Chicago: Medinah Temple, 1984.

Melish, William B. *The History of the Imperial Council, 1872–1921.* Cincinnati: Abingdon Press, 1921.

Melville, Herman. *Redburn: His First Voyage.* 1849. Reprint, Evanston and Chicago: Northwestern University Press and The Newberry Library, 1969.

The Moorish Palace and its Startling Wonders. Chicago: Metcalf Stationary Co., 1893.

Morris, Rob. Freemasonry in the Holy Land; or, Handmarks of Hiram's Builders. New York: Masonic Publishing Company, 1875.

——. Youthful Explorers in Bible Lands. Chicago: Hazlitt & Reed, 1870.

——. The Faithful Slave. Boston: O. E. Dodge, 1852.

Morris Relief Fund. An Appeal to Generous Masons. N.p., 1862.

Norton, Frank H., ed. Frank Leslie's Historical Register of the United States Centennial Exposition, 1876. New York: Frank Leslie's Publishing, 1877.

Ockley, Simon. History of the Saracens: Comprising the Lives of Mohammed and His Successors. 1718. Reprint, London: George Bell and Sons, 1875.

Olin, Stephen. Travels in Egypt, Arabia Petraea, and the Holy Land, 2 vols. New York: Harper & Brothers, 1843.

Oriental and Occidental Northern and Southern Portrait Types of the Midway Plaisance. St. Louis: N. D. Thompson Publishing Co., 1894.

Oscanyan, Christopher. The Sultan and His People. New York: Derby & Jackson, 1857.

Ottley, Roi. New World A-Coming: Inside Black America. Boston: Houghton Mifflin, 1943.

Pike, Albert. Morals and Dogma of the Ancient and Accepted Scottish Rite of Freemasonry. Charleston: Supreme Council of the Southern Jurisdiction, 1871.

Prime, William C. Boat Life in Egypt and Nubia. New York: Harper and Brothers, 1857.

Proceedings of the Freethinkers Convention, Watkins, New York, August 23–25, 1878. New York: D. M. Bennett, 1878.

Rawson, Albert Leighton. "Palestine Exploration from a Practical Standpoint." Journal of the American Geographical Society of New York 7 (1875): 101–13.

Rawson, Albert Leighton, et al. What the World Believes, The False and the True, Embracing the People of All Races and Nations. New York: Gay and Brothers, 1886.

Robinson, Edward. Biblical Researches in Palestine and the Adjacent Regions: A Journal of Travels in the Years 1838 and 1852, 3 vols., 3rd ed. London: John Murray, 1867.

Robinson, Ira, ed. Selected Letters of Cyrus Adler, 2 vols. Philadelphia: Jewish Publication Society of America, 1985.

Root, George L. The Ancient Arabic Order of the Nobles of the Mystic Shrine. Peoria, Ill.: Mohammad Temple, 1903.

Rule, Lucien V. Pioneering in Masonry: The Life and Times of Rob Morris, Masonic Poet Laureate. Louisville: Brandt and Connors, 1922.

Sale, George. Koran, Commonly Called the Alcoran of Mohammed, tr. into English Immediately from the Original Arabic. London: C. Ackers, 1734.

Salvador-Daniel, Francisco. The Music and Musical Instruments of the Arab: With an Introduction on How to Appreciate Arab Music. New York: Scribner's, 1915.

Senter, Sidney. Pictorial History of Al Malaikah Temple, 1888–1977. Los Angeles: Al Malaikah Temple, 1977.

Smyth, Albert H. Bayard Taylor. Boston: Houghton Mifflin and Company, 1896.

Sobel, Bernard. A Pictorial History of Vaudeville. New York: Citadel Press, 1961.

——. *Broadway Heartbeat: Memoirs of a Press Agent*. New York: Hermitage House, 1953.

——. "The Historic Hootchy-Kootchy." *Dance* 20 (October 1946): 13–15, 46.

——. *Burleycue: An Underground History of Burlesque Days*. New York: Farrar & Rineart, 1931.

Spencer, Jesse A. *Egypt and the Holy Land*, 4th ed. New York: A. S. Barnes & Co., 1854.

Stanton, H. U. Weitbrecht. "The Ahmadiya Movement." *Moslem World* 15 (1925): 10–20.

St. Denis, Ruth. *Ruth St. Denis: An Unfinished Life*. London: George G. Harrap & Company, 1939.

Stephens, John Lloyd. *Incidents of Travel in Egypt, Arabia Petraea, and the Holy Land*. 1837. Reprint, San Francisco: Chronicle Books, 1991.

Taylor, Bayard. *Travels in Arabia*. 1881. Reprint, New York: Charles Scribner's Sons, 1893.

——. *The Poetical Works of Bayard Taylor*. Boston: Houghton, Osgood and Company, 1880.

——. *Views Afoot; or, Europe Seen with Knapsack and Staff*, Revised Edition. London: Sampson Low, Son and Marston, 1869.

——. *India, China, and Japan*. New York: Putnam, 1855.

——. *Lands of the Saracen; or, Pictures of Palestine, Asia Minor, Sicily and Spain*. New York: Putnam, 1855.

——. *Poems of the Orient*. Boston: Ticknor & Fields, 1855.

——. *A Visit to India, China, and Japan, in the Year 1853*. New York: Putnam & Co., 1855.

——. *A Journey to Central Africa; or, Life and Landscapes from Egypt to the Negro Kingdoms of the White Nile*. New York: Putnam, 1854.

Thomas, Wendell. *Hinduism Invades America*. New York: Beacon Press, 1930.

Thomson, William M. *The Land and the Book; or, Biblical Illustrations Drawn from the Manners and Customs, the Scenes and Scenery of the Holy Land*, 2 vols. 1859. Reprint, New York: Nelson and Sons, 1893.

Truman, Ben C. *History of the World's Fair: Being a Complete and Authentic Description of the Columbian Exposition from Its Inception*. Philadelphia: C. R. Parish & Co., 1893.

Trumbull, Charles Gallaudet. *Anthony Comstock, Fighter: Some Impressions of a Lifetime Adventure in Conflict with the Powers of Evil*. New York: Fleming H. Revell, 1913.

Twain, Mark. *Innocents Abroad; or, the New Pilgrim's Progress*. 1869. Reprint, London: Chatto and Windus, 1899.

Ueland, Alexander. *William Jermyn Florence: Shriner and Humanitarian*. Boston: Christopher Publishing, 1958.

Van Deventer, Fred. *Parade to Glory: The Story of the Shriners and Their Hospitals for Crippled Children*. New York: William Morrow and Company, 1959.

Van Stolk, Sirkar, with Daphne Dunlop. *Memories of a Sufi Sage, Hazrat Inayat Khan*. Wassenaar, Netherlands: East-West Publications, 1967.

Walkes, Joseph A. *History of the Shrine: Ancient Egyptian Arab Order Nobles of the Mystic Shrine, Inc.: A Pillar of Black Society, 1893–1993*. N.p.: Ancient Egyptian Arab Order Nobles of the Mystic Shrine, 1993.

Ward, J. S. M. *An Interpretation of Our Masonic Symbols*. n.d., Reprint, Kila, Mont.: Kessinger Books, n.d.

Washington, Booker T. *Up from Slavery*. 1901. Reprint, New York: Oxford University Press, 1995.

Whittier, John Greenleaf. *The Poetical Works of John Greenleaf Whittier*, 2 Vols. Boston: J. R. Osgood, 1870.

Willson, Dixie. *Where the World Folds Up at Night*. New York: D. Appleton & Co., 1932.

Wilmshurst, W. L. *The Meaning of Masonry*, 5th ed. 1927. Reprint, New York: Gramercy Books, 1980.

Wingfield, Marshall. *The Shrine in a Temple*. Memphis, Tennessee: Al Chymia Temple, 1943.

World's Columbian Exposition Portfolio of Views, Issued by the Department of Photography. Chicago and St. Louis: National Chemigraph Company, 1893.

Yogananda, Paramahansa. *Autobiography of a Yogi*. 1946. Reprint, Los Angeles: Self Realization Fellowship, 1979.

X, Malcolm. "The Ballot or the Bullet." In *Malcolm X Speaks: Selected Speeches and Statements*, edited by George Breitman, 23–44. New York: Pathfinder, 1989.

SECONDARY SOURCES

Ackerman, Gerald. Gérôme's Oriental Paintings and the Western Genre Tradition." *Arts Magazine* 60, no. 7 (March 1986): 75–80.

Adams, Bluford. *E Pluribus Barnum: The Great American Showman and the Making of U.S. Popular Culture*. Minneapolis: University of Minnesota Press, 1997.

Addison, James Thayer. "The Ahmadiya Movement and Its Western Propaganda." *Harvard Theological Review* 22, no. 1 (January 1929): 1–32.

Ahmed, Leila. *Edward W. Lane: A Study of His Life and Works and of British Ideas of the Middle East in the Nineteenth Century*. London: Longman, 1978.

Aimes, Hubert H. S. "African Institutions in America." *Journal of American Folklore* 18 (1905): 15–32.

Alderson, Brian. "Scheherazade in the Nursery." In *The Arabian Nights in English Literature*, edited by Peter L. Caracciolo, 81–94. London: Macmillan Press, 1988.

Aldridge, Alan. *Consumption*. Cambridge, U.K.: Polity Press, 2003.

Alexander, H. M. *Strip Tease: The Vanished Art of Burlesque*. New York: Knight, 1938.

Algar, Hamid. *Religion and the State in Iran, 1785–1906*. Berkeley: University of California Press, 1969.

Allen, Ernest, Jr. "Identity and Destiny: The Formative Views of the Moorish Science Temple and the Nation of Islam." In *Muslims on the Americanization Path?* edited by Yvonne Yazbeck Haddad and John L. Esposito, 163–214. New York: Oxford University Press, 2000.

Allen, Robert C. *Horrible Prettiness: Burlesque and American Culture*. Chapel Hill: University of North Carolina Press, 1991.

Allison, Robert J. *The Crescent Obscured: The United States and the Muslim World, 1776–1815*. New York: Oxford University Press, 1995.

Alloula, Malek. *The Colonial Harem*. Minneapolis: University of Minnesota Press, 1986.

al-Mahdi, As Sayyid al-Imaam Isa al-Haadi. *Who Was Noble Drew Ali?* Brooklyn: Ansaaru Allah Publications, 1988.

Alpert, Leo M. "Judicial Censorship of Obscene Literature." *Harvard Law Review* 52, no. 1 (November 1938): 40–76.

Ames, Kenneth L. "The Lure of the Spectacular." In *Theatre of the Fraternity: Staging the Ritual Space of the Scottish Rite of Freemasonry, 1896–1929*, edited by Lance C. Brockman et al, 18–29. Minneapolis: Frederick R. Weisman Art Museum, University of Minnesota Press, 1996.

Anderson, Benedict. *Imagined Communities: Reflections on the Origin and Spread of Nationalism*. London: Verso, 1983.

Annam, Margaret C. "Arabian Nights in Victorian Literature." Ph.D. diss., Northwestern University, 1945.

Aruri, Naseer Hasan, and Muhammed A. Shuraydi, eds. *Revising Culture, Reinventing Peace: The Influence of Edward Said*. New York: Olive Branch Press, 2001.

Ashcroft, Bill, and Pal Ahulwalia, *Edward Said: The Paradox of Identity*. New York: Routledge, 1999.

Ashcroft, Bill, Gareth Griffiths, and Helen Tiffin. *Key Concepts in Post-Colonial Studies*. London: Routledge, 1998.

Ashley, Kathleen M. " 'Strange and Exotic': Representing the Other in Medieval and Renaissance Performance." In *East of West: Cross-Cultural Performance and the Staging of Difference*, edited by Claire Sponsler and Xiaomei Chen, 77–92. New York: Palgrave, 2000.

Austin, Allan D. *African Muslims in Antebellum America: Transatlantic Stories and Spiritual Struggles*. New York: Routledge, 1997.

Baer, Hans A. *The Black Spiritual Movement: A Religious Response to Racism*. Knoxville: University of Tennessee Press, 1984.

Bailey, Clinton. "The Ottomans and the Bedouin Tribes of the Negev." In *Ottoman Palestine, 1800–1914*, edited by Gad G. Gilbar. Leiden, Netherlands: E. J. Brill, 1990.

Barbas, Samantha. *Movie Crazy: Fans, Stars, and the Cult of Celebrity*. New York: Palgrave MacMillan, 2001.

Barth, Gunther. *City People: The Rise of Modern City Culture in Nineteenth-Century America*. New York: Oxford University Press, 1980.

Batkin, Jonathan. "Tourism is Overrated: Pueblo Pottery and the Early Curio Trade, 1880–1910." In *Unpacking Culture: Art and Commodity in Colonial and Postcolonial Worlds*, edited by Ruth B. Phillips and Christopher B. Steiner, 282–99. Berkeley: University of California Press, 1999.

Bay, Mia. *The White Image in the Black Mind: African-American Ideas about White People, 1830–1925*. New York: Oxford University Press, 2000.

Bayard, S. P. "Witchcraft Magic and Spirits on the Border of Pennsylvania and West Virginia." *Journal of American Folklore* 51 (March 1939): 47–59.

Beaulieu, Jill, and Mary Roberts, eds. *Orientalism's Interlocutors: Painting, Architecture, Photography.* Durham: Duke University Press, 2002.

Bederman, Gail. *Manliness and Civilization: A Cultural History of Gender and Race in the United States, 1880–1917.* Chicago: University of Chicago Press, 1995.

Behdad, Ali. *Belated Travelers: Orientalism in the Age of Colonial Dissolution.* Durham: Duke University Press, 1994.

Bell, Michael Davitt. *Culture, Genre, and Literary Vocation: Selected Essays on American Literature.* Chicago: University of Chicago Press, 2001.

Benchérif, Osman. *The Image of Algeria in Anglo-American Writings, 1785–1962.* Lanham, Md.: University Press of America, 1997.

Bergmann, Hans. "Panoramas of New York, 1845–1860." *Prospects* 10 (1985): 119–37.

Bernstein, Matthew, and Gaylyn Studlar, eds. *Visions of the East: Orientalism in Film.* New Brunswick, N.J.: Rutgers University Press, 1997.

Beynon, Erdmann Doane. The Voodoo Cult Among Negro Migrants in Detroit." *American Journal of Sociology* 43, no. 6 (May 1938): 894–907.

Beynon, John. *Masculinities and Culture.* Philadelphia: Open University Press, 2002.

Bhabha, Homi. "Of Mimicry and Man: The Ambivalence of Colonial Discourse." *October* 28 (Spring 1984): 125–33.

Blackstone, Sarah J. *Buckskins, Bullets, and Business: A History of Buffalo Bill's Wild West.* Westport, Conn.: Greenwood Press, 1986.

Bode, Carl. *American Lyceum.* New York: Oxford University Press, 1958.

Boime, Albert. *The Magisterial Gaze: Manifest Destiny and the American Landscape Painting, 1830–1865.* Washington D.C.: Smithsonian Institution, 1991.

Bond, Beverley W., Jr. "Civilization Comes to the Old Northwest." *Mississippi Valley Historical Review* 19, no. 1 (1932): 3–29.

Bontemps, Arna, and Jack Conroy, *Anyplace but Here.* 1945. Reprint. New York: Hill and Wang, 1966.

Boskin, Joseph. *Sambo: The Rise and Demise of an American Jester.* New York: Oxford University Press, 1986.

Bourdieu, Pierre. *Distinction: A Social Critique of the Judgment of Taste.* Translated by R. Nice. London: Routledge, 1984.

Bousquet, G. H. "Moslem Religious Influences in the United States." *Moslem World* 25 (1935): 40–44.

Braden, Charles S. "Islam in America." *International Review of Missions* 48 (1959): 309–17.

——. "Why Are the Cults Growing?" *Christian Century* 61, no. 1 (January 12, 1944): 45–47.

Brands, H. W. *The Reckless Decade: America in the 1890s.* New York: St. Martin's Press, 1995.

Braude, Anne. "Women's History Is American Religious History." In *Retelling U.S. Religious History,* edited by Thomas A. Tweed. Berkeley: University of California Press, 1997.

Breen, T. H. *The Marketplace of Revolution: How Consumer Politics Shaped American Independence.* New York: Oxford University Press, 2004.

Brendon, Piers. *Thomas Cook: 150 Years of Popular Tourism*. London: Secker and Warburg, 1991.

Brettell, Caroline B. "Nineteenth Century Travelers' Accounts of the Mediterranean Peasant." *Ethnohistory* 33, no. 2 (May 1986): 159–73.

Brockman, C. Lance, ed. *Theatre of the Fraternity: Staging the Ritual Space of the Scottish Rite of Freemasonry, 1896–1929*. Minneapolis: Frederick R. Weisman Art Museum, University of Minnesota Press, 1996.

Brody, David Eric. "Fantasy Realized: The Philippines, Orientalism, and Imperialism in Turn-of-the-Century American Visual Culture." Ph.D. diss., Boston University, 1997.

Brotz, Howard M. *The Black Jews of Harlem: Negro Nationalism and the Dilemmas of Negro Leadership*. New York: Schocken Books, 1964.

Broun, Heywood, and Margaret Leech. *Anthony Comstock: Roundsman of the Lord*. New York: Literary Guild of America, 1927.

Browder, Laura. *Slippery Characters: Ethnic Impersonators and American Identities*. Chapel Hill: University of North Carolina Press, 2000.

Brown, Emily C. *Har Dayal: Hindu Revolutionary and Rationalist*. Tucson: University of Arizona Press, 1975.

Brown, Richard D. "From Cohesion to Competition." In *Printing and Society in Early America*, edited by William L. Joyce, David D. Hall, Richard D. Brown, and John B. Hench, 300–309. Worcester, Mass.: American Antiquarian Society, 1983.

Budd, Louis J. *Our Mark Twain: The Making of His Public Personality*. Philadelphia: University of Pennsylvania Press, 1983.

Burke, Marie Louise. *Swami Vivekananda in America: New Discoveries*. Calcutta: Advaita Askrama, 1966.

Burke, Peter. *Popular Culture in Early Modern Europe*. New York: New York University Press, 1978.

Burns, Sarah. "The Price of Beauty: Art, Commerce, and the Late Nineteenth-Century American Studio Interior." in *American Iconology: New Approaches to Nineteenth-Century Art and Literature*, edited by David C. Miller, 209–38. New Haven: Yale University Press, 1993.

Butler, E. M. *The Myth of the Magus*. Cambridge: Cambridge University Press, 1943.

Butler, Jon. "Magic, Astrology, and the Early American Religious Heritage, 1600–1760." *American Historical Review* 84, no. 2 (April 1979): 322–39.

Butler, Judith. *Gender Trouble: Feminism and the Subversion of Identity, 10th Anniversary Edition*. New York: Routledge, 1999.

———. "Performative Acts and Gender Constitution." *Theatre Journal* 40, no. 4 (1988): 519–31.

Buzard, James. *The Beaten Track: European Tourism, Literature, and the Ways to "Culture," 1800–1918*. Oxford: Clarendon Press, 1993.

Calder, Lendol. *Financing the American Dream: A Cultural History of Consumer Credit*. Princeton: Princeton University Press, 1999.

Campbell, Colin. *The Romantic Ethic and the Spirit of Modern Consumerism*. Oxford: Basil Blackwell, 1987.

Campbell, I. C. "The Culture of Culture Contact: Refractions from Polynesia." *Journal of World History* 14, no. 1 (March 2003): 63–86.

Campbell, William C. *From the Quarries of Last Chance Gulch: A "News-History" of Helena and Its Masonic Lodges*, 2 vols. 1951. Reprint, Butte, Mont.: William C. Campbell, 1964.

Caracciolo, Peter L., "Such a Storehouse of Ingenious Fiction and Splendid Imagery." In *The Arabian Nights in English Literature*, edited by Peter L. Caracciolo, 1–80. London: Macmillan Press, 1988.

Carey, James. *Communication as Culture*. Boston: Unwin Hyman, 1989.

Carlson, Gustav G. "Number Gambling: A Study of a Culture Complex." Ph.D. diss., University of Michigan, 1940.

Carlton, Donna. *Looking for Little Egypt*. Bloomington, Ind.: IDD Books, 1994.

Carnes, Mark C. *Secret Ritual and Manhood in Victorian America*. New Haven: Yale University Press, 1989.

Carnes, Mark C., and Clyde Griffen. *Meanings for Manhood: Constructions of Masculinity in Victorian America*. Chicago: University of Chicago Press, 1990.

Carrier, James. *Gifts and Commodities: Exchange and Western Capitalism since 1700*. London: Routledge, 1995.

Carroll, Noel. "Performance." *Formations* 3, no 1 (1986): 63–81.

Cary, Richard. *The Genteel Circle: Bayard Taylor and His New York Friends*. Ithaca: Cornell University Press, 1952.

Cayton, Mary Kupiec. "The Making of an American Prophet: Emerson, His Audiences, and the Rise of the Culture Industry in Nineteenth-Century America," *American Historical Review* 92, no. 3 (June 1987): 597–620.

Çelik, Zeynep. *Displaying the Orient: Architecture of Islam at Nineteenth-Century World's Fairs*. Berkeley: University of California Press, 1992.

Çelik, Zeynep, and Leila Kinney. "Ethnography and Exhibitionism at the Expositions Universelles." *Assemblage* 13 (December 1990): 34–59.

Charvat, William. *The Profession of Authorship in America, 1800–1870*, edited by Matthew J. Bruccoli. Columbus: Ohio State University Press, 1968.

——. *Literary Publishing in America, 1790–1850*. Philadephia: University of Pennsylvania Press, 1959.

Chireau, Yvonne. *Black Magic: Religion and the African American Conjuring Tradition*. Berkeley: University of California Press, 2003.

Chireau, Yvonne, and Nathaniel Deutsch, eds. *Black Zion: African American Religious Encounters with Judaism*. New York: Oxford University Press, 2000.

Christison, Kathleen. *Perceptions of Palestine: Their Influence on U.S. Middle East Policy*. Berkeley: University of California Press, 1999.

Christy, Arthur. "The Orientalism of Whittier." *American Literature* 5, no. 3 (November 1933): 247–57.

——. *Orient in American Transcendentalism: A Study of Emerson, Thoreau and Alcott*. New York: Columbia University Press, 1932.

——. "Orientalism in New England: Whittier." *American Literature* 1, no. 4 (January 1930): 372–92.

Clawson, Mary Ann. *Constructing Brotherhood: Class, Gender, and Fraternalism*. Princeton: Princeton University Press, 1989.

Clegg, Claude Andrew. *An Original Man: The Life and Times of Elijah Muhammad*. New York: St. Martin's Press, 1997.

Codell, Julie F., and Dianne Sachko Macleod, eds. *Orientalism Transposed: The Impact of the Colonies on British Culture*. Brookfield, Vt.: Ashgate, 1998.

Cohen, Lizabeth. *A Consumer's Republic: The Politics of Mass Consumption in Post-War America*. New York: Alfred A. Knopf, 2003.

——. *Making a New Deal: Industrial Workers in Chicago, 1919–1939*. Cambridge: Cambridge University Press, 1990.

Cohodas, Marvin. "Elizabeth Hickox and Karuk Basketry: A Case Study on Debates on Innovation and Paradigms of Authenticity." In *Unpacking Culture: Art and Commodity in Colonial and Postcolonial Worlds*, edited by Ruth B. Phillips and Christopher B. Steiner, 143–61. Berkeley: University of California Press, 1999.

Conant, Martha Pike. *The Oriental Tale in England in the Eighteenth Century*. 1908. Reprint, New York: Octagon, 1966.

Conner, Patrick. *Oriental Architecture in the West*. London: Thames and Hudson, 1979.

Conroy, Mark. *Muse in the Machine: American Fiction and Mass Publicity*. Columbus: Ohio State University Press, 2004.

Conzen, Kathleen Neils, David A. Gerber, Ewa Morawska, George E. Pozzetta, and Rudolph J. Vecoli. "The Invention of Ethnicity in the United States: A Perspective from the USA." *Journal of American Ethnic History* 12, no. 1 (Fall 1992): 3–41.

Cook, James W. *The Arts of Deception: Playing with Fraud in the Age of Barnum*. Cambridge: Harvard University Press, 2001.

Cornell, Stephan, and Douglas Harman, eds. *Ethnicity and Race: Making Identities in a Changing World*. Thousand Oaks, Calif.: Pine Forge Press, 1998.

Cray, Robert E., Jr. "Remembering the USS *Chesapeake*: The Politics of Maritime Death and Impressment." *Journal of the Early Republic* 25 (Fall 2005): 445–74.

Cronon, William. *Nature's Metropolis: Chicago and the Great West*. New York: W. W. Norton & Co., 1991.

Cross, Gary. *An All-Consuming Century: Why Commercialism Won in Modern America*. New York: Columbia University Press, 2000.

——. *Time and Money: The Making of Consumer Culture*. London: Routledge, 1993.

Crowder, Ralph F. " 'Don't Buy Where You Can't Work': An Investigation of the Political Forces and Social Conflict Within the Harlem Boycott of 1934." *Afro-Americans in New York Life and History* 15, no. 2 (July 1991): 7–44.

Cullen, Jim. *The Art of Democracy: A Concise History of Popular Culture in the United States*, 2nd ed. New York: Monthly Review Press, 2002.

Curtis, Edward E., IV. "African-American Islamization Reconsidered: Black History Narratives and Muslim Identity." *Journal of the American Academy of Religion* 73, no. 3 (September 2005): 659–84.

———. "Islamicizing the Black Body: Ritual and Power in Elijah Muhammad's Nation of Islam." *Religion and American Culture* 12, no. 2 (Summer 2002): 167–96.

Daniel, Robert L. "American Influences in the Near East before 1861." *American Quarterly* 16, no. 1 (Spring 1964): 72–84.

Daniels, Roger. *Guarding the Golden Door: American Immigration Policy and Immigrants since 1882*. New York: Hill and Wang, 2004.

Davidson, Cathy N. *Revolution and the Word: The Rise of the Novel in America*. Oxford: Oxford University Press, 2004.

Davis, Clark. *Company Men: White-Collar Life and Corporate Cultures in Los Angeles, 1892–1941*. Baltimore: Johns Hopkins University Press, 2000.

Davis, Janet M. *The Circus Age: Culture and Society Under the Big Top*. Chapel Hill: University of North Carolina Press, 2002.

Davis, John. *The Landscape of Belief: Encountering the Holy Land in Nineteenth-Century American Art and Culture*. Princeton: Princeton University Press, 1996.

Davis, Natalie Z. *Society and Culture in Early Modern France*. Stanford: Stanford University Press, 1975.

Davis, Susan G. *Parades and Power: Street Theatre in Nineteenth-Century Philadelphia*. Berkeley: University of California Press, 1986.

Dawson, Michael. *Selling British Columbia: Tourism and Consumer Culture, 1890–1970*. Vancouver: University of British Columbia Press, 2004.

de Certeau, Michel. *The Practice of Everyday Life*. Translated by Steven F. Randall. 1984. Reprint, Berkeley: University of California Press, 1984.

Deloria, Philip J. *Playing Indian*. New Haven: Yale University Press, 1998.

Denning, Michael. *Mechanic Accents: Dime Novels and Working-Class Culture in America*. New York: Verso, 1987.

Deringil, Selim. *The Well-Protected Domains: Ideology and the Legitimation of Power in the Ottoman Empire, 1876–1909*. London: I. B. Tauris, 1998.

Desmond, Jane. "Dancing Out the Difference: Cultural Imperialism and Ruth St. Denis's 'Radha' of 1906." *Signs* 17, no. 1 (Autumn 1991): 28–49.

Deveney, John P. "The Travels of H. P Blavatsky and the Chronology of Albert Leighton Rawson." *Theosophical History* 10, no. 4 (October 2004): 8–30.

———. "Nobles of the Secret Mosque: Albert L. Rawson, Abd al-Kader, George H. Felt and the Mystic Shrine." *Theosophical History* 8, no. 9 (July 2002): 250–61.

Diamond, Elin, ed. *Performance and Cultural Politics*. New York: Routledge, 1996.

DiNapoli, Mary Ann Haick. "The Syrian-Lebanese Community of South Ferry." In *A*

Community of Many Worlds: Arab Americans in New York City, edited by Kathleen Benson and Philip M. Kayal, 11–27. New York and Syracuse: Museum of the City of New York/Syracuse University Press, 2002.

Dirlik, Arif. "Chinese History and the Question of Orientalism." *History and Theory* 35, no. 4 (December 1996): 96–118.

Douglas, Ann. *Terrible Honesty: Mongrel Manhattan in the 1920s*. New York: Noonday Press, 1995.

——. *The Feminization of American Culture*. New York: Knopf, 1977.

Douglas, Mary, and Baron Isherwood. *The World of Goods: Toward an Anthropology of Consumption*, 2nd ed. New York: Routledge, 1996.

Douglas, Susan J. *Inventing American Broadcasting, 1899–1922*. Baltimore: Johns Hopkins University Press, 1989.

Doumani, Beshara. *Rediscovering Palestine: Merchants and Peasants in Jabal Nablus, 1700–1900*. Berkeley: University of California Press, 1995.

Drake, St. Clair, and Horace R. Cayton. *Black Metropolis: A Study of Negro Life in a Northern City*. 1945. Reprint, New York: Harper & Row, 1962.

Dumenil, Lynn. *The Modern Temper: American Culture and Society in the 1920s*. New York: Hill and Wang, 1994.

——. *Freemasonry and American Culture, 1880–1930*. Princeton: Princeton University Press, 1984.

Dunch, Ryan. "Beyond Cultural Imperialism: Cultural Theory, Christian Missions, and Global Modernity." *History and Theory* 41, no. 3 (October 2002): 301–25.

Edwards, Holly. "A Million and One Nights: Orientalism in America, 1870–1930." In *Noble Dreams, Wicked Pleasures: Orientalism in America, 1870–1930*, edited by Holly Edwards, 28–31. Princeton: Princeton University Press and Sterling and Francine Clark Institute, 2000.

——. "Portrait of an Orientalist." In *Noble Dreams, Wicked Pleasures: Orientalism in America, 1870–1930*, edited by Holly Edwards, 120–23. Princeton: Princeton University Press and Sterling and Francine Clark Institute, 2000.

——, ed. *Noble Dreams, Wicked Pleasures: Orientalism in America, 1870–1930*. Princeton: Princeton University Press and Sterling and Francine Clark Institute, 2000.

Edwards, Rebecca. *New Spirits: Americans in the Gilded Age, 1865–1905*. Oxford: Oxford University Press, 2006.

Eilts, Hermann Frederick. "Ahmad bin Na'aman's Mission to the United States in 1840, The Voyage of al-Sultanah to New York City." *Essex Institute Historical Collections* 98 (October 1962): 219–77.

Ellis, Edward Robb. *A Nation in Torment: The Great American Depression, 1929–1939*. 1970. Reprint. New York: Kodashansa International, 1995.

"Enforcement of Laws against Obscenity in New York." *Columbia Law Review* 28, no. 7 (November 1928): 57–90.

Engh, Michael E. "Practically Every Religion Being Represented." In *Metropolis in the*

Making: Los Angeles in the 1920s, edited by Tom Sitton and William Deverell, 201–19. Berkeley: University of California Press, 1999.

Erenberg, Lewis A. *Steppin' Out: New York Nightlife and the Transformation of American Culture, 1890–1930*. Chicago: University of Chicago Press, 1981.

Essien-Udom, E. U. *Black Nationalism: A Search for an Identity in America*. Chicago: University of Chicago Press, 1962.

"Evidence: Judicial Notice that Voltaire's Works are not Immoral or Obscene Literature." *Michigan Law Review* 8, no. 2 (December 1909): 156–57.

Ewen, Stuart. *Captains of Consciousness: Advertising and the Social Roots of the Consumer Culture*. New York: McGraw Hill, 1976.

Fabian, Ann. *Card Sharps, Dream Books and Bucket Shops: Gambling in 19th-Century America*. Ithaca: Cornell University Press, 1990.

Fahmy, Khaled. "Prostitution in Egypt in the Nineteenth Century." In *Outside In: Marginality in the Modern Middle East*, edited by Eugene Rogan, 77–103. London: I. B. Taurus, 2002.

Farmer, David. "American Orientalism." *Apollo* 15, no. 2 (November 2000): 55–56.

Fauset, Arthur Huff. *Black Gods of the Metropolis: Negro Religious Cults of the Urban North*. Philadelphia: University of Pennsylvania Press, 1944.

Fenton, John Y. "Hinduism." In *Encyclopedia of the American Religious Experience: Studies of Traditions and Movements*, 2 vols., edited by Charles H. Lippy and Peter W. Williams, 683–98. New York: Charles Scribner's Sons, 1996.

Fenton, Steve. *Ethnicity*. Cambridge, U.K.: Polity Press, 2003.

Ferguson, Charles W. *The Confusion of Tongues: A Review of Modern Isms*. Garden City, N.Y.: Doubleday, Doran & Co., 1929.

Filene, Peter. *Him/Her/Self: Sex Roles in Modern America*, 2nd ed. Baltimore: Johns Hopkins University Press, 1986.

Finnie, David H. *Pioneers East: The Early American Experience in the Middle East*. Cambridge: Harvard University Press, 1967.

Fluck, Winfried. "The Modernity of America and the Practice of Scholarship." In *Rethinking American History in a Global Age*, edited by Thomas Bender, 343–66. Berkeley: University of California Press, 2002.

Foner, Eric. "The Meaning of Freedom in the Age of Emancipation." *Journal of American History* 81 (September 1994): 458–60.

Foster, Gaines M. *Ghosts of the Confederacy: Defeat, the Lost Cause, and the Emergence of the New South*. New York: Oxford University Press, 1987.

Foster, Stephen William. "The Exotic as a Symbolic System." *Dialectical Anthropology* 7 (1982): 21–30.

Fox, Charles Philip, ed. *American Circus Posters in Full Color*. New York: Dover Publications, 1978.

Frazier, E. Franklin. *The Negro in the United States*. Chicago: University of Chicago Press, 1938.

———. *The Negro Family in Chicago*. Chicago: University of Chicago Press, 1932.

Friedman, Walter A. *Birth of a Salesman: The Transformation of Selling in America*. Cambridge: Harvard University Press, 2004.

Friedmann, Yohanan. *Prophecy Continuous: Aspects of Ahmadi Religious Thought and Its Medieval Background*. Berkeley: University of California Press, 1989.

Gamm, Gerald, and Robert D. Putnam. "The Growth of Voluntary Associations in America, 1840–1940." *Journal of Interdisciplinary History* 29, no. 4 (Spring 1999): 511–57.

Gandhi, Leela. *Postcolonial Theory: A Critical Introduction*. New York: Columbia University Press, 1998.

Garber, Marjorie. *Vested Interests: Cross-Dressing and Cultural Anxiety*. New York: Routledge, 1992.

Gardiner, W. R. W. "The Ahmadiya Movement." *Moslem World* 10 (1920): 59–64.

Ghareeb, Edmund, ed. *Split Vision: The Portrayal of Arabs in the American Media*. Washington, D.C.: Arab-American Affairs Council, 1983.

Gifra-Adroher, Pere. *Between History and Romance: Travel Writing on Spain in the Early Nineteenth-Century United States*. Madison, N.J.: Fairleigh Dickenson University Press, 2000.

Gilbert, Douglas. *American Vaudeville, Its Life and Times*. New York: Whittlesey, 1940.

Gill, James. *Lords of Misrule: Mardi Gras and the Politics of Race in New Orleans*. Jackson: University Press of Mississippi, 1997.

Gilmore, Michael T. *American Romanticism and the Marketplace*. Chicago: University of Chicago Press, 1985.

Gilmore, Paul. *The Genuine Article: Race, Mass Culture, and American Literary Manhood*. Durham: Duke University Press, 2001.

Gist, Noel P. "Structure and Process in Secret Societies." *Social Forces* 16, no. 3 (March 1938): 349–57.

———. "Culture Patterning in Secret Society Ceremonials." *Social Forces* 14, no. 4 (May 1936): 497–505.

Glassberg, David. *Sense of History: The Place of the Past in American Life*. Amherst: University of Massachusetts Press, 2001.

———. *American Historical Pageantry: The Uses of Tradition in the Early Twentieth Century*. Chapel Hill: University of North Carolina Press, 1990.

Gleason, Philip. "Identifying Identity: A Semantic History." *Journal of American History* 69, no. 4 (March 1983): 910–31.

Godwin, Joscelyn. *The Theosophical Enlightenment*. Albany: State University of New York Press, 1994.

Goffman, Erving. *The Presentation of Self in Everyday Life*. Garden City, N.Y.: Doubleday, 1959.

Gomes, Michael. *The Dawning of the Theosophical Movement*. Wheaton, Ill.: Theosophical Publishing Company, 1987.

Gordon, Ian. *Comic Strips and Consumer Culture*, 2nd ed. Washington, D.C.: Smithsonian Institution Press, 1998.

Gorn, Elliot J. "The Wicked World: The National Police Gazette and Gilded-Age America." *Media Studies Journal* 6, no. 1 (Winter 1992): 1–15.

Gould, Harold. *Sikhs, Students, Swamis and Spies: The India Lobby in the United States, 1900–1944*. New York: Sage, 2006.

Grabar, Oleg. "Roots and Others." In *Noble Dreams, Wicked Pleasures: Orientalism in America, 1870–1930*, edited by Holly Edwards, 3–9. Princeton: Princeton University Press and Sterling and Francine Clark Institute, 2000.

Graham-Brown, Sarah. *Images of Women: The Portrayal of Women in Photography of the Middle East, 1860–1950*. New York: Columbia University Press, 1988.

Graziano, John. "Music in William Randolph Hearst's *New York Journal*," *Notes* (2) 48, no. 2 (December 1991): 383–424.

Greef, Robert J. "Public Lectures in New York, 1851–1878: A Cultural Index of the Times." Ph.D. diss., University of Chicago, 1945.

Greenberg, Cheryl Lynn. *"Or Does It Explode?" Black Harlem in the Great Depression*. Oxford: Oxford University Press, 1991.

Greenhalgh, Paul. *Ephemeral Vistas: The Expositions Universelles, Great Exhibitions and World's Fairs, 1851–1939*. Manchester, U.K.: Manchester University Press, 1988.

Grier, Katherine. *Culture and Comfort: People, Parlors and Upholstery, 1850–1930*. Washington, D.C.: Smithsonian Institution Press, 1997.

Grigsby, Darcy Grimaldo. *Extremities: Painting Empire in Post-Revolutionary France*. New Haven: Yale University Press, 2002.

Griswold, H. D. "The Ahmadiya Movement." *Moslem World* 2 (1912): 373–79.

Griswold, Wendy. "The Fabrication of Meaning: Literary Interpretation in the United States, Great Britain, and the West Indies." *American Journal of Sociology* 92, no. 5 (March 1987): 1077–1117.

Grossman, James R. *Land of Hope: Chicago, Black Southerners, and the Great Migration*. Chicago: University of Chicago Press, 1989.

Haddad, Yvonne Yazbeck, and Jane Idleman Smith. *Mission to America: Five Sectarian Communities in North America*. Gainesville: University Press of Florida, 1993.

Haider, Gulzar. "Muslim Space and the Practice of Architecture: A Personal Odyssey." In *Making Muslim Space in North America and Europe*, edited by Barbara Daly Metcalf, 31–45. Berkeley: University of California Press, 1996.

Hajji, Abdelmajid. "The Arab in American Silent Cinema: A Study of a Film Genre." Ph.D. diss., University of Kansas, 1994.

Hall, Catherine, ed. *Cultures of Empire, A Reader: Colonizers in Britain and the Empire in the Nineteenth and Twentieth Centuries*. New York: Routledge, 2000.

Hall, David D. *Cultures of Print: Essays in the History of the Book*. Amherst: University of Massachusetts Press, 1996.

——. *Worlds of Wonder, Days of Judgment: Popular Religious Belief in Early New England.* Cambridge: Harvard University Press, 1989.

Hall, Richard. "The Wilder Shores of Art." *Connoisseur* 204, no. 821 (1980): 194–201.

Halttunen, Karen. *Confidence Men and Painted Women: A Study of Middle-Class Culture in America, 1830–1870.* New Haven: Yale University Press, 1982.

Hammons, Terry B. " 'A Wild Ass of a Man': American Images of Arabs to 1948." Ph.D. diss., University of Oklahoma, 1978.

Hangen, Tona J. *Redeeming the Dial: Radio, Religion, and Popular Culture in America.* Chapel Hill: University of North Carolina Press, 2002.

Hansen, Chadwick. "Jenny's Toe: Negro Shaking Dances in America." *American Quarterly* 19, no. 3 (Autumn 1967): 554–63.

Hansen, Miriam. *Babel and Babylon: Spectatorship and American Silent Film.* Cambridge: Harvard University Press, 1991.

Hanssen, Jens. "Public Morality and Marginality in Fin-de-siécle Beirut." In *Outside In: Marginality in the Modern Middle East,* edited by Eugene Rogan, 183–210. London: I. B. Taurus. 2002.

Harris, Neil. *Cultural Excursions: Marketing Appetites and Cultural Tastes in Modern America.* Chicago: University of Chicago Press, 1990.

Harvey, Bruce A. *American Geographics: U.S. National Narratives and the Representation of the Non-European World, 1830–1865.* Stanford: Stanford University Press, 2001.

Hatch, Nathan O. *The Democratization of American Christianity.* New Haven: Yale University Press, 1989.

Heaman, E. A. *The Inglorious Arts of Peace: Exhibitions in Canadian Society During the Nineteenth Century.* Toronto: University of Toronto Press, 1999.

Hebdige, Dick. *Subculture: The Meaning of Style.* 1979. Reprint, London and New York: Routledge, 1988.

Henkin, David. *City Reading: Written Words and Public Spaces in Antebellum New York.* New York: Columbia University Press, 1998.

Heyrman, Christine Leigh. *Southern Cross: The Beginnings of the Bible Belt.* Chapel Hill: University of North Carolina Press, 1997.

Hickey, Dennis, and Kenneth C. Wylie. *An Enchanting Darkness: The American Vision of Africa in the Twentieth Century.* East Lansing: Michigan State University Press, 1993.

Higham, John. "Integrating America: The Problem of Assimilation in the Nineteenth Century." *Journal of American Ethnic History* 1, no. 1 (Fall 1981): 7–25.

Hilton, Matthew. *Smoking in British Popular Culture, 1800–2000: Perfect Pleasures.* Manchester: Manchester University Press, 2000.

Hinsley, Curtis M. "The World as Marketplace: Commodification of the Exotic at the World's Columbian Exposition, Chicago, 1893." In *Exhibiting Cultures: The Poetics and Politics of Museum Display,* edited by Ivan Karp and Steven Lavine. Washington, D.C.: Smithsonian Institution Press, 1991.

Hitti, Philip K. "America and the Arab Heritage." In *The Arab Heritage*, edited by Nabih Amin Faris, 1–24. Princeton: Princeton University Press, 1944.

Hodin, Mark. "The Disavowal of Ethnicity: Legitimate Theatre and the Social Construction of Literary Value in Turn-of-the-Century America." *Theatre Journal* 52, no. 2 (May 2000): 211–26.

Hodson, Joel C. *Lawrence of Arabia and American Culture: The Making of a Transatlantic Legend.* Westport, Conn.: Greenwood Press, 1995.

Hoffert, A. T. "Moslem Propaganda: The Hand of Islam Stretches Out to Aframerica." *The Messenger* (May 1927): 140, 167.

Hoganson, Kristin. *Consumers' Imperium: The Global Production of American Domesticity, 1865–1920.* Chapel Hill: University of North Carolina Press, 2007.

———. "Cosmopolitan Domesticity: Importing the American Dream, 1865–1920." *American Historical Review* 107, no. 1 (February 2002): 55–83.

Holmes, Sean P. " 'All the World's a Stage!': The Actors' Strike of 1919." *Journal of American History* 91, no. 4 (March 2005): 1291–1317.

Horowitz, Helen Lefkowitz. *Rereading Sex: Battles over Sexual Knowledge and Suppression in Nineteenth-Century America.* New York: Alfred A. Knopf, 2002.

Howe, Stephen. *Afrocentrism: Mythical Pasts and Imagined Homes.* London: Verso, 1998.

Hower, Ralph M. *The History of an Advertising Agency: N. W. Ayer and Son at Work, 1869–1949.* Cambridge: Harvard University Press, 1949.

Hunt, Michael H. *Ideology and US Foreign Policy.* New Haven: Yale University Press, 1987.

Hunter, F. Robert. "The Thomas Cook Archive for the Study of Tourism in North Africa and the Middle East." *Middle East Studies Association Bulletin* 36 (Winter 2003), 157–64.

Hunter, Gary Jerome. " 'Don't Buy From Where You Can't Work': Black Urban Boycott Movements during the Depression, 1929–1941." Ph.D. diss., University of Michigan, 1977.

Irwin, Robert. *The Arabian Nights: A Companion.* London: Taurus Parke, 2004.

Isani, Mukhtar Ali. "The Oriental Tale in America through 1865: A Study in American Fiction." Ph.D. diss., Princeton University, 1962.

Ismaeal, Hani. "Creating an Imagined Community: Self-Representation in an Arab-American Journal, *The Syrian World*, 1926–1935." Ph.D. diss., Southern Illinois University, 2003.

Jackson, Carl T. *Vedanta for the West: The Ramakrishna Movement in the United States.* Bloomington: Indiana University Press, 1994.

Jackson, Sherman A. *Islam and the Blackamerican: Looking toward the Third Resurrection.* Oxford: Oxford University Press 2005.

Jacobson, Matthew Frye. *Barbarian Virtues: The United States Encounters Foreign Peoples at Home and Abroad, 1876–1917.* New York: Hill and Wang, 2000.

Jenkins, Iredell. "The Laisser-Faire Theory of Artistic Censorship." *Journal of the History of Ideas* 5, no. 1 (January 1944): 71–90.

Johnson, Guy B. "Some Factors in the Development of Negro Social Institutions in the United States." *American Journal of Sociology* 40, no. 3 (November 1934): 329–37.

Johnson, Paul K. *The Masters Revealed: Madame Blavatsky and the Myth of the Great White Lodge.* Albany: State University of New York Press, 1994.

———. "Albert Leighton Rawson." *Theosophical History* 2, no. 7 (1988): 229–51.

Jones, Alan. "The Loss of Orientalism: *Matisse in Morocco* Came and Went at MoMA, but Does Anyone Remember Bob Hope in a Fez?" *Arts Magazine* 65, no. 4 (December 1990): 23–24.

Jones, Raymond Julius. "A Comparative Study of Religious Cult Behavior Among Negroes." *Howard University Studies in the Social Sciences* 2, no. 2 (1939): 1–125.

Jowitt, Deborah. *Time and the Dancing Image.* Berkeley: University of California Press, 1988.

Kabbani, Rana. *Europe's Myths of Orient: Devise and Rule.* London: Macmillan, 1986.

Kahf, Mohja. *Western Representations of the Muslim Woman: From Termagant to Odalisque.* Austin: University of Texas Press, 1999.

Kamalipour, Yahya R. *The U.S. Media and the Middle East: Image and Perception.* Westport, Conn.: Greenwood Press, 1995.

Karim, Karim H. *Islamic Peril: Media and Global Violence.* Montreal: Black Rose Books, 2000.

Karpat, Kemal H. "The Ottoman Emigration to America, 1860–1914." *International Journal of Middle East Studies* 17, no. 2 (May 1985): 175–209.

Kasson, John F. *Houdini, Tarzan, and the Perfect Man: The White Male Body and the Challenge of Modernity in America.* New York: Hill & Wang, 2002.

Kasson, Joy S. *Buffalo Bill's Wild West: Celebrity, Memory, and Popular History.* New York: Hill and Wang, 2000.

Kearney, Helen McCready. "American Images of the Middle East, 1824–1924: A Century of Antipathy." Ph.D. diss., University of Rochester, 1975.

Kennedy, Charles A. "When Cairo Met Main Street: Little Egypt, Salome Dancers, and the World's Fairs of 1893 and 1904." In *Music and Culture in America, 1861–1918,* edited by Michael Saffle, 271–98. New York: Garland, 1998.

Kennedy, Valerie. *Edward Said: A Critical Introduction.* Cambridge, U.K.: Polity Press, 2000.

Khalaf, Samir. *Cultural Resistance: Global and Local Encounters in the Middle East.* London: Saqi Books, 2001.

Khater, Adram Fouad. *Inventing Home: Emigration, Gender and the Middle Class in Lebanon: 1870–1920.* Berkeley: University of California Press, 2001.

Kibler, M. Alison. *Rank Ladies: Gender and Cultural Heirarchy in American Vaudeville.* Chapel Hill: University of North Carolina Press, 1999.

Kidd, Kenneth B. *Making American Boys: Boyology and the Feral Tale.* Minneapolis: University of Minnesota Press, 2004.

Kimmel, Michael. *Manhood in America: A Cultural History.* New York: Free Press, 1996.

King, Richard. *Orientalism and Religion: Post-Colonial Theory, India, and "The Mystic East."* New York: Routledge, 1999.

Kitch, Carolyn. *The Girl on the Magazine Cover: The Origins of Visual Stereotypes in American Mass Media.* Chapel Hill: University of North Carolina Press, 2001.

Kuklick, Bruce W. *Puritans in Babylon: The Ancient Near East and American Intellectual Life, 1880–1930.* Princeton: Princeton University Press, 1996.

Laird, Pamela Walker. *Advertising Progress: American Business and the Rise of Consumer Marketing.* Baltimore: Johns Hopkins University Press, 1998.

Lancaster, Clay. *The Incredible World's Parliament of Religions at the Chicago Columbian Exposition of 1893: A Comparative and Critical Study.* Fontwell, U.K.: Centaur Press, 1987.

Lant, Antonia. "The Curse of the Pharaoh, or How Cinema Contracted Egyptomania." *October* 59 (Winter 1992): 87–112.

Laurie, Joe, Jr. *Vaudeville: From Honky-Tonks to the Palace.* Port Washington, N.Y.: Kennikat Press, 1953.

Leach, William. *Land of Desire: Merchants, Power, and the Rise of a New American Culture.* New York: Vintage, 1993.

Lears, T. J. Jackson. *Fables of Abundance: A Cultural History of Advertising in America.* New York: Basic Books, 1994.

———. *No Place of Grace: Anti-Modernism and the Transformation of American Culture, 1880–1920.* New York: Pantheon Books, 1981.

Lee, Robert G. *Orientals: Asian Americans in Popular Culture.* Philadelphia: Temple University Press, 1999.

Leed, Eric J. *The Mind of the Traveler: From Gilgameth to Global Tourism.* New York: Basic Books, 1991.

Lehuu, Isabelle, *Carnival on the Page: Popular Print Media in Antebellum America.* Chapel Hill: University of North Carolina Press, 2000.

Levine, Lawrence W. *Highbrow/Lowbrow, The Emergence of Cultural Hierarchy in America.* Cambridge: Harvard University Press, 1988.

———. "Marcus Garvey and the Politics of Revitalization." In *Black Leaders of the Twentieth Century,* edited by John Hope Franklin and August Meier, 105–38. Urbana: University of Illinois Press, 1982.

Lewis, James R. "Savages of the Seas: Barbary Captivity Tales and Images of Muslims in the Early Republic." *Journal of American Culture* 13, no. 2 (1990): 75–84.

Lewis, Reina. *Rethinking Orientalism: Women, Travel and the Ottoman Harem.* New Brunswick, N.J.: Rutgers University Press, 2004.

———. *Gendering Orientalism: Race, Feminism, and Representation.* London: Routledge, 1996.

Limerick, Patricia Nelson. *The Legacy of Conquest: The Unbroken Past of the American West.* New York: W. W. Norton, 1987.

Lincoln, C. Eric. *The Black Muslims in America,* 3rd ed. 1961. Reprint, Grand Rapids, Mich.: Wm. B. Eerdmans, 1994.

Lippmann, Walter. *Public Opinion*. New York: Macmillan, 1922.

Lipsitz, George. *Time Passages*. Minneapolis: University of Minnesota Press, 1990.

Little, Douglas. *American Orientalism: The United States and the Middle East since 1945*. Chapel Hill: University of North Carolina Press, 2002.

Lockman, Zachary. *Contending Visions of the Middle East: The History and Politics of Orientalism*. Cambridge: Cambridge University Press, 2004.

Long, Carolyn Morrow. *Spiritual Merchants: Religion, Magic, and Commerce*. Knoxville: University of Tennessee Press, 2001.

Lorini, Alessandra. *Rituals of Race: American Public Culture and the Search for Racial Democracy*. Charlottesville: University Press of Virginia, 1999.

Lott, Eric. *Love and Theft: Blackface Minstrelsy and the American Working Class*. New York: Oxford University Press, 1993.

Lowe, Lisa. *Critical Terrains: French and British Orientalisms*. Ithaca: Cornell University Press, 1991.

Luedtke, Luther S. *Nathaniel Hawthorne and the Romance of the Orient*. Bloomington: Indiana University Press, 1988.

Luskin, John. *Lippmann, Liberty and the Press*. Tuscaloosa: University of Alabama Press, 1972.

Lutz, Catherine A., and Jane L. Collins. *Reading National Geographic*. Chicago: University of Chicago Press, 1993.

Lynd, Robert S., and Helen Merryll Lynd. *Middletown: A Study in Contemporary American Culture*. New York: Harcourt Brace & Company, 1929.

Macfie, A. L. *Orientalism*. New York: Longman, 2002.

MacKenzie, John M. *Orientalism: History, Theory and the Arts*. Manchester and New York: Manchester University Press, 1995.

MacLeod, Anne Scott. *American Childhood: Essays on Children's Literature of the Nineteenth and Twentieth Centuries*. Athens: University of Georgia Press, 1994.

Macleod, Dianne Sachko. "Cross-Cultural Cross-Dressing: Class, Gender and Modernist Sexual Identity." In *Orientalism Transposed: The Impact of the Colonies on British Culture*, edited by Julie F. Codell and Dianne Sachko Macleod, 63–85. Brookfield, Vt.: Ashgate, 1998.

Majaj, Lisa Suhair. "Arab-Americans and the Meaning of Race." In *Postcolonial Theory and the United States*, edited by Amritjit Singh and Peter Schmidt, 320–37. Jackson: University of Mississippi Press, 2000.

Makdisi, Ussama. *Artillery of Heaven: American Missionaries and the Failed Conversion of the Middle East*. New York: Cornell University Press, 2008.

———. "Ottoman Orientalism." *American Historical Review* 107, no. 3 (June 2002): 768–96.

———. *The Culture of Sectarianism: Community, History, and Violence in Nineteenth-Century Ottoman Lebanon*. Berkeley: University of California Press, 2000.

———. "Reclaiming the Land of the Bible: Missionaries, Secularism, and Evangelical Modernity." *American Historical Review* 102, no. 3 (June 1997): 680–713.

Mani, Lata, and Ruth Frankenberg. "The Challenge of Orientalism." *Economy and Society* 14, no. 2 (May 1985): 174–92.

Marchand, Roland. *Advertising the American Dream: Making Way for Modernity, 1920–1940.* Berkeley: University of California Press, 1985.

Marr, Timothy Worthington. *The Cultural Roots of American Islamicism.* Cambridge: Cambridge University Press, 2006.

Martin, Richard, and Harold Koda. *Orientalism: Visions of the East in Western Dress.* New York: Metropolitan Museum of Art, 1994.

Martin, Tony. *Race First: The Ideological and Organizational Struggles of Marcus Garvey and the Universal Negro Improvement Association.* Westport, Conn.: Greenwood Press, 1976.

Mason, Peter. *Deconstructing America: Representations of the Other.* London: Routledge, 1990.

Matar, Nabil. *Turks, Moors and Englishmen in the Age of Discovery.* New York: Columbia University Press, 1999.

———. *Islam in Britain, 1558–1685.* Cambridge: Cambridge University Press, 1998.

McAlister, Melanie. *Epic Encounters: Culture, Media, and U.S. Interests in the Middle East, 1945–2000.* Berkeley: University of California Press, 2001.

McClintock, Anne. *Imperial Leather: Race, Gender and Sexuality in the Colonial Contest.* London: Routledge, 1995.

McCloud, Aminah Beverly. *African American Islam.* New York and London: Routledge, 1995.

McCracken, Grant. *Culture and Consumption: New Approaches to the Symbolic Character of Consumer Goods and Activities.* Bloomington: Indiana University Press, 1988.

McGovern, Charles F. *Sold American: Consumption and Citizenship, 1890–1945.* Chapel Hill: University of North Carolina Press, 2006.

McKennon, Joe. *A Pictorial History of the American Carnival.* Sarasota, Fla.: Carnival Publishers, 1971.

McLaren, *Trials of Masculinity: Policing Sexual Boundaries, 1870–1930.* Chicago: University of Chicago Press, 1997.

McLean, Albert F., Jr. *American Vaudeville as Ritual.* Lexington: University Press of Kentucky, 1965.

McNamara, Brooks. *Step Right Up,* rev. ed. Jackson: University Press of Mississippi, 1995.

Mead, David. *Yankee Eloquence in the Middle West: The Ohio Lyceum, 1850–1870.* East Lansing: Michigan State College Press, 1951.

Mehaffy, Marilyn Maness. "Advertising Race/Racing Advertising: The Feminine Consumer(-Nation), 1876–1900." *Signs* 23, no. 1 (Autumn 1997): 131–74.

Metwalli, Ahmed M. "Americans Abroad: The Popular Art of Travel Writing in the Nineteenth Century." In *America: Exploration and Travel,* edited by Steven Kagle, 69–82. Bowling Green, Ohio: Bowling Green State University Popular Press, 1979.

Meyer, B. H. "Fraternal Beneficiary Societies in the United States." *American Journal of Sociology* 6, no. 5 (March 1901): 646–61.

Meyer, Moe. "Reclaiming the Discourse of Camp." In *The Politics and Poetics of Camp*, edited by Moe Meyer, 1–22. London: Routledge, 1994.

Mills, James H. *Cannabis Britannica: Empire, Trade, and Prohibition, 1800–1928*. New York: Oxford University Press, 2003.

Mitchell, Timothy. *Colonizing Egypt*. Cambridge: Cambridge University Press, 1988.

Montgomery, Benilde. "White Captives, African Slaves: A Drama of Abolition." *Eighteenth-Century Studies* 27, no. 4 (Summer 1994): 615–30.

Moon, Krystyn R. *Yellowface: Creating the Chinese in American Popular Music and Performance, 1850s–1920s*. New Brunswick, N.J.: Rutgers University Press, 2005.

Moore, James. *Gurdjieff, A Biography: The Anatomy of a Myth*. Rockport, Mass.: Element Books, 1991.

Moore-Gilbert, Bart. *Postcolonial Theory: Contexts, Practices, Politics*. New York: Verso, 1997.

Moses, L. G. *Wild West Shows and the Images of American Indians, 1883–1933*. Albuquerque: University of New Mexico Press, 1996.

Moses, Wilson Jeremiah. *Afrotopia: The Roots of African American Popular History*. Cambridge: Cambridge University Press, 1998.

Mott, Frank Luther. *Golden Multitudes: The Story of Best Sellers in the United States*. New York: MacMillan, 1947.

Moussa-Mahmoud, Fatma. "English Travellers and the *Arabian Nights*." In *The Arabian Nights in English Literature*, edited by Peter L. Caracciolo, 95–110. London: Macmillan Press, 1988.

Mullen, Bill V. *Afro-Orientalism*. Minneapolis: University of Minnesota Press, 2004.

Mullick, Sunrit. "Protap Chandra Majumdar and Swami Vivekananda at the Parliament of Religions: Two Interpretations of Hinduism and Universal Religion." In *A Museum of Faiths: Histories and Legacies of the 1893 World's Parliament of Religions*, edited by Eric J. Ziolkowski, 219–34. Atlanta: Scholars Press, 1993.

Mullins, Paul R. "Race and the Genteel Consumer: Class and African-American Consumption, 1850–1930." *Historical Archaeology* 33, no. 1 (1999): 22–38.

Mumford, Kevin J. *Interzones: Black/White Sex Districts in Chicago and New York in the Early Twentieth Century*. New York: Columbia University Press, 1997.

Murdock, Catherine Gilbert. *Domesticating Drink: Women, Men, and Alcohol in America, 1870–1940*. Baltimore: Johns Hopkins University Press, 1998.

Naff, Alixa. "New York: The Mother Colony." In *A Community of Many Worlds: Arab Americans in New York City*, edited by Kathleen Benson and Philip M. Kayal, 3–10. Syracuse: Museum of the City of New York/Syracuse University Press, 2002.

——. *Becoming American: The Early Arab Immigrant Experience*. Carbondale: Southern Illinois University Press, 1985.

Nance, Susan. "The Ottoman Empire and the American Flag: Patriotic Tourism before the Age of Package Tours, 1830–1870." *Journal of Tourism Research* 1, no. 1 (forthcoming, 2009).

——. "A Facilitated Access Model and Ottoman Empire Tourism," *Annals of Tourism Research* 34, no. 4 (October 2007): 1056–78.

——. "Respectability and Representation: The Moorish Science Temple, Morocco, and Black Public Culture in 1920s Chicago." *American Quarterly* 54, no. 4 (December 2002): 623–59.

Napier, James. "Some Book Sales in Dumfries, Virginia, 1794–1796." *William and Mary Quarterly* 10, no. 3 (July 1953): 441–45.

Nead, Lynda. "Strip: Moving Bodies in the 1890s." *Early Popular Visual Culture* 3, no. 2 (September 2005): 135–50.

Obeidat, Marwan M. *American Literature and Orientalism*. Berlin: Klaus Schwartz Verlag, 1998.

Obenzinger, Hilton. "Holy Land Narrative and American Covenant: Levi Parsons, Pliny Fisk, and the Palestine Mission." *Religion and Literature* 35, no. 2-3 (Summer/Autumn 2003): 241–67.

——. *American Palestine: Melville, Twain, and the Holy Land Mania*. Princeton: Princeton University Press, 1999.

Olney, Martha L. "When Your Word Is Not Enough: Race, Collateral, and Household Credit." *Journal of Economic History* 58, no. 2 (June 1998): 408–31.

Oren, Michael B. *Power, Faith, and Fantasy: America in the Middle East, 1776 to the Present*. New York: Norton, 2007.

Orvell, Miles. *The Real Thing: Imitation and Authenticity in American Culture, 1880–1940*. Chapel Hill: University of North Carolina Press, 1989.

Osgerby, Bill. *Playboys in Paradise: Masculinity, Youth and Leisure-style in Modern America*. London: Berg, 2001.

Owen, Roger. *The Middle East in the World Economy, 1800–1914*. London: Metheun, 1981.

Ownby, Ted. *American Dreams in Mississippi: Consumers, Poverty, and Culture, 1830–1998*. Chapel Hill: University of North Carolina Press, 1999.

Palmer, Edward Nelson. "Negro Secret Societies." *Social Forces* 23, no. 2 (December 1944): 207–12.

Parkes, H. B. "New England in the Seventeen-Thirties." *New England Quarterly* 3, no. 3 (July 1930): 397–419.

Parsons, Elaine Frantz. "Midnight Rangers: Costume and Performance in the Reconstruction-Era Ku Klux Klan." *Journal of American History* 92, no. 3 (December 2005): 811–36.

Pascoe, Peggy. "Miscegenation Law, Court Cases, and Ideologies of 'Race' in Twentieth-Century America." *Journal of American History* 83, no. 1 (June 1996): 44–69.

Peiss, Kathy. *Hope in a Jar: The Making of America's Beauty Culture*. New York: Metropolitan Books, 1998.

——. *Cheap Amusements: Working Women and Leisure in Turn-of-the-Century New York*. Philadelphia: Temple University Press, 1986.

Peters, Rudolph. "Prisons and Marginalization in Nineteenth-Century Egypt." In *Outside In: Marginality in the Modern Middle East*, edited by Eugene Rogan, 31–52. London: I. B. Taurus, 2002.

Phillips, Ruth B., and Christopher B. Steiner. "Art, Authenticity, and the Baggage of Cultural Encounter." In *Unpacking Culture: Art and Commodity in Colonial and Postcolonial Worlds*, edited by Ruth B. Phillips and Christopher B. Steiner, 3–19. Berkeley: University of California Press, 1999.

Poignant, Roslyn. *Professional Savages: Captive Lives and Western Spectacle*. New Haven: Yale University Press, 2004.

Porterfield, Todd. "Baghdad on the Hoosic: American Orientalism." *Art in America* 89, no. 2 (February 2001): 110–17.

Prashad, Vijay. *The Karma of Brown Folk*. Minneapolis: University of Minnesota Press, 2000.

Quataert, Donald. *The Ottoman Empire, 1700–1922*. Cambridge: Cambridge University Press, 2000.

———. *Ottoman Manufacturing in the Age of the Industrial Revolution*. Cambridge: Cambridge University Press, 1993.

———, ed. *Consumption Studies and the History of the Ottoman Empire*. Albany: State University of New York Press, 2000.

Rabinovitz, Lauren. *For the Love of Pleasure: Women, Movies, and Culture in Turn-of-the-Century Chicago*. New Brunswick, N.J.: Rutgers University Press, 1998.

Rabinowitz, Dan. "Themes in the Economy of the Bedouin of South Sinai in the Nineteenth and Twentieth Centuries." *International Journal of Middle East Studies* 17 (1985): 211–28.

Radway, Janice A. *Reading the Romance: Women, Patriarchy, and Popular Literature*, 2nd ed. Chapel Hill: University of North Carolina Press, 1991.

———. "Reading Is Not Eating: Mass-Produced Literature and the Theoretical, Methodological, and Political Consequences of a Metaphor." *Book Research Quarterly* 2 (Fall 1986): 7–29.

Raibmon, Paige. "Theatres of Contact: The Kwakwaka'wakw Meet Colonialism in British Columbia and at the Chicago World's Fair." *Canadian Historical Review* 81, no. 2 (June 2000): 157–90.

Ramsaye, Terry. *A Million and One Nights: A History of the Motion Picture*. London: Frank Cass & Co., 1926.

Reed, Christopher Robert. *"All the World Is Here!": The Black Presence at White City*. Bloomington and Indianapolis: Indiana University Press, 2000.

Reel, Guy. *The National Police Gazette and the Making of the Modern American Man, 1879–1906*. London: Palgrave, MacMillan, 2006.

Register, Woody. *The Kid of Coney Island: Fred Thompson and the Rise of American Amusements*. Oxford: Oxford University Press, 2001.

Reid, Donald Malcolm. *Whose Pharaohs?: Archaeology, Museums, and Egyptian National Identity from Napoleon to World War I*. Berkeley: University of California Press, 2002.

Rice, Edward. *Captain Sir Richard Francis Burton*. New York: Scribner, 1990.

Rich, Paul, and Guillermo De Los Reyes. "The Nobles of the Shrine: Orientalist Fraternalism." *Journal of American Culture* 21, no. 4 (Winter 1998): 9–19.

Richardson, Alan, ed. and comp. *Three Oriental Tales*. Boston: Houghton Mifflin, 2002.

Richter, Daniel K. *Facing East from Indian Country: A Native History of Early America*. Cambridge: Harvard University Press, 2001.

Roach, Joseph. "Kinship, Intelligence, and Memory as Improvisation: Culture and Performance in New Orleans." In *Performance and Cultural Politics*, edited by Elin Diamond, 219–38. New York: Routledge, 1996.

Robbins, William G. *Colony and Empire: The Capitalist Transformation of the American West*. Lawrence: University Press of Kansas, 1994.

Roberts, Mary. "Contested Terrains: Women Orientalists and the Colonial Harem." *Orientalism's Interlocutors: Painting, Architecture, Photography*, edited by Jill Beaulieu and Mary Roberts, 179–204. Durham: Duke University Press, 2002.

Rogan, Eugene L. *Frontiers of the State in the Late Ottoman Empire: Transjordan, 1850–1921*. Cambridge: Cambridge University Press, 1999.

Romano, Renee. "No Diplomatic Immunity: African Diplomats, the State Department, and Civil Rights, 1961–1964." *Journal of American History* 87, no. 2 (September 2000): 546–79.

Rosa, Joseph G., and Robin May. *Buffalo Bill and His Wild West: A Pictorial Biography*. Lawrence: University Press of Kansas, 1989.

Rose, Jonathan. "Rereading the English Common Reader: A Preface to a History of Audiences." *Journal of the History of Ideas* 53, no. 1 (January–March 1992): 47–70.

Rosenberg, Emily S. *Spreading the American Dream: American Economic and Cultural Expansion, 1890–1945*. New York: Hill and Wang, 1982.

Rothenberg, Winifred. *From Market-Places to Market Economy: The Transformation of Rural Massachusetts, 1750–1850*. Chicago: University of Chicago Press, 1992.

Rothfels, Nigel. *Savages and Beasts: The Birth of the Modern Zoo*. Baltimore: Johns Hopkins University Press, 2002.

Rotter, Andrew. "In Retrospect: Harold R. Isaacs' Scratches on Our Minds." *Reviews in American History* 24 (March 1996): 177–88.

———. "Gender Relations, Foreign Relations: The United States and South Asia, 1947–1964." *Journal of American History* 81 (September 1994): 518–42.

Rotundo, E. Anthony. "Boy Culture: Middle-Class Boyhood in Nineteenth-Century America." In *Meanings for Manhood: Constructions of Masculinity in Victorian America*, edited by Mark C. Carnes and Clyde Griffen, 15–36. Chicago: University of Chicago Press, 1990.

Russell, Don. *Lives and Legends of Buffalo Bill*. Norman: University of Oklahoma Press, 1960.

Ruth, David E. *Inventing the Public Enemy: The Gangster in American Culture, 1918–1934*. Chicago: University of Chicago Press, 1996.

Ryan, Mary P. *Civic Wars: Democracy and Public Life in the American City during the Nineteenth Century*. Berkeley: University of California Press, 1997.

——. *Cradle of the Middle Class: The Family in Oneida County, New York, 1790–1865*. Cambridge: Cambridge University Press, 1981.

Rydell, Robert W. *All the World's a Fair: Visions of Empire at American International Expositions, 1876–1916*. Chicago: University of Chicago Press, 1984.

Rydell, Robert W., and Nancy Gwinn, eds. *Fair Representations: World's Fairs and the Modern World*. Amsterdam: VU University Press, 1994.

Said, Edward W. *Culture and Imperialism*. New York: Chatto and Windus, 1993.

——. "Orientalism Reconsidered." *Cultural Critique* 1, no. 1 (Autumn 1985): 89–107.

——. *Orientalism*. London: Routledge, 1978.

Sandage, Scott A. *Born Losers: A History of Failure in America*. Cambridge: Harvard University Press, 2005.

Sandoval-Sánchez, Alberto. *José, Can You See?: Latinos on and off Broadway*. Madison: University of Wisconsin, 1999.

Saxon, A. H. *Enter Foot and Horse: A History of Hippodrama in England and France*. New Haven: Yale University Press, 1968.

Schacker-Mill, Jennifer. "Otherness and Otherworldliness: Edward W. Lane's Ethnographic Treatment of *The Arabian Nights*." *Journal of American Folklore* 113, no. 448 (Spring 2000): 164–84.

Schlesinger, Arthur M., Jr. "Walter Lippmann: The Intellectual v. Politics." In *Walter Lippmann and His Times*, edited by Marquis Childs and James Reston, 189–225. Freeport, N.Y.: Books for Libraries Press, 1959.

Schlundt, Christena L. *Professional Appearances of Ruth St. Denis and Ted Shawn: A Chronology and Index of Dances, 1906–1932*. New York: New York Public Library, 1962.

Schölch, Alexander. *Palestine in Transformation, 1856–1882*. Translated by William C. Young and Michael C. Gerrity. Washington, D.C.: Institute for Palestine Studies, 1993.

Schueller, Malini Johar. *U S. Orientalism: Race, Nation, and Gender in Literature, 1790–1890*. Ann Arbor: University of Michigan Press, 1998.

Schwab, Raymond. *The Oriental Renaissance: Europe's Rediscovery of India and the East, 1680–1880*. New York: Columbia University Press, 1984.

Schwarz, Henry and Sangeeta Ray, eds. *A Companion to Post-Colonial Studies*. Malden, Mass.: Blackwell, 2000.

Scott, Donald M. "Print and the Public Lecture System, 1840–1860." In *Printing and Society in Early America*, edited by William L. Joyce, David D. Hall, Richard D. Brown, and John B. Hench, 278–99. Worcester, Mass.: American Antiquarian Society, 1983.

——. "The Popular Lecture and the Creation of a Public in Mid-Nineteenth-Century America." *Journal of American History* 66, no. 4 (March 1980): 791–809.

Seager, Richard Hughes. *The World's Parliament of Religion: The East/West Encounter, Chicago, 1893*. Bloomington: Indiana University Press, 1995.

——, ed. *The Dawn of Religious Pluralism: Voices from the World's Parliament of Religions, 1893.* LaSalle, Ill.: Open Court, 1993.

Sernett, Milton C. *Bound for the Promised Land: African-American Religion and the Great Migration.* Durham and London: Duke University Press, 1997.

Shaffer, Marguerite S. *See America First: Tourism and National Identity, 1880–1940.* Washington D.C.: Smithsonian Institution Press, 2001.

Shaheen, Jack. *Reel Bad Arabs: How Hollywood Vilifies a People.* Brooklyn, N.Y.: Olive Branch Press, 2001.

——. *The TV Arab.* Bowling Green, Ohio: Bowling Green University Popular Press, 1992.

Shamir, Milette. " 'Our Jerusalem': Americans in the Holy Land and Protestant Narratives of National Entitlement." *American Quarterly* 55, no. 1 (March 2003): 29–60.

Sharafuddin, Mohammed. *Islam and Romantic Orientalism: Literary Encounters with the Orient.* London: I. B. Taurus, 1993.

Shively, JoEllen. "Cowboys and Indians: Perceptions of Western Films among American Indians and Anglos." *America Sociological Review* 57, no. 6 (December 1992): 725–34.

Silbey, Joel H. *Storm Over Texas: The Annexation Controversy and the Road to the Civil War.* New York: Oxford University Press, 2005.

Simon, Reeva S. *The Middle East in Crime Fiction: Mysteries, Spy Novels, and Thrillers from 1916 to the 1980s.* New York: Lilian Barber Press, 1989.

Slotkin, Richard. "Buffalo Bill's 'Wild West' and the Mythologization of the American Empire." In *Cultures of United States Imperialism,* edited by Amy Kaplan and Donald E. Pease, 164–84. Durham: Duke University Press, 1993.

Smith, Cecil, and Glenn Litton. *Musical Comedy in America.* 1950. Reprint, New York: Theatre Arts Books, 1981.

Smith, George Winston. "A Strong Band Circular." *Mississippi Valley Historical Review* 29, no. 4 (March 1943): 557–64.

Smith, Jane Webb. *Smoke Signals: Cigarette Advertising and the American Way of Life.* Chapel Hill: University of North Carolina Press, 1990.

Snyder, Monroe B. "Survivals of Astrology." *Journal of American Folk-Lore* 3 (1890): 127–31.

Snyder, Robert W. *Voice of the City: Vaudeville and Popular Culture in New York.* New York: Oxford University Press, 1989.

Sobel, Robert. *Machines and Morality: The 1850s.* New York: Thomas Y. Crowell, 1973.

Spann, Edward K. *Gotham at War: New York City, 1860–1865.* Wilmington, Del.: Scholarly Resources, 2002.

Spencer, Thomas M. *The St. Louis Veiled Prophet Celebration: Power on Parade, 1877–1995.* Columbia: University of Missouri Press, 2000.

Spiller, Robert E. "Pilgrim's Return." In *Literary History of the United States: History,* edited by Robert E. Spiller et al., 2:827–42. New York: Macmillan Company, 1963.

Sponsler, Claire and Xiaomei Chen, eds. *East of West: Cross-Cultural Performance and the Staging of Difference.* London: Palgrave, 2000.

Spooner, Brian. "Weavers and Dealers: The Authenticity of an Oriental Carpet." In *The Social Life of Things: Commodities in Cultural Perspective*, edited by Arjun Appadurai, 195–235. Cambridge: Cambridge University Press, 1988.

Steadman, John. *The Myth of Asia*. New York: Simon and Schuster, 1969.

Stearns, Peter N. *Consumerism in World History: The Global Transformation of Desire*, 2nd ed. New York: Routledge, 2006.

Steel, Ronald. *Walter Lippmann and the American Century*. Boston: Little, Brown & Company, 1980.

Steet, Linda. *Veils and Daggers: A Century of National Geographic's Representation of the Arab World*. Philadelphia: Temple University Press, 2000.

Steinbrink, Jeffrey. "Why the Innocents Went Abroad: Mark Twain and American Tourism in the Late Nineteenth Century." *American Literary Realism* 16 (Autumn 1983): 278–86.

Steiner, Christopher B. "Authenticity, Repetition, and the Aesthetics of Seriality: The Work of Tourist Art in the Age of Mechanical Reproduction." In *Unpacking Culture: Art and Commodity in Colonial and Postcolonial Worlds*, edited by Ruth B. Phillips and Christopher B. Steiner, 87–102. Berkeley: University of California Press, 1999.

Stern, Bernard Saul. "American Views of India and Indians, 1857–1900." Ph.D. diss., University of Pennsylvania, 1956.

Sterngass, Jon. *First Resorts: Pursuing Pleasure at Saratoga Springs, Newport and Coney Island*. Baltimore: Johns Hopkins University Press, 2001.

Stockton, Ronald. "Ethnic Archetypes and the Arab Image." In *The Development of Arab-American Identity*, edited by Ernest McCarus, 119–53. Ann Arbor: University of Michigan Press, 1994.

Stoddart, Helen. *Rings of Desire: Circus History and Representation*. Manchester and New York: Manchester University Pres, 2000.

Stokes, Melvyn, and Stephen Conway, eds. *Market Revolution in America: Social, Political, and Religious Expressions, 1800–1880*. Charlottesville: University Press of Virginia, 1996.

Stoler, Ann Laura. *Haunted By Empire: Geographies of Intimacy in North American History*. Durham: Duke University Press, 2006.

Stowe, William W. *Going Abroad: European Travel in Nineteenth-Century American Culture*. Princeton: Princeton University Press, 1994.

Studlar, Gaylyn. " 'Out-Salomeing Salome': Dance, the New Woman, and Fan Magazine Orientalism." In *Visions of the East: Orientalism in Film*, edited Matthew Bernstein and Gaylyn Studlar, 99–129. New Brunswick, N.J.: Rutgers University Press, 1997.

——. *This Mad Masquerade: Stardom and Masculinity in the Jazz Age*. New York: Columbia University Press, 1996.

Suleiman, Michael W. "Impressions of New York City by Early Arab Immigrants." In *A Community of Many Worlds: Arab Americans in New York City*, edited by Kathleen Benson and Philip M. Kayal, 28–45. Syracuse: Museum of the City of New York/Syracuse University Press, 2002.

——. *The Arabs in the Mind of America*. Brattleboro, Vt.: Amana, 1988.

Sutherland, Robert Lee. "An Analysis of Negro Churches in Chicago," Ph.D. diss., University of Chicago, 1930.

Sweetman, Jonathan. *The Oriental Obsession: Islamic Inspiration in British and American Art and Architecture, 1500–1920*. Cambridge: Cambridge University Press, 1988.

Swiencicki, Mark A. "Consuming Brotherhood: Men's Culture, Style and Recreation as Consumer Culture, 1880–1930." *Journal of Social History* 31 (Summer 1998): 773–808.

Taylor, William R. *In Pursuit of Gotham: Culture and Commerce in New York*. New York: Oxford University Press, 1992.

Tchen, John Kuo Wei. *New York Before Chinatown: Orientalism and the Shaping of American Culture, 1776–1882*. Baltimore: Johns Hopkins University Press, 1999.

Tenorio-Trillo, Mauricio. *Mexico at the World's Fairs: Crafting a Modern Nation*. Berkeley: University of California Press, 1996.

Terry, Janice. *Mistaken Identity: Arab Stereotypes in Popular Writing*. Washington, D.C.: American-Arab Affairs Council, 1985.

Tibawi, A. L. *American Interests in Syria, 1800–1901*. Oxford: Clarendon Press, 1966.

Tilley, Nannie M. *The R. J. Reynolds Tobacco Company*. Chapel Hill: University of North Carolina Press, 1985.

Tone, Andrea. "Black Market Birth Control: Contraceptive Entrepreneurship and Criminality in the Gilded Age," *Journal of American History* 87 (September 2000): 435–59.

Toy, C. H. "The Thousand and One Nights." *Atlantic Monthly* 63, no. 380 (June 1889): 756–64.

Trachtenberg, Alan. *The Incorporation of America: Culture and Society in the Gilded Age*. New York: Hill and Wang, 1982.

Trafton, Scott. *Egypt Land: Race and Nineteenth-Century American Egyptomania*. Durham: Duke University Press, 2004.

Trentmann, Frank. "Knowing Consumers—Histories, Identities, Practices." In *The Making of the Consumer: Knowledge, Power and Identity in the Modern World*, edited by Frank Trentmann, 1–27. Oxford, U.K.: Berg, 2006.

Tucher, Andie. *Froth and Scum: Truth, Beauty, Goodness, and the Ax Murder in America's First Mass Medium*. Chapel Hill: University of North Carolina Press, 1994.

Turner, Richard Brent. *Islam in the African-American Experience*. Bloomington and Indianapolis: Indiana University Press, 1997.

——. " 'What Shall We Call Him': Islam and African American Identity," *Journal of Religious Thought* 51, no. 1 (1995): 1–28.

——. "The Ahmadiyya Mission to Blacks in the United States in the 1920s." *Journal of Religious Thought* 44, no. 2 (Winter/Spring 1988): 50–66.

Ullman, Sharon R. *Sex Seen: The Emergence of Modern Sexuality in America*. Berkeley: University of California Press, 1987.

Van Nieuwkerk, Karin. *"A Trade Like Any Other": Female Singers and Dancers in Egypt*. Austin: University of Texas Press, 1995.

Vincent, Theodore G. *Black Power and the Garvey Movement*. Berkeley, California: Ramparts Press, 1971.

Vogel, Lester I. "Staying Home for the Sights: Surrogate Destinations in America for Holy Land Travel." In *Pilgrims and Travelers to the Holy Land*, edited by Bryan F. Le Beau and Menachem Mor, 251–67. Omaha: Creighton University Press, 1996.

——. *To See a Promised Land: Americans and the Holy Land in the Nineteenth Century*. University Park: Pennsylvania State University Press, 1993.

Voorhis, Harold Van Buren. *Negro Masonry in the United States*. Washington, D.C.: n.p., 1939.

Walker, Franklin. *Irreverent Pilgrims: Melville, Browne, and Mark Twain in the Holy Land*. Seattle: University of Washington Press, 1974.

Walkowitz, Judith R. "The 'Vision of Solome': Cosmopolitanism and Erotic Dancing in Central London, 1908–1918." *American Historical Review* 108, no. 2 (April 2003): 337–76.

Walter, Howard A. *The Ahmadiya Movement*. Oxford: Oxford University Press, 1918.

——. "The Ahmadiya Movement To-Day." *Moslem World* 6 (1916): 66–78.

Walton, James, ed. *The Faber Book of Smoking*. London: Faber and Faber, 2000.

Warnock, Robert. "Unpublished Lectures of Bayard Taylor." *American Literature* 5, no. 2 (May 1933): 123–32.

Warraq, Ibn. *Defending the West: A Critique of Edward Said's Orientalism*. Amherst, N.Y.: Prometheus Books, 2007.

Warren, Louis S. *Buffalo Bill's America: William Cody and the Wild West Show*. New York: Knopf, 2005.

Washington, Joseph R., Jr. *Black Religion: The Negro and Christianity in the United States*. Boston: Beacon Press, 1964.

Watkins-Owens, Irma. *Blood Relations: Caribbean Immigrants and the Harlem Community, 1900–1930*. Bloomington and Indianapolis: Indiana University Press, 1996.

Weeks, Emily. "About Face: Sir David Wilkie's Portrait of Mehemet Ali, Pasha of Egypt." In *Orientalism Transposed: The Impact of the Colonies on British Culture*, edited by Julie F. Codell and Dianne Sachko Macleod, 46–62. Brookfield, Vt.: Ashgate, 1998.

Weems, Robert E., Jr. *Desegregating the Dollar: African American Consumerism in the Twentieth Century*. New York: New York University Press, 1998.

Wegelin, C. "The Rise of the International Novel." *Publications of the Modern Language Association of America (PMLA)* 77, no. 3 (1962): 305–10.

Weiss, Melville J. "Don't Buy Where You Can't Work: An Analysis of Consumer Action against Employment Discrimination in Harlem, 1934–1940," M.A. Thesis, Columbia University, 1941.

Wermuth, Paul C., ed. *Selected Letters of Bayard Taylor*. Lewisburg, Pa.: Bucknell University Press, 1997.

——. *Bayard Taylor*. New York: Twayne Publishers, 1973.

Wheeler, Leigh Ann. *Against Obscenity: Reform and the Politics of Womanhood in America, 1873–1935*. Baltimore: Johns Hopkins University Press, 2004.

White, Kevin. *The First Sexual Revolution: The Emergence of Male Heterosexuality in Modern America.* New York: New York University Press, 1993.

White, Shane. "Pinkster: Afro-Dutch Syncretization in New York and the Hudson Valley." *Journal of American Folklore* 102 (1988): 68–75.

Wiebe, Robert H. *The Search for Order, 1877–1920.* New York: Hill and Wang, 1967.

Williams, Loretta J. *Black Freemasonry and Middle-Class Realities.* Columbia: University of Missouri Press, 1980.

Wilmore, Gayraud S. *Black Religion and Black Radicalism: An Interpretation of the Religious History of Afro-American People,* 2nd ed. New York: Orbis Books, 1984.

Wilson, Verity. "Studio and Soirée: Chinese Textiles in Europe and America, 1850 to the Present." In *Unpacking Culture: Art and Commodity in Colonial and Postcolonial Worlds,* edited by Ruth B. Phillips and Christopher B. Steiner, 229–42. Berkeley: University of California Press, 1999.

Wolcott, Victoria W. "The Culture of the Informal Economy: Numbers Runners in Inter-War Black Detroit." *Radical History Review* 69 (1997): 46–75.

——. "Mediums, Messages, and Lucky Numbers: African-American Female Spiritualists and Numbers Runners in Interwar Detroit." In *The Geography of Identity,* edited by Patricia Jaeger, 273–305. Ann Arbor: University of Michigan Press, 1996.

Wollen, Peter. "Fashion/Orientalism/The Body." *New Formations* 1 (Spring 1987): 5–33.

Woodberry, George Edward. *Nathaniel Hawthorne.* Boston: Houghton Mifflin, 1902.

Yamanaka, Yuriko, and Tetsuo Nishio. *The Arabian Nights and Orientalism: Perspectives from East and West.* London: I. B. Taurus, 2006.

Yoshihara, Mari. *Embracing the East: White Women and American Orientalism.* New York: Oxford University Press, 2003.

Younis, Adele L. "The Arabs Who Followed Columbus." *Arab World* 12, no. 3 (March 1966): 13–14.

Yu, Henry. *Thinking Orientals: Migration, Contact, and Exoticism in Modern America.* Oxford: Oxford University Press, 2001.

Zakim, Michael. *Ready-Made Democracy: A History of Men's Dress in the American Republic, 1760–1860.* Chicago: University of Chicago Press, 2003.

Zboray, Ronald J. *A Fictive People: Antebellum Economic Development and the American Reading Public.* New York: Oxford University Press, 1993.

Ziff, Larzer. *Return Passages: Great American Travel Writing, 1780–1910.* New Haven: Yale University Press, 2000.

WEBSITE SOURCES

"Christopher Oscanyan." The Vault at Pfaff's: An Archive of Arts and Literature by New York City's Nineteenth-Century Bohemians, <http://digital.lib.lehigh.edu/pfaffs/people/individuals/85/htm>. July 1, 2007.

"Egyptian Dance," May 9, 1895. Maguire & Baucus catalogue, Early Motion Pictures,

1897–1920, American Memory, Library of Congress, <http://hdl.loc.gov/loc.mbrsmi/edmp.4035>. February 9, 2008.

Hicks, Thomas. "Portrait of Bayard Taylor," 1855. NPG 76.6, National Portrait Gallery, Smithsonian Institution, Washington, D.C., <http://www.npg.si.edu/cexh/brush/index/portraits/taylor.htm>. January 12, 2006.

"Posed group of officers of Mecca Temple of the Ancient Arabic Order of Nobles of the Mystic Shrine of New York." LC-USZ62-63681, Oversize Miscellaneous Photographs and Prints, Prints and Photographs Division, Library of Congress, <http://hdl.loc.gov/loc.pnp/cph.3b11295>. November 2, 2006.

"Princess Rajah dance," 1904. American Variety Stage: Vaudeville and Popular Entertainment, 1870–1920 Collection, American Memory, Library of Congress, <http://memory.loc.gov/cgi-bin/query/D?varstg:28:./temp/ammem_Vwun::@@@mdb=manz,eaa>. January 12, 2006.

"Robert Levy, a Shriner, standing outdoors," Chicago Daily News Collection, American Memory, Library of Congress, image no. DN0005277, <http://memory.loc.gov/ammem/ndlpcoop/ichihtml/cdnhome.html>. January 17, 2008.

"Shriner Robert Levy, standing with silk curtains that he presented to the Medinah Temple," 1907. Chicago Daily News Collection, American Memory, Library of Congress, image no. DN-0005279, <http://memory.loc.gov/ammem/ndlpcoop/ichihtml/cdnhome.html>. January 17, 2008.

"Turkish Dance, Ella Lola." 1898, American Variety Stage: Vaudeville and Popular Entertainment, 1870–1920 Collection, American Memory, Library of Congress, <http://memory.loc.gov/cgibin/query/D?varstg:2:./temp/ammem_2IAe::@@@mdb>.

"View of a woman gipsy/dancer posing outside at Coney Island." Byron Collection of Coney Island, 1896–98, Museum of the City of New York, image no. 93.1.1.3388, <http://museumofnyc.doetech.net/Detlobjps.cfm?ObjectID=17362&rec_num=12&From=obj_key.cfm#42>. May 1, 2008.

"View of a woman gipsy/dancer seated in her side show theatre at Coney Island." Byron Collection of Coney Island, 1896–98, Museum of the City of New York, image no. 93.1.1.3386, <http://museumofnyc.doetech.net/Detlobjps.cfm?ObjectID=46953&rec_num=48&From=obj_key.cfm>. May 1, 2008.

"Wild West Georgians." <http://www.georgians.ge/all.htm>. January 7, 2007.

index